JOURNAL FOR THE STUDY OF THE OLD TESTAMENT
SUPPLEMENT SERIES
276

Sheffield Academic Press

Economic Keystones

The Weight System
of the Kingdom of Judah

Raz Kletter

Journal for the Study of the Old Testament
Supplement Series 276

Copyright © 1998 Sheffield Academic Press

Published by Sheffield Academic Press Ltd
Mansion House
19 Kingfield Road
Sheffield S11 9AS
England

Printed on acid-free paper in Great Britain
by Bookcraft Ltd
Midsomer Norton, Bath

British Library Cataloguing in Publication Data

A catalogue record for this book is available
from the British Library

ISBN 1-85075-920-0

CONTENTS

LIST OF FIGURES

ACKNOWLEDGMENTS

This study would not have been possible without the encouragement and patience of Professor Pirhiya Beck and Professor Nadav Na'aman of Tel Aviv University. The study originated as a chapter in my PhD dissertation in Hebrew (Kletter 1995), revised and significantly enlarged since. I have benefited from many talks with Dr G. Barkay, who shares my interest in these small artifacts, though our opinions sometimes differ.

I have received considerable help from many scholars and institutions in Israel and abroad, for which I am greatly indebted. Included among them are many of my teachers and friends at Tel Aviv University, namely Professor M. Kochavi (Malhata); Professor D. Ussishkin (Lachish and Tel Jezreel); Professor I. Beit Arieh (Aroer, Malhata, Tel 'Ira); Dr Z. Herzog (Arad and Beer Sheba); Professor I. Singer; E. Brand (Tel Hadid); and Neta Halperin who helped with weighing. Special thanks are due to Professor J. Yakar for his understanding and efficiant help during my years of study.

Many of my friends and collegues at the Israel Antiquities Authority contributed to this work, among them Dr Z. Gal (Rosh Zayit); A. de-Groot (Ramot and Moza); Y. Meitlis (Nahal Zimri); B. Brandl and the team of the Romema Stores; Y. Nadelman (Pisgat Zeev); Nurit Feig (Beit Safafeh); G. Edelstein (Mevaseret Jerusalem); U. Galili and Y. Sharvit (Palmahim); Y. Dagan (Lachish and the Shephelah Survey); O. Katz, F. Sontag and O. Salama (Beer Sheba); and E. Shukrun (Mamila). I thank also Y. Levi and all my colleagues at the Tel Aviv branch of the Israel Antiquities Authority.

Among others, I wish to thank all the following scholars: Professor A. Mazar of the Hebrew University, Jerusalem (Tel Batash); Mrs O. Rimon of the Hecht Museum; Dr R. Reich, University of Haifa (Mamila); Dr A. Kindler, Uzah Zevulun and Cecilia Meir of the Eretz Israel Museum, Tel Aviv; and Dr Y. Meshorer and Michal Dayagi-Mendels of the Israel Museum, Jerusalem.

Outside Israel, I have benefited from the encouragement and knowledge of Dr J. Seger and Dr O. Borowski (Tel Halif); Dr A.J. Spencer, Keeper of Egyptian Antiquities, the British Museum; Dr R. Chapman, the Palestine Exploration Found, London; Dr K. Tasso, University of Tartu, Estonia; Dr K. Wright, London University College; and Pamela Magrill, Lachish Collection, British Museum. I also wish to thank Ms Orna Zimhoni but, sadly, I can no longer express my thanks to her in person.

I am greatly indebted to the British Council for a post-PhD scholarship for 1995–96 at Oxford University, England. The kindness and advice of Professor P.R.S. Moorey, Keeper of Antiquities at the Ashmolean Museum, and Professor H.G.M. Williamson, Regius Professor of Hebrew at Oxford University, were most helpful. Thanks are also due to Yad Ha-Nadiv which provided a fund for 1997–98, and thereby helped in bringing this manuscript to press.

At the Department of the Land of Israel Studies, University of Haifa, I have found a warm home. I wish to thank the head of the department, Professor Y. Ben Artzi, and all the members of the department for their kindness and help.

In the preparation of this book I was assisted by the skills of Marina Rapeport (drawings) and Susan Menache (English copy-editing). I am indebted to my friends, Y. Mizrahi and Irit Ziffer, and to Kristel for her tolerance of my recent mode of living, which might be likened to that of a hermit.

This book is dedicated to my father, Reuben.

Raz Kletter

ABBREVIATIONS

ABD	David Noel Freedman (ed.), *The Anchor Bible Dictionary* (New York: Doubleday, 1992)
AOAT	Alter Orient und Altes Testament
AASOR	*Annual of the American Schools of Oriental Research*
ADAJ	*Annual of the Department of Antiquities of Jordan*
AfO	*Archiv für Orientforschung*
AJA	*American Journal of Archaeology*
AJBI	Annual of the Japanese Biblical Institue
BA	*Biblical Archaeologist*
BARev	*Biblical Archaeology Review*
BASOR	*Bulletin of the American Schools of Oriental Research*
BN	*Biblische Notizen*
EAEHL	*Encyclopaedia of Archaeological Excavations in the Holy Land* (2 vols.; 1970) (Hebrew; rev. ET: 4 vols.; 1975–78).
EAEHLnew	*The New Encyclopaedia of Archaeological Excavations in the Holy Land* (4 vols.; 1993) (Hebrew; rev. ET: 1994).
EI	*Eretz Israel*
EncMiqr	*Encyclopedia Miqrait* (8 vols.) (Hebrew).
GM	*Göttinger Miszellen*
HadArch	Hadashot Archaeologiot (Jerusalem: IAA) (Hebrew).
HUCA	*Hebrew Union College Annual*
IAA	Israel Antiquities Authority
IEJ	*Israel Exploration Journal*
IES	*Israel Exploration Society*
INA	Israel Nautical Archaeology
JAOS	*Journal of the American Oriental Society*
JBL	*Journal of Biblical Literature*
JCS	*Journal of Cuneiform Studies*
JEA	*Journal of Egyptian Archaeology*
JESHO	*Journal of the Economic and Social History of the Orient*
JNES	*Journal of Near Eastern Studies*
JNSL	*Journal of Northwest Semitic Languages*
JPOS	*Journal of the Palestine Oriental Society*
JSOT	*Journal for the Study of the Old Testament*
JSOTSup	*Journal for the Study of the Old Testament*, Supplement Series
Numen	*Numen: International Review for the History of Religions*
OA	*Oriens Antiquus*

OBO	Orbis biblicus et orientalis
OLA	Orientalia Lovaniensia Analecta
OTL	Old Testament Library
PEFA	Annual of the Palestine Exploration Fund
PEFQS	*Palestine Exploration Fund, Quarterly Statement*
PEQ	*Palestine Exploration Quarterly*
QDAP	*Quarterly of the Department of Antiquities in Palestine*
RA	*Revue d'assyriologie et d'archéologie orientale*
RB	*Revue biblique*
REg	*Revue d'égyptologie*
RLA	E. Ebeling and B. Meisner (eds.), *Reallexikon der Assyriologie* (Berlin)
SIHAJ	K. Amr, F. Zayadine and N. Zaghlul (eds.), *Studies in the History and Archaeology of Jordan* (5 vols.).
SMEA	*Studi Micenei ed Egeo-Anatolici*
UF	*Ugarit-Forschungen*
VT	*Vetus Testamentun*
ZA	*Zeitschrift für Assyriologie*
ZAW	*Zeitschrift für die alttestamentliche Wissenschaft*
ZDMG	*Zeitschrift der deutschen morgenländischen Gesellschaft*
ZDPV	*Zeitschrift des deutschen Palästina-Vereins*

INTRODUCTION

When excavators understand, and will pay two piasters for each weight found in their excavations, the history of trade will begin to take its proper place (Petrie 1937: 13).

It was a world without coins, without money—or nothing that we today define as money. No coins of gold or silver with heads of rulers, no cheque books, no banknotes and no plastic credit cards. The value of commodities was largely determined by contents in volume or weight. This is why the study of ancient weights gives a rare glimpse into the economic structure of ancient societies.

My interest in ancient weight systems has grown during the past years and continues to do so. The first paper that I read on the Judaean inscribed limestone weights (henceforth JILs) took me by surprise. I stumbled upon a maze of different calculations, bewildering assumptions and conclusions. Amid the great variety of assumed fractions, sub-units, multiples, percents and standards offered, I wondered how an ancient culture could make sense of it all. Indeed, that paper explained why the study of metrology had often been neglected. Studying an ancient weight system in simple terms might be considered to be bordering on the eccentric.

My aim in this book is to offer a full analysis of the weight system of Iron Age II Judah. This analysis is based, first and foremost, on a detailed archaeological study of hundreds of scale weights found in Judah. These weights were never the object of a monographic study, though they must be studied as a whole, and not as separate, isolated parts—the whole is much more than the mere sum of its parts. Surprisingly, this view is contrary to the mainstream of current metrology, which limits its interest to metrological aspects alone. This narrow viewpoint has set the JILs apart from the historical, archaeological and cultural background. However, there was only one past: archaeology, history and theology are merely modern dichotomies. I will try to portray the JILs *as a whole system,* and to discuss the relations of this system with the biblical, historical and archaeological settings. I hope that presenting the Judaean weight system in this way makes it a little better understood. Some wider implications for the economy of Judah are discussed in the concluding chapter, but the scope of this study is obviously limited. I hope to return to this field in the future.

I will not discuss in detail the relations between the JILs and the borders of Judah, nor theoretical works about archaeology and political borders, since I have dealt with this subject elsewhere (Kletter 1996: chap. 4; Kletter 1997). The data about each weight are presented in the catalogues (Appendices 1 and 2). The weights are arranged according to weight units, numbered by their unit and running numbers (e.g. Pym. 7; Nsf. 5; 4 Gerah. 6). The structure of the catalogue and the key terms used there are explained in the notes preceding Appendix 1. Weighing is given in grams, unless marked otherwise. Whenever possible, I checked the weights, either at the IAA laboratories (using Precisa scales, with 0.01 gram precision) or at Tel Aviv University (using electronic scales, with the help of Neta Halperin). A selection of drawings of JILs follows the other figures, after the text (the figures are not to scale, since the size of the weights is given in the catalogue). The names of the JIL units are given in the following English forms: Kikar or Talent, Maneh, Shekel, Nsf, Pym, Beqaᶜ and Gerah. In Hebrew, these are: גרה, בקע, פים, נצף, שקל, מנה, כיכר. I have not used plural endings with the English spellings, except in very few cases when it seemed desirable. I followed the common English name 'Shekel', rather than the more accurate 'Sheqel' (cf. Aviezer 1993). Place names are given in their common English spelling and are not exact scientific transliteration. For the sake of convenience, I use the form 'Tel' and not 'Tell'. All the literature is given in the Bibliography, but a few minor, secondary sources appear in shortened form in the catalogues (e.g. preliminary reports in *Hadashot Archeologiot*).

Spelling mistakes, slips of hand and errors of calculation have probably occurred. I have done my best to limit such errors, but a few are almost inevitable in a study that deals with so many artifacts and calculations. My belief is that they do not affect the main conclusions of this work.

Chapter 1

THE HISTORY OF RESEARCH

More than a hundred years have passed since the discovery of the first Judaean inscribed limestone weights (henceforth JILs). I have distinguished four phases of research within this period, though there is not always a sharp separation between each phase. The phases are: (1) early days, 1882–1911; (2) consolidation of research, 1912–39; (3) Lachish—an intermediate phase, 1940–58; (4) between calculations and explanations, 1959–96. The last phase can be divided into two stages (1959–75; 1976–96).

1.1. *The Early Days (1882–1911)*

1.1.1. *The Phase and its Character*
The first JILs were discovered in Jerusalem by Guthe (1882). Weights had been found earlier, but published in a way that prevents their exact identification today (e.g. Warren 1870: 330; Chester 1871: 491-92). The quantity of JILs found throughout this phase was very small (Fig. 1), so each new weight caused great interest and excitement. At this stage, geographical distinctions between different weights were not possible. For example, an inscribed weight from Samaria, part of the kingdom of Israel, was defined as Hebrew because of the script (Sayce 1894; Chaplin 1890); but it is not a JIL (cf. Delavault and Lemaire 1979). Because of the small number of JILs, scholars could not understand their unique nature as a local weight system. Therefore, efforts to connect the JILs with foreign weight systems were common. This also resulted from the underlying method of 'comparable metrology' ('vergleichende Metrologie'), discussed below.

At first, even the inscriptions on the JILs were not well understood. They were regarded as Roman numerals (Guthe 1882: 373) or Cypriot signs (Sayce 1904: 357-85; Bliss and Dickie 1898: 268). The sign ୪ was sometimes drawn upside-down (Macalister 1904b: 35; Guthe 1882: Pl. 10) and assumed to be the Cypriot script sign *ro* (𐘇, thus Sayce 1904: 357; contra Macalister 1904b: 358; 1905: Pl. 10). Petrie suggested that the א is a shortened form of the Greek word for the unit ounce (in Macalister 1904a: 210 n. 1); however, he quickly dismissed this idea (Macalister 1904b: 357 n. 1). The word Nsf was read *nzf* (Bliss 1899: 108), *nsg* (Sayce 1893: 32; 1894: 284-85) or even *ksf* (literally, Hebrew for 'silver'; Legrange, according to Bliss 1899: 108; cf. Clermont-Ganneau 1901: 25-26; Raffaeli 1920). Some suggestions betray over-imaginative minds. For example, Barton (1903: 358-59) suggested that Pym means *[l]fy m[šql]*, 'according to weight', or perhaps one should read instead *gym*, which is *g[rh] y [l]m[qdš]* ([קדש]מן[ל] ׳ [גרה]ג), meaning '10 Gerah to the temple'.

It is worthwhile returning to such obscure and early studies since, in some cases, later publications include mistakes or omissions that only the original publications can clarify. There are even cases where weights have been totally forgotten. For example, a weight from Gezer was published only in a preliminary report (Macalister 1904b: 359). It was mentioned by Viedebannt (1923), but escaped the attention of subsequent scholars (Appendix 1: 8 א.34). A similar fate befell a weight from Tel Abu-Sleimeh (Petrie 1937: Pl. 39; Appendix 1: Pym 21), perhaps overlooked because of the distance of this site from Judah.

Varied patterns of study already appeared during the first phase of research: publications of weights from excavations and antiquities markets (Guthe 1882; Barton 1903); studies of specific weight units (Clermont-Ganneau 1901), and even a first general review of the JILs (Dalman 1906). The relation between the JILs and the Old Testament sources was established, for example, when the Beqaᶜ weights were identified with Exod. 30.13 and the sign א with the biblical Shekel (Macalister 1904a: 210-11 n. 1; Dalman 1906: 93-94). A basic understanding that the א weights are part of a whole system was reached near the end of this phase, largely by Macalister (1904a: 209) and Dalman (1906: 93-94). Common reading was reached for the units Nsf, Beqaᶜ and Pym, though all were still equated with foreign weight units. The date of the JILs remained problematic (for paleographic dating, see S.A. Cook 1909: 292). Macalister dated them back to the postexilic period (1904a: 209; 1904b: 359; 1909: 282).

Scholar and Year	ℬ Series — 1	2	4	8	12–40	ℬ?	All ℬ	Nsf	Pym	Beqaʿ	Gerah	Mute/ Other	Total JILs
Guthe 1882		1	1				2						2
Clermont-Ganneau 1901								5					5
Macalister 1904–1905	1	1	3	2			7						7
Dalman 1906	1	1	3	6			11	3		3			17
Macalister 1912	2	2	3	2			10	+	+	+	few		10
Pilcher 1912	+	+	+	+			4	2	3				9
Viedebannt 1921	1	2	3	4			9	5	2	3			19
Barrois 1932	2	4	4	7			17	6	4	3	5		35
Diringer 1934	+	+	+	+			+	9	4	4	few		17
Diringer 1953	+	+	+	+			23	14	7	7	6		57
Scott 1959	+	+	+	+			17						17
Yadin 1960	2	6	5	10			23				few		23
Stern 1963	4	8	8	14			34	13	8	6	few		61
Scott 1964										10	21		31
Scott 1965	+	+	+	24	1		62	18	9		few		89
Aharoni 1966	+	+	+	+	+		3						3
Scott 1970													21
Dever 1970				14	16		30	18	12	11	+		71
Segal 1970											45		
Ben-David 1970								36	28				64
Barkay 1981											31		31
Scott 1985	2	7	9	7	1		26	2	3		3	60	34
Eran 1987											62		62
The present study	42	42	56	51	11	3	202	59	52	35	83	196	434

Notes: '+' indicates that weights of this unit were mentioned without precise quantitative data. 'Few' means that few weights were mentioned, usually not discussed. There is some overlapping, and scholars used different definitions of JILs.

The column 'ℬ?' includes 3 weights from Accho and Ekron (see note at the end of Appendix 2).

Figure 1. *The development of research—quantity of JILs*

1.1.2. *Comparable Metrology*

A method of study dictates, to a large extent, the frame of study and the questions that are perceived as worthy of research. The first phase of the JIL research was dominated by the method of 'comparable metrology'. It is important to understand this method in order to understand the phase, and also because it subsequently influenced a few scholars (even today, Eran 1985, 1987).

Comparable metrology was developed by A. Boeckh, and reached its zenith under Lehman-Haupt and Hultsch at the end of the nineteenth century (Hultsch 1882; 1898). It was based on the assumption that in some remote stage of human development there was one basic metrological system, from which all the different systems derived. This was stated clearly by Hultsch (1898: 4): 'Ancient weights stand in simple and minimally-differentiated relationship with each other, in which the younger [i.e. later] weights always derive from the older ones' (author's translation). It is stressed again in the following page (Hultsch 1898: 5): 'The initiative that tries to show the relationship between ancient weights, that outwardly appear so varied, can achieve success if it is able to relate all these weights to one common Mass [gemeinsames Maass].' If all the ancient measure systems are interrelated, whether through actual contemporaneous relationships or through early, mutual 'birth', the aim of comparable metrology was to find these interrelations.

Lehman-Haupt (1893, 1910) mainly discussed the Babylonian system and the relations between standards of gold and silver. It was perceived at that stage that separate standards and weights were used for each expensive metal (cf. also Lehman-Haupt 1956, posthumously).

In 1882, Hultsch mentioned the 'Hebrew' weight system. This study is interesting as a reconstruction based on written sources, from the same year that the first JILs were published (for a study that reflects an even earlier stage, see Herzfeld 1863). Hultsch (1882: 456-74) dealt mainly with later periods in Judah. He modelled the early 'Hebrew' system on the Babylonian one, assuming the existence of different standards of gold and silver in a relation of 1 to $13^1/_3$ (1882: 457; cf. Lehman-Haupt 1910, 1956). Hultsch (1882: 457-60) assumed three Hebrew Shekel standards: (1) 'mosäische' Shekel with 20 Gerah (this is the 'holy Shekel' or 'Shekel of the sanctuary'); (2) light Shekel of 10 Gerah, called 'Kopfsteuer' or 'poll-tax' Shekel; (3) the Old Testament 'Keshita', an early Shekel of $^1/_4$ 'mosäische' Shekel. A substantial part of his discussion dealt with large weights, the Maneh (Mina) and Kikar (Talent). The Maneh was seen as a postexilic addition to the system (Hultsch 1882: 458). Calculating from later sources, with great complication (1882: 468-72), Hultsch estimated the Hebrew Shekel at 13.644-14.93 grams, with a 'minimal norm' of 14.93 grams.

Later, Hultsch (1898: 43-44) returned to the Hebrew system with the same method (only now the 'mosäische' Shekel was given as 14.55 grams, with another standard of 14.30 grams). He did not incorporate the new JILs found after 1882. The comparative metrology was common until the beginning of the twentieth century (occasionally also later, for example, Berrimen 1955: 193-94). It also influenced scholars of Israel, such as Warren (1903: Chap. 9; strangely, the JILs are not even mentioned in this book; for criticism, see 1.2.2 below).

1.2. *The Consolidation of Research (1912–39)*

1.2.1. *The Definition of the Phase and its Character*

The year 1912 marked a new phase in the study of the JILs. The final report of Gezer almost doubled the quantity of published JILs, yet throughout that phase the number of known JILs did not rise above a few dozen (mostly found out of context; see Fig. 1). The consolidation of research was expressed in a large number of general reviews of the JILs, starting with Pilcher (1912) and followed closely by Barton in 1916 (Barton 1937), Viedebannt (1923), Raffaeli (1920) and Diringer (1934). The first publication of a Museum collection also appeared (Rockefeller Museum 1940). The consolidation of research is marked by the growing awareness of metrological limitations. Many scholars during this phase began their studies with an introduction about the inability to weigh exactly in antiquity, the problem of how to define different standards and discover ancient fraud (Viedebannt 1923: 1; Pilcher 1912: 136; Barrois 1932: 59).

The final report of Gezer (Macalister 1912) offers a good example of the state of research in 1912. It was influenced by comparable metrology, in that Macalister tried to identify the JILs with foreign standards. It was also the first attempt to date the JILs by stratigraphy, though to the Persian or 'Maccabaean' levels (Macalister 1912: 280; cf. Macalister 1904a: 211 n. 1; 1904b: 359). Doubts with regard to this dating surfaced only later (Barrois 1932: 64; Sellers and Albright 1931: 9). Not many are aware that Macalister had also found evidence for the production of stone weights in Gezer, but unfortunately his description of this find was very laconic and inadequate (Macalister 1912: 257-58).

There were important improvements in the understanding of the ﬡ series during this period. Some scholars avoided the sign ﬡ (Barton 1937; Raffaeli 1920), but others suggested an identification with the biblical Shekel (not unequivocally, Pilcher 1912: 136). Diringer (1934: 283 n. 1) stated clearly the opinion that it is the Shekel sign. Concerning the metrological side, scholars still tried to identify the ﬡ weights with Babylonian or late standards (Macalister 1912: 190; Pilcher 1912: 136). Duncan's study (1931) was noteworthy in emphasizing the uniformity of the ﬡ weights in shape and material, but it did not receive its due attention. Strangely, Noth (1934: 242-43) understood that the numerals on the Samaria ostraca are Hieratic numerals, but no one noticed that similar numerals appear on the JILs (before

Aharoni, some 30 years later, cf. §1.4.1 below).

Scholars noted for the first time that the word 'Pym' is mentioned in 1 Sam. 13.21. It was noticed by Reifenberg (quoted in Pilcher 1914: 99), though M.H. Segal claimed the discovery as his own (1915). Pilcher (1915, 1916) also discussed this subject extensively. Barrois (1932) offered the most detailed study of the biblical weight system. He suggested that the Nsf weights represented 'a Shekel Nsf', that is, an independent Shekel standard which is different from the 'ℵ Shekel' (Barrois 1932: 72). This idea was extensively developed by Scott in the 1960s (see §1.4.3 below).[1]

1.2.2. *The Collapse of Comparable Metrology*
Sharp criticism of the comparable metrology method appeared during the early decades of the twentieth century (Weissbach 1907, 1916; Viedebannt 1923; Barrois 1932: 60-61), and the attempts to maintain comparable metrology (Lehman-Haupt 1910, 1912, 1956 [posthumously]) were futile (for a review, see Powell 1979: 74-77). The comparable metrology method ignored time and space, and related different systems solely by assumed mathematical connections. Any mathematical relation, even if remote or unlikely, was perceived as proof of a connection between different standards. Indeed, there might be a common, early origin for different standards (e.g. Powell 1979: 87-88; 1984: 33), but mathematical equations alone do not prove relationship, because they can be purely accidental. They must be supported by solid evidence of relations in space and time.

For the time being, many scholars continued to equate the JILs with foreign standards. Pilcher (1912) equated the Pym weights with $^2/_3$ *daric* (Persian stater), the Nsf weights with an Assyrian standard, the Beqaᶜ weights with an Egyptian gold standard, and so on. He did not foresee trouble when he assumed a contemporaneous appearance of all these standards in the land of Israel, though also offering a chronological distinction. In his view, the 'Babylonian' Nsf appeared in the Babylonian period, the Pym in the Persian period and the ℵ is a Greek standard of the classical periods. Petrie suggested similar theories (cf. §1.2.5 below). Viedebannt (1923: 2-4) opposed comparable metrology, but equated the JILs with foreign standards. He saw the obvious

---

1. Gandz (1933) discussed numerals and believed that there were archaic Hebrew numerals (for numerals in general, see Ifrah 1981). Other studies of this phase were made by Raffaeli (1920) and Reifenberg (1925, 1936).

relations between the ४, the Pym and the Beqaᶜ, but suggested that the Pym is ¹⁄₂ of a Phoenician standard, since this equation was mathematically more accurate. It did not matter to him that this Phoenician standard first became known much later, nor was he concerned about neglecting the Old Testament evidence (Exod. 38.26, 'a Beka a head, that is, half a shekel, after the shekel of the sanctuary').

1.2.3. *Flinders Petrie and Mathematical Metrology*
Petrie made an enormous contribution to the study of ancient Egyptian metrology. Not only did he alone publish some 4,000 weights from Egypt (Petrie 1926), but he also developed a unique method of study which can be termed 'mathematical'. Its nature and the way in which it was published make it difficult to understand, but it must be carefully reviewed, since it influenced the study of ancient Israel. Furthermore, Petrie himself found JILs in his excavations in Israel, and there are connections between the JILs and the Egyptian weight system.

Petrie's point of departure was a complete negation of comparable metrology, which he perceived to be speculative and a complete waste of paper (1926: 2). He first discovered 19 weights from Tanis (Sin el-Hajar), and here lie the foundations of his method (Petrie 1885). Petrie tried to find the 'original weight' by sampling the patina on metal weights, calculating the specific gravity of the patina, and thus finding how much metal turned into patina. From this, he found how much weight was lost and finally the 'original' weight (Petrie 1885: 52). This is a very cumbersome process, and it is hard to tell how much Petrie actually used this method. Since all the weights from Sin el-Hajar were uninscribed, Petrie (1885: 52-53) was forced to find the standards 'solely by trial'. He identified a few standards and named them after well-known, mostly foreign standards (Assyrian Shekel, Persian silver standard, etc.; 1885: 53). Petrie offered no definite proof (such as written sources or inscribed weights) that these standards were widely used in ancient Egypt.

The next significant step was the discovery of approximately 500 weights in Naukratis (Petrie 1886: ch. 9) and approximately 870 weights from Naukratis, Defnneh and Nebeshe (Petrie 1888: 80-93). Again, most of these weights were uninscribed, and Petrie sorted the standards by mathematical considerations: 'we should treat ancient weights as we should a set of astronomical observations' (Petrie 1886: 70). This is true despite of the lack of accuracy in ancient times, since

Petrie believed that we can use our exact instruments in order to find
the mistakes of the ancients (1886: 70). Compare the rather different
method of Griffith (1892, 1893).

Petrie used material and shape to a certain extent, but weight was his
most crucial consideration. The few inscribed weights were not used in
order to identify the standards (Petrie 1886: 70). The data was presented graphically and one of Petrie's aims was to create a definite
corpus. At this stage, Petrie (1886: 75-83) recognized nine different
standards and identified them with famous foreign standards[2] that were
supposedly used in daily Egyptian life. Petrie was aware of historical
development, and tried to find a chronological order of standards.
Unfortunately, he had acquired most of the weights in return for
bakshish, and he did not register their exact context. Other weights
were collected by locals from the surface of nearby sites (Petrie 1888:
80-81; cf. Hemmy 1937: 42).

The zenith of Petrie's method is found in a monumental corpus of
weights (Petrie 1926). The neglect of the inscribed weights is very
obvious there. It was conscious, and justified by the assumption that
most of the inscriptions (including numeral signs) on weights are
'secondary', not original. For example, one weight carries the numeral
9 (Petrie 1926: catalogue no. 2640). Petrie claimed that it is a weight of
10 *daric*, which equaled 9 *qdt*. It is not simply 9 *qdt*, since a multiplication of 9 is not typical of the *qdt* standard (being a unit in a
decimal system). But such a claim is, to a large extent, tautological: this
weight can reflect mistake or fraud, or an original 9 *qdt* weight, which
was inscribed precisely because it is a rare multiple. In another
example, Petrie (1926: 3) read the numeral ||| as 4 [× 5 *qdt*], that is, 20
qdt, but in other weights he read the very same sign, ||||, as 4. Thus, the
same sign is used for two numeric values (4, 20). This is against the
basic logic of any numeric system. The Egyptians could not know
when |||| is 4 and when it is 20. Furthermore, Petrie did not explain why
the existing Hieratic numeral 20 (ㅅ) was not used in this case. Petrie
(1926: 3) tried to claim that the same standard names (Shekel, Maneh)
were used in different times and places, not necessarily for the same
quantities of weight. This may be true, but it does not justify the neglect
of the inscribed weights.

2.   These are: Egyptian qat (= *qdt*), Attic drachma, Phoenician shekel, Persian
siglos, Aegean drachma, Roman ounce, Arabian durham and an '80 grains standard' (ancient name unknown).

If we examine the inscribed weights published by Petrie, severe doubts arise regarding his conclusions. For example, let us look at a weight inscribed ⦀⦀, which is one of eight identified as 'Pym weights' (Petrie 1926: 9, catalogue no. 2107). Its weight is 1834 grains (approximately 119 grams). Where is the Pym? It is 'hidden': Petrie read the numeral ⦀⦀ as 4 × 4; that is, 16 Pym of 7.43 grams each. The rest of Petrie's 'Pym' weights are similar: none is 'a primary Pym'. Even more unlikely is Petrie's explanation of weight no. 2086, which carries the sign ∩. Its weight fits one whole Pym, but Petrie explained it as half of a double unit ($\frac{1}{2} \times 2 = 1$).

There remained cases of doubtful standards, even after using such calculations, and the sorting of sub-standards was even more complicated. I will cite just one example, to show how Petrie separated '$\frac{1}{8}$ Beqaᶜ' from '$\frac{1}{5}$ Pym'. The reader should remember that Petrie applied these names to weight units, which are different from those of the JILs. Petrie's (1926: 7) argument went thus:

- $\frac{1}{5}$ Pym cannot be heavier than 25 grains, since the heaviest 'standard Pym' weighs 125 grains.
- If both units ($\frac{1}{5}$ Pym and $\frac{1}{8}$ Beqaᶜ) exist, then there will be more weights in the range of both these units (23.5–25 grains), than in the range of $\frac{1}{8}$ Beqaᶜ alone (25–26.5 grains).
- Actually, the quantities of weights in both ranges are equal, thus $\frac{1}{5}$ Pym does not exist.

This is a problematic line of argument. How can we be sure that the Pym standard is never heavier than 125 grains? What exactly is this 'standard Pym'—were there Pym weights that are not standard, and how can one find this out? Petrie also used exact mathematical calculations, but these require a large quantity of weights of each sub-unit, otherwise the statistic is not reliable. To sum up, Petrie's corpus of weights (1926) is a monumental piece of work, but it is arranged by theoretical calculations (as Petrie himself admitted, 1926: 1).

1.2.4. *The Catalogue of Weigall*

While Petrie followed his 'mathematical metrology' throughout his life, Weigall (1908) suggested a simpler method for sorting the collection of weights in the Cairo Museum. Weigall found only six standards in ancient Egypt, of which he defined two as foreign in origin and rare in distribution. It seems that the difference between Weigall and Petrie is partly a result of the different databases. The collection at the Central Museum in Cairo included many inscribed weights, which had a major role in Weigall's classification (1908: xv), whereas Petrie had to be content mainly with uninscribed weights.

1.2.5. *Petrie and the JILs*

As we saw earlier, Petrie (1926) identified Egyptian weights with the names Beqaᶜ, Pym and Nsf. At the same time, he suggested that the sign ୪ is a Greek monogram *kh* + *o*, denoting the word *khoirine*. This is the Greek name for cowry shell, which in his view served as a unit of weight. That created a confusing situation: the JILs are found in a late period in Judah, but the standard is found much earlier in Egypt, while the name is Greek. Similarly, the Beqaᶜ was detached from the Hebrew Shekel system (Petrie 1926: 17-18) and explained as an Egyptian golden standard—despite the facts that its weight does not fit this Egyptian golden standard and that it is mentioned in direct relation with the Shekel in Exod. 38.26.

Petrie found JILs in his excavations in Israel, in Tel Jemmeh, Tel el-Far'ah (south) and Tel abu-Sleimeh (Petrie 1928: 25-26; 1930: 15; 1937: 12). He continued to ignore the inscriptions, since these did not always agree with his exact mathematical calculations. For example, he commented that a Nsf of 9.28 grams from Gezer was 'clearly' an Egyptian *qdt* standard. He explained its inscription as a fraud, or a Nsf in origin that was devalued secondarily into a *qdt* (cf. Appendix 1: Nsf 10). It must be acknowledged that there are mathematical relationships between the JILs and Egyptian weights, but the nature of these relationships only became clear much later, in the 1960s.

One or two later scholars claimed that there were ୪ (JIL) weights in Egypt (e.g. Eshel 1986: 358-67). Eshel referred especially to one weight inscribed 'V.୪' (Petrie 1926: no. 5152). This is a mistake: the material, shape, weight and inscription are different from the JILs; it is a Roman ounce weight (cf. Qedar 1981: nos. 108-109).

1.3. *Lachish: A Transitional Phase (1939–58)*

During the years 1939–58 only a few studies were published on the JILs. This is not surprising, as World War II and the Israeli–Arab war in 1948 were hardly conducive to archaeological work. Of the few excavations published (Y. Aharoni 1956: 137-38; McCown 1947; Wampler 1947), Lachish was the most important with regard to the

JILs (preliminary report by Diringer [1942]; later in the Iron Age Report [Diringer 1953]).

This publication did not provide a breakthrough in method, nor in quantity of published JILs (Fig. 1). The major contribution concerned the dating of the JILs to level II of the late Iron Age, though the excavators did not reject completely the possibility that some JILs date later, to the Persian period or even to the Hellenistic period. The problem was that many JILs were found out of context, and the debate about the date of level III added to the uncertainty. Otherwise, Diringer's study (1953: 349) was conservative. For example, he took the Pym to be ^{2}/$_3$ of a Shekel (following Speiser 1967 [1940]), but he did not identify the ୪ with the Old Testament Shekel, nor did he question where those two-thirds came from (Diringer 1958: 229-30). He identified the Beqa‘ with an Egyptian gold standard (following Petrie, but see §1.2 above). Diringer tried to date the JILs by paleography to the same period of the *lmlk* stamps (Diringer 1953: 349). He even claimed that ୪ weights were earlier than other JILs, on archaeological and paleographical grounds (1953: 352). This is unlikely: archaeology demonstrated nothing of the sort, and there are no Hebrew letters on the ୪ weights. Thus epigraphic comparisons to Hebrew inscriptions are impossible.

During this phase of research, Moscati (1951) published a short summary, strengthening the dating of the JILs to the Iron Age II period. Barrois (1953) offered a short summary of his earlier studies. A somewhat exceptional work was published by Einzig (1949), concerning the beginning of money. Einzig thought that the Israelites used a developed monetary system even before the invention of coins (1949: 222). Silver was used as a standard of value, but not as a unit of account to facilitate barter, nor as a standard for deferred payments (1949: 221). However, Einzig made no reference at all to the JILs.

1.4. *Between Calculations and Explanations, Part I (1959–79)*

1.4.1. *The Phase and its Character*
The two decades between 1959 and 1979 were fruitful years for the study of the JILs. Many new weights were published (especially from Jerusalem; Fig. 1), matched by important contributions to the understanding of the JILs. The first study that was dedicated wholly to uninscribed weights from Israel appeared during this period (R. Segal 1971), and JILs appeared in auction catalogues (Agora 1974, 1975). I

will review the developments according to the different series of the
JILs.

1.4.2. *Heavy JILs and the Problem of the Sign* ষ

During the 1920s one heavy weight of 40 ষ was found in Jerusalem
(Duncan 1931: 216-17). Later, more weights were discovered in Jerusalem (Scott 1965: 134-35) and Samaria (Kerkhof 1966, 1969;
Y. Aharoni 1971b). Their weight clarified that the ষ series is built on
multiples of 8 or 4 (16 ষ, 24 ষ and 40 ষ), and the inscriptions were a
great aid in understanding the Hieratic numerals (below).

Scott (1959a) suggested that the ষ sign is a schematic representation
of the Old Testament *Ṣeror* (צְרוֹד), which was the sack, or bag, where
lumps of silver were held (e.g. Gen. 42.35). However, according to the
Old Testament, the weights (called literally 'stones') were carried in a
'pocket' (בכּיס) and not in the *Ṣeror* (cf. Deut. 25.15; Mic. 6.11; etc.).
Scott tried to overcome this difficulty by claiming that what is important is not the exact keeping-place of the weights, but that of the silver;
and that the weights were related to silver (1959a: 34). This suggestion
was rightly rejected, but it included an important note by Albright (in
Scott 1959a: n. 14), that ষ is an Egyptian Hieratic sign, *šs*.

Yadin (1960) translated the ষ sign as a symbol of the royal, official
standard of Judah. This was based on a weight from Gezer, inscribed
'‖ *lmlk*'. Yadin claimed that the sign ষ on the JILs is interchangeable
with the word *lmlk* on the Gezer weight, and on the *lmlk* jar impressions. Furthermore, he suggested that the ষ is a schematic form of the
scarab (or 'sun-disc') of the *lmlk* seal impressions. Yadin (1960)
thought that this was the royal symbol of the kingdom of Judah, and
that hence the weights are royal weights (cf. Rainey 1965: 34-35).[3] It
must be said that the resemblance between the ষ and the *lmlk* scarab is
very doubtful (for the symbols, see Goff 1979; Parayre 1993). Although
the symbolism of the sign ষ remained vague, all the scholars agreed
that the sign meant the Shekel (Stern 1963: 866; Scott 1959a: 32).
Henceforward, the argument was limited to the question of which
Shekel was it: royal or commercial? heavy or light? Most scholars preferred the view that it was a royal, heavy Shekel (including Scott and
Yadin).

---

3.   Yadin also found the ষ sign in the Babylonian and Persian periods, but the
relationships between the later signs and the JILs are not clear (cf. Kochman 1982:
27-28; Stern 1992: 70; Di Segni 1990: 214).

1.4.3. *Understanding the Hieratic Numerals of the ʊ Series*
I have already mentioned Albright's note about the similarity of the ʊ
and the Hieratic sign *šs* (in Scott 1959a: n. 14). Yadin ignored this clue,
and explained the numerals of the ʊ weights (and the Samaria ostraca)
as 'Hebrew numerals' for the values of 1, 2, 4, 8 and so forth (Yadin
1960). If these are Hebrew numerals, why the strange base of 4 or 8,
instead of a decimal base? Yadin (1960) wrote that each unit multiplies
the former, but this is not an explanation. He claimed that this is the
most economical base, since it enabled the weighing of 1 to 15 whole
Shekels with the help of only four weight stones. But was this feature
so important? In the larger units (16, 24 Shekel), the multiples of 8 are
very peculiar. In any case, many scholars accepted Yadin's view. Stern
(1963: 876; cf. Kisch 1965: 218-19) looked for a proof of this theory in
an ostracon from Mesad Hashavyahu, '*šql ʾrbʿ ksf* ٦ ʊ', concluding that
Hieratic ٦ is 4 in this ostracon and on the JILs.

Scott (1965: 135) made an important step forward. He saw that the ʊ
series is built on multiplication of 8, and the 8 ʊ weights are the most
common. Since 8 ʊ equals more or less the weight of 1 Egyptian *dbn*
(= 10 *qdt*), the hexagonal multiples were deliberately chosen to conform to the Egyptian weight system in order to facilitate international
trade. Then Y. Aharoni (1966) identified the JIL numerals as Hieratic
numerals. In fact, Noth (1934) had preceded Aharoni by more than 20
years, but Noth failed to connect the numerals of the Samaria ostraca
with the JILs. Aharoni saw that one ostracon from Arad carries a
monthly date, '𝕏 ‖‖', that is, '𝕏 + 4'. This sign can be only 10 or 20
(there are no more than 31 days per month, and Aharoni assumed that it
is a decimal system). Aharoni (1966: 14-16) found that this sign (𝕏) is
the Hieratic numeral 20. He saw that all the ʊ weights carry Hieratic
numerals, which fit the Egyptian *qdt*, not the Judaean Shekel. For
example, the Hieratic numeral 20 appears on weights of 16 Judaean
Shekel; and the numeral 10 on weights of 8 Judaean Shekel.

Aharoni's breakthrough brought to the surface new problems. In the
metrological field, weights of 1 and 2 Shekel do not match the Egyptian
qdt, but directly fit the Judaean Shekel (ʊ). Aharoni did not refer to this
fact, which raises the problem of the use of the numerals on the JILs.
Were these 'face-value' Hieratic numerals, or did they have a unique
value on the JILs, different from their original one? For example, how
should we read the Hieratic numeral ٦ on 8 Shekel weights: 10, or perhaps 8 (according to the weight)? This question has wide implications—

for example, for the Samaria ostraca, should one read ٦ as 5 (as Aharoni) or as 4 (as Yadin)? Supporters were found for both methods. Stern and Dever followed Yadin, and presented an ostracon from Mesad Hashavyahu as proof (see above; Stern 1963: 876; Dever 1970: 177-78). Kaufman (1967) followed Aharoni, but his argument was based on the Gerah series, where Hieratic numerals appear as well. He thought that here they appear in their face value (٦ is 5 Gerah; ٦ is 10 Gerah; etc.). It should be mentioned that the Gerah series is difficult, and could hardly be used as proof in this matter during the 1960s and 1970s. Another problem were two extra signs on the base of one Beqaᶜ weight, one above the other: ٦ and ٦. It looks like the Hieratic numerals 10 + 5, but the Beqaᶜ cannot hold 15 Gerah. Kaufman found an excuse, that here the signs mean '$2/3$', thus '$2/3$ *qdt*', still at 'face value' (1967: 41 n. 21; cf. Demski 1976: 119-21). This is not very convincing.

1.4.4. *Developments in the Other Series*
During this phase, some scholars separated the Nsf from the ۵ and the other JILs. Diringer (1958: 227-28, following Barrois 1932) suggested that the Nsf is a 'common Shekel', which originated from a heavy Shekel of 20 grams. Stern (1963: 870-71) accepted this view but, unlike Diringer, identified the ۵ with the Old Testament Shekel. It turned the Nsf into a totally independent standard, with no connection to the ۵ or the Old Testament Shekel. Scott took a similar view: the Nsf is a 'light Shekel', half of a heavy Syrian Shekel of approximately 20 grams. The ۵ belonged to a later system, while, in a third stage of development, the Nsf returned as the Old Testament 'holy Shekel' (שקל הקדש; Scott 1964, 1965). Similar views were adopted by De Vaux (1961: 309-13), Dever (1970: 18), and Ben-David (1979). Ben-David (1979) regarded the Nsf as a royal standard, but this was based on one exceptional weight from an unknown origin (see Appendix 1: Nsf.a).[4]

Lane (1961: 2-3) found the Pym unit in weights marked with the letter *p* from Cyprus and Carthage, and in the word παιμα on a Cretan coin from the fifth century BCE. This led him to conclude that Pym was not an original Hebrew word. However, it seems to me that Lane's analogies are doubtful. Apart from some semblance of sound, the

---

4.   He also trusted a basalt object (Ben-David 1975), which is probably forged (cf. Delavault and Lemaire 1979: 33).

words are not the same, not to mention the different periods, weights, materials and places.

The Beqa^c was identified as $^1/_2$ of the Old Testament Shekel by all scholars during this stage of research, and as $^1/_2$ ષ by most of them. Scott (1964: 58; 1965: 136) was aware that on average, the Beqa^c weights are a little heavier than $^1/_2$ ષ. He explained this fact as a general tendency of small-scale weights (also Stern 1963: 871). Noteworthy is an iron Beqa^c weight (Shany 1967); as far as I know, it is the only JIL made of iron that has been discovered.

Scholars did not manage to provide a satisfactory explanation of the Gerah series during this period. They could not formulate a valid, general explanation, and made many offers for each sub-unit, often involving weird calculations without the ability to choose between them. Scott (1964; 1965: 136-37; cf. Stern 1963: 872-73) was no different in this regard. The problem was that these calculations were launched from faulty points of departure, spreading to many paths, but leading nowhere in particular.

1.4.5. *Date, Distribution and Historical Significance*
In the late 1950s, few scholars still adhered to a late dating of the JILs; the dating to the late Iron Age II was dominant and soon became accepted (Scott 1965: 137; Stern 1963: 866). Until the 1970s, the separation of the eighth and seventh centuries BCE was not clear, and a finer dating of the JILs was impossible. Yadin (1960) was the first scholar to connect the JILs specifically with the kingdom of Josiah. He defined the JILs as the official, royal standard of Judah, and saw their distribution pattern as another piece of evidence to support the theory that Judah had become a large, important kingdom under King Josiah. This theory gained momentum at precisely the same time, owing to the excavations of Mesad Hashavyahu, which was explained as a fortress of Josiah (Naveh 1962: 32). Therefore, JILs from Gezer were seen as evidence for Josiah's control over this city (Yadin 1960). Many scholars accepted Yadin's view, but Scott (1965: 133) went even further. He believed that Josiah's reform (2 Kings 23) included a standardization of the weight system by creating a unified, 'standard' system of weights. This was an 'amendment' to a supposedly old and devalued Shekel system, made according to the deuteronomistic demand of 'just balances' and 'just weights' (Deut. 25.15; Lev. 19.35-36). Similar views became common (Kenyon 1967: 104; 1974: 163;

Dever 1970: 104, though he knew about the discovery of further JILs outside Judah; Cross 1962: 21-22).

Dever (1970: 186-87) dated the JILs back to a period later than the fall of the kingdom of Israel (720 BCE), arguing that they are not on Israel's territory (cf. a similar argument about the *lmlk* stamps, Diringer 1949: 84). This claim cannot be substantiated: if the JILs are Judaean weights, there is no reason for them to appear in the area of Israel, regardless of their chronology.

Even Aharoni (1966) accepted Yadin's dating, as well as the connection of the JILs with Josiah's reform. Aharoni saw no difficulty in the fact that JILs were found outside Judah: on the contrary, it strengthened the notion of a great kingdom of Josiah. This 'nation-alistic-Josiahnic' explanation went hand in hand with the explanation of the base of 8 with regard to international trade. The JILs were supposedly part of a national, religious reform of 'justice', and at the same time an economical means of international relations. The two poles thrived happily together in the literature of that period.

1.4.6. *Scott and the 'Many Standards' Method*

Scott was the prominent scholar of the JILs in the 1960s. I have termed his theory a 'many standards' method, and present it as follows in detail because I hold a very opposite viewpoint. Scott and his followers always separated the JILs into different standards, which were seen as independent entities. Each series (ﬡ, Nsf, Pym, etc.) was explained independently—and often even each unit. For example, one 4 ﬡ weight from Gibeon is heavier than the other 4 ﬡ weights (Appendix 1: no. 31; Pritchard 1959: 30), so it is taken to be an independent 'heavy Shekel' standard.

What is the advantage of a many standards theory? The answer is simple: it is an easy way to explain the existence of weights that are similar in shape and material and carry the same signs, but still vary in weight. Multi-standard explanations were not new to the JILs (e.g. Diringer 1958: 22), and Scott held them from the beginning of his work (Scott 1959b). I will review the metrological aspect here (for the Old Testament aspects, see Chapter 6). Scott's main conclusion was that the JILs incorporate three different weight systems:

1.	The ﬡ Shekel, defined also as a common Shekel of 24 Gerah.
2.	The Nsf, which is a 'light Shekel' of 20 Gerah. This is the holy Shekel of Ezekiel and the Priestly source, valued at $^5/_6$ of

the ⊗ Shekel (Scott 1959b: 32-33, 39). The proof that it is a different standard is found in two inscribed weights from Samaria (discussed below).

3. A heavy Shekel of approximately 13 grams, deduced from a few ⊗, Nsf and Beqaᶜ weights, which are supposedly too heavy to belong with standards 1 and 2 (1959b: 39).

Weight was the most important factor for Scott (1959b: 39), and even very small differences of weight became overwhelmingly important. He also believed that heavier weights are earlier, because standards deteriorate with time, going through a process of gradual devaluation (1959b: 39). Yet Scott was well aware of the lack of accuracy in ancient weight metrology (1959b: 23, 32, 39). Scott presented his method in the fullest terms in a paper about the Gerah (1964). Three inscribed weights formed the basis of all the discussion:

1. A tortoise-shaped weight of 2.5 grams from Samaria, inscribed with the numeral 5 (5 vertical lines). Scott read this as '5 Gerah', hence 1 Gerah = c. ¹/₂ gram, and 1 Shekel of 24 Gerah = 11.976 grams, thus corresponding to the ⊗ weights.

2–3. A weight of 2.54 grams inscribed *rbᶜ Nsf rbᶜ šl* ('¹/₄ Nsf ¹/₄ šl'), and a weight of 2.63 grams inscribed *plg rbᶜt* ('*plg* of ¹/₄?') were explained by Scott as ¹/₄ Nsf weights. This means that the Nsf included 20 Gerah (its ¹/₄ equals 5 Gerah), so that the turtle weight (no. 1 above) is also a ¹/₄ Nsf weight.

From these three weights alone, Scott already deduced two standards: ⊗ of 24 Gerah, which is the 'royal Shekel', and 'Shekel Nsf' of 20 Gerah, which is a 'light Shekel' (Scott 1959b: 56-57). These standards were equated with Old Testament sources: the ⊗ with the 'weight of the king' (אבן המלך) and the Nsf with the 'holy Shekel' (שקל הקדש).

1.4.7. *Criticism of Scott's Explanation of the Gerah Series*
Even a superficial reading of Scott is enough to cast doubts. One discrepancy concerns the Nsf. Scott (1959b: 57) believed that the Nsf originated in Ugarit, where it was half of a heavy Shekel of approximately 20 grams. If so, why is the Nsf of the JILs equated with a light Shekel? Another problem concerns the Beqaᶜ series. Scott agreed that the Beqaᶜ is half an ⊗, but in Exod. 30.13 Beqaᶜ is half of a 'holy Shekel', not half of a royal, 'heavy Shekel'. Scott (1959b: 58) gave unconvincing excuses, such as that Exod. 30.13 is a secondary gloss or misspelling, or that the Old Testament word half (חצי) is not

equal in meaning to our modern half.

These are trifles in comparison with the main issues that concern the Gerah weights. Scott mingled assumptions and conclusions, Old Testament sources and archaeological objects. His method is based on three inscribed weights, which were found outside Judah, in Samaria and near Gaza. They are totally different in material, shape and inscription from the JILs, and therefore cannot be used as foundation for the understanding of the JILs. Their names alone (Shekel, Nsf) do not prove relation with the JILs, since these are common names in different places and periods (cf. Petrie 1926: 3). These three weights are probably Phoenician, or at least related to Phoenicia (according to their inscriptions; Delavault and Lemaire 1979). Furthermore, there are problems concerning the understanding of these three weights: for example, the words *plg* and *šl*. Nor should one forget the notorious lack of accuracy of small weights, and their tendency towards the heavy side (cf. Scott himself, 1964: 58; 1965: 136). Scott assumed the existence of two Shekel standards, differing in the number of Gerah (20 and 24). But the Old Testament recognizes only 20 Gerah in the 'holy Shekel'; and the three weights from Samaria and the region of Gaza hardly indicate the nature of the Old Testament Shekel (whether royal or holy). Scott did not identify the numerals on the Gerah weights as Hieratic numerals. He assumed that almost any sub-unit is possible ($^2/_6$, $^3/_8$, $^2/_{12}$) for each unit of weight (Nsf, Beqaᶜ and ৪). Therefore, he was left with many possible calculations, unable to choose between them (Scott 1959b: 57-62). I find it hard to follow a method that fails to explain most of the objects under study. Other scholars fared no better at that time, and understanding the structure of the Gerah series was achieved only later.

1.4.8. *The Weights from Jerusalem (Scott 1965, 1985)*

The culmination of Scott's studies came with the publication of the weights from Kenyon's excavations in Jerusalem. Scott (1965) made only few, minor changes in method. He sorted the weights according to their state of preservation, and believed that one weight is representative of the original ৪ standard, because it is in 'mint' condition (1965: 132; here Appendix 1; ৪ 4.2). The other ৪ weights from Jerusalem are less well preserved, but some are lighter and some are heavier than this 'mint' weight. Scott (1965: 134) explained these variations by the existence of two separate ৪ standards. One standard was approximately

1.7 per cent heavier than the other, which was a later, lighter 'copy', made during Josiah's reform. Its makers used a devalued specimen as a prototype, thus reaching the lighter weight (Scott 1965: 133).

This theory is not convincing. First, there is no evidence whatsoever to prove that the 'mint' weight is the most accurate representation of the ชุ standard. Its excellent state of preservation state is no guarantee, since it does not rule out factors such as forgery or mistake in the manufacture. Second, Scott ignored the lack of accuracy in ancient metrology, recognized as up to 3 per cent by many scholars and for different systems (Egypt: Hemmy 1935: 83-85; 1937: 40; Skinner 1967: 33, 39; Mesopotamia: Powell 1979: 83). Written sources from Mari indicate the same phenomenon (Joannès 1989: 121; for the Aegean world cf. Petruso 1992: 6-7, 75-76). It was also acknowledged by Scott himself elsewhere, when he accepted weights with a 5 per cent deviation as ordinary JILs (e.g. Scott 1985: list no. 27). What, then, is the logic of assuming two standards with a difference of only 1.7 per cent in weight? Such standards could not be used at all in ancient periods, since they were not measurable. Variations of 1.7 per cent in ancient weights should be explained on other grounds (e.g. forgery, mistake in manufacture, wear by use), especially since the weights look the same (whereas different standards call for different shapes, materials or inscriptions, to guarantee their identification by users).

Scott (and his followers) overstressed the metrological factor in the study of ancient weights. On one hand, Scott identified slight variations as different standards, but on the other hand, he discarded weights as exceptional if their weight did not fit those assumed 'standards'. A small difference of weight was enough for that purpose. For example, one 2 ชุ weight (Appendix 1: ชุ 2.10) implies an ชุ of 10.88 grams. This was 'too light' for Scott (1965: 133), so he defined the ชุ sign on this weight as an exception and took the weight out of the discussion. Pym weights were called abnormal on the pretences that their script is crude and they are perhaps unfinished (Scott 1965: 135), but their only 'sin' seems to be that one is 7.4 per cent heavier than the other. For Scott, it is a huge difference that requires an explanation of different standards or abnormality. One Nsf weight weighs only 9.33 grams (1965: 136), when Scott's norm is 9.929 grams. So it was said to be a damaged specimen, copied from an earlier specimen, which was in itself very worn. There are more examples, but the these are enough to illustrate my point.

Furthermore, Scott had no stratigraphical evidence that some of the weights from Jerusalem are early and others are late. Many weights were found out of context (not through any fault of the excavators), others belong to one period—the late Iron Age. Scott did not even discuss the context of these weights. Finally, Scott (and practically all scholars of the JILs so far) assumed the existence of 'standards of weights' in ancient Judah, in the modern sense of this term. That is, scholars believed a weight unit was kept somewhere in Judah, regarded as an 'original norm' and used consistently to check other weights, through the power of a centralized, authoritative government. This is theoretically possible, but there is no evidence to prove it.

1.4.9. *Other Studies by Scott and a Summary*

Scott saw no problem with the existence of many different standards at the same time in Judah, but in a study about the Nsf he presented a chronological development (Scott 1970). Its main lines are shown in Figure 2. First there was a 'Nsf Shekel', originating from a heavy Ugaritic unit which had gradually devalued. The ୪ standard was introduced with the reform of Josiah, in order to reconstitute the devalued 'Nsf Shekel' by adding $\frac{1}{6}$ to its value (i.e. from 20 to 24 Gerah; Scott 1970: 62-63). The old 'Nsf Shekel' continued to be use as a 'light Shekel', side by side with the new ୪ Shekel. Finally, during the times of Ezekiel and the Priestly source, there was a return to the old 'Nsf Shekel' of 20 Gerah, now named 'holy Shekel'. This was achieved by reducing $\frac{1}{6}$ of the value of the ୪ standard. Throughout all these

System 1 **'Nsf-Shekel' of 20 Gerah** (originated from a Syrian 'heavy' standard)	→ → → → ↓
	System 2 ୪ **Shekel of 24 Gerah** (a $\frac{1}{6}$ was added to no. 1, during Josiah's reform)
System 3 **'Holy Shekel' (='Nsf-Shekel' of 20 Gerah)** (devaluation of a $\frac{1}{6}$ from no. 2, post exilic period)	↓ ← ← ← ←

Figure 2. *The Judean weight-standards according to Scott*

stages, the Kikar remained the same weight, but with different numbers of Shekel (at first it included 3,000 light 'Nsf Shekel', then 2,500 heavy ﬡ Shekel; Scott 1970: 63-64).

Theoretically, it is all possible. But where is the evidence? On the one hand, there is no archaeological evidence for temporal differences between ﬡ and Nsf weights. Scott himself (1970: 62) stressed that all the weights from Kenyon's excavations in Jerusalem belong to the same period. On the other hand, the Beqaᶜ appears in the Old Testament in relation with the holy Shekel, while its weight fits that of a ¹/₂ ﬡ.

The final publication of the weights from Kenyon's excavations in Jerusalem (Scott 1985) was probably written much earlier, and reflects no substantial changes in method. On the contrary, Scott (1985: 290) separated the ﬡ series even further, into three standards: one Josiahnic, the others earlier and heavier by 3 per cent and 1.8 per cent. These two heavier standard were supposedly a result of Assyrian influence, or the need to pay taxes to Assyria [*sic*]. The evidence for this theory was found in the inscribed *shema'* (שמע) weight (Avigad 1968, but it is an exceptional object, if not a forgery; Delavault and Lemaire 1979: 33).

Many aspects of Scott's studies are problematic, such as the simplified use of Old Testament sources, the method of many standards and the abuse of exact mathematical calculations. Scott neglected, to a large extent, the archaeological context of the JILs. Scott's major contribution was the understanding of the multiples of the ﬡ weights and their connection with the Egyptian *dbn/qdt* system.

1.5. *Between Calculations and Explanations, Part II (1976–96)*

1.5.1. *The Phase and its Character*
Abundant studies of the JILs appeared during this phase of research. I have chosen 1976 as its start because the separation of the eighth and seventh centuries BCE became more or less clear at this time through the work of Y. Aharoni (1976) and the renewed excavations at Lachish (Ussishkin 1976, 1977).

Starting in the 1970s, many JILs appeared in auction catalogues (Qedar 1978, 1979, 1981, 1983; Kroha 1980). This is a mixed blessing: these weights are likely to originate from robbers' activities, inflicting severe damage on sites. Date, origin and contexts are lost, and the information supplied by antiquities merchants cannot be trusted. Weights not sold in one auction may reappear in a later auction, and ultimately they disappear into collections. The few that reach public collections are republished, usually without reference to the auction catalogues, and one runs the danger of 'duplicating' the same weights by mistake. Furthermore, forgeries are possible, since it is not difficult to forge these simple stone objects. Identifying forgeries is not an easy task, unless genuine traits, that are unlikely to be known to forgers, appear (cf. the 12 ४ weight) and forgers can also improve and learn, like scholars.

During this period, two major views crystallized regarding the ४ series. One (Lemaire 1976: 33-34; Lemaire and Vernus 1978: 56) followed Scott in seeing the ४ as a royal Shekel of 24 Gerah, while the Nsf is the 'holy Shekel', that is, a 'light Shekel' of 20 Gerah. The other view (Barkay 1981a, 1987) identified the ४ with the Old Testament Shekel of 20 Gerah, which is also the 'holy Shekel'; and claimed that there was never a Shekel of 24 Gerah in Judah. Lemaire and Vernus (1978: 56-58) stressed the Egyptian influence on the JILs. Following Albright, they saw that ४ is the Hieratic sign *šs*, which has several meanings in Egypt. In their view, it means a denominator of alabaster on the JILs, in the sense of 'a standard of alabaster'. It must be pointed out that alabaster is not found naturally in Israel, and that the JILs are made of limestone, while in Egypt the sign ४ is not found on weights.

The discovery of one ४ weight in Tel Keisan and the full publication of the ४ weight from Tel el-Far'ah (north) brought the question of the distribution of the JILs to the surface again (Puech 1980, 1984). Puech (1984: 81) claimed that the few JILs from Tel Keisan, Tel el-Far'ah (north) and Transjordan are not connected with the Judaean Shekel. He also dated the weight from Tel el-Far'ah (north) earlier than the JILs from Judah. Yet these weights are identical to the JILs in every sense, and it is therefore unnatural to separate them from the JILs.

Regarding the Nsf, Lemaire and Vernus (1978: 56) followed Scott in relying on the *rbᶜ Nsf rbᶜ šl* weight from Samaria. They explained the Nsf as a 'light Shekel', which is the Old Testament 'holy Shekel'. This standard is supposedly later than the ४ Shekel. Lemaire and Vernus added that the Nsf was equal to the Egyptian *qdt*, and therefore the numerals of the ४ series indicated quantities of *qdt*.[5]

A systematic explanation of the Gerah series was made by Barkay (1981a), following Aharoni and Kaufman. Barkay took the Hieratic

---

5.   Crucial to the study of the JILs are the ostraca from Kadesh Barnea, published by Lemaire and Vernus (1980, 1983). These are discussed in Chapter 8 below.

numerals in this series at their face value. The average of the Gerah weights led him to the conclusion that there were only 20 Gerah in the ४ Shekel (1981a: 288-89). He believed that a Shekel of 24 Gerah never existed in Judah; nevertheless, the Gerah series is related to the ४ series and not to the Nsf. Barkay did accept the common dating of the JILs to the seventh to early sixth centuries BCE.

For some reason (perhaps the growing number of JILs), general reviews are rare in the present phase of research. One review is outstanding (Meshorer 1976). Meshorer suggested that all the JILs are part of the same system, and not many independent standards. However, this very short study (in Hebrew) did not receive its due attention.

1.5.2. *Ben-David and the Continuation of the 'Many Standards' Method*

Following a few short studies which need not be discussed (Ben-David 1973, 1975), Ben-David (1979) dedicated a long study to the units Pym and Nsf. It was a distinctively 'many standards' study. Ben-David reached the following main conclusions: (1) The Pym is a Philistine Shekel, and a gold standard of approximately 7.89 grams; (2) the Nsf is a Philistine 'light silver Shekel' of approximately 9.25 grams.

The Philistine 'ethnicity' of the Pym was taken from a very simplistic reading of 1 Sam. 13.21. The rest was built upon a complicated chain of arguments, as follows: a Ugaritic document (RS.1957.701) equates 5 Talents of Ugarit with 7 Talents of Ashdod (Ben-David 1979: 31-32). There were 3000 Shekel of 9.25 grams in one Ugaritic Talent, while an Ashdodite Talent was divided into 2500 Pym Shekels of 7.89 grams (1979: 31-32). Thus, we reach the approximate equation $2500 \times 7 \times 7.89 = 3000 \times 5 \times 9.25$. This equation is presented by Ben-David as proof of the theory.

In my view, this is not so simple. The Pym weights are found in Judah, not in Philistia. Ben-David (1979: 45) explained that the Philistines penetrated Judah during their battles with the Israelite tribes. However, this happened in the Iron Age I period, which was hundreds of years before inscribed Pym weights appeared. The Ugaritic document (RS.1957.701) is 700 years earlier than the JILs and its meaning is disputed (cf. Liverani 1972; Parise 1984). The equation reached by Ben-David is based on preconceptions about the Ugaritic and Philistine Shekels; it furnishes no decisive proof of this theory. There is no evidence on the number of Shekels in an Ashdodite Talent, and the weight system (or even basic standards) of Iron Age Philistia are barely known. Ben-David (1979: 41) acknowledged the fact that the Pym seems to be ^{2}/$_3$ ꙍ, but he believed that ꙍ is a silver standard and Pym is a gold standard, and 'it is famous' that silver and gold standards do not relate to the same system. Such a separation of gold and silver standards was once common, but is no longer acceptable today. Attributing the Pym to 'gold standard' was based on one, exceptional weight (Appendix 1: Pym.a).[6] Ben-David's lists of weights leave much to be desired—many details are missing (size, photographs or drawings), making it hard to identify some weights clearly. He also included doubtful artifacts, which do not seem to be JILs at all (e.g. Ben-David 1979: Nsf list nos. 13, 14, 26, 35, Pym list no. 25).

1.5.3. *Eran and the Extreme Many Standards Metrology*

Eran applied such an extreme many standards method to the study of the JILs, that it is, in fact, a return to the comparable metrology of the nineteenth century AD. This is clearly seen from his first publications (Eran and Edelstein 1977; Eran 1982). For example, Eran believed that 6–7 standards existed in every stratum in Ashdod, and each had its own multiples and subdivisions (Eran and Edelstein 1977: 54-56). The names of the standards were taken from Petrie (cf. §1.2 above). An abundance of standards is grasped as the natural, indeed the only possible, situation (Eran 1982: 95-96). Otherwise, Eran did not make any effort to prove his many standards approach, since he presented it as fact, which needs no further explanation.

Thus, Eran and Edelstein (1977) assumed that both a light Babylonian Shekel and a heavy Babylonian Shekel were used in Late Bronze Age Accho, not only as some rare imported weights, but in everyday life and with locally made weights. Eran never wondered what trade relations existed between Accho and Babylon during this period, if at all. The logic is obvious, though crude: if 6 or 7 standards are possible at the same time and place, and if each is independent (having its own multiples and sub-units), then there is no end to the possibilities of calculations. The metrologist remains happy, for if one weight will not fit, say, ^{2}/$_6$ Pym, then it will surely fit ^{3}/$_8$ Nsf, or ^{5}/$_{10}$ Shekel. Should even such possibilities fail, the metrologist, like a necromancer, will

---

6.   Ben-David calculated averages differently (using the heaviest and the lightest weight in each unit, rather than all existing specimens), but this is not a crucial difference.

consult any remote standard, from Rome to Greece and Persia, for 'seek and you shall find'. Notwithstanding the joys of calculations, it is an easy method but, to be honest, it makes it possible to ascribe almost any small weight to more than one standard. If one adds factors of fraud, mistake in manufacture and wear by usage, how can a certain weight be ascribed to a certain standard? *Mathematical equations themselves prove nothing.*

While dealing with the *dbn*, Eran (1985: 2-3, 5) criticized Petrie for suggesting too few standards [*sic*], and praised Hultsch from the nineteenth century for finding that the Roman *libra* was common in ancient Egypt. Not surprisingly, a study on the Gerah (Eran 1987) is dedicated to Lehman-Haupt of the 'comparable metrology'. The 'innovation' of Eran is the dichotomy of the Gerah weights into not less than six independent standards, simply because Gerah weights with the same signs vary too much in his view (Eran 1987: 5, and the Table). Thus, Eran found among the Gerah weights a heavy Nsf of 10.49 grams; a light Nsf of 9.41 grams; a ὄ of 11.39 grams (which derives from an ¹/₈ Egyptian *dbn* [*sic*]; a Phoenician Shekel of 14.57 grams; a Judaean Pym of 7.56–7.668 grams; and a 'holy Judaean Shekel' of 13.34 grams.

There is no problem: if a certain Gerah weight will not fit the first, second or third standard, it is bound to fit the fourth, fifth or sixth, or Eran will add a seventh as he pleases. We are also not bored, since each standard is subdivided differently into 24, 20, 12 or 10 units. As long as a mathematical equation is found (it does not matter which), it 'proves' the method. The uniformity, achieved by the remarkable study of Barkay (1981a), was shattered by Eran. Eran also presented a chronological scheme (abusing Scott): first there was a Shekel of 20 Gerah, which was turned to a new heavy Shekel of 24 Gerah, and later reduced back to 20 Gerah, and this made for a clear separation between the 'holy Shekel' and the heavy Mesopotamian Shekel of 13.38 grams, which also had 24 Gerah (Eran 1987: 7). One mistake indicates the nature of the problem: Eran gave one weight as 10 Gerah of 0.52 grams, and another as 11 Gerah of 0.4736 grams each. He did not notice that it is the same weight, published twice (Eran 1987: Appendix C, No. 30 = No. 34; here Appendix 1: 10 Gerah.12). However, the mistake is not the problem—the method is: it shows how Eran separated 'standards' on the basis of calculations alone.

Recently, Eran discussed the treasure from Eshtamo'a (1990; for treasures, see Arnaud, Calvet and Huot 1979; Bjorkman 1993, 1994). He also published objects from Shiloh (Eran 1994), which demonstrate another feature—his tendency to identify weights according to their weight only, regardless of shape, material and context. Many are natural pebbles or pestle stones which were never used as weights.

The publication of the weights from the City of David (Eran 1996) is not worth discussing (the catalogue is useful, though it includes pebbles, natural stones and other *varia* that Eran collects). One weight (Eran 1996: w308) is perhaps nothing but a roller stone (Cré 1892). It seems that Eran is determined to ignore the last hundred years and return to the comparable metrology method of the late nineteenth century.

1.5.4. *Other Studies and a Summary*

Di Segni (1990) published a long review of weight systems in Israel. Her method is, again, that of many standards, but she relies on old literature. She did not present a fresh study of the material, but a mixture of speculations and assumptions, a few examples of which would suffice. Di Segni mentioned (1990: 215) the difference in the quantities of Talents taken by Sennacherib from Judah after 701 (300 in his annals versus 800 in the Old Testament). She takes this as an indication that 'in the 8th century BCE Judah, the gold was weighed in Babylonian Shekels, while the silver was weighed in Talents which were $3/8$ of the Babylonian Talents' [*sic*; my free translation from the Hebrew]. There is not even one word of caution about the reliability of ancient sources, their tendency to exaggerate numbers, or the possibility of a simple mistake in one source (without any relevance to actual weight standards in Judah and Assyria). It is also pointless to ask Di Segni why the people of Judah should weigh their gold in Babylonian Shekels (and not in Judaean Shekels, as the JILs indicate). Di Segni's discussion of the Old Testament sources was interesting, since she simply took the scripture literally. In one place Di Segni (1990: 213) wrote, 'one should identify the holy Shekel with the light Nub, a standard that the Israelites brought with them from Egypt' [free translation from Hebrew].[7]

Heltzer (1996) discussed the 'unification' of weight standards in the Mediterranean in a short summary. I wish to point out that I have not discussed the Kikar and the Maneh (Kletter 1991), and the conclusions

---

7. For a few other general reviews, see Ridgeway 1970; Cooper 1980; Thompson 1986; Fritz 1994.

of Heltzer do not stem directly from my work. On the whole, Heltzer's article is welcomed and useful for the Late Bronze Age period. Heltzer mentioned the Egyptian unit *Sniw* (or *Šᶜty*), which I have mentioned in relation to Iron Age weights (Kletter 1994: n. 4, but read *Šᶜty* instead of the misspelling *Šᶜṭy*).

The study of Ronen (1996) is a different story. He invented two chronological phases of the JILs: before 700 BCE (supposedly a Shekel of 9.06 grams) and afterwards (the ⴲ of 11.33 grams). The evidence for this idea is scanty, to put it gently, and consists of two weights from unknown origins. Stratigraphy is neglected, and the 'historical' explanation (a major monetary change from Egypt to Assyria) is nothing but speculation.

A study of royal weighing in Mari, according to written sources (Joannès 1989), is remarkable. It shows different methods of weighing in a royal context, and is important for understanding ancient Near-Eastern weight systems. Finally, Powell (1992) offered a general review, but still thinks that the Nsf is separated from the ⴲ.

I have reviewed more than a hundred years of research in this chapter, and presented different metrological methods, each against the background of its period. During most of the times, an unfortunate separation existed between the metrological aspects (studied in great detail) and the archaeological/historical aspects (largely neglected). This criticism should not hide the fact that I could not have written this book without the existence of those former contributions, the best of which I will discuss again in the following chapters. Interestingly, some studies that involved only a few weights made important contributions (e.g. Y. Aharoni 1966; Barkay 1981a), so we can see that quantity was never a sign of quality (Fig. 1).

Chapter 2

THE DATE

I will try to date the JILs on the basis of archaeological evidence as much as possible, rather than on written sources, which will be discussed separately. The dating is based on the common chronology of the late Iron Age II period in Judah: that is, I follow the dating of Lachish level III to 701 BCE (Y. Aharoni 1976; Ussishkin 1976, 1977, 1982, 1983; Wightman 1985a; Zimhoni 1985, 1990). Other sites are dated accordingly, but need not be discussed here (cf. Kletter 1996: 7-9, with more references). Only 211 JILs (out of 434) are useful for dating, since their site of origin is known. This number includes all the JILs in the addenda, as well as three weights from Accho and Ekron, whose units are not clear (see note at the end of Appendix 2).

2.1. *Postexilic Dating*

A meagre number of JILs can be dated to periods later than 586 BCE (Fig. 3). Aharoni dated one weight from Ramat Rahel to level IV (Appendix 1: 8 ४.20). This level is somewhat disturbed, mainly composed of pits that contain mixed materials ranging from the Persian period to the first century BCE (Y. Aharoni 1956: 138-39, 1962, 1964). Thus, the date of this particular weight is not very clear. A few JILs were dated to Persian or to Hellenistic levels in the early excavations of Gezer (Macalister 1904a: 209; 1904b: 358; 1912: 280). This was not a systematic excavation, and we lack full details of the contexts of the finds. It seems that Macalister had a preconception about the date of the JILs, and his dating was not archaeologically based. One weight (Appendix 2: 16 ४.4) from the City of David was dated to the Persian level 9, but it is broken and the level is not yet fully published.

It seems that the JILs went out of use after 586 BCE. The very few JILs that were dated to later periods are likely to be intrusive or misdated artifacts. There are other arguments in favour of the same conclusion. Judah lost its independence in 586 BCE, and it is likely that the use of its local, independent weight system ceased. Its place was probably taken by the Babylonian/Persian weight system (cf. Stern 1973b: 135ff; Brewer 1991). At the same time, coins appeared and soon became widespread, transforming the nature of the economy. The invention of coins made weighing less critical (on local coinage in Israel during the Persian period, see Betlyon 1986; Mildenberg 1985a, 1988, 1991).

Date BCE	ŏ1	ŏ2	ŏ4	ŏ8	ŏ12–40	ŏ?	Nsf	Pym	Beqaʿ	Gerah	Total	%
Until 701	1	2	1				1			1	6	3%
700–586	9	13	23	21	1		4	8	1	5	85	40%
After 586				1?	1						2?	1%
Other date	8	14	15	20	4	3	16	16	12	10	118	56%
Total with origin	18	29	39	42	6	3	21	24	13	16	211	100%
Total JILs	42	42	56	51	11	3	59	52	35	83	434	

Notes: the column 'ŏ?' includes the weights from Accho and Ekron, whose unit is not clear.

Figure 3. *The date of the JILs*

2.2. *Dating to the Seventh Century* BCE *(700–586)*

Many of the JILs definitely belong to this period—at least 85 weights (40 per cent of the 211 JILs from known origins). These weights were found in clear levels of the seventh century BCE—that is, Lachish level II and its derivatives: Tel Batash II, Ein Gedi V, Arad VI–VII, Ramat Rahel V, Ekron I and the contemporary levels at Tel ʻIra, Aroer, Tel Malhata, the City of David level 10, Mesad Hashavyahu, and so on. Of course, the date of these levels is not totally accurate; there is place for factors such as the distance from Lachish, the nature of the level (if it was deserted or violently destroyed), and the method and quality of each publication (Kletter 1996: 7-9). A few weights from the seventh century BCE could have been manufactured earlier, at the end of the eighth century BCE, and continued to be used. This could have happened, especially in sites that were not destroyed during 701 BCE (e.g. Jerusalem and Ein Gedi). The possibility is a rather theoretical one, which cannot encompass a large number of weights. For this reason, I have retained the seventh-century-BCE dating for the JILs from Kenyon's excavations in Jerusalem (Kenyon 1967: 104; 1974: 162-63; Scott 1965: 128; 1985; though many of these weights were found out of context).

At present, the inner subdivision of the seventh century BCE is not clear. There have been different suggestions (Yadin and Geva 1983; Eshel 1986; for Philistia, see Oren 1986a, 1993). I suggested elsewhere that there are only two historical periods, dependent on the Assyrian withdrawal from the west, and perhaps two archaeological phases (Kletter 1996: 7-9). An example is Jerusalem levels 11–10 (Shiloh's excavations), but most of the JILs were found in older excavations and cannot be dated accurately.

2.3. *Dating to the Eighth Century BCE*

There are at least six JILs that were found in levels of the eighth century BCE or, more exactly, levels dated to that period by the excavators. Because of the great importance of these weights, I will discuss them in detail.

1-2. *Tel Beer Sheba*. Two weights, ४ 4.23 and Nsf.13. The Nsf weight was found in one of the storeroom houses near the gate (locus 282, Y. Aharoni 1973: chap. 6; *HadArch* 40 [1972]: 31-32). Part of the pottery of this locus was published, and the weight definitely belonged to level II. The ४ 4 weight was found in locus 808, a room in a four-roomed house on the north side of the Tell. The house was partially excavated, and only one vessel from locus 808 had been published so far (Y. Aharoni 1973: Pl. 84, Pl. 45.4). Again, the weight clearly belonged to level II, dated to the end of the eighth century BCE by the excavators (Y. Aharoni 1973: 5-6, 76; for the identification, see Na'aman 1987: 4 n. 2). I follow the chronology of the excavators, not the seventh-century-BCE dating suggested in the past by Kenyon (1976), Eshel (1986: II, 43) and Yadin and Geva (1983: Table). There are other suggestions for Tel Beer Sheba II: for example, by Na'aman (1979: 75; 1986a: 13), but the difference is not very significant for our purpose.

There was no real settlement in Tel Beer Sheba in the seventh century BCE, other than one wall and scanty remains defined as level I, which do not have real substance. Thus, the weights definitely belonged to level II and to the eighth century BCE. New studies of Tel Beer Sheba, such as Jericke (1992), Herzog and Singer-Avitz (1995) and Chapman (1995), do not effect this date. One cannot even assume that the weights were left by some seventh-century-BCE traveller, when the site itself was ruined: not only would it be a very unlikely theory, but the weights were found in loci of level II and not on the surface or in mixed loci. In his latest book, Y. Aharoni (1978: 225) suggested that the צ weights belonged to the time of Hezekiah. He did not explain his reasons for this dating, but perhaps it was related with the finding of JILs in the eighth-century-BCE contexts in Tel Beer Sheba.

3. *Lachish*. Weight 8 Gerah: 1. In a preliminary report, this weight was reported to come from locus H.18.1084, but in the final report the locus appears as H.18.1085 (Diringer 1942: 96 versus Diringer 1953: 349). This does not really matter: locus 1085 is a room in a house of level III, north of the road from the gate to the palace (Tufnell 1953: plan 114). A few *lmlk* impressions were found in this room. Locus 1084 is found south of the same road, and is also part of a whole building of level III (Tufnell 1953: 123). In any case, a date of level III is certain.

4. *Arad*. Weight 2 צ no. 16. It was found in square E/12, locus 418. The excavators ascribed it to level VIII of the late eighth century BCE (M. Aharoni 1981: 126). It is the only weight from Arad that was dated to this level. Locus 418 appears in the general plan as one of the casemate rooms. The acute problems of the stratigraphy of Iron Age Arad are well known. The date of the casemate wall, the temple and the separation of levels VII–VI are debated (for the excavators' view, see Y. Aharoni 1971a; Herzog *et al.* 1984; Herzog 1987; for criticism, see Mazar and Netzer 1986; Ussishkin 1988).[1] So far, the date of level VIII had not been debated, and its date to the eighth century BCE is valid. On the other hand, it seems that the casemate wall is indeed late, and removing it makes the distinction between levels VII–VI less clear (but their seventh-century-BCE date is not disputed). The full report on the excavations of Arad may help solve these problems, but currently there is no evidence against the dating of weight צ 4: 16 to the eighth century BCE.

5. *Tel el-Far'ah* (north). Weight צ 1 no. 13. I am not sure whether this weight was found in locus 113 or in locus 153. Locus 113 is a small room, inside a large building near the gate (Puech 1984: 79, 101, 109, plans 5-6). Locus 153 is a small installation of unclear stratigraphy inside room 113. The dating of the weight is not unequivocal (1984: 79,

---

1. In a lecture in London on 16 April 1996, Herzog accepted the late date of the casemate wall, but not the suggestion that the temple functioned only in the late Iron Age II.

101, 109, plans 5-6): it is mentioned in relation to both phases 7d and 7e. The excavators dated the end of phase 7d to the Assyrian conquest of 720 BCE (1984: 12), while phase 7e was dated mainly to the seventh century BCE. Yet 7e is a very disturbed phase and near the surface (1984: 47). 'Assyrian' pottery was found in both these phases (Chambon 1984: 69-70, Pl. 61), and it is the most indicative pottery of the late eighth and mainly seventh century BCE in northern Israel. Puech (1984: 81) claimed that the weight from Tel el-Far'ah is earlier than the other JILs, but the published evidence is not very clear, and a seventh-century-BCE date has not been ruled out.

6. *Beth Shemesh*. Weight ℧ 2: no. 20. This is the only JIL from Beth Shemesh. It was found in locus 351, a room in the centre of the 1933 area (Grant 1934: map 1). It was ascribed to level II (Grant and Wright 1939: 159, Pl. 53.50; Grant 1934: 55, Pl. 54.2). This is an Iron Age II level that has a few phases, defined after the end of the excavation (by Wright, in Grant and Wright 1939). This level was probably destroyed by Sennacherib in 701 BCE (Wightman 1985a: chap. 10, esp. 857-61). Beth Shemesh hardly existed in the seventh century BCE (Bunimovitz and Lederman 1993: 252). A few sherds of this period were collected in the nearby ruins of the Muslim village (Dagan, personal communication; Dagan 1992: 84, site no. 15). Grant (Grant 1931: 29; Grant and Wright 1939: 77-78, 144-45) found one tomb, no. 14, of the sixth century BCE. Mackenzie's short-lived 'squatters' phase perhaps continued a little after 701 BCE (Mackenzie 1912–13: 99f; see now Momigliano 1996: 161-64). The finds from the new excavations of the Bar Ilan University team have not yet been published.

2.4. *The Other Weights*

The rest of the JILs, a total of 118 weights of known origin (56 per cent of the 211 weights with origin), do not help much with the dating. Some of them can be dated to a general range of both the eighth and the seventh centuries BCE, or even the whole Iron Age II. Most of these weights, however, lack clear dating (I have been strict in judging dating data, in order to prevent mistakes). They were found during surveys, on the surface of excavated areas, or in uncertain loci (such as fills, mixed debris, and various secondary contexts).

Most of the 118 JILs mentioned above were found in sites that were occupied in the seventh century BCE, but this is not very helpful.

Usually, remains of the eighth century BCE are also present in these sites. Tel Beit Mirsim was probably not settled in the seventh century BCE, but JILs were not found there. A few JILs were found in Tel el-Far'ah (south), which may have seen a settlement gap during the same period (Yisraeli 1978: 1080, 1082 [Hebrew]). Distinctive seventh-century-BCE artifacts are not apparent in the report (Petrie 1930; Macdonald 1932; versus Eshel 1986: 358-59, but it is because his chronological scheme is different). In any case, it would be better not to place too much emphasis on this sort of evidence, and the few weights that can be dated through the settlement history of their sites do not change the general picture.

2.5. *Conclusion*

Following the available data, the JILs can be dated mostly to the seventh century BCE, with a likely *terminus ante quem* of 586 BCE. The very few weights that were dated later than 586 BCE are negligible in number and in importance. The crucial question is when the use of the JILs began. The answer depends on the few weights that were dated to the end of the eighth century BCE (above). We saw there that some doubts remain concerning the early date of the weights from Arad and Tel el-Far'ah (north). Even the date of the weight from Beth Shemesh is not completely free from doubt. We are left with three weights, or only 3.2 per cent of the 93 securely dated JILs (or, approximately 1.4 per cent of the 211 JILs that have clear archaeological origin).

This point forms a major crossroads in the study. It is tempting to dismiss these few early weights as exceptions, on pretences of mistakes in stratigraphy, intrusive objects that 'immigrated' from later levels, etc. This is no real explanation, but forced conclusion based on the preconception that the JILs belong exclusively to the seventh century BCE. It seems to me that one must accept the stratigraphy of these weights, unless there is solid evidence to the contrary. Since such evidence is lacking, the conclusion is clear: the JILs began to function *as a system* at the end of the eighth century BCE at the latest. I stress the word 'system', for even if one JIL existed, it implies the use of a whole system. Sub-units and the multiples are dependent one upon the other, and cannot exist independently in an early void. For example, it is inconceivable that only one unit, say 8 Gerah, was used without any other unit (indeed, the three secure JILs of the eighth century BCE

Economic Keystones

include the Nsf, 8 Gerah and 4 Shekel units). By definition, weight systems must include different units in order to enable the weighing of a certain range of weight (for the JILs, between 2 and 3 Gerah and a few dozen Shekels). The new JILs from Tel Halif (Lahav) strengthen this conclusion, since the site was not settled during the seventh century BCE (Borowski 1995; see now Seger 1997). The scale beam from Lachish level III indicates weighing in Judah at this period (Barkay 1996, though it does not necessarily prove the use of inscribed weights).

The JILs appeared at the end of the eighth century, but they were not yet in common use. Their use became widespread in the seventh century BCE. Therefore, the JILs are not an innovation of King Josiah and have nothing to do with his reform. Are they perhaps connected with Hezekiah? I will discuss this question later.

Chapter 3

DISTRIBUTION PATTERNS AND THE BORDERS OF JUDAH

I base the study of the distribution patterns of the JILs on the assumption that there are enough weights to render a reliable picture. Future finds may change some details, but it seems that the major conclusions are valid. Many sites were excavated, and today there is no area in Judah that remains unexplored. Factors such as the nature and extent of excavations, and the quality of publications, have their say, but do not change the general picture.

3.1. *Distribution Data*

Only 211 JILs have a known archaeological origin, that is, their site of origin is known. This number includes the three ﬡ weights from Ekron and Accho (see note at the end of Appendix 2). The data is presented in Figures 4–6 and a map, Figure 7 (below). In Figure 6, I have listed the sites according to geographical areas, as follows: (1) Judaean mountains and Judaean desert, including Benjamin; (2) biblical Negev, that is, the Arad and Beer Sheba valleys; (3) the Shephelah of Judah; (4) the southern coastal plain (Philistia); (5) other areas (Samaria, the Galilee, the northern coastal plain and Transjordan). The Shephelah was divided into two regions. The eastern, high Shephelah is considered part of Judah, while the western or low Shephelah is considered part of Philistia. The reasons for this division are explained below.

3.2. *Inner Hierarchy in Judah (Figs. 4, 6–7)*

The distribution of the JILs may provide insight into the settlement pattern inside Judah. Without doubt, Jerusalem forms the major site in regard to the distribution of the JILs (Fig. 5). A total of 67 weights have been found in this city so far (approximately 32 per cent of all the JILs with known origins). Most of the JILs from Jerusalem were found in various areas in the City of David and the 'Ophel' (mainly in Kenyon's excavations). The importance of Jerusalem as a capital city is widely recognized through its physical size and its rich archaeological remains (G. Barkay 1985), as well as from Old Testament sources. JILs have been found in Jerusalem by many excavators, since 1882 (Fig. 5). A group of JILs has also been found in the near vicinity of Jerusalem (Fig. 5), to which one can add the JILs from Ramat Rahel. Most of the JILs from Jerusalem are author weights, but all the different units have been found (the Beqaᶜ is the rarest).

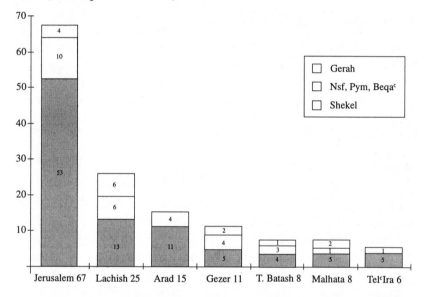

Figure 4. *Distribution pattern: site hierarchy in Judah*

Other than in Jerusalem, and to nowhere near the same extent, large groups of JILs appear in few sites, which can be termed regional centres. These are Lachish (25 weights or 12 per cent of all weights with origin), Arad (15 weights or 7 per cent) and Gezer (11 weights or 5 per cent). Lachish usually features as the capital of the Judaean Shephelah in the reconstruction of site hierarchy in Judah (e.g. Garfinkel 1984, 1985). No doubt, the sources on Sennacherib's campaign are a major factor for this, since in size and wealth Lachish does not differ greatly from neighbouring sites, such as Tel beit-Mirsim (cf. Kletter 1996: 47-48). The large number of JILs from Lachish can be partly explained as a result of the large area of the British excavations at this site. Arad may have functioned as a royal centre in the Negev in the seventh century BCE, when Tel Beer Sheba was deserted. It is possible that the area of the Bedouin *suq* of Beer Sheba today was ancient Beer Sheba (Na'aman 1987: 4 n. 2). In any case, it is likely that Arad was a royal fortress on a road leading south and east of Judah. Among the second-level sites, Gezer is an exception, since it is the only city outside Judah (it belonged to Israel and later to the Assyrian province Samaria). The large number of JILs in Gezer may be connected with its large size, and the huge extent of excavations by Macalister (see further below).

Excavations/sites	1ℵ	2ℵ	4ℵ	8ℵ	Other ℵ	Total ℵ	Nsf	Pym	Beqaᶜ	Gerah	Total Per site
Crowfoot				2		2					2
Duncan		3	3	4	1	11					11
Guthe		1	1			2					2
Kenyon	2	7	9	7	1	26	2	3		3	34
Mazar				1	1	2		1	1		4
Reich (Mamila)								1			1
Siloam village								1			1
Shiloh (city of David)	1	3	3	1	1	9					9
Zion Mt		1				1	1			1	3
Total Jerusalem	**3**	**15**	**16**	**15**	**4**	**53**	**3**	**6**	**1**	**4**	**67**
Anathot (a tomb near)							1				1
Armon Ha-Naziv				1		1					1
Beit Safafeh					1	1					1
Mevaseret Jerusalem	1					1					1
Moza							1				1
Pisgat Zeev								1			1
Ramot		1				1					1
Rephaim Valley								1			1
Shu'eifat									1		1
Total Vicinity of Jerusalem	**1**	**1**		**1**	**1**	**4**	**2**	**2**	**1**		**9**

Notes: The totals appear again in Figure 6 (below). In 'vicinity of Jerusalem', I have included most of the sites near Jerusalem, except a few that were listed separately, i.e. Ramat Rahel that appear in Figures 6,7.

Figure 5. *Distribution table: Jerusalem and its vicinity*

The third step in the hierarchical ladder is taken by sites where small groups of JILs have been found, between four and eight weights at each site. This group includes seven sites: Ekron, Tel Batash, Beth Zur,

Azeka, Tel 'Ira, Malhata and Tel Jemmeh. Ekron was a Philistine city (Gitin and Dothan 1987; Gitin 1990: 41; 1993). The number of JILs at the Ekron site is at least five, but possibly more (we have only preliminary reports so far). Tel Batash is situated on the border between Judah and Philistia and exhibits a mixed culture (Kelm and Mazar 1982; 1991; A. Mazar 1985). Cahill (1995: 247 n. 18) suggested that it was a Philistine city (see Kelm and Mazar 1995: 141, 168). I have not included Ein Gedi here, since the JILs there come from different sites and not only from Tel Goren.

The fourth and last level of hierarchy includes all the other sites, where few JILs (between one and three) have been found. There are 28 sites in this category (and, if we include the separate sites that were grouped into the category 'vicinity of Jerusalem' [Fig. 5], we reach 37 sites). I have included Kh. el-Kom in this group, since only three weights were found in it (and even they were not found in scientific excavations or surveys). If one was to include the other weights reported by Dever 1970, which were bought from a merchant in Jerusalem, Kh. el Kom would hold a much more important place on the map (Fig. 7). The fact that the southern Judaean mountains are barely attested (Fig. 7) strengthens the doubts about the origin of these weights.

Area and Site	1ℵ	2ℵ	4ℵ	8ℵ	Other ℵ	Total ℵ	Nsf	Pym	Beqaᶜ	Gerah	Total per site
Beth Zur							2	1	1		4
En Gedi	1		2	1		4					4
Gibeon			1			1					1
Jericho (?)			1			1					1
Jerusalem	3	15	16	15	4	53	3	6	1	4	67
Vicinity of Jerusalem	1	1		1	1	4	2	2	1		9
Ramat Rahel				2		2			1		3
Tel en-Nasbeh							2	1			3
Total Area I	**5**	**16**	**20**	**19**	**5**	**65**	**9**	**10**	**4**	**4**	**92**
Arad	2	3	2	4		11	2	2			15
Aroer			1			1					1
Kh. Uzah									1		1
Tel Beer Sheba			1			1	1				2
TelꜤIra	1		2	2		5		1			6
Tel Malhata	2	1		2		5	1			2	8
Total Area II	**5**	**4**	**6**	**8**		**23**	**4**	**3**	**1**	**2**	**33**

Area and Site	1ẛ	2ẛ	4ẛ	8ẛ	Other ẛ	Total ẛ	Nsf	Pym	Beqaʿ	Gerah	Total per site
Azeka			2			2	3				5
Beth Shemesh		1				1					1
Gezer	2	1		2		5	1	2	1	2	11
Kh. el.-Kom		1	1			2			1		3
Lachish	1		4	8		13	1	2	3	6	25
Nahal Elteke									1		1
Tel Batash		1	1	2		4		3		1	8
Tel ej-Judeideh			1			1					1
Total Area III	**3**	**5**	**9**	**13**		**32**	**5**	**7**	**7**	**9**	**60**
Ashdod							1	1	1		3
Mefalsim							1				1
Mesad Hashavyahu			1			1					1
Nebi Rubin		1				1					1
Tel es-Sleimeh								1			1
Tel el-Far'ah south				2		2				1	3
Tel Jemmeh	1	2	1			4	1				5
Tel Haror							1				1
Total Area IV	**1**	**3**	**2**	**2**		**8**	**2**	**4**	**1**	**1**	**16**
Accho						1*					1
Bethel	1					1					1
Dor	1					1					1
Samaria			1			1					1
Shechem					1	1					1
Tel el-Far'ah north	1					1					1
Tel Keisan	1					1					1
Buseirah							1				1
Kh. el Biara			1			1					1
Tel Deir Alla		1				1					1
Total Area V	**4**	**1**	**2**		**1**	**9**	**1**				**10**
Grand Total	**18**	**29**	**39**	**42**	**6**	**137**	**21**	**24**	**13**	**16**	**211**

Notes: Areas are: I. Judaean mountains and Benjamin; II. Negev; III. Shephelah; IV. Coastal plain; V. Other areas. Vicinity of Jerusalem and Jerusalem are detailed in Fig. 5 (above). I have included three weights from Accho and Ekron in the column 'total ẛ', since their units are not clear (see note at the end of Appendix 2).

Figure 6. *Distribution table: sites and regions*

It is important to stress that the JILs alone cannot indicate exact size or wealth of sites, partly because their status is under debate (royal weights? or 'private' ones?) and partly because of the many factors involved in establishing size and wealth of sites (extent of excavation, method of publication, choice of areas excavated, existence of

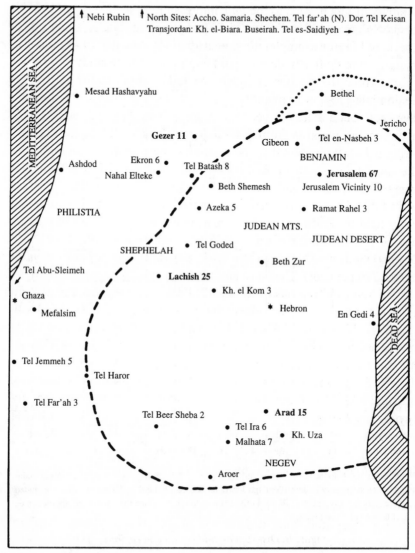

Figure 7. *Distribution Map*

destruction layers, etc.). The JILs' distribution pattern should be compared with that of other artifacts, in order to achieve a more representative picture. Usually, scholars chose 'official' remains to study the hierarchy in Judah, such as the *lmlk* impressions (Garfinkel 1984, 1985; versus Na'aman 1986a; 1988: 75-76). It is appropriate to study other aspects of life: for example, the 'pillar figurines' (Kletter 1996) or daily objects, but to do this in detail would require a separate study.

Concerning the regions of Judah, the Judaean mountains are by far the dominant region in quantity of JILs. Indeed, a total of 87 weights have been found there (41 per cent of the 211 weights with origin), not including the weights from Ein Gedi and Jericho. In fact, only the northern Judaean mountains and Benjamin are prominent on the map. The mountains south of Bethlehem and around Hebron are almost empty (Fig. 7). In second place, but far behind, comes the Shephelah (a total of 60 JILs, or 29 per cent). One must remember that this area was partly held by Philistia, so that from the eastern Shephelah, which is related with Judah, there are only 35 JILs (approximately 12 per cent; for the definition of this area, see §3.3 below). The Negev is third with 33 JILs (16 per cent). The Judaean Desert is negligible (only 5 JILs).

In all sites and regions (a total of 211 JILs with origin), the Shekel series is the most common, especially in its middle range (that is, 4 and 8 Shekel). Then come 2 Shekel, Pym and Nsf. Interestingly, relatively few 1 Shekel weights are known from excavations and surveys, though this was the basic unit. There are fewer weights of this unit than of the Nsf and Pym. One reason for this could be that 1 Judaean Shekel was practical only for inner Judaean transactions, since it did not fit Egyptian or Mesopotamian standards (see Chapter 5 below). The Beqa^c is also not very common, surprisingly less than Pym and Nsf (though as $1/2$ Shekel we would expect it to be more common than $2/3$ or $5/6$ Shekel). Again, it is a unique Judaean unit, not compatible with foreign weight systems. A certain measure of caution is required here, since we have too few JILs of each unit to reach reliable statistical conclusions.

In summary, the inner distribution of the JILs in Judah seems to show a similar picture to that of the pillar figurines, rosette impressions (Kletter 1996), *lmlk* impressions (Garfinkel 1984, 1985, though I do not agree with his conclusions) and other Judaean finds. On this basis, as well as on the study of the size of sites and the written sources, there is no doubt that Jerusalem (and the northern Judaean mountains) functioned as the 'hub' of economic activity in Judah.

3.3. *The 'Heartland of Judah' and the JILs outside Judah*

In order to discuss the relation between the JILs and the borders of Judah, it is necessary first to define these borders independently.[1] Otherwise, we run the risk of circular arguments. We can define the border of Judah according to the historical sources or, rather, a certain interpretation of those sources. There were various changes in Judah's border throughout the seventh century BCE. Hezekiah took control of certain areas of Philistia—at least over Ekron—before 701 (for a 'maximalistic' expansion, see Mittmann 1990). Sennacherib tore away areas of Judah, probably in the Shephelah (Na'aman 1979: 83; 1986a: 17; Rainey 1983; Dagan 1992: 260-62). We have very little evidence from the *pax Assyriaca* period. Manasseh perhaps restored the borders of Judah (Ginsberg 1950; Bulbach 1981; Finkelstein 1993: 64). However, this is based on accepting 2 Chron. 33.10-17, and a later restoration, under Josiah, is more likely. Many scholars think that Josiah acted independently and established a kind of a mini-empire in Palestine, and that Mesad Hashavyahu was seen as part of his kingdom (for some of the latest additions to this theory, see Galil 1992; Stern 1994; Suzuki 1992: 32-37; Laato 1992: 76). However, it seems that the site is somewhat later than his reign (Wenning 1989). According to another view, Josiah was a vassal king of Egypt (Na'aman 1989). After the Assyrian withdrawal (approximately 630–620 BCE), Palestine entered a period of upheaval, and Judah may have suffered the loss of certain areas before 586 BCE, through the hands of Edom or Babylon. I have also discussed elsewhere in detail the sources concerning the border of Judah (Kletter 1996: 43-44).

Since historical sources are debated, a concept of 'the heartland of Judah' may help to define Judaean finds. According to this concept, I am defining a minimal region that was clearly part of Judah. All scholars agree about the political affiliation of this area. This is more or less 'traditional' Judah, as it existed, with stable borders from the tenth century to the end of the eighth century BCE. Judah ruled this 'heartland', and most of the population was no doubt Judaean. I must stress that I speak here of Judah in a political sense, and will not discuss the problematic definition of ethnicity in ancient periods. The 'heartland of

---

1.   I will not discuss the theoretical question of the relationships between artifacts and political borders, which is studied elsewhere (Kletter forthcoming d).

Judah' included the Judaean mountains and Benjamin, and the northern border was from Miṣpa (Tell en-Nasbeh) to just south of Jericho. The Dead Sea formed the eastern border, and the Arad-Beer Sheba valleys the south border (the Negev). The western border was the least stable (see above), but the heartland of Judah included the eastern Shephelah (Azeka, Lachish, Beth Shemesh, Tel Goded), while the western Shephelah is considered part of Philistia/Israel (Ekron, Gezer, Gat [Tell es-Safi], perhaps Tel Batash). Using the written sources and the concept of the heartland area, it is possible to discuss the distribution of finds in relation to Judah. Even if Judah had expanded out of its heartland, it would only strengthen the conclusions (because more JILs would be directly related to Judah), while it does not seem likely that Judah lost large areas of this heartland until 586 BCE.

It is clear that Transjordan and northern Israel (Samaria, Galilee, the Jezreel Valley, the Jordan Valley, the Sharon and the northern coastal plain) are negligible with regard to the JILs. The quantity of JILs found in these areas is so meagre that they are clearly not the homeland of the JILs (altogether 10 JILs, or 4.7 per cent of the 211 JILs from known origins). Furthermore, the few JILs from these areas appear as solitary, 'foreign' finds within local assemblages. They are almost always 1 ୪ weights, other than one Nsf from Buseirah which is exceptional in form and script (Appendix 1: Nsf.21) and one 2 ୪ from Tell es-Sa'idiyeh.

A total of 160 JILs were found in the area defined as the heartland of Judah. They include areas 1–2 (Fig. 5), and the eastern Shephelah (part of area 3: Azeka, Beth Shemesh, Kh. el-Kom [actually more in the mountains], Lachish, and Tel Goded, altogether 35 JILs). These 160 weights form approximately 76 per cent of the 211 JILs with known origins. It is the large majority, and the meaning is clear: these weights are *Judaean weights*. This definition means that the JILs were manufactured in Judah and used by Judaeans. I am speaking about the picture as a whole, not about each and every JIL, and I am defining Judah and the Judaeans here as a political entity. This conclusion fits the material (limestone) and the Hebrew script on the Nsf, Pym and Beqaᶜ series (with due caution, since the Philistine script is not clearly defined; see Naveh 1985; Kempinski 1987; Na'aman and Zadok 1988).

The sum of 25 JILs (12 per cent of the 211 JILs from known sites) were found in the western Shephelah and 16 JILs (or approximately 7.6 per cent) on the southern coastal plain. The JILs from the coastal plain were found in small groups, and it is suggested that they reached

Philistia by trade. These JILs may have been used for international trade, and their small number is not in keeping with the assumption of a Judaean control over this area. In the western Shephelah, there are concentrations of JILs in Gezer (11 JILs) and Ekron (5 JILs at least; also Tel Batash with 8 JILs, but its political affinity is not clear). Various explanations can be offered for this fact. Ekron was controlled by Hezekiah before 701 BCE. Gezer was settled by Israelites until 722/720 BCE, and perhaps influenced by Hezekiah—as the evidence of many *lmlk* stamps suggests, though almost all of them were found in the older excavation of Macalister (1912), out of context (for Gezer, see Seger 1987: 124-25, Na'aman 1988: 74; Becking 1992: 114-18; Reich and Brandl 1985). Tel Batash was situated on the border of Judah. Still, the quantities of JILs at those sites are not very high, and do not prove any conquest or political domination of Judah in this area—nor do they refute such a theory, of course. The explanation of trade seems the most plausible, but perhaps Gezer and Ekron reflect Judaean interference during Hezekiah's revolt. One should remember that weights were used in sets, and there could be up to ten weights or so in one set (for examples from Egypt, see Skinner 1967: 5-6). If so, a few weights at a certain site may indicate only the existence of one or two merchants there. In comparison with the Judaean pillar figurines, the Judaean weights are more widespread outside Judah (96 per cent of the Judaean pillar figurines were found in Judah; Kletter 1996: chap. 5). This is not so surprising, since weights are intended to be used in trade, and reflect trade relations.

In summary, the JILs must be defined as a Judaean weight system. There is a clear connection between the JILs and the borders of Judah. However, the weights cannot indicate exact border-lines or small-scale changes within short time-spans. Outside Judah, JILs are found mainly in Philistia, and this may be the result of border changes in the Shephelah area. It can also be a result of trade relations, and this seems to be the best explanation for coastal sites such as Ashdod. In all the other areas outside Judah, the JILs are scarce and do not confirm any idea of conquest or expansion by Judah.

Chapter 4

THE TYPOLOGY

4.1. *The Material (Fig. 8)*

Of the 431 JILs, 423 JILs are made of limestone, that is, 98 per cent
(Fig. 8). Specific types of limestone, such as dolomite, are sometimes
indicated in the publications, but often there are no further specifica-
tions. It is likely that the JILs were made of local Judaean limestone
(called *mizi akhmar* in Arabic), found in the vicinity of Jerusalem, but
this cannot be proved for each weight. Weights from other sites could
have been made from other variations of local limestone. Most of the
weights are white or white-brown (*café au lait* colours), but there are
also yellow, pink, reddish, grey and even black weights (ᵈ 1.6). A few
weights are said to be made of hematite (Nsf: 50-51) or steatite (8
Gerah.17). Two weights are said to be made of clay: Pym.20 from Tel
Haror and ᵈ 4.31 from Gibeon.

Only eight weights in Appendix 1 are made of metals, always bronze
except the one iron Beqaᶜ (for which, see Shany 1967; Appendix 1,
Beqaᶜ: 10). The bronze weights include three ᵈ weights (ᵈ 2.a from
Gezer, marked 'Ⅱ *lmlk*'; ᵈ 4.47; ᵈ 4.a), three Pym weights (nos. 44-
46) and one Gerah weight (7 Gerah.2). A few of the bronze weights are
different from the JILs, not only in material, but in other aspects, and it
seems best to define these as exceptional. That is, their definition as
JILs is not secure. I have not excluded these weights from the catalogue, but marked them with ordinals (a, b, etc.) instead of the usual
catalogue numbers. As far as I know, the structure and the content of
the metal weights were not analysed (for an analysis of a metal weight
from Kh. Rosh Zayit, see Kletter 1994: 37-38 no. 6).

Three JILs have depressions in their bases (Nsf.6 from Tel en-
Nasbeh; ᵈ 1.2 from Jerusalem; cf. Scott 1985: 202, Pl. 79.10, and ᵈ
4.48 from an unknown origin). The ᵈ 1.21 and ᵈ 4.48 weights retain a
lump of lead inside this depression. Another weight (not a JIL) securely

dated to Iron Age II bearing the same phenomenon was found at Tel
'Ira (not yet published, courtesy of Y. Beit Arieh). Because of its heavy
weight, lead was used in this way to balance or correct the weight of
the stone. The custom is very rare among the JILs, and known better
from later periods and other areas. Finally, one weight has white paint
to stress the engraved script (ᴆ 2.39).

Weight unit	Material			Shape		Total
	Limestone	Metal	Clay	Dome	Cube	
ᴆ1	42			41	1	42
ᴆ2	42			42		42
ᴆ4	55		1?	55	1	56
ᴆ8	51			51		51
ᴆ12–40	11			11		11
Nsf	59			58	1	59
Pym	48	3	1?	49	3	52
Beqaʿ	34	1		34	1	35
Gerah	82	1		81	2	83
Total JILs	**423**	**6**		**422**	**9**	**431**
(Exceptions)		2			2	

Note: Three weights from Accho and Ekron (note end of Appendix 2) are not
included.

Figure 8. *Typology: material and shape*

4.2. *The Form*

Of the 431 JILs, 422 (or approximately 98 per cent) are dome-shaped
(Fig. 8). They have flattened, rounded bases. The sides protrude a little
outwards, and curve or bend inward at roughly two-thirds of their
height. The upper third of the weight is shaped as a rounded dome.
There are some variations in the exact shape of the dome: some weights
have high, vault-like domes, while others are rounded and a section
looks like a half-ball (cf. Scott 1985: 198).

Dome-shaped weights are known from practically all over the
ancient Near East, including Mesopotamia and Ugarit. They flourished
mainly in the first millennium BCE, and were especially common in
Egypt (Petrie 1926: 4-6; Cour-Marty 1983: 29; 1985: 191-92). Many of
the dome weights in Egypt are characterized by a carination, or a sharp
bend, between the sides and the domes (Petrie 1926: Pl. 4.31-34). The
limestone weights from Kh. Rosh Zayit (Kletter 1994: nos. 1-5), which
are probably Phoenician, have the same shape. There are also many
dome weights in Egypt, which are practically identical in shape to the

JILs (Petrie 1926: Pls. 4-5 forms 36.8-45, with a few exceptions).

Among the 431 JILs, only 10 are not domed, but shaped as truncated pyramids (trapezoids), or as rectangular cubes. Many of these are metal weights, already mentioned in §4.1 above (these are ƍ 2.a, ƍ 4.47, Pym.44-46; Beqaᶜ.20). One limestone weight from Buseirah (Nsf.21) is an irregular cube shape, and its script is exceptional. The other weights are 2 Gerah.1 and 8 Gerah.2 from Lachish, and Pym.4 from the Siloam village (Jerusalem). One weight is perforated (Nsf.4), and was perhaps intended to be used secondarily as an amulet.

4.3. *Implications of Material and Shape*

Following the data presented above, the conclusion is clear: there is a very high uniformity of material and shape among the JILs. One can define a JIL as a weight made of limestone and dome-shaped (and inscribed; the inscriptions are also very uniform, as will be shown later).

There are very few exceptions to this definition, namely the eight metal weights, almost all of which are shaped as cubes or trapezoids, and two limestone weights of a similar form. If one relies on the inscriptions, it is better to include these few weights within the JILs (as I have done, with only one or two weights defined as exceptions). This seems preferable than to treat all these weights as exceptions.

Metal weights in the shape of cubes are regarded in the metrological literature as a form typical to Phoenicia, and this is based on a large series of these weights that carries Phoenician inscriptions (Lemaire 1980; Bron and Lemaire 1983: 768 n. 36). These are probably later, perhaps typical to the Persian period (Lemaire 1980). The existence of such weights at the end of the Iron Age is documented from a weight from *Kh.* Rosh Zayit (Kletter 1994: 37-38 no. 6), and now from Ashkelon as well (Stager 1996: 66 Fig. 7; see also Deutsch and Helzer 1994: 63-67). It is highly unlikely that the eight metal weights discussed above are Phoenician, for the reasons listed below, even though our knowledge about the Phoenician weight system(s) is very limited (cf. Kletter 1994). First, a few of these weights were found in Judah (as far as the origins are known). Second, their weight fits the JILs' system. Third, some of these weights carry Hebrew inscriptions (the weight alone is no proof, as these may match other systems, and Hieratic marks were widely used. Also, vertical lines for the numerals 1–3 are shared by many scripts).

What is important is that the number of these metal or cubic weights is so low. I have decided to follow the inscriptions as the main guidance, and included them among the JILs, but it does not matter much if they are excluded. One weight from Lachish is more problematic (Gerah 2: 1). Not only is it cubic, it is the only known weight with the mark 'II'. This mark could belong to a few weight systems, and not necessarily to the JILs. Also, the weight is heavier than the assumed 'standard' of 2 Gerah (but see Chapter 5 below). Until similar weights are found, it is impossible to formulate an unequivocal view regarding this weight.

4.4. *Typology of the Inscriptions*

The marks on the JILs are divided into Hebrew letters on the Nsf, Pym and Beqa^{c} series; and Hieratic numerals on the Gerah and ɤ series. To these, the sign ɤ and a few other exceptional signs must be added.

4.4.1. *The Typology of the Hebrew Script: Nsf, Pym and Beqa^{c} Series (Fig. 9)*

The paleography of the Hebrew script on the JILs involves great difficulties, more than those recognized in the study of other Hebrew inscriptions. The drawings and the photographs of the JILs are often poor and occasionally taken from awkward angles, making comparisons difficult. When more than one photograph has been published, the signs may appear very different. In one case (Meshorer 1976: 53, 54), the marks on two photographs look completely different, but the damaged area near the ɤ sign proves that it is the same weight. The weights are currently scattered in dozens of institutions and museums around the world, and it is impossible to check them all personally. The top of the JILs, where the inscriptions are engraved, is rounded, and this causes peculiarities in the form of signs. Also, it is a very restricted area and difficult for writing. All these problems make it hard to compare the JILs with other inscriptions, such as ostraca.

For those reasons, it is be pointless to try to date the JILs by paleography. Paleography can hardly be exact, as its record proves time and again. Arad can furnish a good example: the excavators (M. Aharoni 1981: 130-31) believed that there was a significant paleographical difference between levels VI and VII, more than that between levels VII and VIII. Today, levels VI–VII should perhaps be amalgamated

Letter	Weights of known origins	Weights of unknown origins	8th-century BCE script	7th-century BCE script
ב	*(script forms)*	*(script forms)*	*(script forms)*	*(script forms)*
י	*(script forms)*	*(script forms)*	*(script forms)*	*(script forms)*
מ	*(script forms)*	*(script forms)*	*(script forms)*	*(script forms)*
נ	*(script forms)*	*(script forms)*	*(script forms)*	*(script forms)*
ע	*(script forms)*	*(script forms)*	*(script forms)*	*(script forms)*
כ	Nsf: *(script forms)* Pym: *(script forms)*	*(script forms)*	*(script forms)*	*(script forms)*
צ	*(script forms)*	*(script forms)*	*(script forms)*	*(script forms)*
ק	*(script forms)*	*(script forms)*	*(script forms)*	*(script forms)*

Notes: The size of the letters is not to scale. The figure is based on published drawings, which are not always of good quality. The Hebrew script is compared to the Siloam inscription, the ostraca of Arad VIII and Samaria (8th century BCE): the ostraca of Arad VII, Mesad Hashavyahu and Lachish II (7th century BCE). This table does not include the weights in the addenda (Appendix 2).

Figure 9. *Typology of the Hebrew letters*

into one level (since the casemate wall is late). Formerly, paleographers ascribed significance to very small variations in letter forms (e.g. Cross 1962; for criticism, see S.A. Kaufman 1986: 1-2). Lately, Naveh (1989: 73, 88) and Avigad (1986: 102-104) stressed that typological differences do not have to be chronological. Only eight Hebrew letters appear on the JILs, a narrow base for discussion. Furthermore, any paleographical dating is dependent on the archaeological dating of those inscriptions that have contexts, while for the JILs we already have an independent archaeological dating. Difficulties should be explored, and I will therefore present the data and make a few preliminary observations, hoping that they will be useful for scholars of paleography.

I have gathered most of the letters from the Nsf, Pym and Beqaᶜ weights (Fig. 9). Letters that were not clear on the surface of the weights were omitted (the figure is not drawn to scale). Clearly, there is no uniformity in the shape of the letters, although the JILs are mostly dated to the same period (seventh century BCE). The differences in writing may be explained as variations, due to the difficulty of writing on an irregular, small space; as different hands involved in the writing; or perhaps both.

The script on the JILs is similar to eighth-century-BCE ostraca rather than to seventh-century-BCE ostraca, though most of the JILs are dated in the later period (e.g. the lower horizontal line still existing in the letter Y, or the transcending upper line of the M. The Q and the N are also similar to eighth-century-BCE forms). The best explanation of this fact is conservatism on behalf of the writers (expressed also in Hebrew seals and in the *bullae* from the City of David; cf. Avigad 1986: 102-103 group 1). The closest form of writing to the JILs is found on seals and seal impressions, since these also involved writing on limited, hard surfaces. The seals were engraved, of course. Evidence for this assumption is found in a few instances, where signs on the JILs are 'mirrored' (left to right). Another notable example is the 'mirror' writing on the Nebi Rubin weight (Appendix 1: ठ 4.20). See also the left-to-right direction of the letter Q in some instances (ϙ instead of ϙ) and the S in Nsf.20 from Ashdod.[1] Such mistakes are natural for those who are used to *intaglio* writing (as on seals). Apart from conservatism, there is a tendency for careless writing, which is also apparent among Hebrew seals (Avigad 1986: 102-104, groups 2-3).

Exceptional writing appears occasionally. One weight has confused

1.   While an upside-down sign appears in ठ 4: 47.

letters (*n-f-s* instead of *n-s-f*; Appendix 1: Nsf.44). Some weights carry a shortened form of the name of the unit: *b* for Beqaᶜ (Beqaᶜ.6), *py* for Pym (Pym nos. 7, 21).[2] The Nsf from Buseirah (no. 21) is exceptional, not only in shape. It has the letter *n* on one side and *nṣ* crossed by a line on another side (denoting abolishment of the inscription?). There are very few instances of inscriptions in ink instead of engraved (Pym.20 from Tel Haror, possibly 6 Gerah.2 from Lachish and ४ 4.31 from Gibeon). The word Shekel (שקל) was inscribed on one metal weight from an unknown origin, but its weight does not fit the Judaean Shekel (Deutsch and Heltzer 1994: 65-66 Fig. 31).

The placement of the script is always standard: on the dome, but not necessarily on its exact centre. The dome is the most prominent part, while the base is hidden from view, at least during weighing. This is probably the reason for writing on the dome (although the flattened base is more convenient for writing). Bases are inscribed with additional inscriptions in a few cases (but never instead of the regular inscription on the dome). These are: ४ 1.9, inscribed 'to Nedavyah' (לנדביה); ४ 2.b; ४ 4.38 (Fig. 32 below); Beqaᶜ.12 (an inscribed rosette; for the motif, see Kletter forthcoming d) and Beqaᶜ.14 (discussed in Chapter 5 below).

4.4.2. *Names on JILs*
Three JILs carry personal names in the Hebrew script. The first, 'to Nedabyah' (לנדביה) is written in two lines on the base of weight ४ 1.9 from Lachish. The second, 'to Barki' (לברכי), is written on ४ 2.23 from Nebi Rubin, and the third, 'to Zecharyahu [son of] Ya'ir' (לזכריהו [ב]ן יאר), is found on Pym no. 44. The name Barki was written 'left to right', as if in a mirror, perhaps an indication that this weight was used (secondarily) as a seal, or that the writer was a seal engraver.

All these names, or very similar names (and components), are well known from the Old Testament. Nedabyah is quite common as a name (Exod. 6.23; 1 Kgs 14.20, 31; 15.25, 27; 1 Chron. 3.18; 8.30; 9.36; etc.). Similar forms (Yehonadav or Yonadav) are also known. Zecharyahu or Zecharyah are even more common (2 Kgs 14.29; 15.11; 18.2; 2 Chron. 24.20; 26.5; etc.). Ya'ir is also known (Deut. 3.14; Judg. 10.3-5; 2 Sam. 20.26; etc.). An exact comparison to the name *Brky* is missing from the Old Testament, but close forms are known (Berachyahu or

---

2.   In the last case, maybe the last letter (*m*) was eroded. The letter *m* (Pym. 22) may also be a shortened form.

Berachyah, Zech. 1.1, 7; 1 Chron. 9.16; 15.23; 2 Chron. 2.28; etc.). Ya'ir and Zecharyahu/Zachar appear on Hebrew Iron Age seals (Lawton 1984: 337, 338). Berachyahu and Zachar appear on the city of David *bullae* (Avigad 1986: nos. 9, 50, 51). All this fits the dating of the JILs quite well.

The habit of inscribing personal names on weights is known from Egypt (Cour-Marty 1985: 195 nn. 39-42) and Mesopotamia (Powell 1979: 8 n. 48). The names are probably ownership marks. The names on the JILs cannot be identified with biblical figures, and it is rather vague as to whether these are private persons or officials in some governmental role. Thus, the names do not imply that the JILs are necessarily private weights (cf. the so-called 'private' seal impressions that are related to the *lmlk* jars: Garfinkel 1985; Na'aman 1988; Kletter 1995: 229-32).

4.4.3. *The Sign* ୪

The typology of this sign shows some variations. It is mostly rounded (୪), but sometimes flattened (୪). Sometimes the upper line curves (୪). In a few weights, the lower part is pointed (୪, e.g. ୪ 8.12 from Lachish). In one case, the lower part seems to be open, but this is judged only from a photograph, Yadin and Geva 1983: 254). Three weight have a sign that is similar to an English *G*: Ɛ (୪ 1.2), Ϭ (୪ 1.25 and ୪ 2.20). It is not clear if these variations are meaningful, since inscribing on small, hard and curved surfaces is bound to be difficult and to cause variations. It can also be the result of different hands with different experiences in writing.

Eshel (1986: 346) claimed that all the forms of the ୪ appear in the Cypriot sign *ro*, returning to an explanation from the end of the nineteenth century (§1.1.2 above). I fail to see the advantage of such an identification, since what connection is there between the JILs and a Cypriot sign? What meaning could such a sign have on the local JILs, or vice versa? It does not appear on Cypriot weights at all (for the meaning of this sign, see Chapter 8 below)

The Hieratic numerals are usually situated to the left of the ୪. This is the same order that is found in the Hebrew ostraca: for example Kadesh Barnea no. 6, Samaria no. 1101 ('barley...*x*'); Mesad Hashavyahu ('ℸ ୪'); and various ostraca from Arad and Lachish (letter *B* and numeral, presumably the unit of volume *bat*, for which see Mittmann 1992). A few JILs have an opposite order, whereby the numeral is to the right of the 𐤀 sign (𐤀 1.12, 33; 𐤀 2.2, 23; 𐤀4.10, 28, 43 and perhaps 𐤀 8.40). This can also be compared with Hebrew ostraca: for example, 'the [silver] s[heqels] (שקל[ים] ה[כסף]) in Arad ostracon no. 16, line 5 (M. Aharoni 1981); or '*x* Gerah' in ostracon 3 from Kadesh Barnea (Lemaire and Vernus 1980). The same instability is found in biblical Hebrew: usually, numerals precede units (Josh. 7.21; 2 Sam. 14.26; 2 Kgs 15.19-20), but sometimes the order is reversed (2 Sam. 24.24; Neh. 5.15; 7.70).

4.4.4. *Notes on the Hieratic Numerals*
Hieratic script was used in Late Bronze Age Cana'an under the Egyptian rule (Goldwasser 1984, 1991). It is not clear when Israel and Judah adopted Hieratic numerals (see Na'aman 1996: 172). The numerals on the JILs belong to the Hieratic 'a-normal' script, which is not well known (but this is a late form of Hieratic, so perhaps the borrowing was done in the Iron Age). There are few inscriptions in this script and they indicate varied ways of writing (Malinine 1972). The basic typology of this script is still the book by Möller (1936). I have used his work in order to make a few observations. When signs from the 26th dynasty are not recorded, I have compared with signs from the nearest periods that exist in Möller's plates.

1. *The numeral 2*: ‖ (Möller 1936: no. 615). There is only one weight with this numeral (2 Gerah.1), and its exact definition is not clear (above, §4.3). The use of vertical lines for the numerals 1–4 is not common to many ancient scripts. Thus, it is not necessarily indicative of the Hieratic script.

2. *The numeral 3*: ‖‖ (Möller 1936: no. 616). On the JILs, this numeral is usually marked by three simple lines. One weight is marked Ͷ (3 Gerah.8) and another ꟼꟼ (3 Gerah.9). The Hieratic sign is ‖‖ or ꟼꟼ.

3. *The numeral 4*: ‖‖‖ (Möller 1936: no. 617) is very uniform on the JILs, always four vertical lines.

4. *The numeral 5*: ꓶ (Möller 1936: no. 618). The usual Hieratic form is the most common on the JILs (e.g., weight 𐤀 4.1). Other forms appear, such as the pointed, angular line ꓶ or ꓩ (e.g. 𐤀 4.2, 𐤀 4.39); and 'T' shape with crossing horizontal line (e.g. 𐤀 4.37-38, 5 Gerah.5). In two

cases the numeral is found to the right of the unit sign, and then it is written 'left to right': Γ (ȣ 4.10, 28).

5. *The numeral 6*: ⌐ (Möller 1936: no. 619). The regular Hieratic form appears on JILs 6 Gerah.6, 10, but variations are common: ⌐ (6 Gerah.8-9); ⌐ (6 Gerah.7) and even ⌐ (6 Gerah.12-13).

6. *The numeral 7*: ⌐ (Möller 1936: no. 620). There are very few JILs of this unit, and generalization is therefore impossible. On one weight, which was published with a fine photograph, the numeral is equal in shape to Möller's form.

7. *The numeral 8*: ⌐ (Möller 1936: no. 621). The sign on the JILs is different from that of Möller, as if formed from two separate lines: ⌐ . Sometimes, these lines are connected and look very close to the Hieratic original form (8 Gerah.3, 7, 14). An identical sign to the Hieratic is found on 8 Gerah.16. Sometimes the little 'ticks' are missing, and there are only two parallel lines (8 Gerah.9, 12). One weight seems exceptional (8 Gerah.5), in that the sign looks like three sides of a rectangle: ⊏. Perhaps it should be turned the other way, and thus is close to the regular sign on these weights.

8. *The numerals 9 and 11*. The number of weights known with these numerals is meagre, and there is not much point in comparisons.

9. *The numeral 10*: ⌐ or ⌐ (Möller 1936: no. 623). The JILs' sign can lean to the right: ⌐ (ȣ 8.10), or, more commonly, to the left: ⌐ (ȣ 8.14-15, 18, 29, 35, 37). A very straight form, like English *T*, is also common (ȣ 8.11, 13, 25, 33). Two weights carry a peculiar sign, ⌐ or ⌐ (ȣ 8.38-39, but they were not found in scientific excavations). One weight carries a sign that is shallow engraved and uncertain: ⌐ (ȣ 8.29 from Tel 'Ira). In all the 10 Gerah weights, the sign is very uniform and straight (like the English *T*).

A phenomenon of 'left-to-right' numerals is found on weights, but only rarely. The numeral *5* is written as L or ⌐ on two weights (ȣ 4.28, 43). The same left-to-right writing is found in the numeral 1000 (⌐) of Kadesh Barnea ostracon no. 6.

4.4.5. *Unusual Marks*
The list (below) compiles other, unusual marks that appear on the JILs.

1. Weight ষ 1.16 has a peculiar mark (𐤌 ষ), while a similar mark appears on weight ষ 4.a (𐤌). The last is published with a poor photograph, which shows only part of the inscription. Weight ষ 4.a is irregular only in its shape and material. Lemaire suggested that the sign in ষ 1.18 (𐤌, according to the text) includes the Hebrew letter *m*, that is, *ma'ah* (מעה) as a unit of silver. However, it is a late coin without any connection to the JILs.

2. An additional line appears in a few weights, for example ষ 4.12. The weight is not affected, and the meaning of the line is not clear. For an additional line in numerals in the Kadesh Barnea ostracon, see Chapter 8 below.

3. The base of weight ষ 2.c carries the marks ₩. This may stand for '2 Shekels' (Lemaire 1976: 41), but the suggestion of Babylonian Shekels is hardly convincing. It could also mean a late, secondary mark on an early weight, which is not very likely (Lemaire 1976: 41).

4. Hieratic numerals appear on the base of Beqa'.13. This is discussed in Chapter 5 (below).

5. A peculiar 'S'-shaped sign (𐤎) appears above the numeral in weight 10 Gerah.4. Its meaning is not clear (G. Barkay 1981a: 292).

6. A rosette is engraved on the base of Beqa'.12 weight.

7. A man holding hand-scales is engraved on the base of weight ষ 4.38 (Fig. 32).

Chapter 5

THE METROLOGY OF THE WEIGHTS

5.1. *The 'One-Standard Method'*

Every metrological study must include calculations, but my aim here is
not to reach absolute mathematical accuracy, nor to suggest a new statistical method. Mathematical calculations should serve as the means,
and not the goal, of metrological studies. I find little merit in presenting
ancient weights with many digits after the decimal point (i.e. to the
nearest $1/1000$ grams), or in the obsession with exact norms, for reasons
that will be explained below. I will try to present the metrological facts
in the simplest way, with simple statistics. For the calculation of
averages, I have included almost all the weights that are defined as JILs
in Appendix 1 (weights from the addenda are mentioned whenever
necessary). I have been very cautious in defining exceptional weights;
by this term I mean broken or badly damaged weights and weights that
are significantly different from the regular JILs. Concerning the weight,
an exception means more than 5 per cent difference from the average of
the relevant unit. Exceptional weights have been defined mostly on
grounds of more than one aspect (e.g. both form and material, or form
and inscription). I have used the definition of exceptions very sparingly
for the lighter series, and avoided it completely for the Gerah series.
The status of the Gerah weights is debated, and it would be methodically wrong to exclude weights *a priori* as 'an exception'. In all the
units where only a few weights were found, one can hardly speak of
averages and deviations (these are the 2, 7, 9 Gerah and all the ช units
above 8 ช). However, I have performed the calculations and presented
them for the sake of completeness.

Two fundamental assumptions guided me throughout the study. One
can be summarized by the saying 'the whole is more than the sum of its
parts'. With this, I do not mean a mathematical formula, but wish to
stress the value of seeing a weight system as a whole. Former studies

usually ignored the whole picture and treated each unit or each series as independent entities. The second assumption is related to the first, and argues that all the JILs are part of the same system, formed around one basic standard. This method is the very opposite of the one that is widely held in the study of the JILs, that of many standards. Below are the arguments in favour of a 'one standard method' approach to the research of the JILs.

1. *Limit of Accuracy*

In ancient times, weighing was not exact. Cautious estimates put the limit of accuracy of weighing to within 3 per cent of the weight, in either direction. This inaccuracy derived from the fact that the balances and the weights themselves were not precise. This is shown in many studies (Skinner 1967; Hemmy 1937: 40; Powell 1992: 899; Petruso 1992: 6-7, 76), and is also documented in ancient written sources (Joannès 1989: 139-40). The concepts of accuracy and exact prices were not similar to our modern, monetary economies. In Egypt, for example, differences of 5 or even 10 per cent of the price were often negligible (Janssen 1975; 1988: 15). If we add other factors, such as wear by use, wear or damage after use, possible forgery and mistakes during manufacture, we may well reach a 5 per cent margin of inaccuracy, if not more (Powell 1992: 899; cf. Scott 1985: 209 Fig. 6 for estimation of wear alone). Therefore, a margin of 5 per cent deviation from an estimated standard must be perceived as a normal deviation, not as evidence for different standards (I use the term 'standard' here for the sake of convenience, defining it simply as the average of all the weights that belong to the same unit). This is the very opposite of Scott's method (followed by many metrologists), who explained differences of a few per cent of weight as different weight standards.

2. *Physical Connections between Units of JILs*

All the JILs, or the overwhelming majority of them, were found in the same geographical areas, sites, levels and sometimes even loci. A preliminary list of JILs from the same loci includes ୪ and Pym weights from Tel 'Ira (*HadArch* 74–75 [1980]: 32); Pym, Nsf and ୪ weights from Jerusalem loci 669.34a (Scott 1985: list nos. 9, 12, 14, 19, 20, 35, 51); Nsf and ୪ weights from loci 34.669 (Scott 1985: nos. 13, 28, 39, 56); ୪ and 5 Gerah weights from locus 672.12 (Scott 1985: 2, 53); and 1 ୪, 2 ୪ weights from Malhata locus 242 (1 ୪.41 and 2 ୪.39). The connections are more elaborate when whole levels or sites are investigated (cf. Figs. 4–6). The conclusion is clear: the JILs form part of one weight system and do not express different geographical, or chronological standards (i.e. different standards for different periods or regions).

3. *The Limited Distribution Area*
The JILs are found in the kingdom of Judah only, with relatively few weights outside this area (mainly in Philistia). This limited distribution area cannot be compared to the vast areas of empires such as Assyria or Egypt. The assumption that regional standards existed in such empires is plausible and perhaps natural, but for the small kingdom of Judah, with its centralized government, it is an unlikely assumption.

4. *The Uniformity of the JILs*
We have seen earlier (Chapter 4) that the JILs are very homogeneous concerning material, shape and script. The quantity of exceptional weights (such as metal cubic weights) is totally negligible. Such a uniformity fits one standard, for, had there been more standards, one would have expected to see them expressed, other than just in the weight. Otherwise, how could the people of Judah themselves tell which scale weight belongs to which standard? A different shape, or a different material, or perhaps different inscriptions on the weights would have been be necessary—but there is nothing of the sort among the JILs.

5. *Requirements for a Definition of a Weight Standard*
I will not discuss here the question of what is a 'standard', but only the problem of how to define a standard according to the evidence of ancient weights. One or two deviant weights (i.e. weights that are more than 5 per cent different from a presumed 'standard') cannot prove the existence of different standards, since they may be the expression of wear, deliberate forgery or mistakes in manufacture. That forgery was a problem is clear from all the condemnations against it in the Old Testament (cf. Chapter 7) and other historical sources. *To define a weight standard one must present many similar weights* that supposedly belong to that standard. As I will demonstrate below, the JILs are so uniform that very few exceptional weights can be found. For example, there is one weight from Gibeon ($\forall$ 4.29), which is approximately 14 per cent heavier than the average of all the other JILs of the same unit.

True, it is unique, but there is no other JIL close to it in weight. Therefore, it would be methodically wrong to postulate the existence of
another standard based on it, for it could signify forgery or mistake as
well.

6. *Simplicity*

The scholars that claimed that the JILs included many different standards failed to explain why all these standards were needed, how they
were formed, and how the Judaeans could differentiate between them
all. Any additional standard further complicates a weight system, and
creates opportunities for forgery and confusion. A one-standard method
is simpler. It does not mean that it is necessarily better. I am merely
pointing out the fact that the Judaean weight system, even with one
basic standard, was quite complicated (e.g. the duality of the Hieratic
numerals and the multiples of 4 and 8 Shekel, discussed in the
following chapters). Many standards for the JILs would make it such a
cumbersome weight system that it could hardly be functional.

7. *Existence of Foreign Standards*

Foreign weight standards appear in Israel during the same period that
the JILs were used. These include 'Assyrian' metal weights in the form
of crouching lions (Fig. 27) and Phoenician weights, shaped as metal
cubes, limestone domes and possibly other forms (Fig. 28). Egyptian
weights possibly also exist in Israel, I suspect, in dome weights that
have carinated sides. In any case, since the JILs were adjusted to the
Egyptian *dbn* system, there was probably no need to use imported
Egyptian weights inside Judah.

I will discuss further some of these other weights in Chapter 9. My
argument here is that a foreign standard could be used simply by using
such 'foreign' weights, thus there was no need to manufacture local
weights in these foreign standards. (This should not be confused with
an adjustment of a local system to a foreign one. In such cases, some
local weight units match the foreign system in weight only, but not in
shape, materials and inscriptions.) This omits the ground under the feet
of all those who claimed that some JILs belong to Mesopotamian,
Phoenician, Babylonian and other standards (notably Scott and Eran).
Nor were all these standards needed for international trade: the JILs
were already adjusted to the Egyptian system, and mediating values
probably existed with other weight systems as well. Transactions
between traders could be based on finding these mathematical

correspondences, or each side could weigh the goods with his own weights. Thus, a Judaean trader would not need to hold sets of weights of all the foreign weight systems.

8. *The Wholeness of the System*

A basic misunderstanding of scholars from the 'many standards' theory was the separation of JILs into independent parts. Thus, the Nsf (but also other units) was understood not only as an independent standard, but called Shekel—which is the name of the major standard in Semitic weight systems. It was then assumed, that each of these 'standards' had its own sub-units and multiples (e.g. Scott 1965). I think that this separation is wrong, and that all the JILs are part of one system only (based on the ४ Shekel). My arguments are as follows: (1) The complete lack of multiples or sub-units of Nsf, Pym and Beqaᶜ among the JILs. So far, not even one inscribed multiple of these units is known (e.g. weights inscribed '‖ Nsf', '⦀ Pym'). Were these independent standards, one would have expected to find at least a few such weights. True, there is the *rbᶜ Nsf* weight from Samaria, but it is not a JIL and not directly related to Judah. (2) The underlying logic of all weight systems is the use of a restricted number of weight units to measure a range of weight by combining different units together. Each unit completes the other. This is exactly what happens with the JILs: each unit takes a certain place in a sequence, between the preceding and the following unit. It is similar to the way a jigsaw puzzle is constructed from interlocking pieces. For that reason, we do not have Gerah weights that are heavier than 10 Gerah, since this brings us into the range of the Beqaᶜ (cf. G. Barkay 1981a: 293; except perhaps one 11 Gerah weight). For the same reason, there are no weights of ¹/₂ Beqaᶜ, ¹/₂ Nsf, 3 ४, 5 ४, etc. They are not needed, since other existing units are available (¹/₂ Beqaᶜ is measured by 6 Gerah; ¹/₂ Nsf by 8 Gerah, etc.), or a combination of existing units (3 ४ by 1 ४ + 2 ४, 7 ४ by 4 ४ + 2 ४ + 1 ४, etc.). The assumption of former scholars, that each unit of JILs can have many multiples and sub-units (cf. Chapter 1), is wrong. The different JIL units (Nsf, Pym, Beqaᶜ, Gerah) are not independent standards—they are all derivatives of the Shekel (४).

I believe that these arguments are decisive, leading to the conclusion that a method of 'one standard' is preferable for the study of the JILs. Let us now check this underlying assumption to see whether it is in keeping with the metrological facts.

5.2. *The Metrological Data (Fig. 10)*

The metrological data (Fig. 10) were reached by accurate calculations, but the limited space in the table necessitated rounding the numbers to two decimal places. Only the average of the 1 𐤔 weights is presented more accurately.

The left part of the table (Fig. 10: columns I–V) includes: I. the signs on the weights; II. the quantity of weights from each unit; III. the quantity of weights used for the calculation of the average; IV. the average of the unit in grams (rounded to three digits, except for the 𐤔1 unit); V. the relation (i.e. the multiple) between the average of the 𐤔1 unit and the unit under discussion). The central part of the table (Fig. 10: columns VI–XI) includes the interpretation of the units, as follows: VI. The interpretation of the unit in relation to the 1 𐤔 unit, according to the result reached in column V. 1 𐤔 is taken to be the Shekel according to the Hebrew ostraca and the Old Testament (discussed in Chapters 6 and 7 below). VII. The mean deviation of the unit, in percentages, calculated in relation to the 1 𐤔 unit. 1 𐤔 is defined as the basic unit in the system, that is, being 100 per cent and 0 per cent deviation (since it appears as the major unit in the Old Testament and in the Hebrew ostraca. From a purely metrological point of view, 4 or 8 Shekel can also be taken as basis of calculation). The deviation is calculated thus:

$$\text{Deviation} = 100 \ - \ \frac{(\text{column V}) \times 100}{\text{column VI}}$$

The results are rounded to two digits (i.e. 0.01 per cent). This is, of course, a mean deviation of all the weights from each unit. Absolute deviations in the 𐤔 series are presented separately (Fig. 12). Columns VIII and X do not require further explanation, while columns IX and XI are similar to column VII. Since the status of the Gerah weights is the subject of debate, I have separated the calculation of this series: first assuming 24 Gerah per 1 𐤔 (Fig. 10: columns VIII–IX) and then assuming 20 Gerah per 1 𐤔 (Fig. 10: columns X–XI).[1]

---

1. Theoretically, one can assume any other number of Gerah units per 𐤔, but these were the only possibilities raised so far, for good reasons.

I	II	III	IV	V	VI	VII	XII	XIII	XIV
Script	No. general	No. for average	Average grams	Multiple (to š1)	Explanation of the unit	Deviation from š1	Hieratic numerals	Qdt units	Dbn units
𐤔 (script)	2	1	454.55	40.110	40 Shekel	0.28%	50	50	5
𐤔 (script)	2	2	274.33	24.207	24 Shekel	0.86%	30	30	3
𐤔 (script)	3	3	184.769	16.304	16 Shekel	1.90%	20	20	2
𐤔 (script)	1	1	129.45	11.422	12 Shekel	-4.81%	15	15	
𐤔 (script)	42	34	90.627	7.997	8 Shekel	-0.04%	10	10	1
𐤔 (script)	47	41	45.239	3.992	4 Shekel	-0.20%	5	5	0.5
𐤔 (script)	34	28	22.617	1.996	2 Shekel	-0.21%	2		
𐤔 (script)	34	27	11.332489	1.0	1 Shekel	0%	1		
Nsf	51	46	9.659	0.852	5/6 (0.833) š	2.28%		1.08	0.1
Pym	47	42	7.815	0.690	2/3 (0.666) š	3.44%		0.87	
Beqaᶜ	29	28	6.003	0.530	1/2 (0.5) š	5.95%		0.67	

Notes: Column III: number of weights used for calculating the average. Columns IV and V are rounded to three decimal places except for the 1 Shekel unit. Columns VII, IX, XI and XIII are rounded to two decimal places.

Figure 10. *Metrology of the š, NSF, Pym and Beqaᶜ series.*

The right side of the table (Fig. 10: columns XII–XIV) treats the adjustment of the JILs to the Egyptian weight system, which will be discussed in Chapter 9 (below).

5.3. *The Metrology of the ಠ Series*

The data in Fig. 10 prove the uniformity of this series. Where large quantities of weights have been found, and the averages can be trusted, the mean deviation is less than 0.5 per cent. This is such a low deviation that it is absurd to assume that there was more than one standard in this series. The small deviations are possibly the result of forgery, mistakes in manufacture, wear during and after use, encrustation of lime, etc. It could therefore be that they stem from a mixture of some of these factors. When only a few weights are known from a certain unit, the average is hardly accurate, but the deviations are small, even in the few known weights of 12 ಠ–40 ಠ. The larger deviation of the one 12 ಠ weight is due to its damaged state of preservation.

A few ಠ weights have larger absolute deviations (Fig. 12). Even among these, deviations of more than 6 per cent are found only in two weights, and deviation of more than 5 per cent in another two (Fig. 12). Otherwise, we are left with weights defined as exceptional and not included in the calculations. There are only 11 such weights (among the 202 weights of the ಠ series, i.e. approximately 5 per cent).[2] Other weights that are not included in Table 10 are simply cases where the weight is unknown or not yet published. The weights that remain are really exceptional, not only in weight but in shape, material or inscription. Many scholars suggested various explanations for these weights, such as unfinished specimens, or results of forgery or modern forgeries. Furthermore, these few exceptional weights are scattered (some are heavier, some lighter than the average of 1 Shekel). They are not centred around any specific value that could be assumed to be another norm. Finally, the numbers of these deviant weights is so low, that they cannot sustain a theory of different standards (see above).

Throughout the metrological discussion of the ಠ series, I have used outside sources (the Old Testament and the Hebrew ostraca) only to identify the ಠ as the Shekel. There is no other choice here, but this

---

2.   These are ಠ 1.2, 4, 18, 20, 29, 42; ಠ 2.12; ಠ 4.31-32; ಠ 8.29. Add weight ಠ 1.42 from the addenda. Interestingly, most are among the ಠ 1 unit, which is the lightest of the series.

identification is accepted by all scholars today, and it is well established from the evidence of the Hebrew ostraca.

5.4. *The Metrology of the Nsf, Pym and Beqaᶜ Series*

Following the data (Fig. 10), it is suggested that the Nsf formed ⁵/₆ ׁ,ש the Pym ²/₃ ש and the Beqaᶜ ¹/₂ ש. In these series, the mean deviations are also small. The biggest deviation appears in the Beqaᶜ series (+ 5.6 per cent), as already noticed by Scott (1964: 58; 1965: 136). However, this fact does not justify an explanation of different standards, nor the detachment of the Beqaᶜ from the ש. Furthermore, since the deviation becomes larger as the weights become lighter, it is a uniform phenomenon. When the weights are lighter, it is more difficult to manufacture them exactly, as each 'chip' removed may be too much. Perhaps this was the reason why the manufacturers tended to err 'on the heavy side' (cf. Hemmy 1937: 45; Powell 1979: 73; 1992: 905-906). In any case, whatever the reasons are, the uniformity of this phenomenon indicates that it is not related to different standards, but to lighter weights in general.

Regarding absolute deviations, the Nsf, Pym and Beqaᶜ are significantly less exact than the larger ש weights. There are many weights with deviations of more than 5 per cent (13 Nsf, 8 Pym and 12 Beqaᶜ). Yet this cannot be taken as evidence of different standards. For example, the 13 deviant Nsf weights are divided into four weights that are heavier than the average (Nsf nos. 2, 14, 17, 43) and nine weights that are lighter than the average (Nsf nos. 4, 13, 40, 44, 45, 48, 51, 59). On either side, there is a whole range of approximately 5–15 per cent deviation from the average, not any specific value around which the weights are centred (nor two or three 'groups' with the same values). Some of these deviant weights are simply badly preserved (e.g. Nsf.4); others may reflect forgeries, mistakes in manufacture, and so on.

It seems to me that there is no compelling evidence that the Nsf was an independent Shekel. It is situated well inside the JIL system, and removing it forms a gap between the Pym and the ש. Understanding the Nsf and the Pym as ⁵/₆, ²/₃ ש also fits a system based on 24 (and not 20) Gerah in the ש, since ⁵/₆, ²/₃ form natural fractions (of ²⁰/₂₄, ¹⁶/₂₄). Mathematically, a system of 20 Gerah per ש is still possible, but then the Nsf and Pym form ¹⁷/₂₀, ¹⁴/₂₀ of the ש. This is very awkward, and there is more to be said on this matter (below).

I	II	III	IV	V	VI	VIII	IX	X	XI	XIII
Script	General No.	No. for average	Average grams	Multiple (to 1)	Meaning of unit	Fraction: 24 Gerah method	Deviation %	Fraction: 20 Gerah method	Deviation %	Qdt units
ፐ	13	13	5.129	0.452	10 Gerah	10/24	8.62%	10/20	- 9.48%	0.57
፰	17	17	4.308	0.380	8 Gerah	8/24	14.04%	8/20	- 4.96%	0.48
ፖ	2	2	3.415	0.301	7 Gerah	7/24	3.32%	7/20	- 13.9%	0.38
ፖ	13	13	2.269	0.288	6 Gerah	6/24	15.40%	6/20	- 3.83%	0.36
ፖ	7	7	2.727	0.240	5 Gerah	5/24	15.50%	5/20	- 3.75 %	0.30
፡፡፡፡	8	8	2.366	0.209	4 Gerah	4/24	25.25%	4/20	3.38%	0.26
፡፡፡	9	8	1.891	0.166	3 Gerah	3/24	33.49%	3/20	11.24%	0.21
፡፡	1	1	1.705	0.150	2 Gerah	2/24	80.54%	2/20	50.45%	0.19

Figure 11. *Metrology of the Gerah series*

Notes: Column III: number of weights used for calculating the average. Columns IV-V are rounded to three decimal places, except for the 1 Shekel unit. Columns VII, IX, XI, XIII are rounded to two decimal places.

Unit	Average grams	Maximum positive deviation	Maximum negative deviation
ᛦ1	11.33249	no. 16, 11.95 g, 5.4%	No. 2, 10.50 g, - 7.3%
ᛦ2	22.617	no. 12, 24.50 g, 8.3%	No. 2, 21.77 g, - 3.7%
ᛦ4	45.239	no. 36, 46.66 g, 3.1%	No. 29, 43.00 g, - 4.9%
ᛦ8	90.627	no. 34, 94.60 g, 4.4%	No. 29, 85.45 g, - 5.7%

Note: In the addenda, only one weight exceeds these maximum deviations (1ᛦ.42, 12.2 grams or 7.6% deviation)

Figure 12. *Absolute deviations in the ᛦ series*

5.5. The Metrology of the Gerah Series (Fig. 11)

The Gerah is more difficult to study. The relation of its units towards the ᛦ 1 (Fig. 11: column V) does not supply an immediate answer about the nature of each unit, since the mathematical results may fit several explanations. Therefore, I have explained the Gerah units according to their Hieratic numerals (column VI).

Formerly, scholars debated whether these numerals are Hieratic numerals at their 'face value' (Kaufman, G. Barkay) or according to a special, 'Judaean' value (thus Yadin, Stern and other scholars). Unlike the ᛦ weights, it is impossible not to read the Gerah numerals at their face values.[3] The reason is the appearance of a complete sequence of numbers from 2 to 10. One cannot read this other than at face value, as a few examples would show. If one reads the Hieratic 10 as 8 (in analogy to Yadin's explanation of the ᛦ 8 weights), then how would one explain the existing 8 Gerah weights (marked with Hieratic 8)? If one reads the Hieratic ܐ as 4, what is to be done with the existing Gerah weights that are marked ⦀? It is impossible that the same value would be written in two ways (⦀ and ܐ) within one system; and the averages of the weights marked ⦀ and ܐ indicate that these are different units. Furthermore, one cannot 'reduce' numerals such as 6, 7 or 9 into whole numbers, as opposed to 5, 10 or 20. Surely no serious scholar would suggest that there were Gerah weights of 4.5, 7.2, etc. Another argument involves one specific weight (5 Gerah.1). Apart from

---

3. The non-face value of the heavier Shekel weights is discussed in §9.1.4 below, in relation to the Hieratic numerals. (For non-face values in the Kadesh Barnea ostraca, see §8.4.)

the usual Hieratic 5 on the dome, it bears five vertical lines on its base. This can only mean the numeral five, a sign shared by many scripts. Both signs appear on the same weight, so they are equal: Hieratic ٦ = five vertical lines = 5. In other words, the Hieratic numerals are taken at face value.

The next step is to calculate the 'norm' of 1 Gerah, which is approximately 0.55 grams (this is based on the series of 5, 6 and 8 Gerah, where the deviations are smaller and the quantities of weights larger).

We now reach the question of the relationship between the Gerah and the ש. According to the 20 Gerah per ש method, the Gerah form part of a decimal system, with relatively uncomplicated fractions ($^3/20$, $^4/20$, $^5/20$, etc.). It is also easy to perceive the Gerah weights as 15 per cent, 20 per cent, 25 per cent, etc. of the ש unit. The deviation in comparison to the ש reaches 14 per cent in one case, but is usually much lower. In fact, in most of the Gerah weights they are lower than the 5 per cent margin (defined above). According to the 24 Gerah per ש method, the Gerah weights do not always form simple fractions ($^3/24$, $^5/24$, etc.). It may appear thus to our modern eye, but perhaps the necessity of a full sequence of weights was more important that simple fractions. Another difficulty is the higher deviations of the Gerah weights, reaching nearly 33 per cent (mean deviation versus the ש1, excluding the unique 2 Gerah weight).

If we had to choose on the basis of the metrological facts alone, the method of 20 Gerah per ש is preferable. However, we must again consider the whole picture. I believe that there were 24 Gerah per ש, based on the following arguments.

1. The deviations in the 24 Gerah per ש method are larger, but they are consistent. There is a uniformity in this phenomenon, that of growing deviations as the weights become lighter (Fig. 11: column IX). This starts with the Nsf and goes through the Pym and the Beqaᶜ (Fig. 10). Thus, it is a general phenomenon, and not something that is limited only to the Gerah weights.

2. The 20 Gerah per ש method creates a dichotomy in the transfer from the Gerah to the Beqaᶜ. The Beqaᶜ is unequivocally 0.5 of the ש, that is $^{10}/20$ (accepted also by G. Barkay 1987). Yet if 1 ש equals 20 Gerah, then 10 Gerah = $^{10}/20$ unit, then that should be equal to the Beqaᶜ. But Beqaᶜ weights are heavier than 10 Gerah weights. One cannot pull the rope from both ends: if the ש had 20 Gerah, then the Beqaᶜ is not part of the ש system. However, tearing the two apart is

problematic on other grounds (above), and contradicts the written evidence (Exod. 38.26).

3. If the Nsf and the Pym formed $5/6$, $2/3$ of the ש, they fit a system of 24 Gerah per ש, but not a decimal subdivision of 20. Similar evidence may be found in 1 Sam. 13.21, where the original verse should perhaps be amended into 'third of a Shekel' (שלש שקל, instead of the corruption תלת הקלשון; for a *midrash* on the third of the Shekels see Nogah 1992: 251-60). Thirds are not compatible with a system of 20 sub-units.

4. Weight Beqaᶜ.13 has additional marks on its base, probably the Hieratic numerals $5 + 10$, i.e. 15. Since 15 does not fit the Beqaᶜ in either system, it seems that here the marks are not face value, but similar to the marks on the larger ש weights (cf. weight ש 12 for the same numerals). One should read here 12, thus the Beqaᶜ is 12 Gerah and the ש is 24 Gerah.

5. Ostracon no. 6 from Kadesh Barnea is a strong indication for 24 Gerah in the ש (discussed in Chapter 8 below).

6. The analogy to other weight systems. A basis of 24 Gerah per ש compares with the Mesopotamian system. On the other hand, there are no comparable weight systems based on 20 sub-units in the standard from the same period in the Near East. Connections between the JILs and the Mesopotamian world are evident in other areas: for example, the names of the units (below).

7. The analogy to the ש series. There, the multiples are 4 or 8, and it is more likely that the same mathematical system would be kept for the whole system (not half of the system decimal and half hexagonal). This is not a decisive argument, but it has some merit.

To sum up, three possibilities exist for explaining the Gerah weights. The first is to break the Gerah series into different 'standards' at will, without direct relation to the ש. It is a simple way to sort weights by weight only and avoid problems of deviations (e.g. Eran 1987). I have tried to show that this method is wrong, and results in complete ignorance of historical and archaeological data (above). The second possibility is to assume that the Gerah formed $1/20$ of the ש. This is more in keeping with the metrological facts (Fig. 11), but creates severe problems and tensions (cf. ostracon 6 from Kadesh Barnea, the Beqaᶜ as half the ש, etc.) that cannot be reconciled without breaking the JIL system. The last possibility is that one Gerah is $1/24$ ש. In my view, this is the best option. The only argument against it is the higher deviations of the smaller weights, but this is not a crucial problem.

The deviations in the Gerah series may seem great in percentages, but as a matter of fact they amount to $1/2$ gram at the most. If buying and selling were made using the same set of weights, the deviation is negligible in the long run for transactions within a local community. The Old Testament indicates that forgery resulted from using two sets of weights ('stones'), one lighter and one heavier. In any case, it is possible to estimate the value of $1/2$ gram of silver in the ancient Near East. This was quite a stable value (excluding times of crisis), approximately 1–1.5 work-days of a hired labourer. This calculation assumes a Mesopotamian Shekel of 8.4 grams and 25 work-days per month. It is calculated from written sources in Syria-Mesopotamia (Janssen 1988: 14; Pritchard 1959: 177 no. 273, no. 195; Klengel 1988; Dandamayev 1988: 53-54; Zaccagnini 1988). The situation in Ugarit is less clear (but see Heltzer 1978; Stieglitz 1979). The equivalent of 1–1.5 work-days of a hired labourer is certainly a small sum of money in the world of today,[4] but one cannot be sure if the same is true for ancient conceptions of price and 'time value'.

The whole JIL system is presented in Figure 13, with a drawing in Figure 14. So far, the basic assumption that ﬡ is the Old Testament Shekel has not been discussed, and this will be done in the following chapters.

Gerah	Beqaᶜ	Pym	Nsf	Shekel (ﬡ)
multiplications	12/24	16/24	20/24	multiplications
2? 3 4 5 6 7 8 9? 10 11?				1 2 4 8 12 16 24 40

Figure 13. *Summary of the JIL system*

---

4.   In Israel's terms (1996), the average salary is approximately $60 per day, and this is based on $17000 per year as an average income; 25 days of work per month, reflects a modern, industrial society, but is probably much too high.

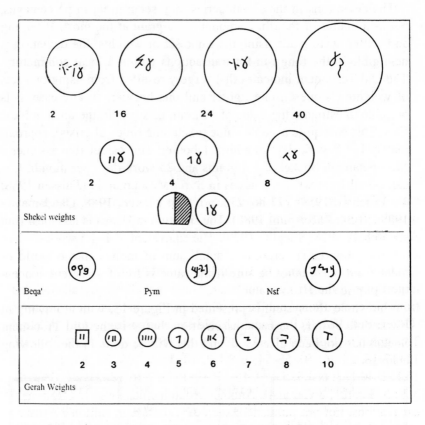

Figure 14. *The JIL system: A schematic drawing*

Chapter 6

THE ARCHAEOLOGICAL CONTEXT

6.1. *Contextual Data (Fig. 15)*

Out of 434 JILs, only 211 have known sites of origins (including three weights from Ekron and one from Accho (see note at the end of Appendix 2).

1. *Unknown Contexts* (75 JILs). Unfortunately, the contexts of the largest part of the JILs are not clear. These include, above all, weights from old excavations, published with very few details about contexts (Gezer, Beth Zur, Tel ej-Judeideh, old excavations in Jerusalem, etc.). This group includes 50 JILs (א 1.5, 10-11, 16; א 2.8-10, 12, 22, א 4.10, 12, 17-18, 25-26, 50, 53-54; א 8.1-2, 10, 15, 27-28, 33, 35, 44, 49; א 16.1; א 40.1, 3; Nsf.3, 5, 8-9, 15-17, 19; Pym: 7.16-18, 21, 52; Beqaᶜ.2-3, 9; 5 Gerah.1; 8 Gerah.4). Another group includes weights from new excavations, not yet published, such as Tel Batash, Shiloh's excavations in Jerusalem (Eran [1996] did not deal with the contexts) and Kh. Uzah (information from other excavations was kindly given to me by excavators). Here, there are 18 JILs (א 1.3; א 2.11, 13, 41-42; א 4.29, 31-32, 55-56; א 8.32; Pym.13-15, 20, 48; Beqaᶜ.7; 4 Gerah.11). Seven other JILs were actually bought and their contexts are vague (א 2.19; א 4.27, 51?; Nsf.4 Pym: 4; Beqaᶜ.1, 8).

2. *Unclear Contexts* (32 JILs). This is another category that is unhelpful. It includes mixed loci (2 JILs, א 2.6 and Pym.6), as well as surface finds and general definitions, such as whole squares, 'debris', 'fills', Lachish D/X' or 'Lachish 500' (25 JILs, א 1.4, 12, 23; א 8.12, 17, 34, 51; Nsf.14, 18, 20, 21; Pym.5, 11, 12, 19; Beqaᶜ.4-6, 10, 30, 34; 2 Gerah.1; 4 Gerah.1; 6 Gerah.2; 8 Gerah:.1, 3). Add three weights from later contexts, probably secondary ones (א 4.11; א 8.11; א 16.4). One weight was found in a foundation trench (א 8.45). Another weight was

found in a layer of ash near a house (ﬡ 88.30).

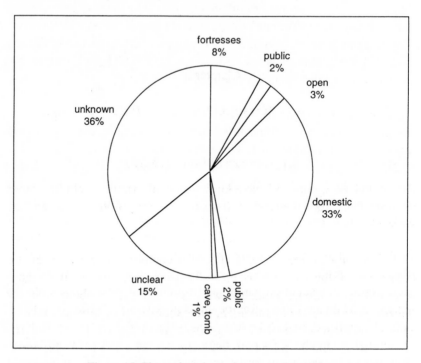

Figure 15. *The archaeological context of the JILs*

3. *Open Areas* (6 JILs). Some weights were found in open areas inside settlements (ﬡ 2.14; ﬡ 4.28; ﬡ 8.21, 50; 6 Gerah.4?), or outside city walls (Pym.10). It does not say much about their function. Although 6 Gerah.2 and 10 Gerah.1 weights were found in Lachish area 500 outside the city, they already appear in the 'unclear' category (above).

4. *Pits, Cisterns, Pools*. Altogether 5 JILs (pits: ﬡ 1.14-15, and perhaps also ﬡ 8.20?; pool: ﬡ 4.31; cistern: Nsf.7). These are probably secondary contexts, since weights cannot be useful in a pool or a cistern. Probably they were thrown, or accidentally fell, into these loci.

5. *Caves and Tombs* (2 JILs). This very small group includes Pym.51 from Mamila and ﬡ 4.52. Perhaps two weights from Kh. el-Kom belong here (ﬡ 82.19; Beqaᶜ.8), but they were actually bought and not excavated. The same is true for the Nsf from Anathot (bought, not found in situ).

6. *Storage Rooms, Public Contexts* (5 JILs). This small group may imply that JILs were used in public contexts. For the problem of separating public from 'private' life in ancient Judah, see §5.1.2 (below). The weights here were found in storehouses (the tripartite buildings: Nsf: 13), and areas of gates (ᛪ 1.8; ᛪ 8.29; Pym.8). One weight was found in an installation or room of a gate (ᛪ 1.13).

7. *Domestic Contexts* (65 JILs). This large group is composed of weights found in clear domestic contexts: for example, the small rooms under the 'sun temple' at Lachish and in other sites (17 JILs: ᛪ 1.9; ᛪ 2.15, 20, 25?; ᛪ 4.14-15, 16?, 19-20, 23; ᛪ 8.13, 18-19, 22; Nsf.6; Gerah 8.1-2). Even here, the details published about these rooms are often minimal, and their nature is left vague, such as from Ein Gedi (we only hear that a weight was found in an area of houses on the slope of the site). Most of these rooms are small and seem to belong to domestic buildings. Many other weights probably belong with them. The first of these are weights from new excavations, which seem to come from domestic contexts, but only final publications will make this certain: for example, Malhata, Ekron, Ramot and Beit Safafeh (15 JILs: ᛪ 1.40-41; ᛪ 2.24, 39-40; ᛪ 4.24, 33?; ᛪ 8.16, 47-48; ᛪ 24.3; Nsf.12; Beqaᶜ.11; 4 Gerah.9; 6 Gerah.3). Second, there is the large group of weights from Kenyon's excavations in Jerusalem (Kenyon 1967, 1974: Scott 1985). Details about the contexts are few (mainly Jerusalem I–II). The weights were found in different loci and areas, mostly in area A (but also AA, K and L). Following the excavators, I assume that almost all this group belonged to domestic loci (but, with the experience of other excavations, some probably come from unclear or surface loci). A few weights were put in other categories, if their context was specified.

8. *Fortresses* (at least 16 JILs). This category is problematic. It includes mainly weights from Arad, but in fact Azeka and Mesad Hashavyahu (4.30) are also fortresses. In Arad, many weights were found in rooms that are part of the casemate wall, or near it (ᛪ 81.6-7; ᛪ 82.16-18; ᛪ 84.21-22, 23?; ᛪ 88.24-26; Nsf.10?, 11; Pym 9). Since this wall is late, they probably belonged to an earlier level, that is, VI or VII, and to small rooms near the walls of the Iron Age fortress. In some cases, the published details are very few (Nsf.10; Pym.9). In one case, the weight was found in 'Elyashiv's house' (ᛪ 8.24), a sort of official context. As for the weights from Azeka, they appear above since their context is not

clear. It is difficult to classify these weights. Should we take them to be 'royal' or 'official', because the fortresses were governed by the kingdom of Judah? Was the function of the Arad fortress, for example, related to royal trade or military acts? Or perhaps some of these weights belonged to 'private' citizens who lived there in non-royal roles? There is no simple answer, but common sense would imply that at least some of these weights belonged to the officials of the king, who worked in such border fortresses. As for Mesad Hashavyahu, see Chapter 3 above.

6.2. Discussion of the Contexts

The clearest conclusion that can be drawn about the context of the JILs is that the data in our hands are very limited. Most of the weights simply do not have clear details of context, since they were found in mixed, secondary loci, or in old excavations that paid little attention to the exact context of each find. For some newly found weights, the details are not yet published. In addition, there are surface finds or general designations, such as whole areas or squares. In view of this situation, the discussion of the contexts remains preliminary.

It is easy to state that most of the JILs were found in domestic contexts. In this I include rooms and courts of domestic buildings, as well as most of the casemate rooms. Architecturally, these form part of public fortifications, but, as a matter of fact, they were usually used for daily activities as part of four-roomed houses. In many cases, the real nature of 'domestic' loci is not clear: we do not know who used a certain room and for what functions. It is also worth remembering that a large proportion of ancient Judaean cities was, after all, domestic; thus it is likely to be excavated and to produce a considerable amount of the corpus of JILs.

Only a few JILs can be connected with public domains. A few were found in the eastern court of the palace at Lachish, and one was found in the court at Ramat Rahel (8 ℵ.14-16, 21, perhaps add Beqaꜥ.5 from Lachish). A few other JILs were found in areas of gates, and at least one in a public storehouse at Tel Beer Sheba. To this add perhaps a few weights from a storehouse near the gate at Tel 'Ira. It is, of course, extremely hard to separate public from private in Iron Age II Judah. We can define the physical places as such, but it does not necessarily reflect the uses of the artifacts found there. For example, not all the artifacts from a palace are royal, since servants and other 'private' persons may visit or work in a palace. Another noteworthy fact is that many weights are related to the destruction of the level where they were found (whatever date it was). This means that their last days of use were extraordinary times, not peaceful, daily lives. During times of crisis, social boundaries are breached, and it is harder to define what is public and what is private. To give one example, the royal *lmlk* jars could have been used to feed all the population during the siege of Lachish level III, not only officials and soldiers. We may have found them in domestic places for such reasons (Ussishkin 1976: 64).

So far, the JILs show no relation at all to religious/cultic contexts. This is not the place to go into the problem of how do to define such contexts. It is sufficient to mention the scarcity of religious contexts in Judah that were found in excavations. Other than the Arad temple, there are only a few vague places, taken to reflect house cult (such as one room at Lahav; but what actually is 'house cult'?), or 'popular religion' (such as Jerusalem cave 1, but what really is 'popular cult'?). I have dealt with those matters elsewhere (Kletter 1996: chap. 7). It seems best to conclude that the JILs had no special connection with religious life. As would be natural, they were used in any place where they were needed for transactions or the weighing of precious metals, and that probably includes temples and cult places.

The JILs had no use in tombs, since they belonged to the world of the living. Only very rarely were they put in tombs, probably as personal items of the deceased. This is similar to grave goods in general, so finding a few JILs in tombs does not mean that they had any religious or funerary meanings (G. Barkay 1994; Kletter 1996: 57, 59).

Some loci are 'mass-loci', which do not tell much about the function of the JILs. For example, pools and pits are likely to be secondary contexts for weights, that were thrown (or fell) into them after use. The same may be true for streets and alleys, or open areas outside buildings.

In summary, it seems that the JILs were used mainly in domestic and public contexts, in living layers of settlements. They have little to do with religion or with burial. They were common in many sites in Judah, and it seems that they were used by the whole population, or, to be more exact, by those sections of the population that needed to weigh (officials of the kingdom, traders and merchants, wealthy citizens). We touch here upon a fundamental question, which is the existence of 'private' economy in Judah (see the concluding chapter).

6.3. *Other Aspects of Context*

Manufacture and Allocation of Weights

There is almost no archaeological data about the manufacture of the
JILs. Was there one, central manufacturing shop in Jerusalem? (cf.
Scott 1985: 201; note 1 above). Was it an official domain, that is, regu-
lated by the state? There is evidence of manufacturing weights in
Gezer, found by Macalister (1912: 257-58). The problem is that the
publication leaves much to be desired. A study of the script may show
whether JILs were produced by many hands, perhaps related to regional
production centres (but it is hard to define the script; Chapter 4 above).
Weights could be produced locally even from 'foreign' materials, as is
perhaps the case of Tel el-Ajjul (Late Bronze Age). Petrie found there
a lump of hematite with few weights in one room, and perhaps the
weights were made there (Petrie 1934b: 13-14; 1952: 16). From neighbouring countries there is some evidence: for example, in Egypt
(Spencer 1993) and Mesopotamia (a seal of an official responsible for
weights: Arnaud, Calvet and Huot 1979: 18, 27, 53-54, but cf.
Bjorkman 1993).

We do not have any data on the allocation of weights after manufacture. Were weights 'sold' to customers as any other commodity, and,
if so, what was their 'price'?

Relationship between Contexts and Weight Units

An interesting question is whether there is a relationship between the
context and the type of weight. Do we find small units, for example, in
different contexts than heavier ones? Are certain units limited to certain
types of context, and why? Are there regional differences within Judah
with regard to different weight units, or concerning different types of
site (for example, are larger units connected with more wealthy or
central sites, or with sites on major trade routes?). It is also possible to
ask about relationships between context and deviation. For example,
are deviations larger (that is, the weights are less accurate) in smaller,
rural sites than in central cities? All these questions are interesting, but
we lack the data required to answer them.

Scientific Excavations versus Antiquities Markets

Let us look briefly into the differences between JILs from excavations
and JILs from the illegal robbery of sites (Fig. 16). There are obvious

differences between these two groups. There are 211 JILs with origins, found in excavations and surveys (though seven of these were also bought; §6.1 above). The JILs from unknown origins are almost equal in number (223), so the comparison is easy. Among JILs from excavations and surveys, the 4 ℧, 8 ℧, are dominant (39 and 42 weights), followed by 2 ℧ and Pym (29 and 24 weights). The Nsf comes only in the sixth place (21 weights) and the smaller units of Beqaᶜ and Gerah are the least common (13 and 16 weights). The picture is quite different among the weights from unknown origins: here, the dominant series are the Gerah (67 weights) and the Nsf (38 weights), followed by Pym, Beqaᶜ and 1 ℧ (28, 22, 24 weights accordingly). The 2 ℧, 4 ℧ and 8 ℧ units are the least common (13, 17, 9 weights only).

Assemblage	1℧	2℧	4℧	8℧	Other ℧	℧?	Nsf	Pym	Beqaᶜ	Gerah	Total
Excavations and surveys	18	29	39	42	6	3	21	24	13	16	211
Unknown origins	24	13	17	9	5		38	28	22	67	223
Total JILs	42	42	56	51	11	3	59	52	35	83	434

Note: Column ℧? Includes three weights from Accho and Ekron (see note at the end of Appendix 2).

Figure 16. *JILs from excavations versus JILs from unknown origins*

It is true that smaller units are harder to find in excavation, but the same would also be true for illegal excavations. It is also true that this picture is not completely reliable, because of various factors (for example, perhaps the fact that there are so many Gerah and Nsf weights from unknown contexts is related also to the fact that Eran and Ben-David dedicated studies to these units, publishing many specimens from private collections). But the picture is still alarming and deserves explanation. One plausible explanation would be that some weights from antiquities markets are simply forged, and the market has a demand for weights that carry Hebrew inscriptions (they are more exotic to buyers than simple Hieratic numerals?). Whims of forgers and dealers may also play a part.

This situation generates an interesting thought. A large percentage of artifacts from illegal excavations originated in robbed tombs. Tombs are easy to rob and often rewarding (being rich in whole finds), while excavation of settlement levels may prove poor. Also, tomb robbing is more safe, since the tombs are usually found in slopes and most of the activity is hidden, while sites on hilltops are much more exposed. Now,

when we study the contexts of the 211 weights from scientific excavations, we see that there are almost no JILs from tombs, though many
tombs from Judah have been excavated and published (G. Barkay
1994). All this strengthens the doubts about the authenticity of weights
from antiquities markets.

It is a sad story: antiquities trade inflicts damage on sites, and the
plundered objects of greed lose their scientific value. If we do not pay
attention, we will reach mistaken conclusions. It is really the 4 and 8
Shekel weights that are common; the Gerah, Nsf and Pym are common
only in robbers' possession. This is also important, since 4 and 8
Shekel are common for good reason—they are precisely the units that
are adjusted to the Egyptian weight system (see Chapter 9 below).

Chapter 7

THE JUDAEAN WEIGHTS AND THE OLD TESTAMENT

In this chapter I will discuss the relationships between the JILs and the Old Testament. Both are connected to the kingdom of Judah at the end of the Iron Age period; and it is therefore sensible to assume that they have things in common. The Old Testament is, of course, a much wider creation in scope, both in time and in space. It is usually focused on the higher classes of society, such as acts of kings and relations between kingdoms, while the JILs reflect day-to-day economic life. Owing to the ideological interests of the Old Testament, it must be treated critically.

7.1. *General Metrology of the Old Testament*

During the Iron Age period, coins were not yet known in Judah, and there was no monetary economy in its modern sense. There was no word for 'money', and even today silver in Hebrew (כסף) stands for both the money and the metal. In the story of Abraham in Hebron, a unique term is given, כסף עבר לסחר (literally, 'silver that goes over to the merchant', Gen. 23.16). This may denote negotiable silver, or a certain quality of silver accepted for trade (Hurowitz 1996). Weight defined the value (i.e. the price) of expensive commodities, mainly gold and silver (most other commodities were measured by volume). Values were also affected by the laws of market economy, such as demand and supply. For example, at times of crisis, prices became sky-high (2 Kgs 6.25). A similar phenomenon is well known from other Near Eastern sites, such as Emar (Zaccagnini 1995; in general, see Eph'al 1996). The Old Testament mentions the weighing of different metals, usually gold and silver, rarely copper (1 Kgs 7.47; 2 Kgs 25.16; 1 Chron. 22.13-16). Most of these references concern transactions, taxes and booty at national and international levels, and not trade between individuals.

This may explain the prominent place of gold and silver. It is not clear to what extent such transactions involved real weighing, even when the Old Testament expressed 'prices' in weight units. Local trade and day-to-day transactions in small communities were most probably made by exchange (barter), which did not necessitate formal weighing and actual exchange of precious metals (cf. in Egypt, Janssen 1975, 1979).

Balances were the technical means of weighing. The Old Testament gives very few details about the shape and the nature of the scales, called מאזנים (also פלס, according to Barrois 1932: 51; Trinquet 1957: 1240). There is not one clear mention of 'balance' in the historiographical literature of the Old Testament. When we find descriptions of weighing, it is often in metaphorical contexts (Isa. 40.12; Ps. 62.10; Job 6.2). Such sources, from the prophetic or wisdom literature placed the emphasis on justice in weighing, expressed in terms of 'falsified balances' or 'wicked balances' (meaning 'balances of deceit') on the one hand, and 'just balances', 'even balances' on the other hand (Amos 8.5; Ezek. 45.10; Hos. 12.8; Mic. 6.11; Prov. 11.1; 20.23; Job 31.6; etc.).

We have archaeological evidence of balances found in Palestine (Eran 1982: 91 [Accho]; Scott 1971; Stager 1996: 66-67 [Ashkelon]) and elsewhere (Glanville 1935; Courtois 1983: 159 Pl. 131; Petruso 1992: 75; cf. also Kisch 1965: chap. 4; Skinner 1967). A beam of an Egyptian type of balances was found in Lachish level III (G. Barkay 1992, 1996). Iconographic sources for balances from Israel amount to one JIL (א 4.48, Fig. 32 below). It has on its base a drawing of a man holding small hand-scales (Briend 1992: Fig. 34). There are scenes of weighing from Egypt, and one limestone relief from Marash (Syria, now in the Louvre) shows a man with balances (Scott 1971: 128; Thompson 1986: 171; Ronen 1996: 122). Finally, we have written sources describing weighing from the Near East (see esp. Joannès 1989: 125-40).

The 'Dust of the Balances'. Isaiah 40.15 gives a peculiar expression, שחק מאזנים, usually rendered in English as 'dust of the balances'. The context of the verse implies a meaning of something negligibly small and worthless, which does not matter at all (cf. the opposition to Isa. 40.12). But what is *shahaq* and how is it connected with scales? Most of the commentators explained it as 'dust' (McKenzie 1968: 20; Westermann 1969: 46). Other scholars suggested more imaginative, but probably mistaken, interpretations (Torczyner 1948; 1952; Dahood 1966). However, there is a technical term for weighing in Mesopotamian sources, *šiqû(m)*, which is linguistically identical to the Hebrew *shaḥaq* (Goetze 1948: 85-86; CAD M/II [1977]: 38-39). In the Mari documents, *šiqû(m)* indicates a small margin of error: the scales stopped in a state of equilibrium, but did not indicate exact weighing. A certain small amount, negligible because it could not be checked, could be added or taken away without changing the equilibrium of the scales. This is expressed by the term *šiqû(m)* (Joannès 1989: 136-39; Veenhof 1985: 303-304). There is, of course, a wide gap of time and place between Isaiah (who used this term because of its symbolic value) and the early Mesopotamian sources. Therefore, it does not necessarily mean direct borrowing, but perhaps reflects a general *milieu* of Near Eastern weighing practices.

Day-to-Day Weighing. The Old Testament describes very few instances of daily, 'ordinary' weighing; thus it is almost impossible to define the prices of goods. One outstanding case is found in Jer. 32.9-10. Jeremiah bought a field for 17 silver Shekel. The weighing actually constituted the act of payment, and, in order to leave no room for doubt that Jeremiah paid for the field and owned it legally, the story described the weighing twice. In this case, it seems that there was actual weighing and paying in silver (at least following the logic of the story), and not a barter transaction. A different case is the story of Absalom's hair (2 Sam. 14.26). The weight of the hair indicates its length, thus preparing the reader for Absalom's tragic death, hanging by his hair (2 Sam. 18.9). This story, though, does not describe ordinary circumstances (see more below).

The 'Stones'. In modern Hebrew, the word *mishkolet* (מָשְׁקוֹלֶת) means a 'weight', but in biblical Hebrew it denotes the weight that hangs down at the lower end of a builder's level (אֲנָךְ). The Old Testament term for weights is simply 'stones' (אֲבָנִים)—occasionally, more accurately, 'pocket stones' (אַבְנֵי כִיס). This combination shows that the weights were usually made of stone, at least in origin. The fact that these weights were carried in a pocket indicates that they were quite small (Deut. 25.23; Mic. 6.11; Prov. 16.11). Precious metals were also carried in the pocket (Isa. 46.6). Similar to verses about scales, we find mostly symbolic or moralistic references to weights. The demand for justice called for the use of 'just stones' or 'whole stones' (אֶבֶן שְׁלֵמָה, אַבְנֵי צֶדֶק; Prov. 11.1; Num. 19.36). Fraud was a problem, to judge from this demand and from the common mentioning of forgery in the Old Testament. It seems that forgery was committed by using different sets of stones, for selling and for buying, one lighter and the other heavier (אבן ואבן; Mic. 6.11; Prov. 20.10, 23). This evidence warns us against hasty identification of 'different standards' when we find small deviations in similar weights.

A Royal Weight and Absalom's Hair. In one place, a royal weight is mentioned, called 'stone of the king' (אבן המלך; 2 Sam. 14.26). This term is the polar opposite of the 'stones', which mean 'ordinary weights', but it is a unique verse that does not specify the exact nature of this measure. The story wanted to stress the heaviness of Absalom's hair, and it may mean that the royal weight unit was heavier than the ordinary one. One the other hand, it is possible that the term 'of the king' was used only in order to add credibility or authority to the story (royal weights were perhaps more accurate, or more trusted, than weights owned by individuals). Furthermore, it is natural to expect that Absalom would have used the king's measure, being the king's son! The whole situation is unique (cf. De Vaux 1961: 312; Pilcher 1916: 188; Powell 1992: 907). Of course, the story might be fictional. Absalom had to cut his hair in order to weigh it properly (excuses were found, but they are not convincing). Weighing hair has no use; it is demanded in order to explain Absalom's death. Furthermore, the 'weight of hair' is clearly a metaphor for its length: the 200 royal Shekel signify here a unit of value, not real weighing with balances (for royal weights in general, see Chapter 10 below).

Uses of Weights. It is impossible to put a finger on the exact uses of weights in the Old Testament. We hear that Yahweh weighed people and nations in metaphorical connotations. Absalom, son of David and the prophet Jeremiah, are mentioned in connection with weighing, but it is not clear whether they were actually those who weighed (for Absalom, see above). Cana'an appears as personification in Hosea (12.1, 8), holding the 'balance of evil', but Ephraim is meant there (and it is theology, not history). In the prophetic and legal literature of the Old Testament, there is no mention of special officials for weighing. Perhaps any person could weigh with his own set of scale weights. In Mari, officials responsible for weighing are mentioned in a royal context (Joannès 1989; Arnaud, Huot and Calvet 1979: 18, 54; cf. Bjorkman 1993, 1994). Nothing of this sort is evident in the Old Testament.

7.2. *Units of Weight in the Old Testament (Fig. 17)*

The Old Testament mentions the weight units Gerah, Beqaᶜ, Pym, Shekel, Maneh and Kikar. A few more peculiar, or late, units are mentioned, and I will discuss these briefly.

1. *Qeshitah, Agora and Peres/Parsin.* All these are units of weight, but they are rarely mentioned and their setting is either late or obscure. The Qeshitah was sometimes seen as an early monetary unit of silver (esp. Einzig 1949: 219-20; cf. Hultsch 1882: 460). Einzig (1949: 219-20) believed that it was equal to the value of one lamb, and that cattle was used widely as a store of value. The word may be related to תכשיט, 'jewel', and does not necessarily mean an established weight unit. The Peres is a postexilic unit of weight. The Agora was a small unit of weight, also late in appearance (De Vaux 1961: 310; Stern 1963: 862; G. Barkay 1981a: 294 n. 65; Cross 1981; Brewer 1991, with references). To the best of my knowledge, there is no weight from Judah that is inscribed with the name of these units.

Some scholars suggested that the Hieratic sign on the 8 Gerah weights is a Hebrew letter, z (ז), meaning the weight unit 'Zuz' (Lemaire and Vernus 1983: 309). Yet the Zuz is never mentioned in the Old Testament, and it is probably a late division of the Mesopotamian Shekel (Mayers 1988).

2. *Gerah, Beqaᶜ and Pym.* The Gerah is mentioned only in the Pentateuch and in Ezekiel (45.12). The name is derived from the Mesopotamian unit *giru*. In the Pentateuch, it is always connected with the holy Shekel (שקל הקודש; Exod. 30.13; Lev. 27.25; Num. 3.47; 18.16). I will use a shorter form, 'holy Shekel', instead of the common 'Shekel of the sanctuary'.

The Beqaᶜ is mentioned only twice (Gen. 24.22; Exod. 38.26). It is related to the holy Shekel in Exodus. The name is related to the verb *b.q.ᶜ* (בקע), which has a clear meaning of 'half' (e.g. Zech. 14.4; cf. Torrey 1903: 207; Barrois 1932: 54; Pilcher 1915: 190-92).

The Pym is mentioned only once, in 1 Sam 13.21. It is a difficult verse, which does not define the meaning of the word clearly. 1 Sam 13.21 may be a secondary interpolation (Smith 1899: 102-103; see also Zippor 1984; Ben-David 1979: 36-37, Pilcher 1914; 1916). It seems that the verse should be amended: the Pym denotes two-thirds of a Shekel, and then one should continue to read 'a third [of a Shekel] for a Qilshon' (Bewer 1942: 45-46; Gordis 1942: 209-211; Polzin 1989: 253

n. 18; Kyle-McCarter 1980: 232, 234-35, 238). The origin of the word 'Pym' is not clear. Clermont-Ganneau (1924: 105-11) suggested that it is a dual form of 'a mouth' (פֶּה). Speiser (1967, originally 1940) thought that it means 'two-thirds', according to an Akkadian analogy, *Šinipu* and the Old Testament expression פִּי שְׁנַיִם (cf. also Albright's notes in Speiser 1967; Rainey in M. Aharoni 1981: 126; Powell 1992: 906; Aberbach 1974; cf. Deut. 21.17; 2 Kgs 2.9; Zech. 13.8).

The Nsf of the JILs is missing from the Old Testament (on its etymology, see Clermont-Ganneau 1901: 30; Barrois 1932: 65-67). A similar unit existed in Ugarit (Parise 1971, 1981, 1984, 1991), but I have not seen evidence that it was half of a Syrian Shekel (cf. also Gordon 1965: 446; Heltzer 1978: 59 nn. 339, 449; 1996).

3. *The Shekel* was the main unit of weight. This is indicated by the overwhelming number of references to it in the Old Testament (as opposed to all the other small weight units). Also, it holds a central position within the weight system (below). Many times, the word 'Shekel' is omitted completely in favour of a short form. Thus the formula '*x* silver' appears instead of '*x* Shekel silver' (e.g. Gen. 37.28; 45.22; Judg. 9.4; 16.5; 2 Sam. 18.12; 1 Kgs 10.29; Isa. 7.23). The same short form exists in legal contexts as well (e.g. Deut. 22.19, 29). A decisive proof that this short form applies to the Shekel is found in Num. 7.11-85. It describes how every Israelite tribe gave a charger (מִזְרָק) of 70 silver holy Shekel, and a bowl of 130 silver. In the summary (Num. 7.85), the twelve tribes gave 2400 Shekel, that is, 12 × (130 + 70). Thus, the bowls and the chargers are valued in the same unit, each bowl weighing 130 silver holy Shekel. We can rely on this story, since the author would not make a mistake in such a simple calculation, and would like us to believe the story by presenting credible calculations. The historical background of the story as a whole is something else, but it need not be discussed here.

Of course, the Old Testament often mentions huge numbers of Shekels, which may be exaggerations or imaginary quantities. There are only a few instances of small amounts that look credible. Quarters and thirds of the Shekel are mentioned, but in theological rather than economical circumstances (related to the Temple: 1 Sam. 9.8; Neh. 10.33; cf. also Jer. 32.9; 2 Kgs 7.16). A third of a Shekel was perhaps part of the original version of 1 Sam. 13.21 as well (see the discussion on the Pym above).

Type of literature	Gerah	Beqaᶜ	Pym	Shekel	Holy Shekel	Stone of the king	Maneh	Kikar
A. Historiographic books								
1. Samuel–Kings				9		1	1	12
2. Joshua–Judges			1	2				
3. Chronicles				2				
4. Ezrah–Nehemiah				2		3		
B. Pentateuch								
1. Genesis		1		1				
2. Exodus	1	1		4	6			7
3. Leviticus	1			9	3			
4. Numbers	2			12	5			
5. Deuteronomy								
Prophetic/Wisdom								
1. Ezekiel	1			3			1	
2. Other				2				2
Total	5	2	1	46	14	1	5	43

Note: The numbers indicate the number of references to each unit. The lines indicate that the units are related to each other in the Old Testament text.

Figure 17. *Weight units in the Old Testament*

Ezekiel (4.10) mentions 20 Shekel as a low daily ration of food. This is interesting, since clearly the object here is the quantity (approximately 230 grams in our terms) and not a 'price'. In this case, the Shekel is used as a general standard of measure, not as a specific weight unit that involves actual weighing (cf. the case of Absalom's hair, Chap. 7.1 above). It is unlikely that the Shekel was used to weigh ordinary food, since scale weights were mainly used for weighing precious metals in small amounts. Agricultural products, such as wine, oil and grains, were measured by volume. In any case, this verse in Ezekiel is unique, and belongs to a late date.

4. *The Maneh*. The Maneh (Mina) is mentioned only five times in the Old Testament, most of them in late contexts (1 Kgs 10.17; Ezek. 45.12; Ezra 2.69; Neh. 7.70, 71). Scholars assumed, therefore, that the Maneh was not original to Judah, but a late, postexilic addition (Barrois 1932: 52, 56-57; Stern 1963: 863-64; Trinquet 1957: 1241; De Vaux 1961: 309; Scott 1959b: 34-35; Thompson 1986: 168; etc.). This was also based on the appearance of large numbers of Shekels in the Old Testament (e.g. 50, 100), explained as evidence for the use of heavy Shekel multiples, instead of the Maneh. A crucial verse is Ezek. 12.45. According to a simple reading of this verse in its MT version, the Maneh included 60 holy Shekel. This verse is difficult, and translations offer different readings. Barrois (1932: 56-57) saw the LXX translation of Ezek. 45.12 as an indication of a reform of the Maneh. In the MT, Maneh is 60 Shekels (15 + 20 + 25), but the fraction of $^{25}/_{60}$ seems

irregular and Barrois explained it as a 'leftover' from an earlier Maneh of 50 Shekel (with fractions of $^{25}/_{50}$, $^{20}/_{50}$, $^{15}/_{50}$). In other words, Ezekiel took these fractions and added them into a new Maneh of 60 Shekels (while the Kikar remained the same, since the quantity of Maneh per Kikar was reduced). Barrois's explanation was adopted, with minor variations, by Scott (1959b), Stern (1963: 863), Trinquet (1957), and Powell (1992: 906), but Barrois himself warned that Ezek. 12.45 is difficult.

5. *The Kikar (Talent)* (כיכר) is very common in all the genres of Old Testament literature, related to huge amounts of silver and gold. Very rarely is it mentioned side by side with copper or iron (1 Chron. 29.7). In one instance, lead (עפרת) is mentioned (Zech. 5.7). There are also cases where one Kikar is mentioned (2 Sam. 12.30; 1 Kings 20.39), or two Kikars (which are כיכרים; 1 Kgs 9.24; 2 Kgs 5.23; etc.). The name may imply a rounded form of weight unit, if an analogy to the use of the same word for 'bread loaf' is allowed. According to Exod. 38.25-26, one Kikar included 3000 holy Shekel: the sum of silver mentioned there is 100 Kikar and 1775 Shekel, received from 603,550 persons that gave $^{1}/_{2}$ Shekel each. Thus, they gave 301,775 Shekel, and 300,000 Shekel formed 100 Kikar. The Talent was called *GÚN=biltu* in Mesopotamia, but the Ugaritic form *Kikarum* is close to the Old Testament.

The names of the units Gerah, Shekel, Maneh and Kikar are basically the same as in Mesopotamia and Syria (as detailed above; cf. Stern 1963: 873-76; Skinner 1967: 13-20; 36-39; Joannès 1989; Arnaud 1967; Powell 1979: 93; 1987–90). The origin of the names Beqaᶜ and Pym is less certain. By analogy to Mesopotamia, we can assume that the position of the units within the system was similar (i.e. the Gerah and Beqaᶜ were subdivisions of the Shekel, and the Maneh and Kikar were multiples of the Shekel). Though in both regions the names are similar, the units could be different in weight (De Vaux 1961: 309-10).

7.3. *Weight Systems in the Old Testament*

The plural of the title is not a mistake, since the Old Testament reflects more than one weight system. By now, readers will surely not suspect me of adopting a 'many standards' method without good reasons. At this point, one must remember that the existence of different standards and systems in the Old Testament does not necessarily prove that they have all been widely used in reality.

7.3.1. *The Holy Shekel System of the Pentateuch*

This system is the easiest to define (Fig. 18). Its basis is the holy Shekel (שקל הקדש). Both words, 'holy' and 'Shekel', are clear; but the Old Testament does not give the exact value of this weight unit. Early translators were uncertain how to interpret this weight unit. They translated it literally (*siglos*), or in terms of their own times (*didrachma* in a few verses in the LXX). The weight cannot be found in the translations (though attempts were made; cf. Barrois 1932: 56-57; Pilcher 1916: 188-90).

Gerah	Beqaᶜ	Holy Shekel	Kikar
$^1/_{20}$ holy Shekel	$^1/_2$ holy Shekel	20 Gerah	3000 holy Shekel

Figure 18. *The 'holy Shekel' system in the Pentateuch*

Clearly, the holy Shekel is always mentioned in the Old Testament in relation to religion and cult. It appears when taxes, vows or gifts are presented to God through the priests, the Levites or the Temple (taxes for building the Temple, Exodus 38; the work in the tabernacle, Exod. 30.13-16; vows to God, Leviticus 27; offerings in the Temple, Numbers 7; cf. also Num. 3.44-51; 18.16). This holy Shekel is therefore a unique weight unit, used only in religious contexts. It has no connection with day-to-day economy, local transactions of individuals, nor with economic activities of kings and kingdoms (Barrois 1932: 53-54; 1953: 253). The authors who used the term 'holy Shekel' wanted to distinguish it from another Shekel, which we shall call, for the time being, 'ordinary Shekel'. For that reason, they stressed time and again that the holy Shekel was made of 20 Gerah. We can assume, therefore, that an 'ordinary Shekel' had a different number of Gerah (since, otherwise, why would the 20 Gerah in the holy Shekel be mentioned time and again?). A similar view was expressed by Pilcher (1916: 188) and Barrois (also later Stern 1963: 864 and De Vaux 1961: 310).

Was there really a weight unit (and system) of a holy Shekel, used in the kingdom of Judah? Barrois (1932: 53-54; 1953: 253) thought that the holy Shekel was an official standard, kept in the Jerusalem Temple. G. Barkay (1987: 218) thought that there was only this Shekel, which always had 20 Gerah. It is not easy to answer this question. Clearly, the holy Shekel appears only in the Pentateuch and in Ezekiel (for which see below). It is limited to the Priestly code in the Pentateuch, whose date has been debated since De Wette in the early nineteenth century.[1] Few critical scholars date it to the end of the First Temple Period, while most date it to the postexilic period. The crucial fact is the complete absence of the holy Shekel from Deuteronomy and the deuteronomistic work. It cannot be waved aside as negative evidence, since the deuteronomistic work had an active interest in religion, cult and religious reforms. Furthermore, the deuteronomistic work mentions the Shekel unit, quite often. If a holy Shekel existed during Iron Age II Judah, why is it never mentioned in this literature?

7.3.2. *The Weight System of Ezekiel 45 (Fig. 19)*
This system is equal to that of the holy Shekel, only it is connected with the Maneh instead of the Kikar. Ezekiel is dated to the first half of the sixth century BCE (chs. 40–48 carry the title year 573 BCE, Ezek. 40.1).

Many scholars perceived Ezek. 45.12 as evidence of a reform in the holy Shekel system. During this reform, the Maneh was changed from 50 to 60 Shekel (Barrois 1932: 56-57; 1953: 254-55; Trinquet 1957; Stern 1963: 863; cf. §7.2 above). However, the verse is very difficult to understand, and the LXX version is not necessarily better than the MT.

Gerah	Beqaᶜ	Shekel	Maneh
$^1/_{20}$ Shekel	$^1/_2$ Shekel	(probably 'holy')	60 Shekel

Figure 19. *The weight system of Ezekiel 45.12*

Scholars claimed that the 50 Shekel in the Maneh fit the many decimal quantities mentioned in the Old Testament (De Vaux 1961: 309-10), but such quantities may be rounded or fictional. Also, one should not expect weight units and 'prices' to be identical—as today our salaries and prices are not identical to units of coins and notes.

Ezekiel 45 seems to be a variant of the Pentateuch holy Shekel system. Both deal with a Shekel of 20 Gerah; both are interested only in the religious realm. It is thus plausible that Ezekiel had in mind the same holy Shekel. The ideological and linguistic ties between Ezekiel and the Priestly code are well known, and strengthen the conclusion above. If so, we can combine Ezekiel and the Priestly code, and present

---

1. In a few places in the Pentateuch, 'holy Shekel' is meant, though only a short form, 'Shekel', is given. In other places, one cannot be certain. I use the term 'Priestly code' for convenience; it does not imply acceptance of the Documents theory as a whole.

a somewhat fuller picture of the holy Shekel system (Fig. 20).

Gerah	Beqaᶜ	Holy Shekel	Maneh	Kikar
$^1/_{20}$ holy Shekel	$^1/_{20}$ holy Shekel	(20 Gerah)	60 holy Shekel	3000 holy Shekel

Figure 20. *The combination of the Pentateuch and Ezekiel 45.12*

7.3.3. *The 'Ordinary Shekel' System*

In most of the places where the word 'Shekel' is mentioned in the Old Testament (except in Ezekiel and the Priestly code), it does not signify the holy Shekel, but another type of Shekel. It is a Shekel used for 'secular' (though not exclusively) aims. True, this cannot be proven for every verse, especially when a short formula, '*x* silver', is used (cf. §7.2 above). This is not the important point; the important fact is that this 'ordinary' Shekel is common in various genres, and was clearly used during the First Temple Period. In view of this, I termed it the 'ordinary Shekel' system. The trouble is that we have no information in the Old Testament on the relationships between its weight units. We can only put the units in an assumed place, but even this is based on analogy to the holy Shekel system and to the Mesopotamian system (Fig. 21).

Gerah	Beqaᶜ	Pym	'Ordinary' Shekel	Maneh	Kikar

Figure 21. *The 'ordinary' Shekel system*

The Beqaᶜ probably existed in the ordinary Shekel system, according to Gen. 24.22 (there the situation is 'secular' and the holy Shekel is not mentioned). The Gerah may be included only if one assumes that the ordinary Shekel was subdivided into Gerah units as well (but not into 20 Gerah; see §7.3.1 above).

7.4. *The JILs and the Old Testament Weight Systems*

If my understanding is right, the Old Testament documented two weight systems which have similar names of units, but different kinds of Shekel ('holy' and 'ordinary'). To this we may perhaps add a royal weight system, implied from the term 'stone of the king' in 2 Sam. 14.26. Which of these systems, if any, should be equated with the JILs?

There is no doubt that the JILs represented the ordinary Shekel system, since this was the system used widely in Judah throughout the

late Iron Age II. This system is the only candidate for identification
with the JILs, which were the common weights of Judah during the
same period.

It is impossible to identify the JILs with the holy Shekel, since they
had no relation with religion or cult. The JILs were found in 'secular'
contexts, public or private (Chapter 6 above). Furthermore, I doubt if
the holy Shekel ever existed in Iron Age Judah. It probably reflects a
utopian plan, which did not exist (even during the times of the Priestly
code and Ezekiel). This statement is based not solely on a late dating of
these sources, but on the nature of the economy of Iron Age Judah. It
seems to me that Judah never had a separate 'Temple economy' during
that period. The Jerusalem Temple was build by the kings of Judah and
was not an independent entity, but part of the royal house. David's sons
were priests (2 Sam. 8.18), and the kings of Judah treated the Temple
as their own property in times of need (2 Kgs 18.16; 24.13). When
silver was collected to rebuild the Temple, the kings supervised its
counting (2 Kgs 12.11; 22.4, 9). The Temple was situated immediately
next to the palace (2 Kings 11). If there was no independent Temple,
there was no place for a separate holy Shekel. Furthermore, so far not
even one inscribed weight from Judah carries an inscription 'holy
Shekel' or the like, though hundreds of inscribed weights are known.
This negative evidence carries some weight, since a few inscriptions
related to the word 'holy' appear on Judaean vessels: for example, in
Arad.[2]

The same holds true for the exilic and postexilic periods. During
Ezekiel's times, there was no Temple, thus no Temple economy could
have existed. Later, we hear about a third of a Shekel in relation to the
Second Temple (Neh. 10.33), but it is impossible for this to be a holy
Shekel of 20 Gerah. It is also strange that a 'holy' Shekel would be
lighter than an 'ordinary' one (on the coinage of Persian period Judah,
see Mildenberg 1985b, 1988; Betlyon 1986; Barag 1987).

The identification of the JILs and the 'ordinary' Shekel system leads
to the following conclusions:

1. The ४ weights are Shekel weights, that is, the Shekel that was
commonly used in Iron Age II Judah. This is further strengthened by the evidence of the ostraca (Chapter 8 below). Hence-

2. Even Mesopotamian temples were not fully independent (Janssen 1979;
Lipiński 1979; Dandamayev 1979; Gelb 1969).

forth, I will use the name 'Shekel' to denote the ordinary Judaean Shekel (ย). When I refer to the JILs, I will add the ย symbol to prevent confusion.

2. The ย Shekel did not include 20 Gerah (which is the measure of the holy Shekel).

Many points of similarity exist between the JILs and the Old Testament ordinary Shekel. In both, weights are made of stone, and share the same unit names and relative status of the units. The Shekel is the main standard, the Pym is $^2/_3$ Shekel and the Beqa^c is $^1/_2$ Shekel. However, there are also differences that require attention.

1. The Nsf is not mentioned in the Old Testament. Yet the Pym and the Beqa^c are also rarely mentioned. This is not a problem, since the Old Testament is not a chronicle of day-to-day life and is a religious creation. Since the Nsf is not even mentioned, there is certainly nothing about a 'Nsf Shekel' (a standard assumed by Scott, Lemaire and others). The idea that the Nsf was a sort of an independent Shekel standard was imposed on the Old Testament. It depends on the metrology of the JILs, and, as we have seen (Chapter 5 above), has no real basis.

2. The central unit is called 'Shekel' in the Old Testament, but inscribed ย on the JILs. The suggestion that it was not easy to write whole words such as 'Shekel' on small weights does not help, since whole words appear on even smaller weights (Pym, Nsf, Beqa^c). The difficulty is rather in the sign ย itself (see §10.1 below). In any case, there is no evidence in the Old Testament on heavy and light, or gold and silver Shekels (see what was already said about the 'Nsf Shekel' above).

3. The Old Testament calls the smallest unit 'Gerah', but only Hieratic numerals appear on the smallest JILs. The identification of these weights as Gerah weights is based on written ostraca (Chapter 8 below). The lack of the word 'Gerah' can be explained by the very small size of the Gerah weights.

4. The JILs are based on multiples of 4 or 8, while the Old Testament gives many decimal quantities of Shekel and Kikar. This is not a significant difference, as explained in regard to the Maneh (§7.3.2 above).

5. The JILs represent one weight system, while three at least are mentioned in the Old Testament. There is no difficulty here: the geographic, temporal and thematic horizons of the Old Testament are much wider than the JILs. The 'holy Shekel' system was perhaps just a utopia. As for the royal weight system, see Chapter 10 (below).

6. The lack of inscribed heavy weights—Maneh (Mina) and Kikar. This is the sharpest difference between the Old Testament and the JILs. The Maneh is mentioned rarely in the Old Testament, but the Kikar is very common. On the other hand, not even one inscribed Maneh or Kikar weight was found in Judah. True, inscribed heavy weights are scarce in the whole ancient Near East, in comparison with smaller weight units; but in Mesopotamia we do find some, from different sites and periods (Lemaire and Vernus 1983: 322; Gibson 1971: 67; Holland 1975; Parise 1981; Molina 1989; Powell 1979: 73, 103-104, 107; 1992: 905-906; the word 'Mina' appears as a loan word in Egypt, Ward 1989: 301 no. 8; for 'Mari' see Joannès 1989). A partial explanation is the different nature of the Old Testament and the JILs. The Old Testament deals mainly with higher levels, kings and kingdoms, while the JILs reflect economic realities. The huge numbers in the Old Testament cannot be taken literally.

It is not accidental that the heaviest Shekel weights of the JILs are 40 Shekels. This is exactly the border-line, one step before the Maneh is reached (whether it had 50 or 60 Shekel). It is possible that the multiples of 4 or 8 continued into heavier units. There are a few uninscribed weights that seem to represent 400 Judaean Shekels (Appendix 4: XVII). It does not indicate that the Maneh was not used, since 400 Shekels equal 8 Maneh (then each Maneh included 50 Shekel).

One important weight from Malhata gives us a clue in this matter (Kletter forthcoming b; I thank I. Beit Arieh for the permission to discuss it here). It is probably a Judaean weight, to judge from the material (limestone), the shape (rounded dome), the period (seventh century BCE) and the place (the Negev). A chip is missing from the edge of the dome, and currently the weight is 1381.2 grams (reg. no. 3633, locus 1507). Restoration with plasticine leads to the conclusion that the original weight was approximately 1450 grams. This fits 16 Egyptian *dbn* of approximately 90 grams each. Some logic must have guided the making of a 16 *dbn* weight, since the Egyptian system was decimal, and 15 *dbn* would have been much more practical. In Judaean terms, the Malhata weight equals approximately 128 Shekel. This leads to a simple solution: that what we have is a weight of 125 Judaean Shekels, or 2.5 Mina (of 50 Shekels).[3] The Judaean Maneh was

---

3. I have not overlooked the possibility that the Malhata weight signifies 2 Maneh of 60 Shekel ($2 \times 60 = 120$), but this seems to be too low compared with the restored weight.

therefore equal to approximately 567 grams. The difference between 125 and 128 Shekels is negligible (and may be due to the reconstruction, for the exact original weight is unknown). Why, then, the multiple of 2.5? Probably because there is no other close point of mediation between the Judaean and the Egyptian systems. The next good match is really 400 Shekels = 8 Maneh = 50 *dbn*. If this is true, the Judaean system could have continued in units of Maneh of 50 Shekels, adjusted to Egyptian *dbn*. The series of weights could be 2.5, 4?, 8, 16? Maneh, corresponding with 16, 25, 50, and 100 *dbn*. Another interesting thing is the rough, but possible, equation of the inscribed 24 Shekel weights with half a Maneh (25 Shekel). I hasten to add that it is risky to rely on one weight, and we must wait for more evidence to ascertain the suggestions offered above.

Even more haphazardous is the understanding of the Kikar. Was it based on 3000 or 2500 Shekels (resulting in values of approximately 34.02 or 28.33 kilograms)? If the Maneh was 50 Shekels, 3600 Shekels in a Kikar are unlikely. As a matter of fact, there is one inscribed Kikar weight from Judah. It was discovered in Jerusalem, and it carries the inscription 'stone of king David' (אבן המלך דוד). The only trouble is that it is a forgery (for the fascinating story of this object, see Cré 1892). In a peculiar way, Eran tries to restore this as an ancient Kikar (1996: W.308). This is not new (Raffaeli 1920), but it is hardly convincing.

Chapter 8

THE JUDAEAN WEIGHTS AND THE HEBREW OSTRACA

7.1. *General Introduction*

In order to compare the JILs and the Hebrew ostraca, we must acknowledge several limitations. First, many of the ostraca lack clear dating. I cannot discuss the date of each ostracon here but, for our purposes, it is suffice to set a general time-span—the eighth–seventh centuries BCE. Most of the ostraca belonged to the seventh century BCE (Millard 1984), and therefore match the date of the JILs. Second, not every weight mentioned in the ostraca denotes a weight unit. Different quantities of weight can be written, without directly reflecting the weight system. Third, the 'ethnicity' of the ostraca is often vague. Only in the last few years have we begun to recognize the Philistine script, thanks to a few inscriptions from sites such as Tel Jemmeh, Ashkelon and Tel Shera' (Naveh 1985; Cross 1995; Stager 1996: 66). There is a debate about the political status of Mesad Hashavyahu (Reich 1989; Na'aman 1989; Wenning 1989), and Kadesh Barnea (Cohen 1983; Na'aman 1989: 61-62 n. 67, with references). One ostracon from Arad provides an example. Y. Aharoni (1981: no. 34) assumed that it was written by an Egyptian, and drew wide historical conclusions based on this assumption. Yet, an Egyptian writer could serve a Judaean king, and it is also a possibility that the writer was a Judaean who learned the Hieratic script. I will define Hebrew ostraca according to the script, but occasionally discuss other ostraca that may belong to neighbouring nations, if they contribute to the understanding of the JILs.

As opposed to the Old Testament, the Hebrew ostraca possess many advantages for comparison with the JILs. These ostraca are more accurately dated than many Old Testament sources, and originated from the same period and area as the JILs. Most important, the ostraca usually reflect daily, economic activities, while the Old Testament is focused on national and international strata, or on religious affairs. The ostraca can reveal much more about the lower levels of administration and local economy, and this makes them closer to the JILs than the Old Testament.

8.2. *Names of Weight Units in Ostraca*

It is rare to find the names of weight units written out in full in Hebrew ostraca. Ostracon 3 from Kadesh Barnea gives a sequence of Hieratic numerals from 5 to 800, next to the word 'Gerah' (Lemaire and Vernus 1980: 342-44). Lemaire and Vernus suggested that this ostracon was an exercise, and I tend to agree; I think that the weighing of hundreds of Gerah is very unlikely, since heavier units (Shekel) are much more practical. Furthermore, each Judaean Shekel included 24 Gerah, so 800 Gerah mean the awkward sum of 33.333 Shekel. This shows that we are dealing with an exercise of registration, not with all the quantities of weight that were ever weighed. Note also the metathesis *hgr* instead of Gerah in column 1.10. Since it is an exercise, the amounts of weight have no practical importance. Lemaire and Vernus (1983: 344 n. 9) suggested that the writing is face value and in units of Nsf, but my opinion is that the Nsf was never used as the basis of an independent Judaean weight system, and did not have multiples or subdivisions of its own (see Chapter 5 above).

The word 'Shekel' is rare on ostraca. It appears as part of a private name in ostracon 3a from Heshbon (Cross 1986: 479 line 9). The verb appears in Mesad Hashavyahu (Naveh 1962: 30). Often, the ostraca carry a short form *Š* for 'Shekel': for example, an ostracon from Arad (Y. Aharoni 1981: no. 16 line 5): 'the silver ⊐ š to the sons of Ge'alyahu' (הכסף ⊐ ש לבני גאליהו) and the Tel Qasileh ostracon: '*š* =' (B. Mazar 1951: 67). Sometimes the whole word 'Shekel' is omitted: for example, in Arad (Y. Aharoni 1981: no. 29.1, 6; 48.2). In such cases, the formula '*x* silver for *nn*' means '*x* Shekels of silver for *nn*'. This is the same formula that is found in the Old Testament (§7.2 above). So far, the words 'Beqaʿ', 'Pym', 'Nsf', 'Maneh' and 'Kikar' are lacking in Hebrew ostraca, though the root *M.n.h* ('to count') appears in ostraca from Jerusalem and Samaria (Lemaire 1972: 569; 1978: 152).

8.3. *Writing of Numerals on the Ostraca*

The Hebrew script did not contain special numeral signs (contrary to Gandz 1933; Yadin 1960), but there were Hebrew words for numerals (very similar to those of other Semitic languages). The use of simple vertical lines to denote the numerals 1 to 4 was universal, and these numerals are not indicative of a specific script (Scott 1964: 64; 1985: 204-205).

1. *Full writing of numerals* (in words) is quite common in the ostraca. It was used to denote monthly dates in the ostraca from Samaria, Lachish, Arad and the inscription from the City of David (Reisner, Fisher and Lyon 1924: ostraca nos. 1, 4, etc.; Torczyner 1938, 1940; Shiloh 1979: 18; Y. Aharoni 1981: no. 7 lines 4, 7). The same writing served for amounts as well: for example, in the Siloam inscription; at Kadesh Barnea (Lemaire and Vernus 1983: no. 6, columns 5.12, 6.6); at Mesad Hashavyahu (Naveh 1962: 30 no. 6); and at Tel Qasileh (B. Mazar 1951: 6 no. 1). A similar method appears in the Mesha inscription (Jackson and Dearman 1989: lines 2, 8, 16, 20). Numerals had the same names, or very similar names, over a wide area of the Near East, and these are not really distinctive Hebrew names. Even fractions were sometimes written in a full way: for example, writing חצי for half (Y. Aharoni 1981: Arad no. 101).

2. *Phoenician and Aramaean numerals.* Phoenician numerals appear in the coastal plain: for example, in Tel Qasileh ('≡ Sh[eqel]', B. Mazar 1951: 67) and Tel Jemmeh ('=', i.e. 20, Naveh 1985: 13-15). This is hardly surprising, since these sites were under considerable Phoenician influence during the Iron Age II period (cf. the evidence from Ruqeish, Oren 1986b; Culican 1973), and the same method was maybe adopted by the local population. On the other hand, Aramaic forms of numerals appear in Transjordan: for example, in the Heshbon ostraca (Jackson 1980: 69; Puech 1985: 13-16; cf. Naveh 1989: 107-11). This was not the only influence of Aramaean on Transjordanian scripts, of course.

3. *Hieratic numerals.* The use of Hieratic for numerals was by far the most common method in Iron Age II Palestine. It is already found in the eighth century BCE, in Tel Beer Sheba (Y. Aharoni [ed.] 1973: 71) and Samaria (the numerals 5 and 10).[1] Numerals II and III appear also in Samaria ostracon C1101 (Lemaire 1972).

---

1.   Samaria ostracon 63 has an odd combination, with a sign that looks like a 'T'. It is often explained as the numeral 5 (Reisner, Fisher and Lyon 1924: 243; Torczyner 1987: 203 n. 1; Yadin 1960; Shea 1985: 16-17). This is strange, since the combination would be 10 + 5 + 2, while the writer could write '10 + 7'. Perhaps the 'T' sign means a unit, thus the reading is: 'in the year 10, 2 [units of] T'. This is difficult, though, and perhaps writing '10 + 5 + 2' was easier for the local scribe.

Hieratic numerals were very common in Hebrew ostraca of the seventh century BCE: for example, in Arad, Lachish, Kadesh Barnea, Tel Haror, Mesad Hashavyahu and the Papyrus from Wadi Murabaʿat. The numerals were used for dates (especially in Samaria) but also for registration of quantities of weight, usually small ones. In Arad, the biggest numerals are 24 and 300 (the last appears only once: Arad ostracon 2.4). In Lachish, the numerals are 10 and perhaps 50. On the Ophel ostraca the numerals are 4, 5, 7, 18, 50(?) and 200 (Lemaire 1978). In Murabaʿat, they are 4, 5 and 10. The Tel Haror inscription gives only the numeral 8 (Oren *et al.* 1991: 17-18). As for quantities of weight, these are also small: 4 Shekel are mentioned in Mesad Hashavyahu (Naveh 1962: 30); 5–10 Shekel in Arad (Y. Aharoni 1981: ostraca nos. 16.5; 29.1, 6; 48.2; 65.2; 81.1?); and 30 Shekel in a sherd from Tel Qasileh (B. Mazar 1951: 67). Heavy weights are listed only in the unique Kadesh Barnea exercises (discussed below). This is not surprising, since most of the ostraca reflect daily registration, probably dealing with affairs of individuals and communities. The Hieratic numerals on the ostraca should always be read at face value, except when dealing with quantities of weight, where there is a possibility of the use of non-face values (see further below).

8.4. *The Ostraca from Kadesh Barnea and Mesad Hashavyahu*

I have already mentioned ostracon no. 3 from Kadesh Barnea, where the word 'Gerah' appears (above). Two other ostraca from Kadesh Barnea and Mesad Hashavyahu are important for understanding the JILs, since they reflect this weight system more directly than usual.

1. *The Ostracon from Mesad Hashavyahu*

Transcription:	*Transliteration:*
1. ...*N*]*tṣbᵓl* [...]	1. ...*N*]*etaṣbaᶜal* [...]
2. ...] *šql. ᵓrbᶜ. ksf.* ٦ ४ *šy*	2. ...] weighed four (Shekels of) silver, ٦ ४, a gift.

Perhaps the first part (missing) included a formula 'before *nn*' (לפני) , thus Netaṣbaᶜal was a witness: 'In front of Netaṣbaᶜal, *nn* weighed four silver, ٦ ४, a gift'.

The ostracon dates to the seventh century BCE. Personal names with 'Baᶜal' components are not Judaean (Naveh 1962: 30-31), but here we may have a 'kosher' Judaean name if it is derived from the verb *n.t.ṣ.* ('to break'). On the other hand, Lemaire (1977: 268; cf. Na'aman 1989: n. 157) reads the name as *ʿnybʿl*. The script is Hebrew and the sign ᵃ fits the JIL system. This ostracon proves that the ᵃ is the sign of the Shekel. The shortening 'four silver' should be read as 'four Shekels of silver', by analogy with the same formula in the Old Testament. The Shekel unit was the only weight unit thus shortened, since it was the major unit and the most common one.

Many scholars claimed that this ostracon proves that the numeral ٦ means 4 (Naveh 1962: 30-31; Yadin 1960; Scott 1959a: 32; 1965: 137). This is not so. The formula in the ostracon, whereby 'four silver' is ٦ ᵃ, is not a mathematical equation. It is a formula of an amount of weight. On the one hand, there are four Shekels written in the full Hebrew script. On the other hand, there is the shortened form of *the same amount, but as it was written on the JILs*: ٦ ᵃ. On the heavier Shekel weights, Hieratic numerals were used not face value: for example, Hieratic 5 is inscribed on 4 Judaean Shekel weights.[2] If we discuss ostraca that do not deal with weights, we cannot read the Hieratic numeral in the same way as we read them on the JILs.

Why did the writer add the signs '٦ ᵃ' to the Mesad Hashavyahu ostracon after he already used the formula 'four silver' earlier? One possibility is that he wanted to prevent any confusion as to how much was given. The writer, as we do today, had to deal with a Judaean system that was dual in its use of numerals. Whereas elsewhere Hieratic numerals were used at face value, in the Judaean weight system, weights of 4–40 Shekel carried non-face value Hieratic numerals. This duality appears clearly in ostracon 6 from Kadesh Barnea: there we find a sequence of Hieratic numerals from 1 to 10,000, including a full sequence from 1 to 10 (columns 1–2). Such a sequence can be only at face value (cf. the same sequence of the Gerah weights, §5.5 above). On the other hand, column 4 of ostracon 6 from Kadesh Barnea gives numerals at non-face value (below).

2. *Ostracon 6 from Kadesh Barnea (Figs. 22–23)*
This is the most important ostracon for the JILs and, luckily, one can rely on the excellent publication of Lemaire and Vernus (1983). I agree with them (1983: 325) that it is an exercise, since it contains mistakes

---

2.   The non-face values of the heavier Shekel wights are discussed in §10.1.4 below.

and a peculiar use of the Hieratic script. More important, it registers amounts that are totally impractical and were never weighed in reality (below). The other ostraca from Kadesh Barnea are also exercises. In ostracon 4, a random number returns again and again. Ostracon 6 offers a didactic sequence, including alphabetic letters and numerals (Lemaire 1980; Lemaire and Vernus 1983: 325-26).

It is not easy to decide who the 'student' who wrote ostracon 6 was. It may have been an Egyptian, but more likely a Judaean. The status of Kadesh Barnea is debated (Cohen 1983; Na'aman 1989: 61-62 n. 167). For our purposes, the important fact is that this ostracon reflects the Judaean weight system, regardless of the identity of the writer. Of course, we must remember that it was an exercise, and not designed to supply an accurate picture of the whole weight system.

It is hard to explain the first column of this ostracon but, starting from line 19 until the end of column 3, there is a sequence of Hieratic numerals from 1 to 10,000 (at face value). A sign similar to ɛ appears next to each numeral, probably indicating a unit of volume (the Kor?—thus Lemaire and Vernus 1983: 313). The same sign appears in other Judaean ostraca, and it serves to strengthen the relationships between writing in Judah and the Kadesh Barnea ostracon.

Columns 4–5 present another sequence of Hieratic numerals, only this time they relate to different weight units (cf. Figs. 22–23). The central part of this sequence deals with Shekels, as the sign ɤ proves. The first part of the sequence (column 4.1-12) deals with weights that are lighter than 1 ɤ. This part includes only Hieratic numerals, without any signs of units, and this fits well the Gerah weights (marked only by Hieratic numerals). The numerals are: 1–6, 8, 10, 12, 16, 18, 20?. Part of the last numeral is missing. It could be composed of two numerals, 20 + *x* (most likely 22; cf. the placement of the numeral 20 to the right side of the column). There are no marked weights of 1 Gerah, nor of 12, 16, 18 and 20 (or 22) Gerah. This is the first hint of the conclusion that the writer did not write a sequence of weight units, but a sequence of quantities of weight. He started with the lowest conceivable quantity, 1 Gerah (whereas the JILs started with 3 Gerah, or with the one exceptional 2 Gerah weight). Still, the writer reflected the JIL system quite closely, by giving the full sequence between 2 and 6 (this is matched by the Gerah weights) and by 'jumping' directly to 8 and then to 10 (following the common weights of 8 and 10 Gerah).

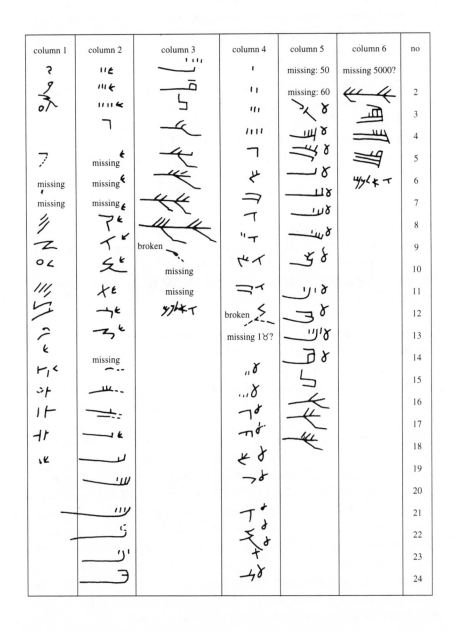

Figure 22. *The units of ostracon 6 from Kadesh-Barnea*

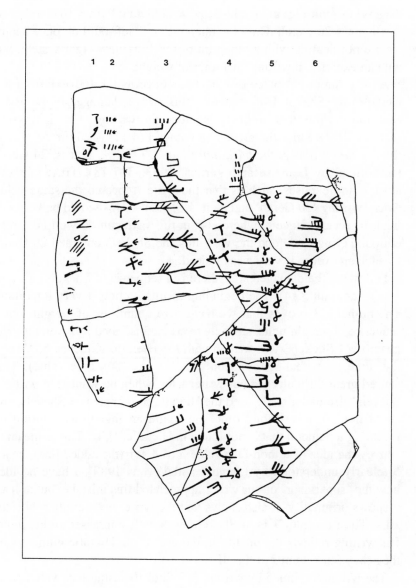

Figure 23. *Ostracon 6 from Kadesh-Barnea*

Ostracon 6 does not give the Judaean weight units Beqaᶜ, Pym and Nsf. The reason for this is not clear, but these units are given in disguise as multiples of Gerah: Beqaᶜ = 12 Gerah; Pym = 16 Gerah; Nsf (perhaps) = 20 Gerah. Only the numeral 18 is left out but, once again, we are not dealing with a blueprint of the Judaean weight system, but with an exercise in writing quantities of weight.

A very important piece of evidence concerns the transfer from the Gerah to the Shekel. Unfortunately, this area is damaged in the ostracon, and the line that probably included the writing '1 ષ' is missing (column 4.12). Since the preceding numeral (4.11) is 20 (or 20 + x), *it follows that 1 Shekel included more than 20 Gerah,* that is, 24 Gerah (as noticed by Lemaire and Vernus, 1983: 317-18). True, one can always find excuses, such as that the writer repeated the same value twice (writing '20 Gerah' and then '1 Shekel'). This would be very difficult to accept, since nowhere else in this ostracon do we find a repetition. Trying to defend the view that the Shekel contained 20 Gerah by such an excuse is very weak indeed.

Following the damaged area, there is a sequence of Shekels (ષ) until 900 ષ (column 5.14). The beginning of this section is very important. The numeral 3 proves that we have here quantities of weight, not a sequence of weight units, since there are no inscribed 3 ષ weights. The quantity '4 Shekels' was written with the Hieratic sequence 5 ('᱈ષ'), the same form that is found on the JILs (i.e. non-face value). This caused great difficulty for our writer later, when he wanted to write '5 Shekels'. He had already used the Hieratic 5 to express 4 Shekels, and could not use it a second time. He found an ingenious solution by inventing a numeral that is not found in Hieratic: '׀᱈'. This is meant to convey the idea of a 'non-face value 5' = 4 + 1 (the added line), hence 5 (clearly understood by Lemaire and Vernus 1983). I have no idea how the 'supervisor' of our writer appreciated this mistake, but at least it shows originality. It also shows that the writer was familiar with the JILs. The idea that ᱈ is '4 Shekels' was well impressed in his mind. His writing reflects the duality in the use of the Hieratic numerals on the heavy Shekel units of the JILs.

The writer continued by writing 6, 7 Shekels, using face-value Hieratic numerals (there are no inscribed weight units in these values). Then, he wrote the numerals 10, 20, 30 (Lemaire and Vernus 1983: 320). This closely follows the JIL system, and here he matched the actual weight units that he knew. Therefore, I think that we should read these numbers as 8, 16, 20 Shekels (similar to the 8 ש and 16 ש weights). This is strengthened by the observation that, if we read 10, 20, 30, it is hard to explain the 'jump' from 7 to 10.

Lemaire and Vernus (1983: 320) suggested that the continuing numbers are also not at face value, and tried to find weight units to match them. For example, they read the combination 900 ש as '720 Shekels'. This is one point where I disagree with an otherwise admirable publication. I think that the writer returned to 'face-value' writing, possibly after 30 ש. It is very difficult to prove this, since we do not know any JIL larger than 40 ש, but, from what we know about the JILs, it is hard to assume the existence of awkward units, such as '720 Shekels'. Again, the writer here meant quantities of weight, not existing weight stones.

The lack of the Maneh and the Kikar is intriguing, but it is negative evidence (cf. §7.4 above). It is best not to jump into hasty conclusions, and leave this matter for future discoveries.

8.5. *Summary: the Ostraca and the JILs*

The Hebrew ostraca help us by showing that the ש is the Judaean Shekel, and that included 24 Gerah. They also help us to define the JILs as Judaean weights. Only a few ostraca directly reflect the structure of the weight system. Perhaps it was obvious, and we should not expect conscious descriptions of such matters in the simple and humble recording of the Hebrew ostraca. The Kadesh Barnea ostraca are exceptional—in fact, the only mathematical exercises from Iron Age Palestine (for mathematical exercises in the ancient Near East, see Hoyrup 1995; Robson 1996).

There was a problem of duality with the use of the Hieratic numerals in Judah. This was due to the marking of 4–40 Shekel weights with Hieratic numerals not at face value. The same duality spread to the Hebrew ostraca that dealt with quantities of weight. There was probably no such problem, in the registration of dates or other measures such as volume and length, where Hieratic numerals were always used at face value.

On the whole, the ostraca and the JILs have many things in common (only one weight system based on the Shekel [ש], dominated by small units and quantities of weight, and lacking evidence about the Maneh and the Kikar). Finding new Hebrew ostraca in the future can improve greatly the understanding of the Judaean weight system.

Chapter 9

THE JUDAEAN WEIGHTS AND OTHER NEAR-EASTERN WEIGHT SYSTEMS

There are thousands of weights known from Egypt and Mesopotamia, but they are scattered over vast areas and divided among many periods. By contrast, the JILs occupy a very specific period and place. Furthermore, most of the Judaean weights are inscribed, a unique phenomenon when compared to other contemporary weight systems. These factors, together with the help of the Old Testament and Hebrew ostraca, make the weight system of Judah the best recognized of all weight systems of the ancient Near East. This forms the basis for evaluation of the relations between the JILs and other weight systems, foremost the Egyptian *dbn/qdt* system.

9.1. *The JILs and the Egyptian Weight System*

1. The Studies of Cour-Marty
Little progress was made in Egyptian metrology in the years following the work of Hemmy (1935, 1937), but during the last decade collections of Egyptian weights were investigated by Cour-Marty (1983, 1985, 1990, 1991). Her studies have significantly added to our knowledge. Important studies appeared on the Egyptian economy as well (Černy 1953; Janssen 1975; 1988; T.G.H. James 1984: 240-67; Castle 1992; Warburton 1997).

The studies of Cour-Marty cannot solve the problem that most of Petrie's weights were found out of context (cf. Chapter 1 above). So far, the quantity of newly published weights from scientific excavations is very limited (e.g. Spencer 1993). Cour-Marty stressed that few standards were used *en masse* in Egypt. One was a 'gold' standard of 12–13 grams, used mainly during the Middle Kingdom period. It was quite rare (Cour Marty 1983: 28-29; 1985: 194; 1990: 19, 22). The main system was the *dbn/qdt* system (1 *dbn* = 10 *qdt*), used throughout many periods in Egypt (Fig. 24). Various weight units were used, but most were not inscribed standards with specific names. Cour-Marty reconstructed the units according to statistical analysis of uninscribed weights (1983: 28; 1990: 22).

Weight grams	1.6	3.1	4.7	9.1–9.5	18–19	(26)	44–45	91–95
Qdt value	$^1/_4$	$^1/_3$	$^1/_2$	1	2	(3)	5	10
dbn value				$^1/_{10}$	$^1/_5$		$^1/_2$	1

Notes: The table is based on the studies of Cour-Marty. The 26 grams value is not certain (Cour-Marty 1985: 91).

Figure 24. *The Egyptian* qdt/dbn *weight system*

The *qdt* was the only standard in the range between 7 and 11 grams, with an average of 8.98 grams (Cour-Marty 1983: 29 graph 3). This value is not a true 'average', but can be taken as an approximate value of the *qdt* (1983: 29; 1985: 190-91). There were inscribed royal weights that belonged to the *dbn/qdt* system (1985: 194-95). About 40 such weights are known (approximately 4 per cent of the weights checked by Cour-Marty). Very few royal weights carry both the *dbn* sign with numerals of units, and the royal name. One is a weight of King Seti I, inscribed '300' in Hieratic, weighing 20,085 grams. Another bears the name Taharqa and the Hieratic number '270', weighing 18,615 grams (Cour-Marty 1985: 194-95, Fig. 5). Both are broken, and cannot be used to calculate the value of the *dbn* (cf. Weigall 1908: 10, 55).

2. *The Dome Shape and the Sign* 𐤔

The similarity of the shape of the JILs and Egyptian dome-shaped weights are well known (§4.2). The shapes are very close, though the JILs lack the carination at the meeting point between the sides and the dome, a common feature of Egyptian weights.

The sign 𐤔 remains enigmatic. Following Albright (in Scott 1964: n. 14; cf. §1.4 above), it seems to be the Hieratic sign *šs*. But what is the meaning of this sign on the JILs? It seems that the most plausible explanation is a phonetic sign with the value *š* (שׁ). In this way, it is a sort of Hieratic shortening for the word 'Shekel', just like the shortening *š* of the Hebrew ostraca (§8.2 above). Such a phonetic use is not common to Hiertaic, of course, and the word 'Shekel' is a Semitic word. It thus seems that this was a local, 'Semitic use' of the Hieratic sign, perhaps by local (Judaean) writers. What was the aim of this

marking? If it was meant for Judaeans, the word 'Shekel', the shortening ǩ in Hebrew, or even a complete omission of the name of the standard would be simpler. These forms for Shekel are widely used in the
Old Testament and Hebrew ostraca. Therefore, perhaps the sign ᴚ was
intended (at least in origin) not for the common people of Judah, but for
readers of Hieratic (officials and scribes?). Definite answers to this
question are not yet available.

3. *The Hieratic Numerals and the Adjustment of Weight*
I have presented the metrological relationships between the JILs and
the *dbn/qdt* system in Figs. 10–11 (columns XII–XIV). This is based on
assuming a *qdt* of approximately 9 grams. It is very clear that the match
between the JILs and the *qdt/dbn* system exists in the heavy units (ᴚ 4–
ᴚ 40). These units are marked in Hieratic numerals that fit quantities of
qdt (5, 10, 20, etc.), and not of Judaean Shekels. This was noted by
Scott (1965: 135) and Y. Aharoni (1966). If we calculate the value of
the *qdt* according to the 4 ᴚ, 8 ᴚ weights, we reach a value very close
to 9 grams (and to Cour-Marty's calculations). The numerals on the
1 ᴚ-2 ᴚ units, as well as their weight, do not conform to the *qdt* standard. The 1 ᴚ–2 ᴚ weights prove, therefore, that the Judaean weight
system is a local, independent one, only partially adjusted to the Egyptian weight system.

The Nsf weights belong to the ᴚ system as ⁵/₆ ᴚ. The average of the
Nsf weights is approximately 7 per cent heavier than that of the *qdt*,
whether we calculate the latter from 4 ᴚ, 8 ᴚ weights or follow the
studies of Cour-Marty. In my method, 7 per cent is not a very crucial
difference, therefore Nsf weights could be used as a crude equivalent to
the *qdt* for international trade. Yet this difference hints that the adjustment between the JILs and the Egyptian *qdt* was not based on the Nsf
weights. In other words, the Nsf was not 'officially' identified with the
qdt, nor were the 4 ᴚ, 8 ᴚ weights considered in Judah as 10, 20 Nsf
(respectively). Scott understood the Nsf as an independent standard
(1959b: 33; 1964: 56-57; 1970: 62-66; 1985: 204-206), followed by
many other scholars (Stern 1963: 870; Lemaire and Vernus 1978: 56;
1980: 344; 1983: 322; Ben-David 1973: 176; 1979: 42-45; Diringer
1958: 227-28; De Vaux 1961; Di Segni 1990: 213-14; Eran 1987: 6-7).
Only Meshorer opposed this view in a short Hebrew article (1976: 54-
55), and now the evidence shows that he was right. I provided strong
arguments (above) against the view that the Nsf was an independent

standard in Judah. Nsf weights do not carry any inscription that indicates a connection with the *qdt* (unlike the heavier Shekel units), and
they lack subdivisions or multiples, such as '2 Nsf', '5 Nsf', etc. The
Nsf was a unit within the JIL system, not an independent standard of a
separate weight system.

Some points of equivalence can be found between the *qdt* and the
Pym, Beqa^c and Gerah (Figs. 10–11, column XIII). For example, 8
Gerah weights are close to a value of $^1/_2$ *qdt*, and 6 Gerah weights can
be equated roughly with $^1/_3$ *qdt*. The inscriptions on these units have
nothing to do with the *qdt*, but are either quantities of Gerah or Hebrew
names of the units. This leads to the suggestion that these equations are
secondary.

4. *Summary: The JILs and the Egyptian Weight System*
The JILs were adjusted to the *dbn/qdt* system by inscribing Hieratic
numerals in values of *qdt* units on the 4 ᛒ–40 ᛒ weights. Some of the
smaller JILs were approximately equal to Egyptian weight units, and
could have been used as mediators between the two systems (e.g. Nsf ≈
qdt). This seems to be a secondary adjustment, never expressed by
writing on the weights.

Since Aharoni and Scott, the adjustment of the JILs to the Egyptian
system was grasped as a deliberate effort, a sort of an official 'reform'
on behalf of the kings of Judah. This reform was made in order to facilitate the trade between Judah and Egypt. Since Yadin (1960), scholars
have connected this 'weight reform' with the famous reform of Josiah
(Cross 1962: 22; Naveh 1962: 31; Scott 1965: 133-34; Dever 1970:
178, 187; Scott 1970: 62, 64; Y. Aharoni (ed.) 1966; Gibson 1971: 67;
Kenyon 1974: 104 Pl. 51; Yadin and Geva 1983: 255; Scott 1985: 204;
Yadin 1985: 24-25; Eshel 1986: 335, 349-50, 360; Stern 1992: 70).
Other scholars did not declare it explicitly, but nevertheless saw the
JILs as official, royal weights of Josiah's reign (Stern 1963: 867; G.
Barkay 1978: 213-14; 1990: Ch. 9 §4.6; Lemaire 1982: 20; Eran 1989:
5). Puech (1984) objected to this view, but he dealt with only one JIL
found outside Judah, which is perhaps earlier than most of the JILs
(Appendix 1: 1 ᛒ 13). Puech did not question the basis of the whole
theory.

Indeed, it is likely that the adjustment between the JILs and the *qdt*
was related to international trade. International trade involves larger
sums of silver or gold (even for small quantities of commodities, if

those are expensive), and this fits in well with the fact that only the heavier Shekel units were adjusted to the Egyptian system. On the other hand, not all the JILs were used for trade with Egypt. The JILs were Judaean weights, and many were probably used within Judah for local trade. The Hieratic inscriptions, once accepted, could become a convention, not necessarily contemplated much by the users of the weights.

The JILs appeared a long time before the reform of Josiah (see Chapter 2), and have nothing to do with it. The metrological and archaeological evidence supports this conclusion. The connection with Josiah was weak from the beginning, since it was based on doubtful historical assumptions. None of the scholars questioned the idea that the JILs were related to a reform, and asked what a 'reform' of weights actually is. I will return to these issues later.

Further comment is required about the duality of the Hieratic numerals on the JILs. In units such as Gerah, 1 ᐯ and 2 ᐯ, the numerals were face value; but in the 4 ᐯ–40 ᐯ units, they indicated quantities of *qdt* (and not of Judaean Shekels). As far as I know, this duality does not appear elsewhere: for example, in registration of dates or in measures of volume and length. The duality could cause confusion, but that was the price paid in order to adjust the JILs to the Egyptian weight system. The traders and the scribes were probably aware of this duality. They knew that ר means 5 in Hieratic, but ר ᐯ on Judaean weights means '4 Judaean Shekel' (which equalled 5 *qdt*). A layperson would recognize the same weight only in its local setting (4 Shekels). This could be the reason for the peculiarities in ostracon 6 from Kadesh Barnea (Chapter 8 above), reflecting the stage of a learning 'student'.

The duality of the numerals of the JILs probably caused fewer headaches to the Judaeans than to modern scholars (including the present one). I am not sure if this brings any comfort to the latter.

9.2. *The JILs and Other Weight System*

1. *The Phoenician Weight System (Fig. 25)*
It is difficult to define Phoenician weights, since the script is not always indicative, and few weights are inscribed. Excavations in Phoenicia are few, and only small groups of weights are known from sites such as Sarepta, Tell Sukas and Tell Tugan. Many weights from Byblos were published, but their chronology is usually unclear. From southern Phoenicia (northern Israel of today), weights are known from Achziv and Tel Keisan. I have discussed the problems of the Phoenician weight

system(s) in relation to an important group of well-dated weights from Kh. Rosh Zayit (Kletter 1994). It was possible to suggest a Phoenician weight unit of 7.6 grams, but this remains tentative at present. Most of the Kh. Rosh Zayit weights are dome-shaped, and it seems that they were adjusted to the Egyptian system (they could also be used with other systems, through equations such as 1 Phoenician unit = 1 Judaean Pym).

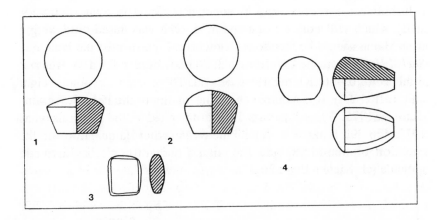

Figure 25. *'Phoenician' weights.* Legend: All the weights are from Kh. Rosh Zayit (Kletter 1994: Figure 1).

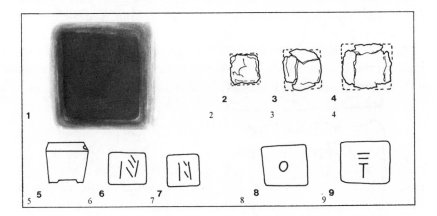

Figure 26. *Bronze cube weights.* Legend: 1. Kh. Rosh Zayit, rentgen photo (Kletter 1994: Fig. 2). 2–4 Ashkelon (after Stager 1996: Fig. 7). 5–7 Near Ashkelon (after Illife 1936: Pl. 34. 10–12). 8–9. Eretz Israel Museum (after Lemaire 1980: Pl. IIa).

Other weights are occasionally called Phoenician: for example, metal weights shaped as tortoises. Such weights are known from Samaria (Delavault and Lemaire 1979: no. 59, with references); Ashkelon? (Delavault and Lemaire 1979: no. 61); Tel Beer Sheba (according to Ben-David 1979: no. 25) and unknown origins (Qedar 1979: nos. 73, 81; Hachlili and Meshorer 1986: no. 60; Kadman collection, nos. K-8905, K-8906, K-8907, K-9420). Their date and identity deserve a separate study.

In between Phoenicia and Mesopotamia, Syria is a large area for study which will not be discussed here. One very interesting weight from Hama should be mentioned, however. It carries the inscription *št Shekel Ḥmt* (Bron and Lemaire 1983: 763-64; Buhl 1983: 108; Riis and Buhl 1990: 65-66; Kletter 1994: 36-37). There is an Egyptian weight unit called *š'ty* (or, sometimes, *sniw*) of approximately 7.5 grams (Janssen 1975: 102-108; 1988: 13; Gardiner 1950: 200 n. 14; Daumas 1977: 426-29). It agrees well with the weight from Ḥama. However, the equation of Semitic *št* and Egyptian *š'ty* is difficult on linguistic grounds (cf. Kletter 1994: 36-37).

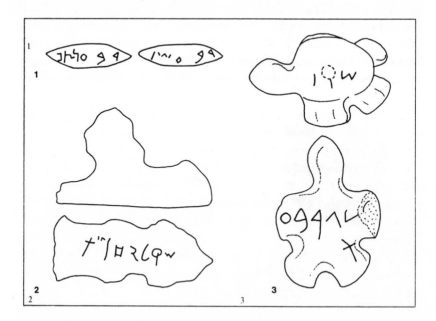

Figure 27. *Other inscribed weights.* Legend: 1 Samaria (after Chaplain 1894: 287). 2. *Šqly Ḥmt* weight (after Bordereuil 1983, Syria 60: 340). 3. *Plg...Šql* weight (after Reifenberg 1936).

2. *Israel, Philistia, and Other Systems*

We have very little information about weight systems in Israel, Transjordan and Philistia. The basic problem is the lack of historical sources concerning these areas in the Iron Age period, as opposed to the rich Old Testament literature and Hebrew ostraca. Furthermore, the archaeological evidence from these areas is limited.

Weights from sites in the kingdom of Israel are rare: Samaria (Reisner, Fisher and Lyon 1924: 344H), Tell el-Far'ah (north) (Puech 1984); Beth She'an (F.W. James 1966) and Tel Jezreel (Kletter 1997). The largest group published was from Megiddo (Lamon and Shipton (eds.) 1939: Pl. 104). Inscribed weights are very few, notably the one from Samaria found in the nineteenth century (Conder 1891; Sayce 1893, 1894, 1904; Delavault and Lemaire 1979: 30-31). The new excavations at sites such as Hazor, Megiddo and Beth She'an may contribute to our knowledge in the future.

Little is known about the Philistine weight system(s). We have already criticized the view of Ben-David (1979), that the Pym was a Philistine standard (Chapter 1 above; for the Ashdodite Talent, cf. Liverani 1972). Few weights from Philistia are known: for example, from Ekron (Naveh 1958: 100), Ashkelon (Stager 1996: 66), a group near Ashkelon (Illife 1936) and Ashdod (Eran and Edelstein 1977). Dothan and Gitin suggested that ingots of silver from Ekron were used as a kind of currency (Gitin 1995: 69-70; but cf. the work of Bjorkman 1993, 1994). The Philistines had close connections with the Phoenician coast, and perhaps the weight systems of both areas had things in common, such as a standard of approximately 7.6 grams, but much more evidence is needed to clarify the situation.

Ugarit is often considered as the 'model' of a Canaanite society. It is usually assumed that the Ugaritic Shekel was equal to approximately 9.4 grams, roughly equivalent to the Egyptian *qdt* (Kletter 1994: 36).

The weight systems of the early Aegean world are not well known. There are many weights, and some carry marks of value or units. These may refer to a weight unit of approximately 60 grams. A basic work was recently offered by Petruso (1992, with further references), but there is no direct connection with the JILs.

3. *Assyrian Lions and the Asherah (Fig. 28)*

A few scholars, especially Dever (1991: 11; 1994: 109), suggest that a bronze object from the Temple of Arad is 'no doubt, an Asherah object'

(Fig. 28.1). Indeed, the object was published as a 'figurine' of a lion in a preliminary report, but this was meant for description only (Y. Aharoni 1971a: 477). Many scholars noticed that it was a type of scale weight common in Assyria (Bron and Lemaire 1983: 765 n. 20; Rose 1975: 192; Holladay 1987: 257, Table 2 G. Barkay 1990: 190; Kletter 1991: 132). The weight of the Arad weight is approximately 82 grams (not yet published; courtesy of Z. Herzog and the Arad team), and it fits in well with 10 Mesopotamian Shekels.

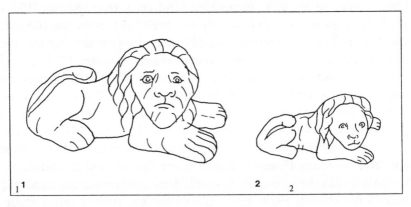

Figure 28. *'Assyrian' lion weights.* Legend: 1 Arad (after Herzog *et al.* 1984: Fig. 20). 2. Tel Jemmeh (after Petrie 1928: Pl. 17.51).

Other weights of this type were found in Palestine, in Ein Shemer (IAA 69-974, currently in the Ein Ha-Shofet Museum); Tel Jemmeh (Petrie 1930: Pl. 17.51) and Hazor (Yadin *et al.* 1959–62: II, 158-59 Pl. 150.4). Another one is held in the Hecht Museum, Haifa (origins unknown, Hachlili and Meshorer 1986: 60; for later periods, cf. Illife 1936: 68; for Syria, see Bordereuil 1983; Bron and Lemaire 1983: 765, table CXLV: 5-6). Weights of this type have been known since the nineteenth century from Assyria, and some carry Aramaean inscriptions (Layard 1853: 513; Mallowan 1966: 109, 170-72; Skinner 1967: 36-37; Powell 1979; 1987–90: 516-17; cf. Mazzoni 1980: 158). The weight from Arad has nothing to do with the Asherah, unless every lion is an Asherah object (see further Kletter 1996: 22).

4. *The Mesopotamian Weight System*

Other than crouching lions, Mesopotamian weights were often made in the forms of grain seeds (often called by other names: spindles, fusiform, parallelpipeds, etc.). In the metrological literature, it is common to speak about a Mesopotamian Shekel of approximately 8.1–8.4 grams. Grain-shaped weights are abundant in Mesopotamian (Uruk, Mari, Larsa; see Arnaud, Calvet and Huot 1979) and Syria (Hama, Ebla, Zinçirly; see Archi 1987; Archi and Klengel-Brandt 1984: nos. 1-9, 12). This shape proved so popular that it became common in Phoenicia (Byblos, Ugarit, Sarepta, Alalakh), Cyprus (Petruso 1984: 296-99; Courtois 1984: 114, Pls. 21-22) and even Egypt (Petrie 1926: Pl. vi; Cour-Marty 1990: 23-24 Fig. 4). Such weights appear in wreckages of trading ships of the Late Bronze Age period (Cape Gelidonia [Bass 1967: 135-36]; Ulu-Burun [Fitzgerald 1996: 7]; and Palmahim [Kletter, Galili and Sharvit forthcoming]).[1] Many grain-shaped weights were found in Palestine, mainly during the second millennium BCE (R. Segal 1971; cf. Heltzer 1996). Another traditional Mesopotamian form is duck-shaped weights, but they are rarely found in Israel (one from Mamila, Jerusalem [courtesy of R. Reich]; another from Athlit [Raban 1992: 49-50 nos. 45-46; cf. Molina 1989]).

A rather surprising fact is the lack of direct correlation between the JILs and the Mesopotamian weight system. The Pym is roughly close to one Mesopotamian Shekel; 2 ४ to 3 Mesopotamian Shekel and 4 ४ to 5 Mesopotamian Shekel. All these equations are far from accurate, and it is doubtful whether they could be used with ease. The lack of correlation with the Mesopotamian weight system is surprising for two reasons. First, the name of some units and their relative positions in the system are similar in both Judah and Mesopotamia. Second, the JILs were used at the time of Assyrian supremacy over Judah (at least until 630/620 BCE). I will return to this subject in the concluding chapter.

---

1. For animal-shaped weights of the Late Bronze Age, see Chavane 1987; for the economy of this period, see Liverani 1990. For Phoenician weights see now J. Elayi and A.G. Elayi, *Recherches sur les poids phéniciens* (Paris: Gabalda, 1997). This book appeared too late to be incorporated into the present work.

Chapter 10

THE QUESTION OF ROYAL WEIGHTS

This chapter is very short, since the idea put forward is, I believe, simple. Therefore, there is no need to hide it behind mountains of scholarly references or elaborate presentations. It is commonly taken for granted that the Judaean inscribed weights are royal weights, and it became a sort of an axiom (Yadin 1960; Rainey 1965). This view has it roots in early stages of research, when it was common to oppose 'official' weights, as against unofficial, 'market' weights (e.g. Pilcher 1912: 138; Barrois 1932: 55). The ৪ weights were always understood as an official, royal standard from the moment they were identified with the Old Testament Shekel (Scott 1959a: 32; 1964: 56). When the JILs were connected with Josiah's reform, it was already based on the preconception that they are royal weights. It was taken for granted that the JILs were invented in the context of royal initiative or royal 'reform'. The relationship with Josiah's reform allegedly strengthened this assumption, but this argument goes around in circles. Even the ৪ sign was explained as a royal Judaean symbol (Yadin 1960). Surprisingly, the concept that the JILs were royal weights was never questioned. Scholars have opposed Yadin's suggestion for the ৪ (Y. Aharoni (ed.) 1966), or Scott's metrological system (Meshorer 1976), but there was no opposition to the idea that the JILs were royal weights.

10.1. *Royal Weights in the Ancient Near East*

One of the reasons for the royal definition of the JILs stems from the discovery of royal weights in the ancient Near East. Royal weights are mentioned in historical sources: for example, the remarkable evidence of weighing in a palatial context in Mari (Joannès 1989). Since Near-Eastern sources are often related to royalty and to economic interest, the combination of economy and royalty is natural. The almost absolute rule of ancient kings determined that a major part of the economy of their kingdoms was royal.

Dozens of royal weights from Mesopotamia and Egypt are known, from different periods and sites (Cour-Marty 1985: 194; Powell 1979: 84-86 n. 48; Rainey 1965). Finkel (1987) even speaks about a unification of weights during the third dynasty of Ur, when official sets of weights were issued. During the early stages of research, it was commonly thought that royal weight systems had special standards, separating them from the 'ordinary' ones (defined as 'common standard', 'market standards', etc.). What defines a weight as royal? When we study royal weights, we find that most of them are not different in weight compared with 'ordinary' weights. The things that determine their 'royal nature' are usually a better quality of craftsmanship, more expensive materials, and especially a royal inscription. Royal weights carry the name of the king, often with the name of the unit and the number of multiples. The inscription is the best evidence we have for identifying weights as royal. Occasionally, 'private' names appear, but these can be individuals that have no relation with the king, or official on his behalf; so in those cases the status of the weights is not very clear.

10.2. *Are the JILs Royal Weights?*

This concept that the JILs are royal weights must be tested again, and I believe that it ought to be rejected. The JILs, or at least part of them, are not royal weights. This statement is based on several arguments.

1. The context of most of the JILs has no connection with royalty. They are common in contexts that seem to be domestic (Chapter 6 above). Only a few weights were found in public contexts, but even these are not necessarily connected with the kings of Judah. A few JILs are connected with graves (Mamila, perhaps Kh. el-Kom and a grave near Anathot), presumably as objects that belonged to the deceased before they died. Thus, they were taken as private property to the graves. The context of the JILs is quite different from that of the Judaean pillar figurines, which were probably religious objects (Kletter 1996).

2. There is no royal inscription on the JILs to mark them as the belongings of the king. Royal marks of this sort are abundant in Judah: for example, the royal *lmlk* jars (Na'aman 1986a; Ussishkin 1977).

Another example is the inscription *bt lmlk* on several vessels, indicating a royal measure of volume (Mittmann 1992; Naveh 1992).

3. Though the Old Testament gives evidence that there were royal weights (below), there is no indication that the royal weight system had special standards, different from those of the JILs.

4. The fact that the JILs have nothing in common with the reform of Josiah somewhat deflates the 'royal' theory. It is no longer necessary to assume that they were invented by a king during a reform.

5. The assumption of a special royal system went hand in hand with the concept of many standards in Judah (see Chapters 1 and 4 above), but the JILs have only one standard (א).

In view of all this, it seems that the JILs served the Judaean population as a whole, and were not a special royal system used solely by the kings of Judah. Yet we must be cautious not to go to the other extreme. There was a royal weight system in Iron Age Judah, though our knowledge about it is poor. This is implied from the appearance of 'the stone of the king' in one Old Testament verse (2 Sam. 14.26; see Chapter 5 above). Unfortunately, the verse does not specify this standard in relation to the 'ordinary' Shekel.

It is likely that the royal house of Judah had a major position in the economy and trade of Judah (on the royal economy in Judah, see De Vaux 1961; Na'aman 1981: 142-43; Lahav 1968; Rainey 1982; Ahlstrom 1982; Mettinger 1971; Rüthersworden 1985). The Judaean kings had to use a royal weight system, since they had to weigh commodities and issue payments. Here the crucial question arises: in what ways was this royal system different from the JILs?

Archaeologically, only one weight from Iron Age Israel can be termed royal, and it was found in Gezer (which was not part of 'the heartland' of Judah). It is a bronze cube, which carries the Hebrew inscription *lmlk* beside two vertical lines. Its value (Appendix 1: 2 א.a) is exactly the same as the common 2 Shekel weights. Another, similar weight was recently published by Deutsch and Heltzer (1994: 66-67 Fig. 32), but its origins are unknown. It is inscribed '*lmlk* ‖ א', and again the value fits the regular Judaean Shekel. If we take the Gezer weight to be representative of the royal Judaean weight system, since at the moment it is the only evidence available, then the royal Judaean standard was the same as the Shekel of the JILs.

I think that this is very plausible. Judah had a royal weight system used by the officials and scribes of the palace. This system had the same value of Shekel as that of the JILs. It was, presumably, different from the JILs in the materials (metal) and shape (cubes). The royal weights were marked to clarify their royal status, with the inscription *lmlk*. Some of the JILs could be used by royal official: for example. in Arad, and thus they were 'royal weights'. But, as a whole, the JILs reflect the 'ordinary' weight system of Judah, used by the population as a whole. Indeed, regarding standards, there was only one system, based on the same Shekel of approximately 11.33 grams.

Chapter 11

THE UNINSCRIBED WEIGHTS OF JUDAH

11.1. *Introduction*

A main question regarding the JIL system concerns its beginning: who initiated this system and under what circumstances? Was the appearance of the JILs related to a reform of weights on behalf of one of the kings of Judah? It is difficult to answer this question because of the meagre quantity of JILs from the first stage (the end of the eighth century BCE; Chapter 2 above). If the dating suggested there is true, most of the JILs belonged to the seventh century BCE and do not reflect the time when the system was introduced.

In this context a simple question arises: *what preceded the JILs in Judah?* It is a wonder that this question was not raised earlier, but perhaps the reason is that scholars were satisfied with the assumption that the JILs were invented during Josiah's reform. However, weighing was surely used long before Josiah's reign, and Judah needed some sort of a weight system earlier. It is possible that weighing was less common at that early period, because of a less developed economy and scarcity of trade relations; yet it is impossible to assume a total lack of a weight system. Any 'polity' or kingdom needs to weigh, and Judah was no exception. This need must have arisen quite early, probably from the creation of a multi-class society and organized political bodies of the state, at the latest. Clear evidence for weighing in Judah exists in the form of a scale beam from Lachish IV (mid eighth century BCE at the latest, G. Barkay 1992; 1996).[1]

At this point I wish to draw attention to a large series of uninscribed limestone weights, which may shed some light on the questions raised above.

1. A weight from Iron Age I Edom is reported from Baraqat el-Hetiye (Feinan area); Fritz 1994b: 148 Fig. 10.12, reg. no. 246/80.

11.2. *The Judaean Uninscribed Limestone Weights*

Different kinds of uninscribed stone weights from Palestine were known from the early stages of metrological research (e.g. Warren 1870). A few casual references, or inclusion in appendices and catalogues, is usually their fate (e.g. Eran 1982; Eran and Edelstein 1977). As a matter of fact, only one study was dedicated completely to uninscribed weights from Palestine (R. Segal 1971, dealing mainly with Bronze Age weights from unknown origins).

A large series of uninscribed weights shows remarkable similarity to the JILs. Surprisingly, this series was never studied thoroughly. This series, like the JILs, has the same shape (a dome), material (limestone) and weight units (based on a Shekel of approximately 11.33 grams). Furthermore, these uninscribed weights were found, roughly speaking, in the same period (eighth–seventh centuries BCE) and place (Judah) as the JILs. The only really significant difference between the JILs and this series is the lack of any inscriptions on the latter; therefore, I have called this series 'Judaean Uninscribed Limestone Weights' (or JULs).

I have collected 196 weights in Appendix 4 (below), of which 160 are defined as JULs. The definition is based on the shared similarities with the JILs and, as for weight, I have included weights with the limit of 5 per cent from the average of the relevant unit (taken from the JILs). I have no doubt that the list (Appendix 4) is only a preliminary one. More JULs exist; they are either not yet published, or published inadequately (in older excavations). In any case, the list is impressive enough to suggest that we are dealing with a significant phenomenon.

Most of the JULs were found in Judah. Some JULs were found outside Judah, in northern Israel (sites such as Samaria, Megiddo, Tel Keisan, Tel Far'ah [north] and Accho) and Philistia (about 20 weights from Tell abu-Sleimeh, Tel Far'ah [south], Ashdod and Tel Jemmeh). Gezer is exceptional, since it is the only site outside Judah where a large number of JULs was found. Unfortunately, many weights from Gezer were inadequately published, and one cannot be certain if they are indeed JULs. The same is true for other weights: for example, from Beth Zur (Sellers *et al.* 1968: Pl. 46a; Sellers 1933: 61-62, 63 Fig. 58). It is not easy to classify such weights, since they lack inscriptions and the weight does not indicate the system (values such as 90 or 45 grams fit more than one weight system in the ancient Near East). If we do not have the full details of the shape and material, the identification is often hazardous. In any case, I believe that there is still a large number of these uninscribed weights from Judah that enables us to offer a general picture, far from complete, but valid in principle.

The JULs exhibit most of the units of the JIL system, from Beqaʿ to 40 ﬡ Shekel (Appendix 4). I have not tried to locate lighter units, since the quantity of the weights from those lighter units are smaller, and they are less exact (and, therefore, more difficult to classify), but probably lighter units also existed in the JULs. The most common units of JULs are the 4 and 8 Shekels (Appendix 4.VII, IX, the values of 4 ﬡ, 8 ﬡ), and this fact fits the picture known about the JILs (Chapter 5 above). Uninscribed Beqaʿ, Nsf and 1 ﬡ are also common, and their existence is not open to doubt. Other units are rare, more or less the same as those rare units of the JILs (the heavy Shekel units is one good example).

In view of the large similarity between the JILs and the JULs, but also according to the metrology of the JULs alone, I think that the JULs are based on the same ordinary Judaean Shekel of approximately 11.33 grams. Apart from the similarity of material, shape, weight and period, there are sometimes physical connections between the two groups of weight. By this, I mean their mutual appearance at the same loci (Malhata locus 242; Kenyon's excavations at Jerusalem locus A.669.11a) and levels (many more examples).

Other than those well-known units, the JULs probably included a few units that are not known among the JILs. These include 3 ﬡ, 5 ﬡ, 10 ﬡ (Appendix 4.VI, VIII; cf. Kletter forthcoming a) and perhaps other units (e.g. 15 ﬡ, 30 ﬡ, 32 ﬡ and 400 ﬡ). It appears that these units could serve as a 'filler' to the units of the JILs, mainly by adding decimal multiples to the inscribed system of weight. This was probably one method of simplifying the act of weighing. The JULs are therefore a sort of a complementary part of the JILs (this was hinted by Duncan 1931: 216; Barrois 1953: 256; Scott 1959a: 32; 1965: 197; R. Segal 1971: 38; G. Barkay 1981a: 294 n. 61; Eshel 1986: 346; Puech 1984: 81; but without thorough investigation). Why were such decimal units never inscribed? There is a simple answer to this: the numerals were occupied! One could not use the Hieratic numerals 5, 10, since they were already used on the 4, 8 Shekel weights. The quantity of the weights from those 'new' units was not great, and—strictly speaking— they were not so vital. The system of the JILs could have functioned well without their help.

11.3. *The Problem of Chronology: The Chicken and the Egg*

Did the JULs precede the JILs in Judah? It is very hard to answer this question, but it is important to try, since understanding the relationships between the two series of weights is vital in order to understand the roots of the inscribed weights, and eventually the development of Judaean economy. The JILs certainly did not appear before the end of the eighth century BCE (Chapter 2 above). Only a few of the JULs can be dated with certainty, to the eighth–seventh centuries BCE. Thus, there is no decisive proof that the JULs existed prior to the beginning of the JILs at the end of the eighth century BCE (for decisive proof, a large body of well-dated specimens is needed). One may construct two possibilities regarding the beginning of the JULs (Fig. 30).

Unit	1ᵛ	2ᵛ	3ᵛ	4ᵛ	5ᵛ	8ᵛ	10ᵛ
JULs	9	13	2	38	6	39	5
Doubtful	3			5		6	1
Total	12	13	2	43	6	45	6

Unit	12ᵛ	15ᵛ	16ᵛ	24ᵛ	30–32ᵛ	40ᵛ	400ᵛ
JULs	3		8	3		4	
Doubtful	1	1	5	2	2	3	3
Total	4	1	13	5	2	7	3

Figure 29a. *The JULs: Shekel weights*

Series	Nsf	Pym	Beqaᶜ	Other	Total All
JULs	12	7	10	1	160
Doubtful			2	2	36
Total	12	7	12	3	196

Notes: doubtful weights are marked by letters (App. 4).

Figure 29b. *The JULs: other units*

Period	Possibility A	Possibility B
Until the 8th century BCE	An early system, other than the ᵛ system	Appearance and use of the JULs
End of the 8th century BCE	Appearance of the JULs and the JILs together	Appearance of the JILs, continuation of the JULs
7th century BCE	JULs and JILs are used together	JULs and JILs are used together

Figure 30. *The beginning of the Judaean weight system*

According to the first possibility (Fig. 30, A), the JILs and the JULs appeared together as complementary parts of the same system. One has to assume, then, that there was an earlier weight system, about which nothing is known. Furthermore, this early system was different from both the JILs and the JULs, since, if it was the same, it is not different from possibility B (below). If we follow this line of thought, the appearance of the JILs and the JULs together must be interpreted as a drastic change of the history of Judaean metrology. This change was not only limited to the appearance of inscriptions, but encompassed further features (e.g. the weight, the relationships between the units, or the typology of the weights).

According to the second possibility (Fig. 30, B), the JULs preceded the JILs. The transfer, which occurred sometime in the late eighth century BCE, involved only the marking of the weights, which were formerly 'mute'. The names of the units and their relative positions, the material, the shape and the weight remained the same. If we follow this possibility, the change from the JULs to the JILs was far less radical than according to possibility A (above). Furthermore, in this scenario, the adjustment to the Egyptian weight system is not new to the JILs, but existed in the earlier system of the JULs (as we have seen, units of 4 ರ, 8 ರ are very common among the JULs).

Theoretically, there is a third possibility: that the JULs are a later phenomenon than the JILs. In this case, the JULs were added as a complementary part to the existing inscribed system. This addition was made in order to simplify weighing by adding decimal (and other) units. This is perfectly possible from the metrological point of view, but we have no evidence whatsoever that the JULs appeared later than the JILs. On the contrary: some JULs clearly belong to the eighth century BCE (Appendix 4.IV.1; 4.VII.13; 4.VIII.1; 4.IX.13, 15, 21-22; 4.X.5; etc.). Furthermore, if the JULs were only an addition to an existing system, why do we find so many units that repeat those of the inscribed weights, and so few 'new' units? We would have expected the very opposite.

Tentatively, possibility B (Fig. 30) seems preferable, and it fits in better with some other aspects. The names of the Judaean weight units are mostly general Semitic names, used in Syria–Mesopotamia as a whole (Shekel, Beqaʿ, Gerah). If we follow possibility A (above), we should assume a very different earlier weight system, but it is unlikely that the names were different. And, if the names were the same, the relative position of the units was probably also similar. This, of course, is not a decisive argument, since the change could have been in the weight of the Shekel unit alone. In any case, there is no archaeological expression of a different weight system early in Judah. At least a few weights from this system should have survived, if it existed. One should also note that many features of the JILs are not a new phenomenon: they already existed in the second millennium BCE (such as the basic Shekel unit, the appearance of the Nsf in Ugarit, and the adjustment to the Egyptian system).

The major obstacle is the situation in Judah during the tenth–ninth centuries BCE. Very little is known about this period, since the material remains are few (there were few destruction levels, since the period was more peaceful than that of 701–586 BCE; on the difficulties of defining this period in Judah see G. Barkay 1990: 90; Wightman 1985a). This prevents us finding the nature of the early weight system of Judah. In my view, it was similar to the later, inscribed system, but at the moment it is impossible to confirm this view.

Whatever possibility we choose, the situation during the seventh century BCE is clear: the JULs and the JILs were used contemporaneously as two parts of one system, which was the ordinary weight system of Judah.

Chapter 12

CONCLUSIONS

12.1. *Summary of Former Chapters*

1. *History of Research.* Since the first discovery of the JILs by Guthe (1882), there have been more than a hundred years of research. The history of research is fascinating and varied, but throughout most of the time, a 'many standards' principle was dominant. Metrologists overstressed accurate calculations, and archaeological, biblical and historical evidences were sometimes neglected, or mixed uncritically into the discussion.

2. *Chronology.* The dating of the weights is based on archaeological data. The stratigraphy of each weight was checked thoroughly. Many weights lack clear context, but the available information shows that most of the JILs were used during the seventh century BCEE. We cannot, at the moment, separate clear sub-phases within this period. A few JILs appear in contexts of the end of the eighth century BCEE, and there is no sense in ignoring this fact (cf. now Seger 1997). Since we are dealing with a weight system, single weights cannot exist in a void. The conclusion is clear: the JILs appeared as a system during the late eighth century BCEE, though at that time they were not widely used. After 586 BCEE, Judah lost its independence and its economy gradually changed into a monetary system, where the JILs were no longer used.

3. *Distribution.* In order to discuss the relationship between the JILs and the kingdom of Judah, historical sources must be consulted. Those sources are open to debate, and it is necessary to state an opinion. I have followed Na'aman (1989) in arguing that Judah was not a sort of 'mini-empire' under Josiah, and that it remained a relatively small kingdom. Another method of sidestepping the historical debate is to define the 'heartland of Judah'. This refers to a minimal area which all the scholars agree belonged to Judah. This heartland area is similar, more or less, to the traditional borders of Judah, as their borders were kept much the same from shortly after the foundation of Judah as a

separate kingdom in the late tenth century BCE.

The majority of the JILs from known origins (approximately 76 per cent) were found in the heartland of Judah; they must therefore be defined as Judaean weights. This definition does not mean that each weight was necessarily used by Judaeans, or in Judah, though most of the weights were. Furthermore, Judah is seen as a polity, and discussed as a political and not an 'ethnic' entity. Very few JILs were found in Transjordan and northern Israel (approximately 4.6 per cent of the JILs). This is a negligible quantity, and indicates sporadic contacts, at the most. The rest of the JILs were found in Philistia and the western Shephelah, but the numbers are small and might indicate peaceful trade relations. Another possibility is the political influence or intervention of Judah in areas close to its western border: for example, at Gezer and Ekron. The JILs certainly do not prove Judaean conquest or rule over parts of Philistia.

Inside Judah, Jerusalem has the largest concentration of JILs (67 weights). It was the capital and the largest and most important settlement for the Judaean economy. There are a few regional centres, such as Lachish (25 JILs) and Arad (15 JILs). Small groups of JILs were found in several other sites; and finally, there are many sites with one weight alone. The dominant area in Judah was the northern Judae-an mountains, centred around Jerusalem. The Shephelah comes second, and the Negev third. All the other areas are marginal in regard to the distribution of the JILs.

4. *Typology*. I have stressed the great homogeneity of the JILs. Almost all the weights are dome-shaped and made of limestone. Not more than a dozen are cubic, metal weights. The uniformity indicates that it is one system, and not many independent standards. The inscriptions are also very uniform in content and location, and the variations are limited to paleography. A few features may imply that those who inscribed the JILs came from the world of seal engraving. A few JILs carry personal names, which is probably an indication of ownership. The names could belong to individual persons, or to officials of the court. The Hieratic numerals bear similarities to the 'a-normal' Hieratic script, but are sometimes written in a peculiar way (left to right, or upside-down).

5. *Metrology*. The metrology of the JILs is investigated from a basic conception of 'one standard'. This is the very opposite of current metrological studies, since most scholars believed in a 'many

standards' approach. Many decisive arguments are offered in favour of the concept that the JILs formed one weight system with only one major standard, the Shekel (something) of about 11.33 grams. All the JILs were found in the same time-span, in the same sites and levels, and some groups are found together in the same loci. The JILs are very homogeneous in shape (dome), material (limestone) and inscriptions. There is no real evidence of different Shekel standards, and most of the deviations of the weights are small—within the range of natural deviations caused by mistakes in production, wear by use, forgeries, and the inability to weigh exactly.

The JIL system is built on multiples of 4 or 8. This made it possible to weigh any weight, without the use of units such as 3, 5 and 7 Shekels. Weights to the value of 4 ᛒ and 8 ᛒ were the most common. The ᛒ series was used to weigh between 1 and 8 ᛒ, which is, approximately 11–90 grams. Occasionally, heavier weights could be used, of up to 40 ᛒ (approximately 450 grams), as well as combinations of different units. This range is suitable for the weighing of precious metals (gold, silver and possibly small quantities of copper). The fact that there are many JILs of an even lighter series of weights (Nsf to Gerah) strengthens this conclusion. Perhaps other expensive commodities were weighed, such as incense and spices, but the JILs were not widely used for weighing other commodities. The reason is clear—weighing was a cumbersome process. Barter was preferred, and it was also easier to measure many commodities by volume.

The Nsf, Pym and Beqaᶜ form an inseparable part of the JIL system, with corresponding values of ⁵/₆, ²/₃ and ¹/₂ ᛒ. There is no metrological evidence that these are independent standards. They have no inscribed multiples and they are placed within the JIL system, in such a way that removing any of them creates a gap in the system. Moreover, written sources do not contribute anything to this theory.

The Shekel ᛒ was divided into 24 (and not 20) Gerah. These Gerah weights carry Hieratic numerals with 'face-value' values. There are deviations in the Gerah series, since smaller weights are less accurate in any system.

6. *The Context*. Only 211 JILs have known origins. The information about the context of these JILs is limited, and the conclusions reached in this chapter are preliminary. Most of the JILs were found in domestic loci, but some weights were found in public places, such as gates and storehouses. Very few weights were found in funerary contexts, and

presumably these were private objects owned by the deceased. Weights from open areas—areas outside the cities, pools, pits, etc.—are not significant, since most of these locations are secondary (that is, the weights were not used in those places). It is very difficult to separate 'public' from 'private' locations, and the limited data on context does not permit generalization about the function of the JIL—that is, whether they belonged to private merchants and wealthy citizens, or to state officials and scribes.

The comparison of the origins of the weights (scientific excavations and surveys against unknown origins) is alarming. There are unresolvable differences between the two groups, and it serves as a warning against relying on artifacts that are bought in the antiquities markets.

7. *Old Testament Metrology.* A study of the Old Testament shows that it recognized three weight systems. The first is the 'holy Shekel' system, with 20 Gerah per Shekel. This system is mentioned in the Priestly code, together with a variation of in Ezek. 45.12. This system is mentioned in contexts of religious activities only. I doubt if it had ever existed in Iron Age Judah. It was perhaps nothing but a utopia. In the time of Ezekiel there was no Temple in Jerusalem, and therefore no use for a sacred weight system. Moreover, the Priestly code is probably also from a late period. Furthermore, the Temple of Jerusalem was not an independent economic unit, but part of the royal establishment of Judah. It was governed by the kings; therefore, there was no place for a 'Shekel of the sanctuary' in Judah. The holy Shekel system may reflect a late, non-historical, writing, influenced by the Mesopotamian Temple economy, but not by the situation in Iron Age Judah.

The second system is that of an 'ordinary' Shekel, but unfortunately we know very little about it. This was the common Judaean system, used for all economic activities that necessitated weighing. Most of the Old Testament sources are ideological or metaphorical, and there are very few sources that describe real weighing and reliable quantities of weight. The JILs must be closely connected with this 'ordinary' Shekel system, and this conclusion is strengthened by the Hebrew ostraca. Differences between the Old Testament and the JILs are partly explained by the different backgrounds: the Old Testament is an ideological creation, focused on national and international levels of society, while the JILs reflect more the day-to-day economy and trade relations. The most significant difference is the lack of the heavy units (Maneh and Kikar) among the JILs.

Finally, there was a royal system, mentioned only in one verse (2 Sam. 14.26) as 'the stone of the king'. This is discussed further in Chapter 10 above.

8. *The Hebrew Ostraca*. I hasten to mention that I am using the term 'Hebrew' here for the sake of convenience, since I discussed a few ostraca that were found outside Judah, or are not written in the Hebrew script, because they help to understand the JILs. The ostraca reflect closer ties with the JILs than the Old Testament, since they deal more with local communities and day-to-day transactions. The way of writing numerals is similar and, throughout Judah, Hieratic numerals were used (there were no special 'Hebrew numerals'). Direct evidence on the weight system is found in a few ostraca that deal with weighing. One ostracon from Mesad Hasahvyahu proves that the ષ is the Shekel. Especially important is ostracon Kadesh Barnea no. 6. It shows that the Shekel held more than 20 Gerah (and the only option left is 24 Gerah). As an exercise, it shows peculiarities in the sequence, which reflect, on the one hand, close knowledge of the JIL system, but, on the other hand, the fact that it was an exercise in writing quantities of weight, not only practical weight units that existed as weight stones. This ostracon also reflects the problem of duality in writing quantities of weights. The writer combined two 'modes' of writing Hieratic numerals: face value and non-face value. This is seen most clearly when he wrote '4 Shekel' as it appears on the JILs ('ㄱ ષ'), and then invented a 'new' numeral, which does not exist in Hieratic, in order to write '5 Shekel' ('lㄱ ષ'), since the face-value Hieratic ㄱ had already been assigned to the '4 Shekel'.

9. *Foreign Weight Systems*. There are many points of contact between the JILs and the Egyptian *dbn/qdt* system: the dome shape of the weights, the sign ષ, the Hieratic numerals, and the fact that heavy Shekel JILs were inscribed with numerals that match the quantities of *qdt*, not of the Judaean Shekel. The marking was meant for the benefit of international trade, but the JILs were the local Judaean system. This is proven by the basic units of 1, 2 Shekel, the names of the units, the location of the weights (Iron Age Judah) and the connections with the Old Testament and the Hebrew ostraca. Most of the JILs were used in Judah, probably for local transactions. The Nsf is approximately equivalent to the *qdt*, and some other small weights could serve as a link with the Egyptian system, but those were not accurate equations. They were

not marked by inscriptions and were probably not of primary importance.

I have briefly mentioned other weight systems, such as the Mesopotamian and the Phoenician. The information about other areas (for example, Philistia and Israel) is very limited, although they are close to Judah.

10. *Royal Weights and the JILs*. Scholars took it for granted that the JILs are royal weights, and some even connected them with the reform of Josiah (2 Kings 23). In light of the available information, it might be concluded that the JILs are not royal weights, strictly speaking. They could have been used by royal officials, but also by the whole population of Judah. They were mostly found in domestic loci, not in 'public' places. There was a 'royal weight system' in Judah, which is mentioned as 'the stone of the king' in 2 Samuel (14.26). My opinion is that this system was was similar in its structure and units, and only different perhaps in the shape and material of its weights. Most significantly, it was marked by 'royal inscriptions', that is, the term *lmlk*, to define it as royal. Unfortunately, only two weights can be considered as an example of this system (one from Gezer, the second from unknown origins).

11. *The Uninscribed Weights*. When we try to understand the circumstances of the appearance of the JILs (sometime towards the end of the eighth century BCE), we must ask what preceded them in Judah. Surprisingly, this question was never raised. A large series of uninscribed limestone weights (JULs) has been studied in relation to this question. I have defined approximately 160 weights as JULs, and actually they are almost identical to the JILs. The main difference is the lack of inscriptions; also, the JULs included a few 'novel' units, such as 3, 5 and 10 Shekels. It is clear that the JULs were used during the late eighth–seventh centuries BCE in Judah, and were thus a complementary part of the inscribed weights, and not a different weight system. It is possible that the JULs and the JILs were 'invented' together, but it is more likely that the JULs preceded the JILs. If so, the creation of the JILs was not a total revolution, but only the marking of a previously unmarked system.

12.2. *Further Implications*

Now that the picture of the Judaean weight system has been explored, I wish to mention a few other topics that have not yet been discussed.

1. *The JILs and the Beginning of Money*

There is a huge amount of literature on the question of 'the beginning of money', but much of it revolves around the understanding of the term 'money' (Einzig 1949; Codrigan 1964; Ridgeway 1970; Balmuth 1975; see especially Pryor 1977: 149-83). Occasionally, it is claimed that a sort of monetary economy existed in Assyrian temples of the seventh century BCE (Lipiński 1979; Dayton 1974). In Egypt, a monetary economy developed at a relatively late stage (Daumas 1977; Lloyd 1983: 329). Coins appeared in Judah only in the sixth century BCE and later. It is true that the JILs are unique in the large quantity of inscribed weights that form a very homogeneous system. This, however, does not mean that Judah had a monetary economy, or was fast approaching this, since the weights were only intended for weighing precious metals. The JILs gave no authoritative guarantee, and weighing was still necessary each and every time silver or gold changed hands.

2. *The JILs and Writing in Judah*

It is not accidental that the JILs are contemporary in time with most of the Hebrew ostraca. Writing became widespread in Judah only during the late eighth and the seventh centuries BCEE (Demski 1976: 19-20; Lemaire 1988; Millard 1984: 305). It is thus natural that writing appeared on weights at the same time. However, this does not explain the creation of the JILs. Writing was known much earlier in Palestine, while neighbouring kingdoms developed script, but not inscribed weight systems (e.g. Edom, Ammon and Philistia).

I do not have a complete answer to this unique phenomenon of the JILs. Why did Philistia or Ammon not develop similar weight systems? Perhaps they adhered to the stage of uninscribed systems out of conservatism, but this is not a valid explanation. We have very few weights from these areas outside Judah, and we do not have Old Testament sources that mention their weight systems. The ostraca reveal that there are no special 'Ammonite' or 'Philistine' numerals (Aramaean numerals were used in Transjordan, Hieratic ones in Judah and Philistia; cf. Chapter 8 above). There were inscribed weights in Egypt and Mesopotamia; thus the people of Judah did not invent writing on weights. It is rather the scope that is surprising—so many inscribed weights from such a small kingdom, whereas in the great empires few of the weights were inscribed. Philistia had trade relations with Egypt for sure, so the reason is not connected to outside policy. Was Judah more literate than its neighbours? This is doubtful. The issue remains open for future studies.

3. *The JILs as a Weight Reform*

As already mentioned, many scholars believed that the JILs signify a reform of the weight system, a reform usually associated with Josiah. While the connection with Josiah must be rejected, the possibility of a reform still exists. It is possible to assume a reform in the weight of the Shekel (from an early Shekel to the later, ඊ Shekel); a change in the multiples of the units (decimal, perhaps, against a later base of 4 or 8), or both (then it is indeed a radical change). Such a sort of change was assumed by former scholars, since they understood the adjustment to Egypt as a reform, that is, a new situation. However, it was not explicitly stated, and I am afraid that little thought has been given to this matter.

I prefer another explanation (Fig. 25, B): that the beginning of the JILs did not include a change in the standard or the status of the units, nor in the adjustment to Egypt, but only the marking of the JILs. This marking could still mean an official effort to standardize the system by making the values explicit. On the other hand, perhaps there was no reform at all, only an invention (by traders?) which later proved useful and became common by a gradual process. What we see is that any question about a 'weight reform' should first clarify what is meant by this term. If the word 'reform' implies an act by a central (or at least a major) authority, do we have evidence that the marking of the JILs was indeed a reform?

Despite the lack of data, the possibility that marking the weights was a reform is the most likely. The fact that the marks of the heavier Shekel weights were made for the benefit of international trade is significant. It does not matter if the weights were adjusted much earlier (in weight); at that time a special effort was made to express this adjustment by marking. If the international trade of Judah was largely controlled by the state, as is most likely, then the reform of the inscribed weights was probably initiated by state officials or scribes. Another indication to substantiate this theory is the uniformity of the markings. There are very few exceptional inscriptions, and it may mean that one hand directed this change (though not that all the weights were written by one hand, of course). It does not look like a case of private invention which was only accepted after a long process. Of course, this is only a very tentative remark.

If the JILs were initiated by royal authority, it may have been an act of Hezekiah. There is no Old Testament evidence for this, but this is not surprising. The JILs have nothing to do with Hezekiah's 'religious reform' (2 Kgs 18.4), which perhaps never existed in reality (Williamson 1982: 360-73; Spieckerman 1982: 170-75). Also, marking weights is not a measure of emergency; and there is no need to connect it with Hezekiah's revolt against Assyria. In times of crisis, one hardly wants to deal with a 'weight reform'. If the adjustment to Egypt existed before, the marking of the JILs was not necessarily related to closer political or economic relations with Egypt, but perhaps the attempt to encourage trade with Egypt was one of the factors involved.

4. *The JILs and Egypt*

What is the reason for the special marking of the heavy JILs with Egyptian *qdt* equivalents? Economic relations between Judah and Egypt existed throughout the Iron Age II period (Elat 1977: 198-201). Neither was Egyptian political involvement in Palestine new: for example, the campaign of Shishak (1 Kgs 14.25-28). Egyptian cultural influence on Israel and Judah is evident in a wide variety of artifacts, not only weights (Williams 1974; De Vaux 1939, but criticism in Kitchen 1986). Relations with Egypt probably intensified during the revolt of Hezekiah, and Assyria later encouraged trade with Egypt (before conquering it). Egypt was again involved in Palestine after the decline of Assyria (Elat 1977: Chs. 8, 10; 1990; Diakonoff 1992; Liverani 1991).

The use of Hieratic numerals in Israel was already known in the Late Bronze Age period (Goldwasser 1984, 1991; cf. Na'aman 1996: 172). The JIL numerals are related to the 'a-normal' Hieratic script of the first millennium BCE (Lemaire and Vernus 1983; Malinine 1972), thus they are not a local continuation of the Late Bronze Age world. The use of Hieratic numerals is evident in the ostraca that preceded the JILs (e.g. the Samaria ostraca), and scribes may have transferred the numerals to the JILs. It was probably a Judaean invention: the system was Judaean, and peculiarities in the marking (numerals written left-to-right, for example) hints at the same conclusion. Moreover, there are no comparable inscribed weights in Egypt (at least not in Weigall's, Petrie's and Cour-Marty's catalogues). Hieratic marks appear on weights from the second-millennium-BCE workmen's village in Deir el Medineh

(Valbelle 1977; Cour-Marty 1985: 193; De Cenival 1982: no. 221). This use was very special, and bore no similarity to the JILs.

5. *The System 'of the Gate'*

Recently, Eph'al and Naveh (1993) suggested that a special measure system 'of the gate' existed. This suggestion is based on three artifacts only: a stone weight from Tel Deir ʿAlla, inscribed אבן שרעה; a jar from the same site inscribed זי שרעא; and jar from Tel Kinrot inscribed כד השער. The first two inscriptions are Aramaic, the third Hebrew. They read those inscriptions as 'weight/jar of the gate', and concluded that there was an official system 'of the gate'. 'It appears that these expressions...designate standard weights and measures of the market place' (Eph'al and Naveh 1993: 62). Furthermore, they imply that this system was different in standards from the royal or sacred ones (taking for granted the existence of a 'Shekel of the sanctuary' system in Judah; 1993: 62-63).[1]

I have certain doubts about this concept. First, the evidence is meagre. Had there been a true 'system of the gate', one would expect many more inscriptions of the kind mentioned above (many gates have been excavated in Palestine). Second, the more simple reading of those three inscriptions is preferred, that is, 'the stone/jar of Shar'ah (private name); 'the jar of the gatekeeper' (שוער). This simpler reading is much more common in ancient inscriptions. Third, even if we accept Eph'al's and Naveh's reading, where is a system? They are right that the gate was a focal point for trade, and possibly measures were held there, but were these special standards that were different from weights and measures held elsewhere? Fourth, one must separate approximated reckoning from established systems. Jars were used for general measurements, but do not signify a 'system'. A present-day comparison would be when we say 'one month' (I cannot offer a good example of weight, since today we tend to measure weight exactly). A month can be 28, 29, 30 or 31 days; it is not an exact measure, but is used since it is convenient when the exact measure is *not* important. Eph'al and Naveh, it seems, did not consider the problem of what a 'standard' was in the ancient world, and whether there really were 'exact' standards (what they call 'true weights and measures'; Eph'al and Naveh 1993: 62).

---

1. Although they did not discuss the measures: for example, the stone from Deir Alla matches 500 units of 7.6 grams.

Despite this, their publication is stimulating and an important contribution to any study of ancient economy.

6. *The JILs and International Trade under Assyria*

I have mentioned that the JILs lack good correlation with the Mesopotamian weight system (Chapter 10 above). This is surprising, since the name of some units and their relative positions within the weight system are similar in both Judah and Mesopotamia (both being Semitic-speaking countries). Furthermore, the JILs were used in the late eighth and seventh centuries BCE, and Assyria ruled the west during most of this period. One would expect a vassal kingdom to show closer relations with the ruling empire, rather than with Egypt.

This puzzling picture may be partially clarified. It is common knowledge that Assyrian sources of international trade are practically nonexistent. There is evidence about only fringe people, where organized states did not exist, such as the Arabs; and Assyria did keep the Phoenician sea trade. For many years, scholars assumed that the Aramaeans had a prominent role in the international trade of Assyria, and since Aramaean (unlike Accadian) was written on perishable materials, the records simply did not survive (Parpola 1981: 121-24, with more references). Now it appears that Aramaeans were not such dominant traders. Furthermore, the Assyrians probably extracted commodities from occupied or influenced lands, not through trade, but by compulsory methods (taxes, booty and 'gifts': Elat 1990: 73-76; 1994). Therefore Judah, a country devoid of sea ports and important natural resources, did not become an important market for Assyrian goods, nor a source of goods traded with Assyria. This is perhaps the reason why the Judaean weight system was not better suited to trade with Assyria.

12.3. *Conclusions: The JILs and the Economy of Judah*

At present, the Judaean weights are unique in many respects. The fact that so many are inscribed, and that they show a uniformity of inscription, material, shape and weight, enable us to present a thorough picture of the weight system of the kingdom of Judah. Such a picture is, as far as I am aware, unmatched by any other Iron Age weight system in the ancient Near East, not even by those of the great cultures of Egypt and Mesopotamia.

The study of the Judaean weight system can provide an important insight into the economy of Judah during the Iron Age period. The scope of such a study requires a separate discussion, so I will present only a few modest notes.

There is no shortage of theoretical works on trade and commerce in the ancient world (Curtin 1984; Kohl 1975, 1978; Renfrew 1969, 1975, 1977; and many others). Some recent works on the economy of Judah can be mentioned (Olivier 1994, without even a mention of the JILs; Silver 1983). The bitter truth is that it is impossible to write a history of the Judaean economy. The written sources are very limited, and satisfactory answers are not to be found in textbooks. What 'mode of economy' did Judah have? What was the role of trade, and that of private trade? Did Judah participate in international trade, such as the south Arabian incense trade (see Finkelstein 1992; Sauer 1995; but see Beck 1996: 112; for the domestication of the camel, see Restö 1991)? What do we actually know about prices, mechanics of manufacturing, markets, distribution patterns, economic development or recession? Archaeological work on these subjects is only just beginning (Eitam 1990; Eitan-Katz 1994).

Judah was a small kingdom, and (in my view) rather unimportant on the 'economic map' of the ancient Near East. It had no sea ports and, owing to its inland location, it had no control over any major trade route (unless we assume periods of expansion, but those could only be few and short-lived). It was an agricultural society, with limited other natural resources. Even its agriculture was dependent on rain, and lacked resources such as a large wood industry or fishing.

The unique importance of Judah is its biblical tradition; therefore, although such a term is unpopular and even despised at the moment, Iron Age archaeology of Judah must be 'biblical archaeology'.

Appendix 1

CATALOGUE OF INSCRIBED JUDAEAN WEIGHTS

Structure and Technical notes

This catalogue lists all the JILs that were published, or became known to me, up until the year 1990. The Addenda to the catalogue (Appendix 2) includes weights that were added afterwards, up until December 1996.

The catalogue is arranged according to the series, in the following order: ૪ first (૪1, ૪2, ૪4, ૪8, etc.), then Nsf, Pym, Beqaᶜ and Gerah (2 Gerah, 3 Gerah, 4 Gerah, etc.). The catalogue number of each weight is a combination of the unit and a running number within the unit (e.g. Nsf.21, Beqaᶜ.3). In the Gerah and ૪ series, the sub-units are identified as well (e.g. ૪16.2, 5 Gerah.5, 8 Gerah.7). This method enables us to give simple references for weights in the textual part of the work, as well as the ability to add new weights to the catalogue without radical change of referencing structure.

I have tried to maintain a geographical order for each unit, giving weights from known origins first (starting with Jerusalem and its environs, the Judaean mountains, the Judaean Desert, the Negev, the Shephelah and finally areas outside Judah). Since so many JILs were found in Jerusalem, I have added names of excavators here as an easy method of definition. Weights from unknown origins follow, and finally doubtful or exceptional items (these are not numbered in the catalogue, but marked by letters: e.g. ૪2.a, Nsf.b). Of course, adding new weights (Appendix 2) disrupts this order.

My aim in the catalogue was to include the fullest data available on each weight. Unfortunately, details are often missing. Photographs, drawings or even the weight (grams) are sometimes not enough for the definitive identification of a weight. It requires full details, such as size and colour. Otherwise, mistakes may occur. For example, weights were sometimes published more than once without cross-references (cf. ૪4.22 and the notes to Nsf.23, 25, 28, 29, 30; Pym.22, 23; Beqaᶜ.24, etc.). I have identified these examples, but it is not always possible to do so. It even happened that weights were lost or stolen, and the preliminary publication is the only source left. Such stolen weights may appear as 'new' weights in antiquities markets.

Unlike the quite formal guidelines for pottery vessels, flint artifacts or coins, there is no strict, accepted way to publish weights. The following catalogue is suggested as a basis. It includes the following data.

The Site. Empty if unknown. The names are given in the common English spelling. 'Tel' is given with one 'l' for the sake of convenience. An alphabetical list of sites is given in Appendix 3 (below).

Weight. Always in grams, as it appears in the original publication (unless weighed again, then this is stated explicitly). Grains were translated into grams (1 grain = 0.00648 grams). If different data exist for one weight, a note is given in the catalogue (unless the difference is negligible).

Registration Number. This is the field number of the excavation (usually basket number).

Location. The present location of the weight, if known. Museum or institution numbers are given separately. I cannot guarantee accuracy in this field, since changes occur often, and the JILs are spread all over the world.

Shape, Material and Colour. Defined in simple terms. I have not tried to define the exact varieties of limestone.

Size. The size is given in millimetres, usually height first, maximal diameter second, diameter of base third.

State of Preservation (PS for short). This is an estimation. In auctions, the natural desire is to overestimate the state of preservation (since it affects the price). I usually left this field blank in such cases.

Context. This field includes details such as level, area and locus. The context and date of each weight were meticulously checked. Exceptional details, comparisons and other notes follow.

Literature. The short references are arranged in chronological order, and full details are given in the Bibliography. A small number of secondary sources are abbreviated in the catalogue without appearing in the bibliography.

Drawings. I have included only a small selection of drawings. Most of the weights are quite homogeneous; many were published earlier, and I had to keep this book within reasonable limits.

ℵ *1 Weights*

ℵ *1.1*
Jerusalem (Kenyon). Reg. no. 3234. 11.31 grams.
Dome, white limestone, 16.5 × 21.5 mm. PS: Good.
Locus A.669.11a, season 1963, area A (eastern City of David).
Context: 35 weights were found in seasons 1962–63 in the excavations, all of the latest Iron Age level (except one, Scott 1965: 128). They were dated, therefore, to the end of the Iron Age. This is strengthened by the fact that 4 weights (from the same locus) show traces of burning, due to the destruction of the level (for the excavations, see Tushingham 1988, 1985; Franken and Steiner 1990; Eshel and Prag 1995).
Literature: Scott 1965: 129; 1985: Pl. 2a, no. 15, Fig. 78.15; Kletter 1991: 140 Table 1.1.
Location: 'Amman 1963'. Weights were left in Jordan, which included then the West Bank. After 1967, some were left in Jerusalem (and could be identified in the

Rockefeller Museum). Those left with the excavator's definition 'Amman' should be in Jordan, but exact locations are not published.

႘ *1.2* (Fig. 31.1)
Jerusalem (Kenyon). Reg. no. 4442. 10.50 grams.
Dome, limestone (size not given). PS: Good.
Locus A.767.1d, season 1965, area A.
Context: Cf. no. 1 above.
Notes: The shape of the sign ႘ is exceptional (somewhat similar to the Roman *libra* sign). The weight has a depression in its base, probably for metal (lead) filling. This may explain its lower weight. Such a filling is very rare among the JILs. There is a second weak line on the dome, probably just a scratch.
Literature: Shiloh 1981: Pl. 32; Scott 1965; 1985: 202 no. 63, Fig. 79.10; Kletter 1991: 140 Table 1.2.
Location: IAA 86-1788, Terra Santa, Jerusalem.

႘ *1.3* (Fig. 31.2)
Jerusalem (Shiloh). Reg. no. G4567. 11.56 grams.
Dome, limestone. $17 \times 29.9 \times 21.8$ mm. PS: Very good.
Context: Level X, locus 790, 7th century BCE.
Literature: Shiloh 1981: Pl. 32; Kletter 1991: 140 Table 1.3; Eran 1996: W122 Fig. 36.10, Pl. 14.8.
Notes: There is a second, weak line, probably just a scratch.
Location: Jerusalem, IAA 86-1788.

႘ *1.4*
Mevaseret Jerusalem (Moza). 7.8121 grams.
Half-ball, limestone. 11×21 mm. PS: Good.
Notes: The weight was found in 1958–59 by Mr Lion in an area of terraces on the southern slope of the site.
Moza is known from graves and excavations as an Iron Age II settlement of the 8th–7th centuries BCE (Negbi 1970: 358-70; De Groot, pers. comm.).
The low weight is perplexing. Barkay suggested that it was reduced too much for a Shekel, and, when it was noticed, the manufacturer continued to reduce and formed a Pym without changing the Shekel mark. This is problematic. The shape is also exceptional.
Literature: G. Barkay 1978: 209; Kletter 1991: 140 Table 1.4.
Location: IAA, currently not clear.

႘ *1.5*
Ein Gedi. Reg. no. 254/30. 11.17 grams.
Half-ball, orange-red limestone, 16×18 mm. PS: A little damaged.
Context: Level V, dated 7th–6th centuries by Mazar *et al.* (1963: 57). Ein Gedi existed in the 8th century BCE as well (cf. G. Barkay 1993).
Notes: The size given by the Romema archive is 18×21 mm, and the weight is

11.21. According to Hestrin, 11.23 grams. There is a damaged area near the Shekel sign. The limestone probably originated in the area of Jerusalem (Ben Tor, note in: Mazar *et al.* 1966).

Literature: *HadArch* 3 (1962): 6; Hestrin 1963: 103 no. 91; B. Mazar *et al.* 1966: 37 Pl. 26.2; Stern 1963: 867 Table A; Meshorer 1976: 53-54 (photographs); Kletter 1991: 140 Table 1.5.

Location: IAA no. 67-522, now at the Israel Museum, Jerusalem.

ɤ *1.6*

Arad. Reg. no. 5705/51. 11.71 grams (?).

Dome, limestone (size not published). PS: Good.

Context: Locus J.9 773. Level VII, 7th century BCE (Y. Aharoni 1971b: 472; M. Aharoni 1981; Herzog *et al.* 1984: 22-26). This date is accepted (cf. Mazar and Netzer 1986: 89-90; Ussishkin 1988: 155-56). Square J.9 is in the south of the citadel, an area of domestic houses next to the wall. Further details of context not yet published.

Notes: This is probably the 1 Shekel weight that appears in Stern (1963: 867 Table). For a few weights from Arad, the weight given by Stern (1963) is different from that given by the excavators (M. Aharoni 1981). I follow the latter, and assume the artifacts are the same.

Literature: M. Aharoni 1981: 126 no. 1; Stern 1963: 867 Table (?); Kletter 1991: 140 Table 1.6.

ɤ *1.7*

Arad. Reg. no. 5705/51. 11.54 grams.

Dome, black limestone (size not published).

Context: Locus 69, square 13. Level VI, 7th century BCE (cf. no. 6 above). The square is in the area of the eastern casemate wall.

Notes: the weight (according to the Museum) is 11.38 grams.

Literature: M. Aharoni 1981: 126 no. 2; Kletter 1991: 140 Table 1.7.

Location: IAA no. 1967-613, at the Israel Museum.

ɤ *1.8* (Fig. 31.3)

Tel 'Ira. Reg. no. E.1110/51. 11.3827 grams.

Dome, pink limestone. Size: 21 × 19 × 14 mm.

PS: Very good, some minor damages on the dome.

Context: Locus 194 in the area of the gate (E). It probably belongs to the 7th century BCE (cf. Biran 1987: 26-29; Beit Arieh 1987: 34-35; for the gate, Beit Arieh 1985: 19-21).

Literature: Beit Arieh 1985: 23 (preliminary report); Kletter 1991: 140 Table 1.8; Kletter forthcoming c: no. 2.

Location: Tel Aviv University.

ɤ *1.9*

Lachish. Reg. no. 6/51. 10.872 grams.

Dome, limestone. Size 16 × 28 × 20 mm.

Context: Locus 5, level II under the 'sun temple' of the Persian period. 7th century BCE.

Notes: The base of the weight carry two inscribed lines with the name *lndb/yh* (cf. 1 Chron. 3.18). This is presumably the name of the owner (Aharoni [ed.] 1975: 19). Cf. weight ʏ 2.23 below.

Literature: *HadArch* 20 (1967): 20-21; Aharoni (ed.) 1975: 19-20 Pl. 17.4; Kletter 1991: 140 Table 1.9.

Location: IAA, no. 1968-259.

ʏ 1.10

Gezer. 11.30 grams.

Dome, limestone.

Context: Not clear. According to the final report, it belongs to the 'Persian-Hellenistic' stratum (Macalister 1912: 285), but formerly it was said to be found in a thin level between the last 'pre-exilic' level and the first 'postexilic' level (Macalister 1904a: 209, 358). This may fit a date at the end of the Iron Age. For Gezer in the 7th century BCE, see Reich and Brandl 1985; for Assyrian evidence, see Macalister 1912: 22; Becking 1992.

Literature: Macalister 1904a: 209, 358; 1912: 285, 287; Viedebannt 1923: no. 4; Barrois 1932: 64 no. 1; Stern 1963: Table 4; Yadin 1960: Table; Kletter 1991: 140 Table 1.10.

ʏ 1.11

Gezer. 11.375 grams.

Dome, quartzite. Either a photograph or a drawing was not published.

Context: Not clear. It was dated to the 'Persian-Hellenistic' period (Macalister 1912: 284).

Literature: Macalister 1912: 285, 287; Barrois 1932: 64 n.2; Stern 1963: Table 4; Yadin 1960: Table; Kletter 1991: 140 Table 1.11.

ʏ 1.12

Bethel. Reg. no. 101. Weight not published.

Dome, limestone.

Context: 'N(orth of 18)', season 1934. This indicates surface debris in the area north of square 18, without clear dating. For Bethel in the 7th century, see 2 Kgs 23.4, 15-19; for archaeological remains, Kelso 1968: 64-67 (perhaps an assemblage of the 6th century BCE, but the city existed earlier as well).

Literature: Kelso 1968: 87 Pl. 44.6; Kletter 1991: 140 Table 1.12.

ʏ 1.13

Tell el Far'ah (north). Reg. no. F.1490. 11.78 grams.

Dome, pink veined limestone. 16 × 20 mm.

Context: On the one hand, the weight was ascribed to locus 113, a room in a large building of level 7e (Puech 1984: 79, 101 Plan 6). On the other hand, locus 153 is

mentioned (Puech 1984: 109 Pl. 67.17). The last is a small installation in the area of the gate, levels 7b-d (Puech 1984: Plan 5). The relationship between these two loci is not clear. Level 7e is dated the 7th century BCE (Puech 1984: 12), while 7d was destroyed in 720 BCE according to the excavators. 'Assyrian' pottery is found in both levels (Puech 1984: 69-70 Pl. 61). Definite pottery of the 7th century BCE, such as *mortaria* bowls and lamps on high bases, is found in level 7e (Puech 1984: Pls. 53, 59). But the excavators compared 7e with Megiddo II, while 7d was compared with Megiddo IV-III (Megiddo III is the Assyrian phase). Locus 153 and level 7e were described as interrupted and/or close to the surface (Puech 1984: 47). Puech dated the weight to the 8th century BCE, but in view of the difficulties it remains an open question.
Literature: Puech 1984: 79-80 Fig. 67.17; Kletter 1991: 140 Table 1.13.
Location: Louvre Museum, Paris, no. AO.23019.

ɤ *1.14* (Fig. 31.4)
Tel Keisan. Reg. no. 6.181. 11.61 grams.
Dome, brown limestone. 16.8 × 21.3 mm. PS: Very good.
Context: Locus 6087, the upper fill level of a pit (Puech 1980: 158 Plan 43). The same area has a few pits with mixed assemblages. The level of the weight is registered as 39.00. The report sometimes connects it with pit 6161 (Puech 1980: 164), but explicitly declares that the exact pit where it was found is not clear (Puech 1980: 164). All the upper part of pit 6087 is ruined, and its stratigraphy is vague (Puech 1980: 164). Both pits 6087 and 6161 were dated to level V, on the basis of ceramic comparisons. This level is dated the end of the 8th century–early 7th century BCE. It included 'Assyrian' pottery (in pit 6078 itself; Puech 1980: 136 Pls. 37.6-130; 39-40). To sum up, a range of the 8th-7th centuries BCE remains possible.
Notes: For the problems of dating the Iron Age II levels in northern Israel, see Wightman 1985a; Finkelstein 1996.
Literature: Puech 1980: 306-308 Pl. 94.12; 1984: 80 n. 60; Kletter 1991: 140 Table 1.14.
Location: IAA, no. 79-333.

ɤ *1.15*
Tel Dor. Weight and size not yet published.
Dome, limestone.
Context: A pit dug into Iron Age levels, near the gate. The pit is later than the 4-roomed gate, and includes pottery of the late Iron Age period (possibly 7th century BCE).
Notes: The publication is preliminary. For Dor in the 7th century BCE, see Forrer 1920: 69; Stern 1992. Stern (1992: 70) still claims that the sign of the Shekel is the royal Judaean sign from the days of Josiah, and that these are royal weights connected. He mentions 11.4 grams (1992: 70), but only as a general average for the Shekel.
Literature: Stern, *HadArch* 86 (1985): 19; *HadArch* 88 (1986): 12; Stern 1992: 70

Photo 89; Kletter 1991: 140 Table 1.15.
Location: Jerusalem University (?).

א 1.16

Tel Jemmeh. Reg. no. 5568. 11.95 grams.
Trapezoid, limestone.
Context: According to Eshel (1978: 251), the weight was found in level V of the
7th century BCE; but it is an old excavation and exact context is unknown (cf.
weight א 2.14).
Notes: Petrie did not publish that this is an inscribed weight, but it is mentioned in
the excavation's diaries (according to Eshel). The weight given here is following
Petrie (184.4 grains).
Literature: Petrie 1928: Pl. 68.5568; Eshel 1978: 251 Pl. 15.30; Kletter 1991: 140
Table 1.16.
Location: London (?).

א 1.17

Site unknown. 11.41 grams. Dome, limestone.
Notes: It is one of a group of 11 weights published by Spaer. They are said to come
from the area of Idna-Tarqumiyeh (Hebron Mountains). A few of these 11 weights
were published by Ben-David under the origin 'Beit Gubrin'. There is some
possibility that the one here is the same weight as no. 32 (below).
Literature: Spaer 1982: 251 Pl. 41c; Kletter 1991: 140 Table 1.17.
Location: Private collection.

א 1.18

Site unknown. 13.43 grams.
Dome, reddish-brown limestone. 17.5 × 22.8 mm. PS: Good. Peculiar script: 'א ﬥ'
Notes: The published photograph is not very clear and the numeral does not appear
in it. There is an exceptional mark on the weight. It was explained as the letter *m*
for 'kingly' (מלכותי), or perhaps *maʿah* (מעה). Lemaire rejected these rather
unlikely explanations. He thought it is a separate א standard because of the heavy
weight (cf. weight א 4.31 from Gibeon).
Literature: Lemaire 1976: 33-34 no. 2, Pl. 1.2; Kletter 1991: 140 Table 1.18.
Location: Private collection.

א 1.19

Site unknown. Museum no. 5045. 11.230 grams.
Dome, brown limestone. 17 × 20.5 × 17 mm. PS: Good.
Literature: Lemaire 1976: no. 23; Kletter 1991: 140 Table 1.19.
Location: Bible et Terre Sainte Museum, Paris.

א 1.20

Site unknown. Museum no. 5047. 9.113 grams.
Dome, reddish limestone. 14.5 × 20 × 17 mm. PS: Damaged.

Notes: Lemaire thought that it may be a forgery because of the reduced weight.
Literature: Lemaire 1976: 42 no. 24, Pl. 2.24; Kletter 1991: 140 Table 1.20.
Location: Bible et Terre Sainte Museum, Paris.

૪ 1.21
Site unknown. 11.67 grams.
Dome, pink limestone.
Further details not published.
Literature: Pritchard 1969: 373 Pl. 1.776c; Kletter 1991: 140 Table 1.21.
Location: Princeton, private collection.

૪ 1.22
Site unknown. 11.55 grams.
Dome, grey limestone. PS: Damaged.
Notes: The weight was offered for sale for 600 *lira* (Israeli currency at the time).
Literature: Agora 1975: no. 387; Kletter 1991: 140 Table 1.22.
Location: Private hands.

૪ 1.23
Site unknown. 11.21 grams.
Dome, white limestone. 20.5×17 mm.
Literature: Qedar 1978: no. 22; Kletter 1991: 141 Table 1.23.
Location: Private hands.

૪ 1.24
Site unknown. 11.02 grams.
Dome, gray limestone. 21×17 mm.
Notes: There are a few light lines, perhaps scratches, on the surface.
Literature: Qedar 1978: no. 23; Kletter 1991: 141 Table 1.24.
Location: Private hands.

૪ 1.25 (Fig. 31.5)
Site unknown. 11.25 grams.
Dome, grey limestone. 28×13 mm. PS: Very good.
Notes: The shape of the ૪ is exceptional, like an English 'G' (cf. weight ૪ 1.2 above).
Literature: Qedar 1979: 26, no. 4048; Kletter 1991: 141 Table 1.25.
Location: Private hands.

૪ 1.26
Site unknown. 11.72 grams.
Dome, reddish limestone. 22×17 mm. PS: Fair.
Literature: Qedar 1979: 26; Kletter 1991: 141 Table 1.26.
Location: Private hands.

ȣ *1.27*
Site unknown. 10.94 grams.
Dome, grey limestone. 22 × 20 mm. PS: Very good.
Notes: The photograph is blurred. There are a few damaged points on the lower sides of the weight.
Literature: Qedar 1979: 27 no. 4051; Kletter 1991: 141 Table 1.27.
Location: Private hands.

ȣ *1.28*
Site unknown. 11.71 grams.
Dome, grey limestone. 16 × 21 mm.
Literature: Qedar 1983: 24 no. 5063; Kletter 1991: 141 Table 1.28.
Location: Private hands.

ȣ *1.29*
Site unknown. 10.60 grams.
Dome, limestone. 16 × 20.5 × 19 mm.
Literature: Kletter 1991: 141 Table 1.29.
Location: Eretz Israel Museum, Tel Aviv, no. K-8908.

ȣ *1.30*
Site unknown. 11.06 grams.
Dome, grey limestone. 15.4 × 21 mm.
Literature: Kroha (ed.) 1980: no. 68; Kletter 1991: 141 Table 1.30.
Location: Private hands.

ȣ *1.31*
Site unknown. 11.65 grams.
Dome, limestone. 21 × 16 mm.
Literature: Meshorer in press: no. 28; Kletter 1991: 141 Table 1.31.
Location: Hecht Museum, Haifa (H-410?).

ȣ *1.32*
Site unknown. 11.48 grams.
Dome, limestone. 21 × 16 mm.
Notes: There is a danger that it is the same weight as no. 17 (above), but the photographs look different.
Literature: Meshorer in press: no. 29; Kletter 1991: 141 Table 1.32.
Location: Hecht Museum, Haifa (H-425?).

ȣ *1.33*
Site unknown. 11.40 grams.
Dome, grey limestone. 20.5 × 16.5 mm.
Notes: The weight was bought in Jerusalem. The numeral is to the right of the Shekel sign.

Literature: Meshorer in press: no. 30; Kletter 1991: 141 Table 1.33.
Location: Hecht Museum, Haifa, H-261.

ﬡ 1.34

Site unknown. 10.90 grams.
Dome, limestone. 20 × 17 mm. PS: Very good.
Literature: Meshorer in press: no. 31; Kletter 1991: 141 Table 1.34.
Location: Hecht Museum, Haifa, H-153 (?).

ﬡ 1.A

Malhata. Reg. no. 2032/50. 10.829 grams.
Flattened dome, fossil limestone. 12 × 16 × 20.5 mm.
Context: Locus 2, probably 7th century BCE.
Notes: The weight is marked with the numeral 1, without the Shekel mark. Barkay suggested that it was planned to be a Shekel weight, and the mark was left though the weight was far too low.
Literature: G. Barkay 1978: 217 Pl. 1.6; Kletter 1991: 141 Table 1.a; forthcoming b: no. 3.
Location: Tel Aviv University.

ﬡ 2 Weights

ﬡ 2.1

Jerusalem (Kenyon). Reg. no. 3258. 21.74 grams.
Dome, pink limestone. 20 × 26.5 mm. PS: Good.
Context: Locus A.669.11a (cf. ﬡ 1.1).
Notes: There is another mark between the Shekel sign and the numerals.
Literature: Scott 1965: Pl. 23.1; 1985: List no. 24, Fig. 78.24; Dever 1970: Fig. 17; Kletter 1991: 141 Table 2.1.
Location: 'Amman 1963'.

ﬡ 2.2

Jerusalem (Kenyon). Reg. no. 3237. 21.77 grams. PS: Good.
Dome, cream limestone with pink veins. 19.5 × 27 mm.
Context: Locus A.669.11a (cf. ﬡ 2.1 above).
Notes: The numerals appear to the right of the Shekel sign. Part of the script is damaged.
Literature: Scott 1965: Pl. 23.3; 1985: 199 no. 18, Fig. 78.18; Dever 1970: Fig. 17; Kletter 1991: 141 Table 2.2.
Location: Oxford, Ashmolean Museum, 1965.461.

ﬡ 2.3

Jerusalem (Kenyon). Reg. no. 3238. 21.80 grams.
Dome, white limestone. 19.5 × 27.5 mm. PS: Bad.
Context: Locus A.669.34 (cf. ﬡ 2.1 above).

Notes: According to Scott (1985), the weight is 21.79 grams.
Literature: Scott 1965: 129; 1985: 199 no. 19, Fig. 78.19; Dever 1970: Fig. 17;
Kletter 1991: 141 Table 2.3.
Location: 'Amman 1963'.

ඊ 2.4

Jerusalem (Kenyon). Reg. no. 3241. 22.26 grams.
Dome, pink limestone. 19.5 × 27.5 mm. PS: Fair.
Context: Locus A.669.34 (cf. ඊ 2.3 above).
Notes: One of the numeral lines is almost erased, but the identification of the unit is
clear (according to the weight).
Literature: Scott 1965: 129; 1985: 199 no. 20, Fig. 78.20; Dever 1970: Fig. 17;
Kletter 1991: 141 Table 2.4.
Location: Royal Ontario Museum, Toronto.

ඊ 2.5

Jerusalem (Kenyon). Reg. no. 4440. 22.57 grams.
Dome, pink limestone. PS: Good.
Context: Locus A.680+, season 1964 (cf. ඊ 1.1 above).
Notes: The numerals appear to the right of the Shekel sign. Part of the script is
damaged.
Literature: Scott 1985: 199 no. 22, Fig. 78.22; Kletter 1991: 141 Table 2.5.
Location: St Andrews.

ඊ 2.6 (Fig. 31.6)

Jerusalem (Kenyon). Reg. no. 93. 22.00 grams.
Dome, pink limestone. PS: Good.
Context: Locus A.1.23a—a mixed locus (season 1961), with material from the 7th
century BCE until the Hellenistic period.
Literature: Scott 1985: 202 no. 59, Fig. 79.11; Kletter 1991: 141 Table 2.6.
Location: Birmingham.

ඊ 2.7

Jerusalem (Kenyon). Reg. no. 491. 22.50 grams.
Dome, limestone with iron colouring. PS: Good.
Context: Locus A.2.7, season 1961 (cf. ඊ 1.1 above).
Literature: Scott 1985: 202 no. 61, Fig. 79.12; Kletter 1991: 141 Table 2.7.
Location: 'Amman 1961'.

ඊ 2.8

Jerusalem (Duncan). 22.21 grams.
Dome, limestone. 21 × 25 mm.
Context: The weight was found in the *Ophel* area, according to Rockefeller's
archive. Such a weight is indeed mentioned in the museum's catalogue from the
British Mandate period (Rockefeller Museum 1940: 43 no. 495, weight stated as

22.12). It is very likely that this is one of the weights found in the excavations of Duncan (cf. Duncan 1931: 31; also 1924; 1925; Macalister and Duncan 1926).
Literature: Rockefeller Museum 1940: 43; Hestrin 1963: 103 no. 92; Meshorer 1976: 54 (upper photograph); Kletter 1991: 141 Table 2.8.
Location: Rockefeller, no. S.2585.

४ 2.9
Jerusalem (Duncan). Weight not published.
Dome, brown limestone.
Context: The weight was found by Duncan, but the context was not published. The Shekel sign is very rounded.
Literature: Duncan 1931: 217 (center of plate); Kletter 1991: 141 Table 2.9.
Location: Not clear. Some weights from Duncan's excavations are registered in the collection of the Hebrew University, Jerusalem, but they were lost afterwards. Other weights are stored in the PEF collection, London, or at Rockefeller (cf. Eran 1996).

४ 2.10
Jerusalem (Duncan). Weight not published.
Dome, brown limestone. PS: Seems to be very good.
Context: Cf. weight no. 9 (above).
Notes: The Shekel sign is very angular.
Literature: Duncan 1931: 217 (plate); Kletter 1991: 141 Table 2.10.
Location: Cf. weight no. 9 (above).

४ 2.11
Jerusalem (Shiloh). Reg. no. 4727. 22.79 grams.
Dome, brown limestone. $19 \times 27 \times 26$ mm. PS: Good.
Context: Area G, level 10, locus 773. 7th century BCE.
Notes: There is a damaged area above the Shekel sign.
Literature: Shiloh 1981: Pl. 32; Kletter 1991: 141 Table 2.11; Eran 1996: W117, Fig. 36.7 Pl. 14.6.
Location: The Hebrew University, Jerusalem.

४ 2.12
Jerusalem (Guthe), Siloam village area. 24.50 grams.
Dome, limestone.
Context: The weight was found in the upper level of the excavations, but a better definition is not possible.
Literature: Guthe 1882: 373 Pl. 109; Bliss and Dickie 1898: 268; Dalman 1906: 93; Viedebannt 1923: no. 5; Barrois 1932: 64 no. 6; Diringer 1934: 284 no. 2; Yadin 1960: Table; Stern 1963: 867 Table; Dever 1970: Fig. 17; Kletter 1991: 141 Table 2.12; Eran 1996: W306.
Location: Not clear.

ƻ 2.13

Jerusalem, Mt Zion. Details not yet published.

Context: The weight was found in the excavations in the Armenian cathedral south-west of Zion gate. Remains of the 7th–6th centuries BCE have been found, but also earlier finds, e.g. *lmlk* and concentric rings stamps (G. Barkay 1985: 168-69).

Notes: No drawing or photograph of the weight has been published.

Literature: *HadArch* 40 (1971): 19-20; *HadArch* 45 (1973): 22; Kletter 1991: 142 Table 2.13.

Location: IAA (?).

ƻ 2.14

Tel Jemmeh. Reg. no. 5557. 23.20 grams.

High dome, light brown limestone.

Context: Locus GJ.192, an open area in Petrie's '20th dynasty city' (Petrie 1928: Plan 7). The height seems too great for this level, however. A few vessels were found in locus GJ (Petrie 1928: Pl. 69: nos. 27, 235, 177), but they do not supply exact date. Eshel (1978: 255-56) dated the weight to level V of the 7th century BCE, but there are doubts whether an exact dating is possible. Tel Jemmeh did flourish in the 7th century BCE (see the Assyrian types of building and pottery; Petrie 1928: 7-8; Van Beek 1973).

Notes: According to Barrois, the weight is 23.23 grams. Petrie included this weight in his *koirine* standard. I have checked the weight at the PEF collection, where the weight is given as 23.22 grams.

Literature: Petrie 1928: Pl. 17.52; Pl. 18.5557; Barrois 1932: 64 no. 4; Yadin 1960: Table; Stern 1963: 867 Table A; Dever 1970: Fig. 17; Eshel 1978: 251 Pl. 15.25; Kletter 1991: 142 Table 2.14.

Location: London, PEF collection.

ƻ 2.15

Tel Jemmeh. Reg. no. 5558. 23.20 grams.

Dome, brown limestone.

Context: Locus AQ.197, a narrow room in a large building from the '26th dynasty city' (Petrie 1928: Plan 11). The building was defined as a fortress (Petrie 1928: 7-8), and is clearly dated to the 7th–early 6th centuries BCE (for the 'Assyrian' pottery, see Petrie 1928: 20-21, 23 Pl. 65).

Notes: This weight was not mentioned by Eshel (1978). According to Barrois, the weight is 23.26 grams.

Literature: Petrie 1928: pls. 17.53, 18.5558; Barrois 1932: 64 no. 5; Yadin 1960: Table; Stern 1963: 867 Table A; Dever 1970: Fig. 17; Kletter 1991: 142 Table 2.15.

Location: London, PEF collection (?).

ƻ 2.16

Arad. Reg. no. C.379/1. 22.568 grams.

Dome, white limestone. 21.5 × 26 mm.

Context: Locus 418 in square E.12, height 74.80 m. This is one of the rooms of the wall in the west side of the fortress (Y. Aharoni 1981: Map). The weight was ascribed to level VIII, and is the only weight dated to the 8th century BCE from Arad (the date of this level is clear: Y. Aharoni 1971, 1981; Herzog *et al.* 1984; Mazar and Netzer 1986).

Notes: According to the museum records, the weight is 22.60 grams. Stern (1963: Table) lists two weights of 2 Shekel from Arad, and I assume that these are the same as nos. 16–17 here (he gives different weights: 22.58, 22.82 grams, but I follow the data published by the Arad excavators).

Literature: M. Aharoni 1981: 126 no. 3; Kletter 1991: 142 Table 2.16.

Location: Eretz Israel Museum, Tel Aviv, K-71925.

ℵ *2.17*

Arad. Reg. no. 6515/50. 22.9022 grams.

Dome, white limestone.

Context: Locus 905, square J.16, height 75.30 m. J.16 is a square in the gate at the north side of the fortress; and 905 is found inside a building north of the Hellenistic fort (Y. Aharoni 1981: General map). Level VII.

Notes: No drawing or photograph of the weight has been published. For the weight, cf. no. 16 (above).

Literature: M. Aharoni 1981: 126 no. 4; Kletter 1991: 142 Table 2.17.

ℵ *2.18*

Arad. Reg. no. 634/1. 22.731 grams.

Dome, light brown limestone.

Context: Locus 360, square D.13, height 74.30 m. It is the inner room of a 'bastion' in the west side of the casemate wall. The date of the wall is disputed (it may be from the Hellenistic period; Mazar and Netzer 1986), but the material from inside its rooms is 7th–early 6th centuries BCE (Herzog *et al.* 1987: 77-79).

Notes: No drawing or photograph of the weight has been published. There is another vertical line, on the right side of the Shekel mark.

Literature: M. Aharoni 1981: 126 no. 5; Kletter 1991: 142 Table 2.18.

Location: IAA 1964-312, now at the Israel Museum, Jerusalem.

ℵ *2.19*

Kh. el-Kom (?). 22.61 grams.

Dome, white limestone. PS: Excellent.

Context: The weight was bought by Dever in Kh. el-Kom itself, reputedly found in a cave inside the village. There is no guarantee that it is really the origin. Only two pottery vessels have been published, not very helpful for an exact dating of the weight (Dever 1970: 169f).

Literature: Dever 1970: 178 Fig. 15.3; Fig. 17; Kletter 1991: 142 Table 2.19.

Location: not clear.

ъ *2.20*
Beth Shemesh. Reg. no. [19]33-3-189. 22.42 grams.
Dome, limestone.
Context: Locus 351, level II (?). It is the only JIL from Beth Shemesh, from a room in the centre of the 1933 area of excavations. Level II includes different Iron Age II phases, sorted *post mortem* by Wright (Grant and Wright 1939). Most of the finds belong to phase IIc, dated to the 8th century BCE; there are very few remains from the 7th century BCE (Wightman 1985a: chap. 10, esp. pp. 857-61). There is one rich tomb (no. 14), a few surface sherds (Dagan, pers. comm.); Mackenzie's 'squatters' phase (its date is not very clear; cf. now Momigliano 1996) and pottery from the water system found in the new excavations.
Literature: Grant and Wright 1939: 159 Pl. 53.50; Grant 1934: 55 Pl. 5.4; Eshel 1986: 355; Kletter 1991: 142 Table 2.20.
Location: Haverford (?).

ъ *2.21*
Tel Batash. Reg. no. 9180. 22.78 grams.
Dome, limestone.
Context: Level II, 7th century BCE (A. Mazar 1985: 309; preliminary publication).
Literature: A. Mazar 1985: 320; Kletter 1991: 142 Table 2.21.
Location: The Hebrew University.

ъ *2.22*
Gezer. 22.50 grams.
Dome, limestone.
Context: Not clear; cf. ъ 1.10.
Notes: No drawing or photograph has been published.
Literature: Dalman 1906: 93; Macalister 1912: 285, 287; Barrois 1932: 64 no. 3; Yadin 1960: 323-24; Stern 1963: 867; Dever 1970: Fig. 17; Kletter 1991: 142 Table 2.22.
Location: Not clear.

ъ *2.23* (Fig. 31.7)
Nebi Rubin. 21.894 grams.
Dome, limestone.
Context: The weight was found on the surface, in a survey (Glueck 1959: 36-38 Fig. 1). Iron Age remains were reported from the site (Dothan 1951: 44).
Notes: The weight is inscribed 'to *brky*', presumably the name of the owner. The script is 'mirrored', indicating perhaps that the writer was a seal engraver. Glueck (1959: 39) suggested that the weight was used as a seal. The numeral is inscribed to the right of the Shekel sign.
Literature: Glueck 1959: 36-38 Fig. 1; Yadin 1960: Table; Stern 1963: 867; Dever 1970: Fig. 17; Kletter 1991: 142 Table 2.23.

ﬡ *2.24*
Ekron. Weight not published.
Dome, limestone.
Context: Locus 13b or 25 (?), the southern industrial area. Probably level Ib, 7th
century BCE (Gitin 1989: 36).
Literature: Gitin 1989: 51; Kletter 1991: 142 Table 2.24.
Location: Hebrew University (?).

ﬡ *2.25* (Fig. 31.8)
Tell Deir 'Alla. Reg. no. DA.2632. 22.74 grams.
Dome, limestone. 24 mm diameter. Season 1978.
Context: Square B/A.8, level VI, 7th century BCE (for the evidence, including
'Assyrian' pottery, see Franken and Ibrahim 1978: 73 Pl. 39.3; Van der Kooij and
Ibrahim 1989: 104 nos. 149, 119, 120).
Notes: The mark in Franken and Ibrahim (1978: Pl. 7b-c) is mistaken.
Literature: Franken and Ibrahim 1978: 73 Pl. 39.4; Van der Koiij and Ibrahim
1989: 106 no. 142; Kletter 1991: 142 Table 2.25.

ﬡ *2.26*
Site unknown. 23.40 grams.
Dome, pink limestone.
Notes: This is one of a group of weights published by Spaer; cf. discussion in
weight 1ﬡ . 17 (above).
Literature: Spaer 1982: no. 2 Pl. 41b; Kletter 1991: 142 Table 2.26.
Location: Private collection.

ﬡ *2.27*
Site unknown. 22.61 grams.
Dome, white limestone. PS: Excellent.
Notes: The weight was bought in the antiquities markets of Jerusalem. One cannot
rely on the dealers, who claimed that it came from Kh. el-Kom.
Literature: Dever 1970: Pl. 9.4, Fig. 17; Kletter 1991: 142 Table 2.27.
Location: Not clear.

ﬡ *2.28*
Site unknown. 23.02 grams.
Dome, white limestone. 17.5 × 28 mm.
Notes: The weight was bought by the Israel Bank.
Literature: Qedar 1979: 26 no. 4047; R. Barkay 1987: 189 Pl. 1e; Kletter 1991: 142
Table 2.28.
Location: Bank of Israel, Jerusalem.

ﬡ *2.29*
Site unknown. 22.35 grams.
Dome, white limestone. 20 × 27 mm.

Notes: There are indentations on the base, perhaps to adjust the weight.
Literature: Qedar 1978: no. 20; Kletter 1991: 142 Table 2.29.
Location: Private collection.

ਠ 2.30
Site unknown. 22.29 grams.
Dome, orange limestone. 23 × 26 mm.
Literature: Qedar 1978: no. 21; Kletter 1991: 142 Table 2.30.
Location: Private collection.

ਠ 2.31
Site unknown. 22.06 grams.
Dome, limestone. 20 × 26 mm.
Notes: There is another 'X' mark on the base of the weight.
Literature: Qedar 1981: 31, no. 72; Kletter 1991: 142 Table 2.31.
Location: Private collection.

ਠ 2.32
Site unknown. 22.62 grams.
Dome, white limestone. 21 × 27 mm.
Literature: Qedar 1983: 24 no. 5602; Kletter 1991: 142 Table 2.32.
Location: Private collection.

ਠ 2.33
Site unknown. 21.91 grams.
Dome, grey-black limestone. 20 × 27.5 mm.
Literature: Kroha (ed.) 1980: no. 67; Kletter 1991: 142 Table 2.33.
Location: Private collection.

ਠ 2.34
Site unknown. 22.85 grams.
Dome, light limestone. 25 mm diameter (following the museum's card, 22 × 19 mm).
Literature: Meshorer in press: no. 27; Kletter 1991: 142 Table 2.34.
Location: Hecht Museum, Haifa, H-451.

ਠ 2.a (Fig. 31.10)
Gezer. 22.28 grams. Inscription *lmlk* with two vertical lines.
Trapezoid (truncated pyramid), bronze.
Context: Cf. ਠ 1.10 (above).
Notes: This famous weight received a lot of attention, and was almost always explained as two royal Shekels. Yadin (1960) claimed that this weight shows that the ਠ is equal to the word *lmlk*.
Literature: Macalister 1912: 285 Fig. 433; Barrois 1932: 65 no. 23; Diringer 1934: 280 no. 19; 1942: 95; Scott 1959a: 32; Stern 1963: 867 Table; Yadin 1960: Table;

Kletter 1991: 142 Table 2.a.
Location: Not clear (Istanbul?).

໐ 2.b
Unknown. Museum no. 5044. 17.363 grams.
Dome, *café au lait* limestone. 15 × 27 × 25.5 mm.
Notes: The weight carries the usual inscription on the dome, but a different mark on the base: **\W**. Lemaire interpreted this mark as an Aramaean letter *s* and two vertical lines, hence '2 Shekels'. This is explained as two Mesopotamian Shekels from the Persian period, perhaps a secondary use of a Judaean weight. Another option is an Attic tetradrachma of 17.4 grams (Lemaire 1976: 41-42). In any case, the weight does not fit 2 Judaean Shekel at all, and I have not included this weight in the calculation of averages.
Literature: Lemaire 1976: List no. 22; Kletter 1991: 142 Table 2.b.
Location: Bible et Terre Sainte Museum, Paris.

໐ 4 Weights

໐ 4.1 (Fig. 32.1)
Jerusalem (Kenyon). Reg. no. 3246. 45.23 grams.
Dome, reddish-brown dolomite. 28 × 32.5 mm.
PS: Fair–good; damaged near the base.
Context: Locus A.669.34, cf. ໐ 1.1. Season 1963.
Literature: Scott 1965: 130; Dever 1970: Fig. 16; Scott 1985: 200 no. 35, Fig. 78.32; Kletter 1991: 143 Table 3.1.
Location: Ashmolean Museum, Oxford, Reg. No. 1965: 459.

໐ 4.2
Jerusalem (Kenyon). Reg. no. 3247. 45.36 grams.
Dome, pink limestone. 25 × 34.5 mm. PS: 'Mint'.
Context: Locus A.669.11a; cf. ໐ 1.1. Season 1963.
Notes: Scott explained this weight as the original Judaean norm from the days of Zedakiah because of its excellent state of preservation. There is no proof for this (see discussion in Chapter 1).
Literature: Scott 1965: 130; Dever 1970: Fig. 16; Scott 1985: 200 no. 36; Kletter 1991: 143 Table 3.2.
Location: 'Amman 1963'.

໐ 4.3
Jerusalem (Kenyon). Reg. no. 3245. 45.55 grams.
Dome, white and rose limestone. 24.5 × 34 mm. PS: Fair.
Context: Locus A.669.11a; cf. ໐ 4.2. Season 1963.
Literature: Scott 1965: 130; Dever 1970: Fig. 16; Scott 1985: 200 no. 38; Kletter 1991: 143 Table 3.3.
Location: Jerusalem, British School of Archaeology.

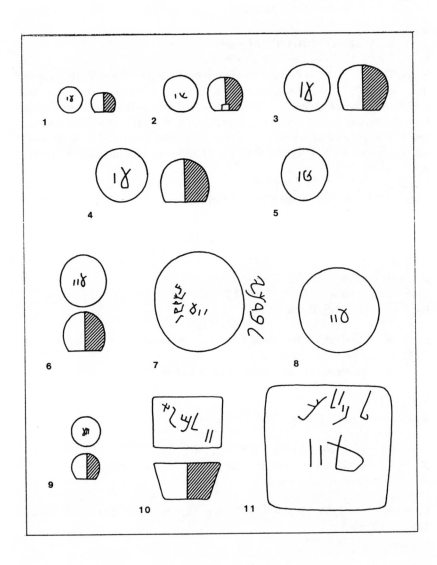

Figure 31. *Selection of 1–2 Shekel weights.* Legend: 1–5: 1 Shekel weights; 1 no. 2; 2. no. 3; 3. no. 8; 4. no. 14; 5. no. 25; 6–11: 2 Shekel weights; 6. no. 6; 7. no. 23; 8. no. 25; 9. no. 42; 10. no. a; 11. after Deutsch and Heltzer 1994: Fig. 32. Drawings not to scale (details are given in Appendices 1 and 2). The weights are referred to according to their catalogue numbers.

ℸ *4.4*
Jerusalem (Kenyon). Reg. no. 3244. 45.56 grams.
Dome, red limestone. 27.5 × 31.4 mm.
PS: Fair (Scott 1965) or very good (Scott 1985).
Notes: No photograph or drawing has been published.
Context: Locus A.669.34; cf. ℸ 1.1. Season 1963.
Literature: Scott 1965: 130; Dever 1970: Fig. 16; Scott 1985: 200 no. 39; Kletter 1991: 143 Table 3.4.
Location: Glasgow.

ℸ *4.5*
Jerusalem (Kenyon). Reg. no. 3245. 45.68 grams.
Dome, red limestone. 27.5 × 32 mm. PS: Fair.
Context: Locus K.15.17. Season 1962.
Literature: Scott 1965: 130; Dever 1970: Fig. 16; Scott 1985: 200 no. 40; Kletter 1991: 143 Table 3.5.
Location: Birmingham.

ℸ *4.6*
Jerusalem (Kenyon). Reg. no. 6776. 44.81 grams.
Dome, black-grey limestone. 27 × 33 mm. PS: Fair.
Context: Locus AA.305.13. Season 1967.
Literature: Scott 1985: 200 no. 34, Fig. 78.31; Kletter 1991: 143 Table 3.6.
Location: Romema, IAA no. 1974-567.

ℸ *4.7*
Jerusalem (Kenyon). Reg. no. 5628. 45.49 grams.
Dome, light-coloured limestone.
Context: Locus L.713.18. Season 1965.
Notes: No photograph or drawing has been published.
Literature: Scott 1985: 200 no. 37; Kletter 1991: 143 Table 3.7.
Location: St Andrews.

ℸ *4.8*
Jerusalem (Kenyon). Reg. no. 7495. 46.27 grams.
Dome, pink-grey limestone. 26 × 34 mm. PS: Very good.
Context: Locus L.16.24a. Season 1967.
Literature: Scott 1985: 200, no. 41, Fig. 79.2; Kletter 1991: 143 Table 3.8.
Location: Romema, IAA no. 1974-568.

ℸ *4.9*
Jerusalem (Kenyon). Reg. no. 3255. 43.19 grams.
Dome, white limestone.
Context: Locus A.669.34a; cf. ℸ 4.4. Season 1963.
Notes: The script is shallow, but the Shekel sign is clear. Part of the numeral can be

seen, and the weight indicates that it is 4 Shekel.
Literature: Scott 1985: 199 no. 28, Fig. 78.28; Kletter 1991: 143 Table 3.9.
Location: St Andrews.

ᵆ *4.10*
Jerusalem (Duncan). Weight not published.
Dome, brown limestone.
Context: Not published.
Notes: The weight was published in a preliminary form only. Duncan described the numeral as ━┥, and the photograph indeed shows this mark. It is perhaps the same as Eran 1996: W.207, reg. no. 50/4846).
Literature: Duncan 1931: 217 no. 5 Pl. next p. 218; Kletter 1991: 143 Table 3.10.
Location: London (?).

ᵆ *4.11* (Fig. 32.2)
Jerusalem (Shiloh). City of David. 46.22 grams.
Dome, limestone. Reg. 4793. 24.8 × 34.2 × 25.5 mm.
PS: Very good, tiny areas of encrustation.
Context: Area G, locus 778. Level 9, Persian period.
Literature: Shiloh 1981: Pl. 32 (photograph only); Kletter 1991: 143 Table 3.11; Eran 1996: W.169, Fig. 38: 12 Pl. 16.2.
Location: Hebrew University.

ᵆ *4.12*
Jerusalem (Guthe), Siloam Village. 46.00 grams.
Dome, limestone.
Context: Unknown. cf. ᵆ 2.12 (above).
Literature: Guthe 1882: 373 Pl. 10h; Dalman 1906: 93 Table; Bliss and Dickie 1898: 268; Viedebannt 1923: no. 8; Barrois 1932: 64 no. 9; Dever 1970: 177 Fig. 16; Kletter 1991: 143 Table 3: 12; Eran 1996: W.307.
Location: Unknown.

ᵆ *4.13*
Lachish. Reg. no. 18/51. 45.0953 grams.
Dome, limestone. 29 × 33 × 24 mm.
PS: Fair, a little damaged.
Context: Locus 3. Level II, 7th century BCE.
Literature: *HadArch* 20 (1967): 20-21; Y. Aharoni (ed.) 1975: 19-20 Pl. 17.3; Kletter 1991: 143 Table 3.13.
Location: Romema, IAA no. 1968-255.

ᵆ *4.14*
Lachish. Reg. no. 73/51. 45.949 grams.
Dome, limestone. 28 × 34 × 26 mm.
PS: Fair, a little damaged. Script: '┓ ᵆ ┣━'

Context: Locus 3 cf. weight no. 13 (above).
Notes: The script is exceptional in that there is another mark to the right of the ชื
(for a similar mark, cf. weight no. 10 above).
Literature: *HadArch* 20 (1967): 20-21; Y. Aharoni (ed.) 1975: 19-29 Pl. 17.7;
Kletter 1991: 143 Table 3.14.
Location: Romema, IAA no. 1968-256.

ชื *4.15* (Fig. 32.3)
Lachish. Reg. no. 114/51. 46.2722 grams.
Dome, limestone. 27.5 × 30 × 26 mm.
PS: Fair, a little damaged.
Context: Locus 3 cf. weight no. 13 (above).
Literature: *HadArch* 20 (1967): 20-21; Y. Aharoni (ed.) 1975: 19-29 Pl. 17.2;
Kletter 1991: 143 Table 3.15.
Location: Romema, IAA no. 1968-254.

ชื *4.16*
Lachish. Reg. no. 142/51. 44.8723 grams.
Dome, limestone. 27 × 31 × 24 mm. PS: Worn.
Context: Domestic?
Notes: The published photograph is not very good. The numeral is completely
worn, but the ชื is clear.
Literature: *HadArch* 20 (1967): 20; Y. Aharoni (ed.) 1975: 19-29 Pl. 17.6; Kletter
1991: 143 Table 3.16.
Location: Romema, IAA no. 1968-257.

ชื *4.17*
Ein Gedi. 44.31 (or 44.27) grams.
Dome, limestone. 22 × 32 mm.
Context: Level V, the northern slope of the site. Exact locus not published.
Notes: Another 4 Shekel weight was found nearby cf. no. 52 (addenda, below). The
weight was given by Hestrin as 44.31 grams.
Literature: *HadArch* 3 (1962): 6; B. Mazar *et al.* 1963: 37; Hestrin 1963: 103 no.
93; Stern 1963: 867 Table; Dever 1970: Fig. 16; Kletter 1991: 143 Table 3.16.
Location: Romema, IAA no. 1967-489.

ชื *4.18*
Aroer. Weight not published.
Dome, limestone.
Context: area A, upper level. Aroer flourished in the 7th century BCE, and the
weight is probably from this period.
Notes: This weight was probably mentioned also in *HadArch* 57–58 (1978): 38-39.
Another weight is mentioned in *HadArch* 63–64 (1977): 6-7.
Literature: *HadArch* 54–55 (1975): 27-28; Biran and Cohen 1975: Pl. 19a; 1978:

21; 1981: 263 Pl. 49.2; Kletter 1991: 143 Table 3.18.
Location: Hebrew University (?).

ℵ *4.19* (Fig. 32: 4)
Tel 'Ira. Reg. No. 4107/50. 45.53 grams. Season 1980.
Dome, pink limestone. 33 × 27 × 26 mm. PS: Excellent.
Context: Locus 510, a room in level VI, 7th century BCE.
Literature: Courtesy of I. Beit Arieh; Beit Arieh 1985: 23-24; Kletter 1991: 143
Table 3.19.
Location: Tel Aviv University.

ℵ *4.20*
Tel 'Ira. Reg. No. 2126/50. 44.2518 grams.
Dome, white limestone. 33 × 24 × 26 mm.
PS: Damaged and partly peeled off. The numeral is now missing.
Context: Locus 330, a room in level VI, 7th century BCE.
Literature: Beit Arieh 1985: 23-24; Kletter 1991: 143 Table 3.20.
Location: Tel Aviv University.

ℵ *4.21*
Arad. Reg. No. 7702/50. 45.866 grams.
Dome, light brown limestone.
Context: Locus 952, a room in the (late) casemate wall in the north of the fortress
(Y. Aharoni 1981: General map). Square J/16, height 74.95 m. The pottery from
this room is not yet published (except one jar; Herzog *et al.* 1984: Fig. 25). Level
VII, 7th century BCE.
Notes: For the date, cf. ℵ 1.6 (above).
Literature: M. Aharoni 1981: 126-27 no. 6; Kletter 1991: 143 Table 3.21.
Location: IAA or the Hebrew University (?).

ℵ *4.22*
Arad. Reg. No. D66/2. 45.806 grams.
Dome, grey limestone.
Context: Locus 607, the (late) casemate wall in the west of the fortress (Y. Aharoni
1981: General map). Square E/13, height 75.40 m. Level VI, 7th century BCE.
Notes: For the date, cf. ℵ 1.6 (above). Stern and Dever list a weight of 45.10 from
Arad. I assume that it is the same as weight no. 21 (above).
Literature: M. Aharoni 1981: 126-27 no. 7; Kletter 1991: 143 Table 3.22.
Location: IAA no. 1964-313, exhibited in the script department, the Israel Museum,
Jerusalem.

ℵ *4.23*
Tel Beer Sheba. Reg. No. 7602/50. 46.6552 grams.
Dome, limestone.
Context: Locus 808, square L/8, height 2.07 m. It is part of a four-roomed house

(Y. Aharoni [ed.] 1973: Plan 84). Level II, 8th century BCE.
Literature: Y. Aharoni (ed.) 1973: 135 Pl. 39.2; Kletter 1991: 143 Table 3.23.
Location: Not clear.

Ȣ 4.24
Ekron. Details not yet published.
Context: Domestic area, level I, 7th century BCE.
Notes: This weight is mentioned briefly in a preliminary report as '5 Shekel' (Gitin 1989: 51). This may mean the Hieratic sign 5, or a mistake (but it is stated to be an inscribed weight).
Literature: Gitin 1989: 51; Kletter 1991: 144 Table 3c.
Location: Hebrew University (?).
Notes:This is not equal to the weight in Kletter 1991: 143 Table 3.24, which was believed to be an inscribed 4 Shekel from Malhata (but is, in fact, an uninscribed 8 Shekel weight, reg. no. 2006/50, 86.3980 grams).

Ȣ 4.25
Azeka. 45.50 grams.
Dome, red limestone.
Context: Not clear. Azeka existed both in the 8th century BCE (Bliss and Macalister 1902: 20 Pl. 56 for many *lmlk* stamps) and later (cf. Jer. 33.7, ostracon 4 from Macalister 1912 and rosette seal impressions from Azeka—Bliss and Macalister 1902: Pl. 56).
Literature: Bliss and Macalister 1902: 145 Fig. 58; Viedebannt 1923: no. 7; Barrois 1932: 64 no. 6; Stern 1963: 867 Table A; Dever 1970: Fig. 16; Kletter 1991: 143 Table 3.25.
Location: Not clear.

Ȣ 4.26
Azeka. 44.60 grams.
Dome, white limestone.
Context: Not clear cf. weight no. 25 (above).
Notes: A drawing of the weight has not been published, only of the script.
Literature: Bliss and Macalister 1902: 145 Fig. 58; Viedebannt 1923: no. 6; Barrois 1932: 64 no. 7; Stern 1963: 867; Yadin 1960: Table; Dever 1970: Fig. 16; Kletter 1991: 143 Table 3.26.
Location: Not clear.

Ȣ 4.27
Kh. el-Kom. 44.57 grams.
Dome, white limestone. PS: Excellent.
Context: Not clear. The weight was not found in scientific excavations, and even the origin is not certain (cf. Ȣ 2.19 above).
Notes: The Hieratic numeral is upside down.

Literature: Dever 1970: 176 Fig. 15.2 Pl. 9.2; Kletter 1991: 143 Table 3.27.
Location: Not clear.

४ 4.28

Tel Jemmeh. Reg. no. 5559. 46.60 grams (my weighing 46.569 grams).
Dome, white-pink limestone. PS: Very good.
Context: BV.192, an open area outside one of the large buildings of Petrie's '26th dynasty' city (Petrie 1928: Pl. 11). The building was called by him 'residency' (the late Greek pottery found in it is probably intrusive (Petrie 1928: 8). For the date, cf. ४ 2.14.
Notes: The numeral appears to the right of the ४.
Literature: Petrie 1928: Pl. 17.54; Barrois 1932: 64 no. 10; Stern 1963: 867; Dever 1970: Fig. 17; Eshel 1978: 251 Pl. 15.28; Kletter 1991: 143 Table 3.28.
Location: PEF collection, London.

४ 4.29

Tel Batash. Reg. no. 6160. 43.00 grams.
Dome, limestone (?).
Context: Level II, 7th century BCE.
Notes: The publication is preliminary.
Literature: A. Maza 1985: 320; Kletter 1991: 143 Table 3.29.
Location: Hebrew University.

४ 4.30

Mesad Hashavyahu. 44.82 grams.
Dome, limestone. 27 × 35 × 30 mm.
Context: Mesad Hashavyahu is a one-period site of the late 7th or early 6th century BCE (Reich 1989; Wenning 1989, with references).
Literature: Naveh 1962: 31 Pl. 6d; Stern 1963: 867 Table A; Dever 1970: Fig. 16; Kletter 1991: 143 Table 3.30.
Location: IAA 1960-56, at the Israel Museum, Jerusalem.

४ 4.31

Gibeon. Reg. no. 257. 51.58 grams.
Dome, limestone (?). 27 × 35 × 29 mm.
PS: The weight is cracked, probably by fire.
Context: The public pool, depth 2.1–3 m. The date of the pool is probably 8th–7th centuries BCE, evidenced by many *lmlk* impressions, but also rosette impressions and pottery typical of the 7th century BCE (*mortaria* bowls, elongated 'carrot' bottles and high-based lamps; Pritchard 1961: pls. 33.7-10, 34.14, 38.7; cf. also the mentioning of the city in Jer. 28.1; 41.12).
Notes: Pritchard (1958: Fig. 24) stated that the weight was made of clay. This is strange, since the size is only slightly larger than the limestone 4 Shekel weights, but the weight is heavier (while clay is lighter; cf. also Pym.20). The heavy weight was explained by Pritchard as a different Shekel standard.

Literature: Pritchard 1958: Fig. 24; 1959: 29 Fig. 12.6-7; Yadin 1960: Table; Stern 1963: 867 Table, 870; Dever 1970: Fig. 16; Kletter 1991: 143 Table 3.31.
Location: Princeton University Museum.

ᕍ 4.32
Kh. Umm el Biara. 42.46 grams.
Dome, limestone. Diameter 35 mm.
Context: Area A.XXI, season 1963. Iron Age, but the exact date is not clear. Bennett thought that it is an export from Judah, by a merchant or traveller.
Literature: Bennett 1966: 395 Pl. 24b; Kletter 1991: 144 Table 3.32.
Location: Jordan (?).

ᕍ 4.33
Site unknown. 45.99 grams.
Dome, limestone.
Notes: Cf. weight ᕍ 2.26.
Literature: Spaer 1982: 251 Pl. 41a; Kletter 1991: 144 Table 3.33.
Location: Private collection.

ᕍ 4.34
Site unknown. 44.89 grams.
Dome, pink limestone. PS: Slightly worn.
Context: The weight was bought in Jerusalem, probably through Hebronite middlemen. The origin in Kh. el-Kom possible but not certain (versus Dever 1970: 174).
Literature: Dever 1970: Fig. 15.1 Pl. 9.1; Kletter 1991: 144 Table 3.34.
Location: Not clear.

ᕍ 4.35
Site unknown. 45.47 grams.
Dome, limestone. 22.5 × 32 × 28 mm. PS: Good.
Literature: Lemaire 1976: 33 Pl. 1.1; Kletter 1991: 144 Table 3.35.
Location: Private collection.

ᕍ 4.36
Site unknown. Museum no. 5042. 46.662 grams.
Dome, limestone. 25 × 33 × 27.5 mm. PS: Good.
Literature: Lemaire 1976: no. 19 Pl. 2.19; Kletter 1991: 144 Table 3.36.
Location: Bible et Terre Sainte Museum, Paris.

ᕍ 4.37
Site unknown. Museum no. 5060. 46.139 grams.
Dome, limestone. 25 × 34 × 25 mm. PS: Good.
Literature: Lemaire 1976: no. 20; Kletter 1991: 144 Table 3.37.
Location: Bible et Terre Sainte Museum, Paris.

ﬡ *4.38* (Fig. 32: 5)
Site unknown. Museum no. 5043. 45.383 grams.
Dome, limestone. 25 × 34 × 25 mm. PS: Very good.
Notes: The base carries the picture of a man with small hand-scales. On the sides of this, there is the inscription 'ﾔ ﾡ'. A photograph was published only recently by Briend (1992).
Literature: Scott 1971: 128; Lemaire 1976: no. 21 Pl. 2.21; Kletter 1991: 144 Table 3.38; Briend 1992: 38 Fig. 34, 2nd right.
Location: Bible et Terre Sainte Museum, Paris.

ﬡ *4.39*
Site unknown. 45.55 grams.
Dome, pink limestone.
Literature: Agora 1975: no. 386; Kletter 1991: 144 Table 3.39.
Location: Private collection.

ﬡ *4.40*
Site unknown. 44.94 grams.
Dome, limestone. 26 × 34 mm.
Literature: Qedar 1978: no. 19; Kletter 1991: 144 Table 3.40.
Location: Not clear.

ﬡ *4.41*
Site unknown. 45.77 grams.
Dome, limestone. 26 × 35 × 32 mm.
Notes: There is another line engraved on the dome.
Literature: Qedar 1979: 25 no. 4040; Kletter 1991: 144 Table 3.41.
Location: Not clear.

ﬡ *4.42*
Site unknown. 44.10 grams.
Dome, red limestone. 26 × 34 mm.
Literature: Qedar 1979: 25 no. 4045; Kletter 1991: 144 Table 3.42.
Location: Not clear.

ﬡ *4.43*
Site unknown. 45.50 grams.
Dome, red-white limestone. 24 × 35 mm.
Notes: The photograph in the catalogue is upside-down. The numeral is to the right of the Shekel mark.
Literature: Qedar 1983: 24 no. 5061; Kletter 1991: 144 Table 3.43.
Location: Not clear.

ﬡ *4.44*
Site unknown. 44.77 grams.

Dome, red-brown limestone. 25.3 × 32.7 mm.

Notes: According to the size, it is not the same as no. 55 (addenda, below).

Literature: Kroha (ed.) 1980: no. 64; Kletter 1991: 144 Table 3.44.

Location: not clear.

४ 4.45

Site unknown. 46.89 grams.

Dome, red limestone. 2.5 × 30 mm.

Notes: The photograph in the catalogue is upside-down. The numeral is to the right of the Shekel mark.

Literature: Meshorer in press: no. 25; Kletter 1991: 144 Table 3.45.

Location: Hecht Museum, Haifa, H-658 (?).

४ 4.46

Site unknown. 44.51 grams.

Dome, limestone. PS: A little damaged.

Literature: Meshorer in press: no. 26; Kletter 1991: 144 Table 3.46.

Location: Hecht Museum, Haifa, H-658 (?).

४ 4.47

Site unknown. 45.45 grams.

Cubic, bronze. 17 × 21 × 21 mm. PS: Good.

Notes: The material and the shape are exceptional. The origin is unknown. I have not included this weight in the statistical calculations of averages.

Literature: Qedar 1983: no. 5060; Kletter 1991: 144 Table 3.47.

Location: Private collection.

४ 4.a

Site unknown. 43.86 grams.

Shallow dome, bronze. 13.5 × 27 mm.

Notes: The shape is squat, but it is definitely a weight. The marks are exceptional: ⅃. It is probably the numeral 5 in Hieratic, with another, problematic, sign.

Literature: Qedar 1978: 11; Kletter 1991: 144 Table 3.a.

Location: Private collection.

४ 4.b

Jerusalem (Duncan).

Limestone vessel, rectangular.

Notes: This is a stone vessel that has a depression (for measuring liquids or paste?). It is inscribed 4४. Duncan thought that it was a small altar (without clear reasons for this). Scales are more versatile for measuring weight, so perhaps the vessel had some use for smelting (?).

Literature: Duncan 1931: Pl. next to p. 228; Kletter 1991: 144 Table 3.b.

Location: PEF London (?).

* breve 8 Weights*

** breve 8.1**

Jerusalem (Duncan?). 87.84 grams

Dome, limestone. 35 × 41 mm.

Context: Not clear.

Literature: Duncan 1931: Pl. next to p. 218, no. 13 (88 grams)?; Rockefeller 1940: 43 no. 497; Hestrin 1963: 103 no. 94; Meshorer 1976: 54 upper left; Kletter 1991: 144 Table 4.1.

Location: Rockefeller, no. S.2672.

breve 8.2

Jerusalem (Duncan). c. 89 grams.

Dome, limestone.

Context: Duncan's excavations, 1927.

Literature: Duncan 1931: Pl. next to p. 218, no. 14; Kletter 1991: 144 Table 4.2.

Location: Probably PEF, London, no. 0.1229 (47, E-9). The colour is light brown-yellow. PS: Very good, except small damages. The numeral is not clear.

breve 8.3

Jerusalem (Kenyon). Reg. no. 3762. 88.93 grams

Dome, red-brown limestone. 36 × 41 mm.

PS: Fair–poor. Season 1964.

Context: Locus A.678.1; cf. weight breve 1.1 (above).

Literature: Scott 1965: 138-39; 1985: 200 no. 43, Fig. 79.5; Kletter 1991: 144 Table 4.3.

Location: Glasgow.

breve 8.4

Jerusalem (Kenyon). Reg. no. 3259. 89.33 grams

Dome, pink-brown limestone. 31.5 × 42.5 mm.

PS: Bad. Season 1963.

Context: Locus A.669.11.a; cf. weight breve 1.1 (above).

Literature: Scott 1965: 130; 1985: 200 no. 50 (89.31 grams); Kletter 1991: 144 Table 4.4.

Location: 'Amman 1963'.

breve 8.5

Jerusalem (Kenyon). Reg. no. 3256. 89.52 grams

Dome, red-brown limestone. 32.5 × 40.5 mm.

PS: Fair-poor. Season 1963.

Context: Locus A.669.34; cf. weight breve 1.1 (above).

Literature: Scott 1965: 130; 1985: 200, no. 51; Kletter 1991: 144 Table 4.5.

Location: Birmingham.

ℵ *8.6*
Jerusalem (Kenyon). Reg. no. 3250. 90.07 grams
Dome, white-brown calcite. 30.5 × 43.5 mm.
PS: Fair. Season 1963.
Context: Locus A.669.11.a; cf. weight ℵ 1.1 (above).
Literature: Scott 1965: 130; 1985: 200 no. 52; Kletter 1991: 144 Table 4.6.
Location: Ecole Biblique, Jerusalem.

ℵ *8.7*
Jerusalem (Kenyon). Reg. no. 3728. 91.88 grams
Dome, white-cream limestone. 31.5 × 41.5 mm.
PS: Poor. Season 1964.
Context: Locus A.677.3; cf. weight ℵ 1.1 (above).
Literature: Scott 1965: 138; 1985: 200 no. 53, Fig. 79.6; Kletter 1991: 145 Table 4.7.
Location: IAA no. 68-856.

ℵ *8.8*
Jerusalem (Kenyon). Reg. no. 3260. 92.79 grams
Dome, white-cream limestone. 36 × 42 mm.
PS: Fair, slightly damaged. Season 1963.
Context: Locus A.669.11.a; cf. weights ℵ 1.1, ℵ 8.6 (above).
Literature: Scott 1965: 131; 1985: 201 no. 54, Fig. 79.4; Kletter 1991: 145 Table 4.8.
Location: ROM, Toronto.

ℵ *8.9*
Jerusalem (Kenyon). Reg. no. 7513. 86.80 grams
Dome, dark grey limestone. Season 1967.
Context: Locus L.14.34. It is a mixed, late assemblage (though called 'early Jewish').
Literature: Scott 1985: 203 no. 89; Kletter 1991: 145 Table 4.9.
Location: Israel (IAA?).

ℵ *8.10*
Jerusalem (Bliss and Dickie). 90.8519 grams.
Dome, limestone.
Context: It was found deep in the Tyropoeon valley, but exact location and date are not clear (for the area, and its Iron Age remains, cf. G. Barkay 1985; *HadArch* 77 [1981]: 26).
Notes: According to Yadin and Stern, the weight is 90 grams.
Literature: Bliss and Dickie 1898: 267-68; Viedebannt 1923: no. 9; Barrois 1932: 64, no. 13; Kletter 1991: 145 Table 4.10; Eran 1996: W.310.
Location: Probably PEF, London. It has an inscription on the base: '2.92 oglroy found in Tyropoeon valley, 1894-7, R267'. I saw only a cast in London. It has a

very high dome, and seems to be a little damaged (c. 40 × 32 × 25 mm).

୪ 8.11
Jerusalem (Crowfoot). 90.5 grams.
Dome, limestone.
Context: It was found in room 47 in the Tyropoeon valley, in a very mixed level (with remains from the Early Bronze to the Hellenistic periods. Iron Age remains are clear, Crowfoot and Fitzgerald 1929: 67 Pls. 10–11).
Literature: Crowfoot and Fitzgerald 1929: 101; Barrois 1932: 64 no. 12; Kletter 1991: 145 Table 4.11; Eran 1996: W.237.
Location: Probably PEF, London. I saw only a cast (c. 43 × 35 × 33 mm).

୪ 8.12
Lachish. Reg. no. 1512. 88.8645 grams.
Dome, grey limestone. 29 × 41 × 34.5 mm.
PS: Fair, but worn and damaged on the base. Remains of burn on the dome.
Context: Locus D/X, i.e. a surface find, or from unidentified stratigraphy (Diringer 1953: 349).
Notes: On the weight is written: 'wall, NE side'.
Literature: Diringer 1942: 92 no. 6; 1953: no. 7 Pl. 51.7; Moscati 1951: 104 no. 16; Stern 1963: 867 Table; Yadin 1960: Table; Kletter 1991: 145 Table 4.12.
Location: Lachish collection, British Museum, London.

୪ 8.13 (Fig. 32.7)
Lachish. Reg. no. 5261. 91.055 grams.
Dome, light brown limestone. c. 37 × 38 × 33 mm.
PS: Good, but slightly worn.
Context: Locus Q.12.106, the central court of the Persian period 'sun temple' (Tufnell 1953: 141, Plan 21). In the same room was found a rosette impression (handle). The weight was registered from a height lower than the floor; thus probably belonged to the Iron Age level underneath the temple (level II, 7th century BCE).
Literature: Diringer 1942: no. 5 Pl. 13.5; 1953: no. 5 Pl. 51.4; Moscati 1951: 101 no. 14; Stern 1963: 867 Table; Yadin 1960: Table; Kletter 1991: 145 Table 4.13.
Location: Lachish collection, British Museum, London.

୪ 8.14
Lachish. Reg. no. 1491a. 91.115 grams.
Dome, limestone. 33 × 39 mm.
Context: Locus E.14. Pal. East Wall—a whole square and the eastern wall of the palace (Tufnell 1953: Plan 119).
Literature: Diringer 1942: no. 4 Pl. 13.4; 1953: no. 4, pls. 50.3, 51.5; Moscati 1951: 104 no. 13; Stern 1963: Table; Yadin 1960: Table; Kletter 1991: 145 Table 4.14.
Location: British Museum, no. 132826.

ﻙ *8.15*
Lachish. Reg. no. 1491. 91.43 grams.
Dome, limestone. 29 × 40 × 35.6 mm.
Context: Locus K.14. Pal. East. Wall, a whole square east of the palace. (cf. weight no. 14 above).
Literature: Diringer 1942: no. 3 Pl. 13.3; 1953: no. 3 Pl. 51.3; Moscati 1951: 104 no. 12; Stern 1963: 867 Table; Yadin 1960: Table; Kletter 1991: 145 Table 4.15.
Location: Not clear.

ﻙ *8.16*
Lachish. Reg. no. 6794. 91.985 grams.
Dome, limestone. 31 × 40 × 35 mm.
Context: Locus L.14.1061, part of a pavement from levels III–II east of the palace (Tufnell 1953: 117 Plan 116). *Lmlk* jars and handles indicate the use of this locus in the 8th century BCE. Continuation into the 7th century BCE is possible.
Literature: Diringer 1942: no. 2 Pl. 13.2; 1953: no. 2 Pl. 51.2; Moscati 1951: 104 no. 15; Stern 1963: 867 Table 5; Yadin 1960: Table; Kletter 1991: 145 Table 4.16.
Location: Not clear.

ﻙ *8.17*
Lachish. Reg. no. 6156. 92.465 grams.
Dome, brown-grey limestone. 36 × 40 × 27 mm.
PS: Very good.
Context: Locus D/X; cf. weight no. 12 above.
Literature: Diringer 1942: no. 1 Pl. 1.1; 1953: no. 1 Pl. 51: 1; Moscati 1951: 104 no. 11; Stern 1963: 867 Table; Yadin 1960: Table; Kletter 1991: 145 Table 4.17.
Location: Lachish collection, British Museum, 160029.

ﻙ *8.18*
Lachish. Reg. no. 48/51. 91.7343 grams.
Dome, limestone. 35 × 31 mm (in the museum's card).
Context: Locus 3, level II, 7th century BCE.
Literature: *HadArch* 20 (1967): 20-21 (Hebrew); Y. Aharoni (ed.) 1975: 19-20 Pl. 17.1; Kletter 1991: 145 Table 4.18.
Location: IAA, no. 68-258.

ﻙ *8.19*
Lachish. Reg. no. 56/51. 91.1327 grams.
Dome, limestone. 35 × 35 mm.
Context: Locus 3, level II, 7th century BCE.
Literature: *HadArch* 20 [1967]: 20-21; Y. Aharoni (ed.) 1975: 19-20 Pl. 17.5; Kletter 1991: 145 Table 4.19.
Location: IAA, no. 68-253.

ᵡ *8.20*

Ramat Rahel. 90.80 grams.

Dome, limestone.

Context: Level IV (other details not clear). It is a very disturbed level, mostly pits with mixed finds from the Persian to the Roman periods.

Literature: Y. Aharoni 1956: 138-39 Pl. 1.9; Stern 1963: 867 Table A; Yadin 1960: Table; Kletter 1991: 145 Table 4.20.

Location: Not clear.

ᵡ *8.21*

Ramat Rahel. 92.28 grams.

Dome, limestone.

Context: Locus 324, square X20. It is a court in the Israelite fort, level V (Y. Aharoni [ed.] 1962: Plan 22). This level is from the 7th–early 6th centuries BCE.

Literature: Y. Aharoni (ed.) 1962: 14 Pl. 10: 2; Y. Aharoni 1960: 44 n 88 Pl. 7.12; Stern 1963: 867 Table A; Kletter 1991: 145 Table 4.21.

Location: Not clear.

ᵡ *8.22*

Ein Gedi. Reg. no. 3492 (?). 88.30 grams.

Dome, grey limestone with red veins. 40 × 34 mm.

Context: The weight was related to buildings of level V in the north slope of the site. Exact details are not clear. The level was dated the 7th–6th centuries BCE, but possibly began earlier, in the 8th century BCE..

Literature: *HadArch* 3 (1963): 6; B. Mazar *et al.* 1963; 8-9, Stern 1963: 867 Table A; Kletter 1991: 145 Table 4.22.

Location: Probably IAA no. 67-488, exhibited in the script section of the Israel Museum, Jerusalem.

ᵡ *8.23*

Arad. Reg. no. 55/1. 90.15 grams.

Dome, grey limestone.

Context: Square K.16 in the north of the fort, locus 21. The weight was dated to level VII, 7th century BCE (cf. weight ᵡ 1.6 above)

Literature: M. Aharoni 1981: 126-27 no. 8; Kletter 1991: 145 Table 4.23.

Location: Not clear.

ᵡ *8.24*

Arad. Reg. no. 5602/51. 89.751 grams.

Dome, white limestone.

Context: Locus 779, square L.9, level VI (height 75.45 m). It is part of the 'Elyashiv house', where the famous archive was found. Probably levels VII and VI are the same level, but this does not matter for the dating—7th century BCE (cf. weight ᵡ 1.6).

Notes: the numeral is peculiar, and is to the right of the Shekel sign: ४ ⊢.
Literature: M. Aharoni 1981: 126-27 no. 9; Kletter 1991: 145 Table 4.24.
Location: IAA 67-632, exhibited in the Israel Museum, Jerusalem.

४ 8.25

Arad. Reg. no. 5689. 90.51 grams.
Dome, white limestone. Height 75.30 m.
Context: Locus 779, square L.9, level VI (cf. weight no. 24 above).
Literature: M. Aharoni 1981: 126-27, no. 10; Kletter 1991: 145 Table 4.25.
Location: Eretz Israel Museum, Tel Aviv, probably no. K-71926.

४ 8.26

Arad. Reg. no. D25/1. 92.725 grams.
Dome, grey limestone. Height 75.10 m. PS: A little damaged
Context: Locus 605, square E.13, level VI. It is a room of the western casemate
wall. 7th century BCE.
Notes: According to the museum's records, the weight is 94.65 grams.
Literature: M. Aharoni 1981: 126-27, no. 11; Kletter 1991: 145 Table 4.26.
Location: Israel Museum, Jerusalem (script section), no. 17.

४ 8.27

Tel el-Far'ah (south). Reg. no. 5640. 89.942 grams.
Dome, limestone.
Context: Only the script on this weight was published. There was perhaps no
settlement at the site during the 7th century BCE (Petrie 1930; Macdonald 1932,
without indicative pottery of this period; but versus Eshel 1986: 358-59).
Notes: Petrie explained this weight as 8 *koirine*. The weight was forgotten, and not
mentioned in most of the studies (except Barrois 1932).
Literature: Petrie 1930: Pl. 49 (1388 grains); Barrois 1932: 64 no. 11; Kletter 1991:
145 Table 4.27.
Location: Not clear.

४ 8.28

Tel el-Far'ah (south). Reg. no. 5646. 94.485 grams.
Dome, limestone.
Context: Locus C.390, level C. This level was dated to the Egyptian 21–22nd
dynasties (Macdonald 1932: Pls. 80–81; Petrie 1930: Pl. 59). The absolute height of
the weight, however, is too great, and better matches the 'Greek' level B. The date
within the Iron Age period is therefore not certain.
Literature: Petrie 1930: Pl. 49 (1458.1 grains); Barrois 1932: 64 no. 12; Kletter
1991: 145 Table 4.28.
Location: Not clear.

४ 8.29

Tel 'Ira. Reg. no. 4113/50. 85.45 grams. Season 1980.

Dome, pink limestone. 42 × 30 × 31 mm.
PS: Very good. The numeral is written 'left to right'
Context: Locus 510, area E. Probably 7th century BCE.
Literature: *HadArch* 74-75 (1980); Kletter 1991: 145 Table 4.29.
Location: Tel Aviv University.

४ *8.30*

Tel 'Ira. Reg. no. 5166a/50. 91.2541 grams.
Dome, pink limestone with purple veins. 42 × 31 × 33 mm.
PS: Good, but a few scratches. The ४ sign can hardly be seen.
Context: Locus 844. Probably 7th century BCE.
Literature: *HadArch* 74–75 (1980); Kletter 1991: 145 Table 4.30.
Location: Tel Aviv University.

४ *8.31*

Tel Batash. Reg. no. 9422. 91.2 grams.
Context: Level II, 7th century BCE.
Literature: A. Mazar 1985: 320; Kletter 1991: 145 Table 4.31.
Location: Hebrew University, Jerusalem.

४ *8.32*

Tel Batash. Reg. no. 9732. 91.16 grams.
Context: Level II, 7th century BCE.
Literature: A. Mazar 1985: 320; Kletter 1991: 145 Table 4.32.
Location: Hebrew University, Jerusalem.

४ *8.33*

Tel ej-Judeideh (Goded). 93.0 grams.
Context: Not clear.
Notes: The numeral is written left to right. Tel Goded is often identified as Moreshet Gat (cf. now Mittmann 1992), which is mentioned in 7th-century-BCE sources (Mic. 1.1, Jer. 26.18). This identification has not been proved and cannot be used for dating the weight, since the site was settled during the 8th century BCE as well (37 *lmlk* impressions).
Literature: Bliss and Macalister 1902: 146; Viedebannt 1923: no. 13; Barrois 1932: 64 no. 15; Stern 1963: Table; Yadin 1960: Table; Kletter 1991: 145 Table 4.33.
Location: PEF, London (?). There is an 8 Shekel weight there from the same site (no. 50/4852), with reference to Bliss and Macalister 1902: 146 no. 6, but only the Shekel sign appears on it and it is grey in colour.

४ *8.34*

Gezer. 94.60 grams.
Dome, quartzite.
Context: Not clear; it was found together with a Greek weight of the 3rd century BCE, close to the surface (Macalister 1908: 282).

Literature: Macalister 1908: 281; 1912: 286; Viedebannt 1923: 12; Barrois 1932: 64 no. 14; Stern 1963: 867; Yadin 1960: Table; Kletter 1991: 145 Table 4.34.
Location: Unknown, perhaps Istanbul.

℧ 8.35
Gezer. 91.47 grams.
Dome, white-yellow limestone. c. $40 \times 33 \times 29$ mm. PS: Excellent.
Context: Not clear; allegedly from the 'Maccabaean level'.
Notes: This weight was forgotten, since it was not mentioned in the final report (Macalister 1912).
Literature: Macalister 1904b: 359-60; Viedebannt 1923: no. 10; Barrois 1932: 64 no. 14; Kletter 1991: 145 Table 4.35.
Location: PEF, London.

℧ 8.36
Site unknown. 88.80 grams.
Dome, red-brown limestone. 35×41 mm.
Notes: Only the Shekel sign is seen in the published photograph.
Literature: Qedar 1978: no. 18; Kletter 1991: 146 Table 4.36.
Location: Private collection.

℧ 8.37
Site unknown. 91.15 grams.
Dome, limestone. 36×40 mm.
Notes: The base is indented, to fix the weight (?).
Literature: Qedar 1981: no. 71; Kletter 1991: 146 Table 4.37.
Location: Private collection.

℧ 8.38
Site unknown. 93.96 grams.
Dome, grey limestone. 32×44 mm.
Notes: The numeral sign is exceptional.
Literature: Kroha (ed.) 1980: no. 60; Kletter 1991: 146 Table 4.38.
Location: Private collection.

℧ 8.39
Site unknown. 90.7 grams.
Dome, white limestone. 35.5×40.3 mm.
Notes: The numeral sign is exceptional.
Literature: Kroha (ed.) 1980: no. 61; Kletter 1991: 146 Table 4.39.
Location: Private collection.

℧ 8.40
Site unknown. 92.90 grams.
Dome, limestone. 31×42 mm (?).

Literature: Meshorer in press: no. 22; Kletter 1991: 146 Table 4.40.
Location: Hecht Museum, Haifa, no. H-733 (?).

४ 8.41
Site unknown. 86.87 grams.
Dome, limestone.
Literature: Meshorer in press: no. 23; Kletter 1991: 146 Table 4.41.
Location: Hecht Museum, Haifa. H-1482 (?).

४ 8.42
Site unknown. 86.82 grams.
Dome, limestone.
Literature: Meshorer in press: no. 24; Kletter 1991: 146 Table 4.42.
Location: Hecht Museum, Haifa (perhaps H-176, but this may be an uninscribed weight).

४ 8.a
Site unknown. 91.05 grams.
Dome, yellow limestone. 35 × 41 mm.
Notes: Only the Shekel sign appears on this weight.
Literature: Qedar 1979: no. 24; Kletter 1991: 146 Table 4.a.
Location: Private hands.

४ 8.b
Site unknown. 91.40 grams.
Dome, grey limestone. 34 × 42 mm.
Notes: Only the Shekel sign appears on this weight.
Literature: Qedar 1979: no. 25; Kletter 1991: 146 Table 4.b.
Location: Private collection.

४ 12–40 Weights

४ 12.1 (Fig. 33.1)
Site unknown. 129.45 grams.
Dome, grey limestone. 38 × 45 mm. PS: Fair.
Notes: Kroha explained it as 12 Shekel, according to its weight, but missed the meaning of the script (which he read as ' Γ Ι ४'). It seems that there is another line in the central sign, ↖, thus the two signs are Hieratic 5 + 10 (5 is either damaged or 'left to right'). As for all other Shekel weights (in units heavier than 2 Shekel), this should be read as 12.

It is the only weight known of this unit, so far, and is unlikely to be a forgery. It leads to the calculation of 1 Shekel = 10.787 grams, but one must remember the far from excellent preservation state.
Literature: Kroha 1980: no. 59.
Location: Not clear.

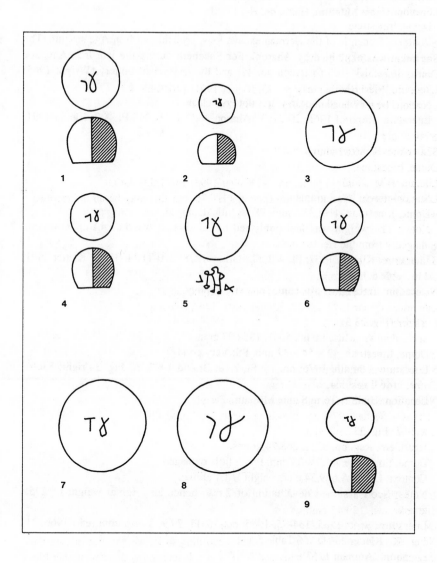

Figure 32. *Selection of 4–8 Shekel weights*. Legend 1–6: 4 Shekel weights. 1. no. 1; 2. no. 11; 3. no. 15; 4. no. 19; 5. no. 38 with drawing on base; 6. no. 50. 7–9: 8 Shekel weights. 7. no. 13; 8. no. 46; 9. no. 51. Drawings not to scale (details are given in Appendices 1 and 2). The weights are referred to according to their catalogue numbers.

ȣ *16.1*
Shechem. 188.5 grams.
Dome, limestone.
Context: Trench R of the German excavations, probably an Iron Age stratum. The
numeral was explained by Aharoni. For Shechem during the late Iron Age, see
Jaros 1976: 104-105 (ostracon no. 44) and the 'Assyrian' pottery (Wright 1965:
164-66; 1978: 1093).
Notes: The published photograph is not very clear.
Literature: Kerkhof 1966: 20-21; Y. Aharoni (ed.) 1966: 313 Pl. A.2; Kletter 1991:
146 Table 5.2.
Location: Rijksmuseum, Leiden.

ȣ *16.2* (Fig. 33.2)
Site unknown. 180.2 grams.
Dome, limestone. 41 × 37.5 mm. PS: A little damaged.
Notes: The weight was first published by Kindler. It was bought in Jerusalem,
allegedly from the Hebron area.
Literature: Kindler 1967: Pl. A.2; G. Barkay 1978: 210-11 Pl. 33c-d; Kletter 1991:
146 Table 5.3.
Location: Eretz Israel Museum, Tel Aviv, K-8899.

ȣ *16.3* (Fig. 33.3)
Site unknown. Museum no. 5041. 185.607 grams.
Dome, limestone. 42 × 54 × 37 mm. PS: Very good.
Literature: Lemaire 1976: no. 18. Pl. 2.18; Briend 1992: 38 Fig. 34 right; Kletter
1991: 146 Table 5.4.
Location: Bible et Terre Sainte Museum, Paris.

ȣ *24.1* (Fig. 33.5)
Jerusalem. Reg. no. 3257. 268.24 grams.
Dome, limestone. 44.5 × 63 mm. PS: A little damaged.
Context: Locus A.669.34a; cf. weight ȣ 1.1 above.
Notes: Scott assumed devaluation of 2.6%, hence an original weight of 275.4
grams.
Literature: Scott 1965: 134-35; 1985: no. 56, Pl. 79.9; Y. Aharoni (ed.) 1966: 313
Fig. 3.3; Kletter 1991: 146 Table 5.5.
Location: 'Amman 1963'.

ȣ *24.2*
Site unknown. 280.42 grams.
Dome, limestone. 55 × 56 mm. PS: Damaged.
Notes: According to the museum's record, the weight is 280.125 grams.
Literature: Meshorer in press: no. 21; Kletter 1991: 146 Table 5.6.
Location: Hecht Museum, Haifa H-294.

 y *40.1* (Fig. 33.6)
Jerusalem. Reg. no. S.2671. 454.55 grams.
Dome, white limestone. 59 × 71 mm.
Context: Duncan's excavations, exact details unknown.
Notes: Duncan (1931: 218) suggested that the numeral is the Hieratic 5. Scott explained it as 40 Shekel according to its weight; but Aharoni was the first to understand the numeral.
Literature: Duncan 1931: 216-17, no. 4, Pl. no. 25; Rockefeller Museum 1940: 43 no. 498; Hestrin 1963: 104; Scott 1965: 135; Y. Aharoni 1971b: 35-36; Kletter 1991: 146 Table 5.7; Eran 1996: W.228.
Location: Israel Museum, Jerusalem.

y *40.2* (Fig. 33.7)
Site unknown. Weight not published.
Dome, red limestone. PS: Badly broken.
Notes: In the text of the publication, the numeral is explained as 40, but drawn more like 24.
Literature: Qedar 1981: 70; Kletter 1991: 146 Table 5.8.
Location: Not clear.

NSF Weights

Nsf.1 (Fig. 34.1)
Jerusalem (Kenyon). Reg. no. 3253. 9.33 grams.
Dome, white limestone. 16.5 × 20.5 mm. PS: Good.
Context: Locus A.699.34.a (season 1963), cf. y 1.1 above.
Notes: Scott (1965: 135) claimed that it is too light for the Nsf, and is therefore a copy from an earlier, much worn specimen.
Literature: Scott 1965: 129 Pl. 24.6; 1970: 62, 65; Dever 1970: Fig. 18; Ben-David 1979: List no. 31; Scott 1985: 199 no. 13; Kletter 1991: 146 Table 6.1.
Location: 'Amman 1963'.

Nsf.2 (Fig. 34.2)
Jerusalem (Kenyon). Reg. no. 3233. 10.63 grams.
Dome, red-brown limestone. 15.5 × 22 mm. PS: Fair.
Context: Locus A.699.34.a (1963); cf. no. 1 above.
Notes: Scott (1965: 135) claimed that it was not finished, because of the weight, and is exceptional. But this is not convincing.
Literature: Scott 1965: 129 Pl. 24.8; 1970: 62-66; Dever 1970: Fig. 18; Ben-David 1979: no. 1; Scott 1985: 199 no. 14, Fig. 78.14; Kletter 1991: 146 Table 6.2.
Location: Jerusalem, British School of Archaeology.

Nsf.3
Jerusalem (Mt Zion?). 9.93 grams.
Details not published.

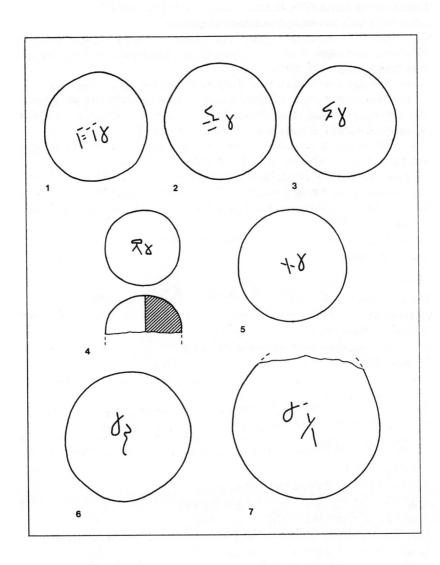

Figure 33. *Selection of 12–40 Shekel weights.* Legend: 1. ୪ 12.1; 2. ୪ 16.2; 3. ୪ 16.3; 4. ୪ 16.4; 5 ୪ 24.1; 6 ୪ 40.1; 7.୪ 40.2. Drawings not to scale (details are given in Appendices 1 and 2). The weights are referred to according to their catalogue numbers.

Notes: Ben-David is the only source for this weight, which probably originated from the excavations at Beit Kaifa; cf. ᵍ 2.13 above.
Literature: Ben-David 1979: 42 no. 21; Kletter 1991: 146 Table 6.3.
Location: Hebrew University (according to Ben-David).

Nsf.4
Near Anatot village. 8.68 grams.
Dome, brown limestone. PS: Damaged and perforated.
Context: Not clear. It was bought by Clark from a local man, who claimed he found it in 1891 in a grave. Later it was bought in Jerusalem by T.E. Wright. For Iron Age II remains at Anatot ('Anata), see *HadArch* 75 (1985): 20-21.
Notes: The weight is perforated, explaining its low weight (restored by some to 10.21 grams). It could have been used as an amulet.
Literature: Sayce 1893: 32-33; Dalman 1906: 93; Pilcher 1912: 181; Raffaeli 1920: 23; Viedebannt 1923: no. 15; Barrois 1932: 66 no. 28; Diringer 1934: no. 1; Scott 1970: 65; Dever 1970: Fig. 18; Ben-David 1979: 42 no. 6; Kletter 1991: 147 Table 6.4; Eran 1996: W.309.
Location: PEF, London.

Nsf.5
Moza. 9.88 grams.
Details not published.
Notes: Scott is the only source for this weight; for another weight from the same area, cf. ᵍ 1.4 above.
Literature: Scott 1965: 65; Kletter 1991: 147 Table 6.5.
Location: Not clear.

Nsf.6
Tel en-Nasbeh. Reg. no. 2512. 9.324 grams.
Dome, limestone. 16 × 18 mm.
Context: Room 475. For the site during the late Iron Age, see 2 Kings 25; Jeremiah 41–42; McCown 1947; Zorn 1993. For 7th century BCE pottery, see Wampler 1947: 142 Pit 325; Pl. 39.
Notes: The letter N is partly worn out.
Literature: McCown 1947: 164 Pl. 57.8; Moscati 1951: 102 no. 4 Pl. 24.5; Scott 1970: 65; Kletter 1991: 147 Table 6.6.
Location: Berkeley University Museum.

Nsf.7
Tel en-Nasbeh. Reg. no. 2552. 9.935 grams.
Dome, limestone. 14 × 17 × 20 mm.
Context: Cistern 370.
Notes: This is probably the Nsf mentioned by Hestrin (1963) as 9.95 grams, and drawn there.
Literature: McCown 1947: 164 Pl. 57: 6; Moscati 1951: 102 no. 3 Pl. 24.4; Scott

1970: 65; Meshorer 1976: 55 (photo); Kletter 1991: 147 Table 6.7.
Location: Rockefeller Museum.

Nsf.8
Beth Zur. 9.80 grams.
Dome, limestone. PS: Good.
Context: Not clear. A general Iron Age II dating is given (Sellers 1933: 60), but a preliminary report (Sellers and Albright 1931: 9) stated that the weight was found during the removal of a Hellenistic wall. *Lmlk* and rosette impressions indicate settlement from 8th–7th centuries BCE (Sellers 1933: 53; for 7th-century pottery, cf. Sellers *et al.* 1968: pls. 18.18, 19.5). Beth Zur is mentioned in 2 Chron. 11.7, but the dating of this list is disputed.
Notes: According to Ben-David, it is 9.76 grams.
Literature: Sellers and Albright 1931: 9; Barrois 1932: 67 no. 2; Sellers 1933: 60 Figs. 53–54; Diringer 1934: 268 no. 9; Stern 1963: 870 Table b; Scott 1970: 65; Dever 1970: Fig. 18; Ben-David 1979: 43 no. 17; Kletter 1991: 147 Table 6.8.
Location: Not clear.

Nsf.9
Beit Zur. 9.54 grams.
Dome, limestone. PS: Good.
Context: Not clear, cf. Nsf.8 above.
Notes: According to Ben-David, it is 9.59 grams.
Literature: Sellers and Albright 1931: 9; Barrois 1932: 67 no. 2; Sellers 1933: 60 Figs. 53–54; Diringer 1934: 268 no. 8; Rockefeller Museum 1940: 43; Stern 1963: 870 Table b; Scott 1970: 65; Ben-David 1979: 43 no. 23; Kletter 1991: 147 Table 6.9.
Location: Rockefeller Museum.

Nsf.10
Arad. 9.6627 grams.
Details not published; no drawing or photograph.
Notes: Nsf weights nos. 10-11 do not appear in publications on Arad (M. Aharoni 1981), nor other works on weights (Scott 1970; Dever 1970; Stern 1963). I did not manage to locate these weights.
Literature: Ben-David 1979: 43 no. 20; Kletter 1991: 147 Table 6.10
Location: Israel Museum, Jerusalem (?).

Nsf.11
Arad. 9.8405 grams.
Details not published; no drawing or photograph.
Notes: Cf. Nsf.10 above.
Literature: Ben-David 1979: 43 no. 15; Kletter 1991: 147 Table 6.11
Location: Eretz Israel Museum, Tel Aviv (?).

Nsf.12
Malhata. Reg. no. 910/1. 10.031 grams.
Dome, limestone. 15 × 20 mm. PS: Good.
Context: Section B, probably 7th century BCE.
Literature: *HadArch* 14 (1968): 5-6; Ben-David 1979: 43 no. 9; Kletter 1991: 147
Table 6.12; Kletter forthcoming b: no. 4 (for the site, see Kochavi 1970).
Location: IAA no. 1972-96.

Nsf.13 (Fig. 34.3)
Tel Beer Sheba. Reg. no. 5151/51. 8.7895 grams.
Dome, limestone.
Context: Locus 282, square Q.18, level II. It is one of the storerooms. 8th century
BCE.
Literature: Y. Aharoni (ed.) 1973: Pl. 39.1; Ben-David 1979: 43 no. 36; Kletter
1991: 147 Table 6.13.
Location: IAA no. 1972-96.

Nsf.14 (Fig. 34.4)
Lachish. Reg. no. 7253. 10.515 grams.
Dome, pink limestone. 16 × 19 × 21.2 mm.
Context: Locus D.7000, surface (Tufnell 1953: 253, 349).
Notes: Diringer thought that it is a local, heavy standard. Ben-David has another
Nsf from Lachish (1979: no. 28), but the reference is mistaken. It seems that there
is no such weight, but it is a mistake originating in Dever (1970), who gave the
same reference for 'two' Nsf weights from Lachish.
Literature: Diringer 1942: 83-84; Moscati 1951: 102 no. 1; Diringer 1953: no. 31,
Pls. 50.7, 51.7; Stern 1963: 870 Table B; Dever 1970: Fig. 18; Scott 1970: 66; Ben-
David 1979: 42 no. 2; Kletter 1991: 147 Table 6.14.
Location: London, British Museum, no. 132827.

Nsf.15
Azeka. 9.447 grams.
Dome, pink limestone. 20 × 15 × 21 mm.
Context: Not clear.
Notes: Slight variations appear regarding the weight—I have chosen Viedebannt's
data, because he weighed anew. Diringer (1949: 266-67) mentioned two Nsf
weights from Azeka in a private collection, but it seems that he meant the same
weights nos. 15–16 here.
Literature: Bliss 1899: 183; Clermont-Ganneau 1901: 25; Bliss and Macalister
1902: 145 Fig. 57; Pilcher 1912: 181-82; Raffaeli 1920: 23; Barrois 1932: 66 no.
24; Stern 1963: 870 Table B; Dever 1970: Fig. 18; Scott 1970; Ben-David 1979: 42
no. 29; Kletter 1991: 147 Table 6.15.
Location: Not clear; cf. location of no. 16 below.

Nsf.16 (Fig. 34.5)
Azeka. 9.998 grams.
Dome, white limestone.
Context: Not clear.
Notes: Some variations appear regarding the weight (Ben-David: 10.10; Bliss and Macalister: 10). I have followed Viedebannt's weighing.
Literature: Bliss 1899: 183; Clermont-Ganneau 1901: 25; Bliss and Macalister 1902: 145 Fig. 47; Dalman 1906: 93; Pilcher 1912: 181-82; Raffaeli 1920: 23; Barrois 1932: no. 17; Rockefeller 1940: 43 no. 494b; Stern 1963: 870 Table B; Dever 1970: Fig. 18; Ben-David 1979: 42 no. 29; Kletter 1991: 147 Table 6.16.
Location: Not clear. A cast of a Nsf weight from Azeka is found in the PEF collection, London, probably of no. 16.

Nsf.17
Azeka. 10.21 grams.
Dome, reddish limestone.
Context: Not clear.
Notes: Slight variations appear regarding the weight—I have followed the excavator's weighing.
Literature: Bliss 1899: 107-108, 183; Clermont-Ganneau 1901: 25; Bliss and Macalister 1902: 145 Fig. 57; Pilcher 1912: 181-82; Raffaeli 1920: 23; Viedebannt 1923: no. 14; Barrois 1932: no. 29; Stern 1963: 870 Table B; Dever 1970: Fig. 18; Scott 1970: 66; Ben-David 1979: 42 no. 5; Kletter 1991: 147 Table 6.17.
Location: PEF collection, London (?).

Nsf.18
Mefalsim. 9.66 grams.
Dome, limestone. 16 × 20.
Context: Found in the vegetable garden of the Kibbutz, c. 8 km east of Gaza. There is a site there, with Iron Age II (7th century BCE) pottery.
Literature: *HadArch* 9 (1964): 14-15; Gophna 1970: 27; Kletter 1991: 147 Table 6.18.
Location: IAA 60-57, exhibited at the Israel Museum, Jerusalem.

Nsf.19
Gezer. 9.28 grams.
Dome, limestone.
Context: Not clear (cf. ૪ 1.10 above).
Literature: Macalister 1912: 285; Diringer 1934: 267 no. 6; Scott 1970: 66; Dever 1970: Fig. 18; Ben-David 1979: 43 no. 33; Kletter 1991: 147 Table 6.19.
Location: PEF, London (?).

Nsf.20 (Fig. 34.6)
Ashdod. 9.8236 grams.
Dome, limestone. 18 × 18 × 15 mm.

Area A, surface find.

Notes: The letter *Z* is written upside-down. Scott gives the weight as 10.85 grams.

Literature: *HadArch* 8 (1964): 17; Dothan 1971: 40 Fig. 7.18, Pl. 12.4; Scott 1970: 66; Ben-David 1979: 43 no. 16; Kletter 1991: 147 Table 6.20.

Location: IAA (?).

Nsf.21 (Fig. 34.7)

Buseirah. Reg. no. 621. 9.5 grams.

Cube, white limestone. 15 × 19 mm.

Context: Surface find, season 1963 (for the site during the Assyrian period, see Bennett 1978; 1983).

Notes: The weight is perforated. The letter *N* is inscribed on one side (short for Nsf?—thus Puech 1977: 16-17). The other side is blurred, but perhaps *NZ* can be read there. The weight fits the Nsf unit of Judah. Puech tried to date it by paleography, but it is doubtful. He did not discuss the location at Buseirah.

Literature: Puech 1977: 15-17 Pl. 6a; Ben-David 1979: 43 no. 27; Kletter 1991: 147 Table 6.21 (for the site, see Bennett 1973, 1978; Bienkowski [ed.] 1992).

Location: Jordan (?).

Nsf.22

Site unknown. 9.947 grams.

Dome, white limestone. 15 × 21 mm. PS: Good.

Notes: It was allegedly found in 1926 in the area of Jerusalem.

Literature: Pritchard 1969: 373 Pl. 1.774b; Scott 1970: 66; Kletter 1991: 147 Table 6.22.

Location: Private collection, Princeton, USA.

Nsf.23

Site unknown. 9.76 grams.

Dome (?), white limestone.

Notes: No photograph or drawing has been published. The weight was allegedly found in the area of Jerusalem. Reifenberg read the inscription as *ksf*. It is probably the same weight that appears under the title 'Jerusalem' in Dever 1970: Fig. 18; cf. Stern 1963: Table B.

Literature: Reifenberg 1925: 107; Scott 1970: 65; Kletter 1991: 147 Table 6.23.

Location: Not clear.

Nsf.24 (Fig. 34.8)

Site unknown. 9.9468 grams.

Dome, red-grey limestone.

Notes: It was bought by Barton in Jerusalem.

Literature: Barton 1903: 386-87; Pilcher 1912: 182; Raffaeli 1920: 23; Viedebannt 1923: no. 16; Barrois 1932: 66 no. 25; Diringer 1934: 267 no. 5; Stern 1963: Table B; Dever 1970: Fig. 18; Scott 1970: 66; Kletter 1991: 147 Table 6.24.

Location: Rockefeller (?).

Nsf.25
Site unknown. 10.044 grams.
Dome, limestone.
Notes: It was found in 1920, allegedly from the area of Gaza. Ben-David included it in his list, giving a weight of 9.95 grams.
Literature: Raffaeli 1920: 23; Barrois 1932: 66 no. 27; Diringer 1934: 267 no. 7; Stern 1963: Table B; Dever 1970: Fig. 18; Ben-David 1979: 42 no. 10; Kletter 1991: 147 Table 6.25.
Location: Not clear.

Nsf.26
Site unknown. 9.19 grams.
Dome, limestone. PS: Good.
Literature: Dever 1970: 180-81 Fig. 15.6, Pl. 9.6; Scott 1970: 65; Ben-David 1979: 43 no. 34; Kletter 1991: 147 Table 6.26.
Location: Not clear.

Nsf.27
Site unknown. 9.66 grams.
Dome, limestone. PS: Excellent.
Notes: This may be the same as no. 18 (above), but it is difficult to be certain, since Dever did not give any further details.
Literature: Dever 1970: 180-81 Fig. 15.5, Pl. 9.5; Scott 1970: 65; Ben-David 1979: 43, no. 21; Kletter 1991: 147 Table 6.27.
Location: Not clear.

Nsf.28
Site unknown. 9.58 grams.
Dome, red limestone. 14.9 × 19.4 × 16 mm. PS: Good.
Notes: Ben-David (1979: no. 20) listed another Nsf with the same weight— probably he reached the very same collection and 're-published' the two Nsf weights there, without noticing Lemaire's work.
Literature: Lemaire 1976: no. 4; Ben-David 1979: 43, no. 25; Kletter 1991: 147 Table 6.28.
Location: Private collection.

Nsf.29
Site unknown. 9.70 grams. PS: Good.
Dome, grey-black limestone. 15.6 × 20.3 × 16.6 mm.
Notes: Ben-David (1979: no. 19) listed another Nsf with the same weight (see note to Nsf.28 above).
Literature: Lemaire 1976: 34 no. 3; Ben-David 1979: 43 no. 18; Kletter 1991: 147 Table 6.29.
Location: Private collection.

Nsf.30
Site unknown. Museum no. 5058. 9.345 grams.
Dome, reddish limestone. 15 × 20 × 17 mm. PS: Good.
Notes: This weight was published by Scott without a photograph, then a second time by Lemaire.
Literature: Scott 1970: 65 List; Lemaire 1976: 43 no. 26, Pl. 3.26; Ben-David 1979: 43 no. 30; Kletter 1991: 147 Table 6.30.
Location: Bible et Terre Sainte Museum, Paris.

Nsf.31
Site unknown. 9.649 grams.
Dome, reddish limestone. 15 × 20 × 17 mm. PS: Fair.
Notes: This weight was published by Scott, then a second time by Lemaire.
Literature: Scott 1970: 65; Lemaire 1976: 42 no. 25, Pl. 3.25; Ben-David 1979: 43 no. 22; Kletter 1991: 148 Table 6.31.
Location: Private collection.

Nsf.32
Site unknown. 9.832 grams.
Dome, white limestone. PS: Fair.
Notes: This weight was published by Scott, who saw it in a private collection (cf. nos. 30–31 above). Scott did not publish a photograph or drawing.
Literature: Scott 1970: 65; Kletter 1991: 148 Table 6.32.
Location: Private collection.

Nsf.33
Site unknown. 9.46 grams.
Dome, white limestone. PS: Fair.
Literature: Scott 1970: 65; Kletter 1991: 148 Table 6.33.
Location: Semitic Museum, Harvard.

Nsf.34
Site unknown. 10.04 grams.
Dome, limestone. 19 mm diameter.
Notes: The photographs published by Meshorer and Ben-David prove that it is the same weight. It has a little damage under the letter *s*. According to Spaer and the Hecht Museum, the weight is 10.05.
Literature: Ben-David 1979: 43 no. 8 ('Beit Gubrin'); Spaer 1982: 251 Pl. 41d ('Idna-Tarqumiyah'); Kletter 1991: 148 Table 6.34; Meshorer in press: no. 32 (10.08 grams).
Location: Hecht Museum, Haifa, H-712.

Nsf.35
Site unknown. 10.10 grams.
Dome, red limestone. 16 × 20 mm.

Literature: Qedar 1978: no. 24; Kletter 1991: 148 Table 6.35.
Location: Not clear.

Nsf.36
Site unknown. 9.99 grams.
Dome, orange limestone. 15 × 21 mm.
Literature: Qedar 1978: no. 25; Kletter 1991: 148 Table 6.36.
Location: Not clear.

Nsf.37
Site unknown. 10.11 grams.
Dome, orange limestone. 16 × 21 mm.
Literature: Qedar 1978: no. 26; Kletter 1991: 148 Table 6.37.
Location: Not clear.

Nsf.38
Site unknown. 9.60 grams.
Dome, limestone. 6? × 22 mm.
Literature: Qedar 1978: no. 27; Kletter 1991: 148 Table 6.38.
Location: Not clear.

Nsf.39
Site unknown. 9.22 grams.
Dome, white limestone. 18 × 18.5 mm.
Literature: Qedar 1978: no. 28; Kletter 1991: 148 Table 6.39.
Location: Not clear.

Nsf.40
Site unknown. 8.77 grams.
Dome, red limestone. 14 × 20 mm.
Literature: Qedar 1978: no. 29; Kletter 1991: 148 Table 6.40.
Location: Not clear.

Nsf.41
Site unknown. 8.24 grams.
Dome, grey limestone. 13 × 20 mm.
Literature: Qedar 1978: no. 30; Kletter 1991: 148 Table 6.41.
Location: Not clear.

Nsf.42
Site unknown. 9.63 grams.
Dome, grey limestone. 13 × 21 mm.
Notes: The photograph (Qedar 1978) is not clear.
Literature: Qedar 1978: no. 31; Kletter 1991: 148 Table 6.42.
Location: Not clear.

Nsf.43
Site unknown. 11.26 grams.
Dome, white limestone. 18 × 21 mm.
Literature: Qedar 1979: 27 no. 4052; Kletter 1991: 148 Table 6.43.
Location: Not clear.

Nsf.44
Site unknown. 9.15 grams.
Dome, limestone. 16 × 19 mm.
Notes: The inscription is *nfs* instead of Nsf.
Literature: Qedar 1979: 27 no. 4053; Kletter 1991: 148 Table 6.44.
Location: Not clear.

Nsf.45
Site unknown. 7.97 grams.
Dome, grey limestone. 13.5 × 20 mm.
Literature: Qedar 1979: 27 no. 4054; Kletter 1991: 148 Table 6.45.
Location: Not clear.

Nsf.46
Site unknown. 9.75 grams.
Dome, white limestone. 16 × 20 mm.
Notes: The photograph is not clear but, according to the description, is it an inscribed Nsf weight.
Literature: Qedar 1979: 28, no. 4055; Kletter 1991: 148 Table 6.46.
Location: Not clear.

Nsf.47
Site unknown. 9.41 grams.
Dome, yellow limestone. 15 × 20 mm.
Literature: Qedar 1981: 31 no. 74; Kletter 1991: 148 Table 6.47.
Location: Not clear.

Nsf.48
Site unknown. 9.15 grams.
Dome, grey limestone. 17 × 19 mm.
Literature: Qedar 1981: 25; Kletter 1991: 148 Table 6.48.
Location: Not clear.

Nsf.49
Site unknown. 9.90 grams.
Dome, limestone. 16.5 × 19 mm. PS: A little damaged.
Notes: It is possible that this weight, of unknown origin, is a duplication of one of the weights above. It is difficult to ascertain this without a good photograph and

more details. Literature: Kletter 1991: 148 Table 6.49.
Location: Kadman K-8910, Eretz Israel Museum, Tel Aviv.

Nsf.50
Site unknown. 9.65 grams.
Dome, hematite (?). 16.2 × 19.2 mm.
Notes: If the material is really hematite, it is exceptional among Judaean weights, since hematite is not a local material.
Literature: Kroha (ed.) 1980: no. 71; Kletter 1991: 148 Table 6.50.
Location: Not clear.

Nsf.51
Site unknown. 6.84 grams.
Dome, hematite (?). 11.3 × 17.3 mm.
Notes: For the material, cf. no. 50 above. Kroha explained the low weight as a result of taking off part of the original base. He suggested that it is a $2/3$ Shekel. The script in the published photograph is not clear.
Literature: Kroha (ed.) 1980: no. 72; Kletter 1991: 148 Table 6.51.
Location: Not clear.

Nsf.a (Fig. 34: 9)
Site unknown. 9.5198 grams.
Dome, brown limestone. 16.7 × 15.1 × 19.4 mm.
Notes: This weight was bough from a merchant in Jerusalem. Ben-David read נ לו 1, and restored it as a royal inscription: '1 n[sf] to the [king]'. This is a very fanciful restoration.
Literature: Ben-David 1973: 176; 1979: 43 Pl. 3.26.
Location: Not clear.

Nsf.b
Site unknown. 29.56 grams.
Half-ball, black hematite. 18 × 20 × 28 mm.
Notes: Ben-David is the only source for this weight. Only the letter *n* is inscribed. He explained it as 3 Nsf, but there is nothing to substantiate this. The weight is badly damaged, the material and the shape do not match the Nsf weights, and there is no comparison to an inscribed multiple of the Nsf unit. The published photograph is not good, and one cannot see any inscription at all.
Literature: Ben-David 1979: no. 14.
Location: Not clear.

Nsf.c
Site unknown. 4.503 grams.
Half-ball, brown-grey limestone. 7.45 × 11.95 mm.
Notes: Ben-David is the only source for this weight. Only the letter *n* is inscribed. He explained it as $1/2$ Nsf, but there is nothing to prove this idea. The photograph is

not good, and one cannot see any inscription.
Literature: Ben-David 1979: 43 no. 35 Pl. 3.39.
Location: Not clear.

Nsf.d
Site unknown. 2.5772 grams.
Half ball, yellow-brown limestone.
Notes: Ben-David is the only source for this weight. It has one mark, the Hieratic numeral 5. Ben-David explained it as ¼ Nsf, only because of the weight, but it is probably a 5 Gerah weight (see below, 5 Gerah.b).
Literature: Ben-David 1979: 42 no. 3, Pl. 3.3.
Location: Private collection.

Nsf.e
Gezer. Reg. no. 569. 10.258 grams.
Dome, light brown limestone. 15.5×18.6 mm.
Context: Locus 2160, level 66.
Notes: Ben-David lists this item as a Nsf, but Eran clarified that it is an uninscribed weight. Eran did mention one inscribed Nsf from Gezer, but he meant the one from Macalister's excavations (no. 19 above).
Literature: Eran 1974: 131 Pl. 41.1; Ben-David 1979: no. 42 no. 4.
Location: Not clear.

Nsf.f
Lachish. 9.45 grams.
Notes: This is a duplication and not another weight. Ben-David probably took the details from Dever, and it is a duplication of weight no. 15 (above).
Literature: Dever 1970: Fig. 18; Ben-David 1979: 43 no. 28.

PYM Weights

Pym.1
Jerusalem. Reg. no. 3231. 7.81 (or 7.80) grams.
Dome, pink-white limestone. 16.5×18.5 mm. PS: Good.
Context: Locus A.669.34.
Literature: Scott 1965: 129; Dever 1970: Fig. 19; Ben-David 1979: no. 12; Scott 1985: 199 no. 9, Fig. 78.9; Kletter 1991: 148 Table 7.1.
Location: 'Amman 1963'.

Pym.2
Jerusalem. Reg. no. 3232. 8.39 grams. Season 1963.
Dome, pink limestone. 16.5×18.5 mm. PS: Good.
Context: Locus A.669.34.
Notes: Scott suggested that it is an unfinished weight, since it is too heavy and the script is not well executed. But this Pym is similar in all respects to the other Pym

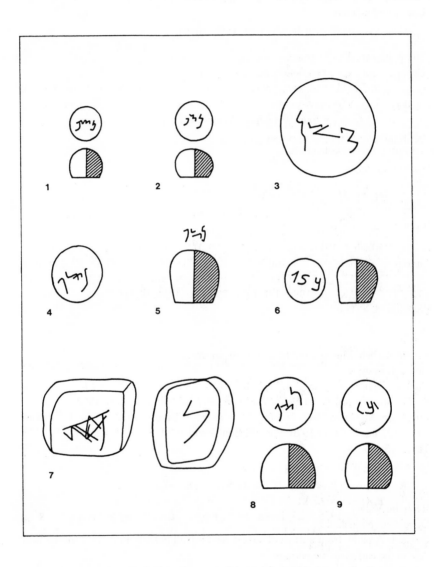

Figure 34. *Selection of Nsf weights.* Legend: 1. Nsf.1; 2. Nsf.2; 3. Nsf.13; 4. Nsf.14; 5. Nsf.16; 6. Nsf 20; 7. Nsf.21; 8. Nsf.24; 9. Nsf.a. Drawings not to scale (details are given in Appendices 1 and 2). The weights are referred to according to their catalogue numbers.

weights, and there is no real justification to regard it as an unfinished weight.
Literature: Scott 1965: 129 Pl. 24.7; Scott 1985: 199 no. 9, Fig. 78.12; Kletter 1991: 148 Table 7.2.
Location: Jerusalem, British School of Archaeology.

Pym.3 (Fig. 35.1)
Jerusalem. Reg. no. 6558. 7.92 grams. Season 1965.
Dome, grey limestone. PS: Very good.
Context: Locus AA.306.2.
Literature: Scott 1985: 199 no. 10, Fig. 79.10; Kletter 1991: 148 Table 7.3.
Location: Royal Ontario Museum, Toronto.

Pym.4 (Fig. 35.2)
Jerusalem (Siloam Village). 7.80 grams.
Shape not clear, limestone.
Notes: The weight was bought by Raffaeli. Different weightings exist for it: 7.71, 7.75, etc. Dever mentioned two Pym weights, of 7.68 and 7.75 grams, referring once to Raffaeli 1920 and then to *PEQ* 46: 99. However, it is the same weight.
Literature: Pilcher 1914: 99; Raffaeli 1920: 22; Barrois 1932: 68 no. 33; Diringer 1934: 372 no. 13, Pl. 23.12; Dever 1970: Fig. 19; Stern 1963: 870; Ben-David 1979: 37 no. 17; Kletter 1991: 148 Table 7.4; Eran 1996: W.315.
Location: Not clear.

Pym.5
Tel en-Nasbeh. Museum no. M.223. 8.591 grams.
Dome, limestone.
Context: Debris in square AK/21, in the south of the city (McCown 1947: 211 Plan P). The stratigraphy is not clear (McCown 1947: 179; cf. now Zorn 1993).
Literature: McCown 1947: 163 Fig. 38.9, Pl. 57.7; Barrois 1932: 69 no. 1; Moscati 1951: 103 no. 7; Dever 1970: Fig. 19; Ben-David 1979: 37 no. 1; Kletter 1991: 148 Table 7.5.
Location: Berkeley.

Pym.6
Rephaim Valley.
Details not published.
Context: Area D, from a cairn of stones with mixed pottery, ranging from the Iron Age to the early Islamic periods.
Literature: *HadArch* 87 (1985): 33-34; Kletter 1991: 148 Table 7.6.
Location: IAA.

Pym.7
Beth Zur. 7.18 grams.
Dome, limestone. Context: Not clear.
Notes: Only *py* is inscribed on the weight. The letter *m* is worn out.

Literature: Sellers and Albright 1931: 9; Sellers 1933: 60 Figs. 53.4, 54; Diringer 1934: no. 14; Stern 1963: 870 Table B; Ben-David 1979: no. 28; Kletter 1991: 148 Table 7.7.
Location: Not clear.

Pym.8
Tel 'Ira. Reg. no. E-1110/50. 8.1796 (or 8.1805) grams.
Dome, yellow limestone. $18.5 \times 13 \times 16$ mm. PS: Excellent. Season 1979.
Context: Locus 194, area E. Room in the gate area. 7th century BCE.
Literature: *HadArch* 74–75 (1980, Hebrew); Beit Arieh 1985: 23; Kletter 1991: 149 Table 7.8.
Location: Tel Aviv University.

Pym.9
Arad. Reg. no. 537/1. 7.952 grams.
Dome, brown limestone.
Context: Not stratified.
Literature: M. Aharoni 1981: 126-27 no. 12; Kletter 1991: 148 Table 7.9.
Location: IAA, Rockefeller Museum (?).

Pym.10
Arad. Reg. no. 6363/50. 7.9030 grams.
Dome, dark grey limestone.
Context: K.18.805, out of the fortress. The stratigraphy is not clear.
Notes: Stern and Dever mentioned only one Pym from Arad, of 8.120 grams. Ben-David and Hestrin listed two Pym weights from Arad, with different weightings (cf. Meshorer 1976: 53, bottom, second from right).
Literature: M. Aharoni 1981: 126-27 no. 13; Kletter 1991: 148 Table 7.10.
Location: IAA no. 64-314, now at the Israel Museum, Jerusalem.

Pym.11 (Fig. 35.3)
Lachish. Reg. no. 6157. 7.805 grams.
Dome, yellow limestone. $14.5 \times 18 \times 13.5$ mm.
Context: D/X, i.e. not stratified.
Literature: Diringer 1942: 86 no. 3, Pl. 13.3; Moscati 1951: 102 no. 6; Diringer 1953: no. 37 Pl. 51.9; Dever 1970: Fig. 19; Ben-David 1979: 37 no. 15; Mitchell 1988: 74 no. 37; Kletter 1991: 149 Table 7: 11.
Location: British Museum, WA 160316.

Pym.12 (Fig. 35: 4)
Lachish. Reg. no. 1505. 8.130 grams.
Dome, limestone. $16.5 \times 18 \times 12$ mm.
Context: D/X, i.e. not stratified.
Literature: Diringer 1942: 86 no. 2 Pl. 13.2; Moscati 1951: 102 no. 5; Diringer 1953: no. 35 Pl. 51.8; Dever 1970: Fig. 19; Ben-David 1979: 37 no. 5; Kletter

1991: 149 Table 7.12.
Location: Not clear.

Pym.13
Tel Batash. Reg. no. 7531. 7.72 grams.
Details not yet published.
Context: Level II, 7th century BCE.
Literature: A. Mazar 1985: 320; Kletter 1991: 149 Table 7.13.
Location: Hebrew University.

Pym.14
Tel Batash. Reg. no. 6197. 7.78 grams.
Details not yet published.
Context: Level II, 7th century BCE.
Literature: A. Mazar 1985: 320; Kletter 1991: 149 Table 7.14.
Location: Hebrew University.

Pym.15
Tel Batash. Reg. no. 5204. 8.02 grams.
Details not yet published.
Context: Level II, 7th century BCE.
Literature: A. Mazar 1985: 320; Kletter 1991: 149 Table 7.15.
Location: Hebrew University.

Pym.16
Tel Jemmeh. Details not published.
Literature: *HadArch* 36 (1971): 23 (Hebrew); Kletter 1991: 149 Table 7.16.
Location: Not clear.

Pym.17 (Fig. 35.5)
Gezer. 7.27 grams.
Dome, limestone.
Context: The so-called 'Persian-Maccabaean' level.
Literature: Macalister 1912: 285 Fig. 431; Pilcher 1912: 187; Viedebannt 1923: no. 22; Barrois 1932: no. 31; Dever 1970: Fig. 19; Ben-David 1979: 37 no. 27; Kletter 1991: 149 Table 7.17.
Location: Istanbul (?).

Pym.18
Gezer.
Dome, limestone. 16 × 18 mm.
Context: Area 20; other details not published.
Literature: *HadArch* 48–49 (1974): 60 (Hebrew); *IEJ* 23 (1971): 251; Kletter 1991: 149 Table 7.18.
Location: IAA no. 74-716, now in Los Angeles.

Pym.19 (Fig. 35.6)
Ashdod. Reg. no. M.21/61. 7.8945 grams.
Dome, limestone. 11 × 19 mm. PS: A little damaged.
Context: Surface, square F.8 (according to the Romema card, levels VII-VI).
Literature: *HadArch* 31–32 (1970): 23-24 (Hebrew); Ben-David 1979: 37 no. 9;
Eran 1982: 96, 99 no. 50, Fig. 31.2, Pl. 39.1; Kletter 1991: 149 Table 7.19.
Location: IAA, no. 69-2073.

Pym.20
Tel Haror. Clay, ink inscription (?).
Other details not yet published.
Context: Level G.III, area G, 7th century BCE.
Notes: According to the preliminary reports, it is made of clay, and the word 'Pym'
is written in ink.
Literature: *HadArch* 84 (1984): 57; cf. *HadArch* 82 (1983): 67-68; 87 (1984): 42-
43; Kletter 1991: 149 Table 7.20; Stern 1995: 465.
Location: Ben Gurion University, Beer Sheba.

Pym.21 (Fig. 35.7)
Tel Abu Sleimeh. Reg. no. 6202. 8.1648 grams.
Dome, pink limestone. Written only *py*.
Context: GP.468, level G, dated by Petrie to 625–500 BCE (dynasty 26). P is the
area, but there are two areas marked 'GP' on the plan (Petrie 1937: Pl. 10). The
absolute height is 468 (or 470, Petrie 1937: Pl. 47), which better matches the earlier
level, H (Petrie 1937: Pl. 11). For the site during the 7th century BCE, see Reich
1984, but the 'sealed Karu' is perhaps Tel Rukeish (Oren 1986b).
Notes: The letter *m* is missing. Petrie explained the writing as 'Pym', but as a
forgery, since the weight in his view was a *daric*. This weight was not mentioned
by any of the scholars that discussed the Judaean weights.
Literature: Petrie 1937: 12 Pl. 39; Kletter 1991: 149 Table 7.21.
Location: Probably Cairo Museum.

Pym.22
Site unknown. 7.42 grams.
Dome, limestone. 15 × 18 mm. Written only *m*.
Notes: Spaer did not refer to Ben-David but, according to the details in Ben-
David's archives (now at the Hebrew University, Archaeology library), it is no. 26
on his list. The origin is, allegedly, 'Idna-Tarqumiyah'.
Literature: Ben-David 1979: no. 26; Spaer 1982: 251 no. 7, Pl. 41.g; Kletter 1991:
149 Table 7.22.
Location: Private collection.

Pym.23
Site unknown. 7.98 grams.
Dome, limestone. 18 × 20 mm. PS: Fair to damaged.

Notes: Spaer did not refer to Ben-David but, according to the photographs, it is the same weight.
Literature: Ben-David 1979: no. 7; Spaer 1982: 251 no. 6, Pl. 41.f; Kletter 1991: 149 Table 7.23.
Location: Private collection.

Pym.24
Site unknown. No details or photograph published.
Notes: This weight was given to the Israel Museum.
Literature: *HadArch* 30 (1969): 33; *Israel Museum News* 3 (1968): 72; Kletter 1991: 149 Table 7.24.
Location: Israel Museum, Jerusalem, no. 68-38.115.

Pym.25
Site unknown. 7.55 grams.
Dome, pink limestone. PS: Good.
Notes: cf. ৬ 2.19 (above).
Literature: Dever 1970: Figs. 19, 16.7; Ben-David 1979: 37 no. 24; Kletter 1991: 149 Table 7.25.
Location: Not clear.

Pym.26
Site unknown. 7.62 grams.
Dome, pink limestone. PS: Damaged near the letter *m*.
Notes: It might be the same as no. 31 (below), but the photographs look different.
Literature: Agora 1975: no. 388; Kletter 1991: 149 Table 7.26.
Location: Private collection.

Pym.27
Site unknown. 7.69 grams. $12.7 \times 18.8 \times 16$ mm.
Dome, red-brown limestone. PS: Good.
Literature: Lemaire 1976: 35 no. 6; Ben-David 1979: 37 no. 20; Kletter 1991: 149 Table 7.27.
Location: Private collection.

Pym.28
Site unknown. 7.70 grams.
Dome, grey limestone. 13.2×15.8 mm. PS: Good.
Literature: Lemaire 1976: 35 no. 5; Ben-David 1979: 37 no. 19; Kletter 1991: 149 Table 7.28.
Location: Private collection.

Pym.29
Site unknown. Museum no. 5049. 7.805 grams.
Dome, yellow limestone. $14 \times 17.5 \times 15.5$ mm. PS: Good.

Literature: Lemaire 1976: 43 no. 28; Ben-David 1979: no. 13; Kletter 1991: 149 Table 7.29.
Location: Bible et Terre Sainte Museum, Paris.

Pym.30
Site unknown. Museum no. 5059. 8.224 grams. PS: Good.
Dome, orange limestone. 15.5 × 14.5 × 18.5 mm.
Literature: Lemaire 1976: 35 no. 27; Ben-David 1979: 37 no. 3; Kletter 1991: 149 Table 7.30.
Location: Bible et Terre Sainte Museum, Paris.

Pym.31
Site unknown. Museum no. H-1484 (?). 7.62 grams.
Dome, limestone. 21 mm diameter.
Notes: Ben-David gives the weight as 6.56 grams. It may be the same as no. 26 (above), but the Xerox of the photographs in my possession does not indicate a clear conclusion.
Literature: Meshorer in press: no. 33; Kletter 1991: 149 Table 7.31.
Location: Hecht Museum, Haifa.

Pym.32 (Fig. 35.8)
Site unknown. 7.832 grams.
Dome, limestone. 13 × 19 mm.
Notes: Ben-David did not give other details. It is probably no. K-8909 of the Museum, and does not look the same as no. 40 (below).
Literature: Ben-David 1979: 37 no. 10; Kletter 1991: 149 Table 7.32.
Location: Eretz Israel Museum, Tel Aviv, K-8909 (?).

Pym.33
Site unknown. 7.9 grams.
Dome, brown limestone. No photograph or drawing has been published.
Literature: Ben-David 1979: 37 no. 8; Kletter 1991: 149 Table 7.33.
Location: *Hechal Shlomoh*, Jerusalem. (the chief Rabbinate of Israel; I have applied for details, but received no answer).

Pym.34
Site unknown. 7.8 grams.
Details not published.
Notes: Ben-David is the only source for Pym nos. 34–35. I have located (in 1993) one Pym bought by the Hebrew University in the 1940s, registered and drawn by Avigad as no. 659. It is possibly no. 34 or 35 here.
Literature: Ben-David 1979: 37 no. 16; Kletter 1991: 149 Table 7.34.
Location: Hebrew University, Jerusalem.

Pym.35
Site unknown. 8.20 grams.
Details not published; cf. Pym.34 above.
Literature: Ben-David 1979: 37 no. 4; Kletter 1991: 149 Table 7.35.
Location: Hebrew University, Jerusalem.

Pym.36
Site unknown. 7.85 grams.
Dome, white limestone. 12 × 19 mm.
Literature: Qedar 1978: no. 32; Kletter 1991: 149 Table 7.36.
Location: Private collection.

Pym.37
Site unknown. 7.53 grams.
Dome, yellow limestone. 16 × 18 mm.
Notes: The script is not clear, especially the letter *y*.
Literature: Qedar 1978: no. 33; Kletter 1991: 149 Table 7.37.
Location: Private collection.

Pym.38
Site unknown. 7.77 grams.
Dome, orange limestone. 14 × 19 mm.
Literature: Qedar 1978: no. 34; Kletter 1991: 150 Table 7.38.
Location: Private collection.

Pym.39
Site unknown. 7.90 grams.
Dome, white limestone. 14 × 18 mm.
Literature: Qedar 1978: no. 35; Kletter 1991: 150 Table 7.39.
Location: Private collection.

Pym.40
Site unknown. 7.95 grams.
Dome, white-red limestone. 13.5 × 20 mm.
Notes: It may equal Pym.32, but the details are not enough to be certain.
Literature: Qedar 1979: 28 no. 4056; Kletter 1991: 150 Table 7.40.
Location: Private collection.

Pym.41
Site unknown. 6.95 grams.
Dome, limestone. 14 × 18 mm.
Literature: Qedar 1981: 31 no. 75; Kletter 1991: 150 Table 7.41.
Location: Private collection.

Pym.42
Site unknown. 7.37 grams.

Dome, pink limestone. 16 × 18 mm.
Notes: the photo is not clear, except the letter *m*.
Literature: Qedar 1983: 25 no. 5065; Kletter 1991: 150 Table 7.42.
Location: Private collection.

Pym.43
Site unknown. 8.35 grams.
Dome, brown-grey limestone. 13.7 × 19.6 mm.
Literature: Kroha (ed.) 1980: no. 73; Kletter 1991: 150 Table 7.43.
Location: Private collection.

Pym.44 (Fig. 35.9)
Site unknown. 7.6095 grams.
Cube, bronze. Inscription on one side: *lzkryhw y'r*.
Notes: Barton bought this weight in Jerusalem. Allegedly, it was found on the Temple Mount. The weight was checked by Pilcher.
Literature: Barton 1903; Pilcher 1912: 186; Barton 1937: 202-203 Pl. 63: 187; Raffaeli 1920: 22; Viedebannt 1923: no. 21; Barrois 1932: 68 no. 32; Diringer 1934: no. 11; Stern 1963: 870 Table B; Dever 1970: Fig. 19; Ben-David 1979: no. 22; Kletter 1991: 150 Table 7.44; Eran 1996: W.314.
Location: Haverford College, USA.

Pym.45
Site unknown. 7.5458 grams.
Cube bronze. 11.1 × 12.9 × 14 mm.
Notes: The sides form a sort of a pyramid, not a complete cube. It is probably Ben-David's no. 18 (but he gives the weight as 7.75 grams). The weight was bought in Jerusalem.
Literature: G. Barkay 1978: 209-10 no. 5, Pl. 34.c-d; Kletter 1991: 150 Table 7.45.
Location: Eretz Israel Museum, Tel Aviv.

Pym.46 (Fig. 35.10)
Site unknown. 7.95 grams.
Cube, bronze. 11.7 × 11.7 × 8 mm. PS: Good.
Literature: Lemaire 1982: 19-20 Pl. 4.6; Kletter 1991: 150 Table 7.46.
Location: Private collection.

Pym.47
Site unknown. 7.6082 grams.
Dome, brown hematite. 13.8 × 16.5 mm.
Notes: Ben-David is the only source. He saw three signs on the base: a letter *p*, a circle and dot (in his view, the sign for gold standards), and a late Phoenician letter *shin*. He read this as: 'P[ym = ²/₃ of a] Sh[ekel]'. This is fanciful. The material is not typical of Judah; the Phoenician letter is problematic, and the inscription bears no '²/₃'. Two bad photographs were published, both of the base (?), but the script is

not seen clearly in either of them. I doubt very much that it is a Judaean weight.
Literature: Ben-David 1979: 37 no. 23, 38-39 Pl. 2; Kletter 1991: 150 Table 7.47.
Location: Private collection.

Pym.a
Tel esh-Shuqaf. 112 grams.
Limestone object, rectangular.
Notes: It carries a late, Aramaean inscription 'Pym'. Stern, followed by Ben-David,
thinks that it is a modern forgery.
Literature: Stern 1973b: 214 Photo 252 n. 7; Ben-David 1979: 32.

Pym.b
Tel Beer Sheba. 45.5 grams.
Tortoise, bronze. Level IX.
Notes: Surprisingly, Ben-David saw 6 Pym here, but everything is foreign to the
Judaean weights: the form, the weight (no other multiples of Pym are known from
Judah), the material. If we follow his method, why should it not be 4 Judaean
Shekels? Ben-David's reference is wrong and the location of the weight today is
not clear.
Literature: Ben-David 1979: 37 no. 5
Location: Private collection.

Beqaᶜ Weights

Beqaᶜ.1 (Fig. 36.1)
Near Shueifat. 6.648 grams.
Dome, limestone. 11 × 15 mm.
Notes: Bought in Jerusalem.
Literature: Dalman 1906: 94 Fig. 4; Pilcher 1912: 188; Viedebannt 1923: no. 1;
Barrois 1932: no. 36; Diringer 1934: no. 17; Raffaeli 1920: 23; Dever 1970: Fig.
20; Kletter 1991: 150 Table 8.1; Eran 1996: W.313.
Location: Not clear.

Beqaᶜ.2
Ramat Rahel. 6.650 grams.
Details not published.
Notes: Stern is the only source, as this weight is not mentioned in Y. Aharoni (ed.)
1962, 1964.
Literature: Stern 1963: 870 Table; Dever 1970: Fig. 20; Kletter 1991: 150 Table
8.2.
Location: Not clear.

Beqaᶜ.3
Beth Zur. 5.80 grams.
Dome, limestone.

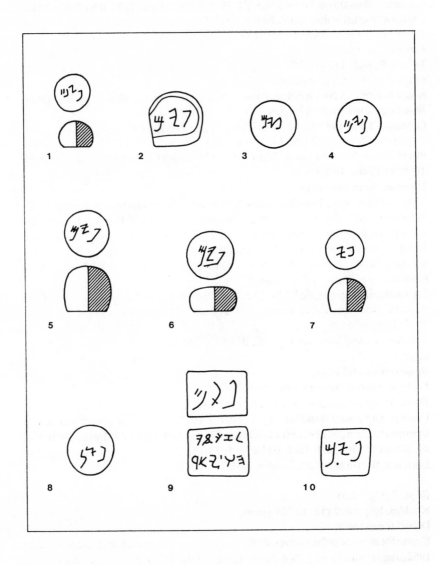

Figure 35. *Selection of Pym weights.* Legend: 1. Pym.3; 2. Pym.4; 3. Pym.11; 4. Pym.12; 5. Pym.17; 6. Pym.19; 7. Pym.21; 8. Pym.32; 9. Pym.44; 10. Pym.46. Drawings not to scale (details are given in Appendices 1 and 2). The weights are referred to according to their catalogue numbers.

Context: The weight was dated to Iron Age II. It does not have a specific locus.
Literature: Sellers and Albright 1931: 9; Barrois 1932: 76; Sellers 1933: 60 Fig. 53.3; Diringer 1934: no. 18; Shany 1967: 54 no. 5; Dever 1970: Fig. 20; Stern 1963: 870 Table B; Kletter 1991: 150 Table 8.3.
Location: Not clear.

Beqaᶜ.4
Lachish. Reg. no. 500. 6.150 grams.
Dome, limestone. 14 × 17 × 15.8 mm. PS: A little damaged.
Context: D/X, not in situ.
Literature: Diringer 1942: 89 Pl. 13.4; 1953: no. 38 Pl. 51.12; Moscati 1951: 103 no. 8; Shany 1967: 54 no. 8; Stern 1963: 870 Table; Dever 1970: Fig. 20; Kletter 1991: 150 Table 8.4.
Location: Not clear.

Beqaᶜ.5
Lachish. Reg. no. 5349. 6.095 grams.
Dome, pink limestone. 15.5 × 16 × 13.5 mm.
Context: Square L.12, north-west area of palace A (Tufnell 1953: Pl. 110), out of context.
Literature: Diringer 1942: 89 Pl. 13.5; 1953: no. 40 Pl. 50.9; Moscati 1951: 103 no. 9; Stern 1963: 870 Table; Dever 1970: Fig. 20; Mitchell 1988: 75 no. 38; Kletter 1991: 150 Table 8.5.
Location: British Museum, London, BM/WA 132828.

Beqaᶜ.6 (Fig. 36.2]
Lachish. 5.660 grams. Inscribed with one letter: *b.*
Dome, limestone. 15.5 × 15 mm. PS: Very good.
Context: D/X, out of context.
Literature: Diringer 1942: 90 Pl. 12.6; 1953: no. 42 Pl. 51.14; Moscati 1951: 103 no. 10; Stern 1963: 870 Table B; Dever 1970: Fig. 20; Kletter 1991: 150 Table 8.6.
Location: British Museum, London, BM/WA 160032.

Beqaᶜ.7 (Fig. 36.3)
Kh. Uza. Reg. no. 2452. 5.8328 grams.
Dome, limestone.
Context: Locus 741. 7th century BCE.
Literature: Courtesy of I. Beit Arieh; Kletter 1991: 150 Table 8.7 (for the site, see Beit-Arieh and Cresson 1991).
Location: Tel Aviv University.

Beqaᶜ.8
Kh. el-Kom. 5.75 grams.
Dome, white limestone. PS: A little worn.
Context: Allegedly from a tomb near the village.

Literature: Dever 1970: 183-84 Fig. 15.8 Pl. 9.8, Fig. 20; Kletter 1991: 150 Table 8.8.
Location: Not clear.

Beqaᶜ.9 (Fig. 36.4)
Gezer. 6.109 grams.
Dome, limestone.
Context: The weight was dated to the Persian period, but its context is not clear (cf. ᵼ 1.10 above).
Literature: Macalister 1904a: 210 Fig. 4; Dalman 1906: 93; Macalister 1912: 285 Fig. 430; Pilcher 1912: 188; Raffaeli 1920: 22; Viedebannt 1923: no. 2; Barrois 1932: 65 no. 35; Diringer 1934: no. 16; Stern 1963: 870 Table B; Dever 1970: Fig. 20; Shany 1967: 54; Kletter 1991: 150 Table 8.9.
Location: Not clear.

Beqaᶜ.10
Ashdod. Reg. no. A.618/69. 5.7067 grams.
Dome, limestone. 10.5 × 16 mm.
PS: The letter *b* is missing, and the other two are not apparent from the photograph.
Context: Surface find, area A.
Literature: Dothan (ed.) 1971: 40 Fig. 7.19, Pl. 13.5; Kletter 1991: 150 Table 8.10.
Location: IAA (?).

Beqaᶜ.11
Ekron.
Details not yet published.
Context: An area of private houses, level I, 7th century BCE.
Literature: Gitin 1989: 51; 1990: 41, 59 n. 17; *EAEHLnew*: III, 1003; Kletter 1991: 150 Table 8.11.
Location: With the excavation team.

Beqaᶜ.12 (Fig. 36.5)
Unknown site. 5.8988 grams.
Dome, limestone. 13 × 11 mm.
Notes: The weight was bought in Jerusalem. It has an eight-leafed rosette inscribed on the base (G. Barkay 1978: 213; cf. Kletter 1995: chap. 5).
Literature: Barkay 1978: 213 Fig. 1.3, Pl. 33.e-g; Kletter 1991: 151 Table 8.12.
Location: Eretz Israel Museum, Tel Aviv, K-8912.

Beqaᶜ.13 (Fig. 36.6)
Unknown site. 5.8698 grams.
Dome, reddish limestone.
Notes: The weight was bought by Torrey in Jerusalem in 1901.
Literature: Torrey 1903; Muller 1904: 179; Dalman 1906: 94; Pilcher 1912: 187; Raffaeli 1920: 22; Viedebannt 1923: no. 3; Barrois 1932: 69 no. 34; Diringer 1934:

no. 15 Pl. 22; Shany 1967: 54 no. 6; Dever 1970: Fig. 20; Kletter 1991: 151 Table 8.13; Eran 1996: W.312.
Location: Not clear.

Beqaᶜ.14 (Fig. 36.7)
Unknown site. 5.927 grams.
Dome, limestone. Inscribed 10 and 5 (in Hieratic) on the base.
Notes: Scott read the base signs as $4 + 8 = 12$, hence ½, a heavy Shekel of 24 Gerah. Kaufman could not explain '$10 + 5 = 15$' here, since Beqaᶜ cannot be 15 Gerah, so he suggested reading '⅔ *qdt*' as a secondary inscription (thus the weight enables transfer between the Beqaᶜ and the *qdt*). This is most unlikely, and it seems to me that one should follow Scott and read '15' at non-face value, i.e. 12 (hence ½ Shekel).
Literature: Scott 1964: 57 no. 20, Fig. 1; Shany 1967: 54 no. 7; Kaufman 1967: 41 no. 20; Dever 1970: Fig. 20; Kletter 1991: 151 Table 8.14.
Location: Not clear.

Beqaᶜ.15
Unknown site. 6.18 grams. PS: Very good.
Dome, limestone. $16.5 \times 17.5 \times 16.4$ mm.
Literature: Lemaire 1976: no. 7 Pl. 1.7; Kletter 1991: 151 Table 8.15.
Location: Private collection.

Beqaᶜ.16
Unknown site. 5.85 grams.
Dome, limestone. $13 \times 16.7 \times 14$ mm. PS: Good.
Literature: Lemaire 1976: no. 8 Pl. 1.8; Kletter 1991: 151 Table 8.16.
Location: Private collection.

Beqaᶜ.17
Unknown site. 5.53 grams.
Dome, limestone. $12.2 \times 17 \times 14$ mm. PS: Very good.
Literature: Lemaire 1976: no. 9 Pl. 1.9; Kletter 1991: 151 Table 8.17.
Location: Private collection.

Beqaᶜ.18
Unknown site. 5.51 grams.
Dome, limestone. $14 \times 16.3 \times 1.03$ mm. PS: Good.
Notes: Only the letters q and ᶜ are seen in the photograph.
Literature: Lemaire 1976: no. 10 Pl. 1.10; Kletter 1991: 151 Table 8.18.
Location: Private collection.

Beqaᶜ.19
Unknown site. Museum no. 5046. 5.826 grams.
Dome, limestone. $13 \times 17 \times 14$ mm. PS: Fair.

Literature: Lemaire 1976: no. 29 Pl. 3.29; Kletter 1991: 151 Table 8.19.
Location: Bible et Terre Sainte Museum, Paris.

Beqaᶜ.20
Unknown site. 5.5505 grams.
Cube, iron. 9 × 7 × 6.5 mm.
Notes: This weight was bought in Jerusalem and published by Shany (1967), who tried to date it paleographically (assuming that the *lmlk* stamps belong to the 7th century BCE). It is the only JIL made of iron, so far.
Literature: Shany 1967: 54-55; G. Barkay 1981b: 42; Kletter 1991: 151 Table 8.20.
Location: The Pontifical Institute, Jerusalem.

Beqaᶜ.21
Unknown site. 5.62 grams.
Dome, limestone.
Notes: This weight was bought by the Israel Bank.
Literature: Qedar 1978: no. 36; R. Barkay 1987: Pl. 1.d; Kletter 1991: 151 Table 8.21.
Location: Collection of the Israel Bank, Jerusalem.

Beqaᶜ.22
Unknown site. 6.46 grams.
Dome, light-grey limestone. PS: Good.
Notes: The published photograph is not good.
Literature: Agora 1974: no. 389; Kletter 1991: 151 Table 8.22.
Location: Private collection.

Beqaᶜ.23
Unknown site. 5.99 grams.
Dome, white limestone. 13 × 17 mm. PS: Good.
Literature: Qedar 1978: no. 37; Kletter 1991: 151 Table 8.23.
Location: Private collection.

Beqaᶜ.24
Unknown site. 6.8 grams.
Dome, yellow limestone. 14 × 17 mm.
Literature: Qedar 1978: no. 38; Kletter 1991: 151 Table 8.24.
Location: Private collection.

Beqaᶜ.25
Unknown site. 5.72 grams.
Dome, yellow limestone. 14.5 × 17 mm.
Literature: Qedar 1978: no. 39 = Qedar 1981: 32 no. 77 (?); Kletter 1991: 151 Table 8.25.

Notes: The weights and size are the same, and it seems to be the same weight (the photographs are poor).
Location: Private collection.

Beqaᶜ.26
Unknown site. 6.04 grams. PS: Good.
Dome, light-coloured limestone. 13.5 × 17 mm.
Literature: Qedar 1978: no. 40; Kletter 1991: 151 Table 8.26.
Location: Private collection.

Beqaᶜ.27
Unknown site. 5.75 grams.
Dome, white limestone. 12.2 × 17.1 mm.
Literature: Kroha (ed.) 1980: no. 69; Kletter 1991: 151 Table 8.27.
Location: Private collection.

Beqaᶜ.28
Unknown site. 6.24 grams.
Dome, red limestone. 14 × 16.5 mm.
Literature: Kroha (ed.) 1980: no. 70; Kletter 1991: 151 Table 8.28.
Location: Private collection.

Beqaᶜ.29
Unknown site. 5.8 grams.
Dome, white limestone. 14 × 16 mm.
Notes: I was informed that this weight was bought in Jerusalem, therefore it is not equal to Beqaᶜ.34 (below). It is probably different from Beqaᶜ.15 (above) as well.
Literature: Hestrin 1963: no. 96; Meshorer 1976: 54, photograph only; Meshorer in press: no. 34; Kletter 1991: 151 Table 8.29.
Location: Hecht Museum, Haifa no. H-57 or H-1483 (?).

Gerah Weights

2 Gerah.1 (Fig. 37.1)
Lachish. Reg. no. 1502. 1.705 grams.
Cube, white limestone. 7 × 9.5 × 9.5 mm. PS: Good.
Context: D/X, out of context.
Notes: Diringer could not decide if it is 2 or ¹/₂ or ¹/₄ Beqaᶜ = ¹/₈ Shekel of the sanctuary (1953: 452). Scott explained it as ²/₈ Beqaᶜ or ²/₁₂ Nsf. The shape is exceptional, and so far no other similar inscribed 2 Gerah unit is known. Thus, the meaning of this weight and it status as Judaean are not certain.
Literature: Diringer 1942: 97 Pl. 12.10; Moscati 1951: 105 no. 22; Diringer 1953: 452 no. 55, Pl. 51.16; Scott 1964: 61 no. ii, Fig. 3c; Eran 1987: App. B.23; Kletter 1991: 151 Table 9A.1.
Location: British Museum, London, Lachish Collection.

Economic Keystones

Figure 36. *Selection of Beqaᶜ weights.* Legend: 1. Beqaᶜ.1; 2. Beqaᶜ.6; 3. Beqaᶜ.7; 4. Beqaᶜ.9; 5. Beqaᶜ.12; 6. Beqaᶜ.14; 8. Beqaᶜ.20. Drawings not to scale (details are given in Appendices 1 and 2). The weights are referred to according to their catalogue numbers.

3 Gerah.1 (Fig. 37.2)
Jerusalem (Kenyon). Reg. no. 6766. 1.93 grams.
Dome, white-cream limestone. PS: Very good.
Context: Locus L.235.5, season 1967.
Notes: Scott suggested it is a 3 Gerah weight, or ⅛ 'royal' Shekel.
Literature: Scott 1985: 199 no. 1, Fig. 78.1; Kletter 1991: 151 Table 9B.1.
Location: IAA (?).

3 Gerah.2
Site unknown. Museum no. 5099. 1.898 grams.
Dome, limestone. 9 × 11 × 10 mm. PS: Good.
Notes: Lemaire explained this weight as ³/20 Shekel.
Literature: Lemaire 1976: Pl. 3.30 Eran 1987: App. B.1; Kletter 1991: 151 Table 9B.2.
Location: Bible et Terre Sainte Museum, Paris.

3 Gerah.3
Site unknown. 1.52 grams.
Dome, limestone.
Literature: Scott 1964: 60 no. 1, Fig. 3a; Barkay 1981a: Table 1; Eran 1987: App. B.2; Kletter 1991: 151 Table 9B.3.
Location: Private collection.

3 Gerah.4
Site unknown. 1.99 grams.
Dome, red limestone. 9 × 12 mm.
Literature: Scott 1964: 60 no. 1, Fig. 3; Kaufman 1967: 39; Kletter 1991: 151 Table 9B.4.
Location: Private collection.

3 Gerah.5
Site unknown. 2.02 grams.
Dome, white limestone. 12 × 9 mm.
Literature: Qedar 1978: 48 no. 4061; Eran 1987: App. C.1; Kletter 1991: 152 Table 9B.5.
Location: Private collection.

3 Gerah.6
Site unknown. 1.97 grams.
Dome, white limestone. 8.8 × 12 mm.
Literature: Kroha (ed.) 1980: no. 86; Eran 1987: App. C.3; Kletter 1991: 152 Table 9B.6.
Location: Private collection.

3 Gerah.7
Site unknown. 1.90 grams.

Dome, orange limestone. 8.8 × 11.3 mm.
Literature: Kroha (ed.) 1980: no. 87; Eran 1987: App. C.5; Kletter 1991: 152 Table 9B.7.
Location: Private collection.

3 Gerah.8
Site unknown. 1.90 grams.
Dome, grey limestone. 8 × 13 mm.
Notes: This weight was bought by the Israel Bank, but Eran was not aware of this, and treated it as two different weights.
Literature: Qedar 1979: 26 no. 4062; R. Barkay 1987: Pl. 1a; Eran 1987: App. C.4 = C.6; Kletter 1991: 152 Table 9B.8.
Location: Israel Bank, Jerusalem.

3 Gerah.9
Site unknown. 1.5968 grams.
Dome, limestone. 9 × 10.5 mm. The script is unique.
Notes: Barkay read the letter as 3 (Hieratic), comparing with Arad ostraca nos. 22, 79.
Literature: G. Barkay 1981a: 288 no. 1, Pl. 55.1; Eran 1987: App. A.1; Kletter 1991: 151 Table 9B.9.
Location: Eretz Israel Museum, Tel Aviv, K-8920.

4 Gerah.1
Jerusalem (Beit Kaifa). 2.120 grams.
Dome, limestone. 11.7 × 9.5 × 8.8 mm. PS: Fair.
Notes: No photograph or drawing has been published. The weight was found on bedrock, under an Iron Age II stratum (not fully published yet). It was stolen afterwards (G. Barkay 1981a: 289).
Literature: *HadArch* 40 (1971): 19; G. Barkay 1981a: 289 Table 2.3; Eran 1987: App. B.3 (?); Kletter 1991: 152 Table 9C.1.
Location: Private collection.

4 Gerah.2 (Fig. 37.3)
Site unknown. Museum no. K-8918. 2.7157 grams.
Dome, limestone. 11 × 13 mm. PS: Good.
Notes: The numeral is 4, but Barkay thought that there are 20 Gerah per Shekel, thus that this weight belongs to a heavy, different Shekel standard.
Literature: G. Barkay 1981a: 289 no. 2, Pl. 55.2; Eran 1987: App. A.2; Kletter 1991: 152 Table 9C.2.
Location: Eretz Israel Museum, Tel Aviv.

4 Gerah.3
Site unknown. 2.30 grams.
Dome, limestone.

Notes: Spaer refers to Scott for a former publication of this weight, but I could not locate it.
Literature: Spaer 1982: 251 Pl. 41.k; Eran 1987: App. C.8; Kletter 1991: 152 Table 9C.3.
Location: Hecht Museum, Haifa, H-711 (?); see 4 Gerah.a (below).

4 Gerah.4
Site unknown. 2.57 grams.
Dome, purple limestone.
Literature: Agora 1975: no. 390; Kletter 1991: 152 Table 9C.4.
Location: Private collection.

4 Gerah.5
Site unknown. 2.25 grams.
Dome, limestone. 8 × 13 mm.
Literature: Qedar 1979: 29 no. 4060; Eran 1987: App. C.10; Kletter 1991: 152 Table 9C.5.
Location: Private collection.

4 Gerah.6
Site unknown. 2.29 grams.
Dome, white limestone. 10 × 13 mm.
Literature: Qedar 1979: 25 no. 5068; Eran 1987: App. C.9; Kletter 1991: 152 Table 9C.6.
Location: Private collection.

4 Gerah.7
Site unknown. 2.52 grams.
Dome, grey limestone. 10.5 × 12 mm.
Literature: Kroha (ed.) 1980: 85; Eran 1987: App. C.7; Kletter 1991: 152 Table 9C.7.
Location: Private collection.

4 Gerah.8
Site unknown. 2.16 grams.
Dome, grey limestone. 8.7 × 12.4 mm.
Literature: Kroha (ed.) 1980: 84; Eran 1987: App. C.11; Kletter 1991: 152 Table 9C.8.
Location: Private collection.

4 Gerah.a
Site unknown. Museum no. H-711. 2.49 grams.
Dome, limestone. Diameter 13 mm.
Notes: This is probably the same weight as 4 Gerah.3 (above), and the difference in weight are due either to mistake or different weighing.

Literature: Meshorer in press: no. 37.
Location: Hecht Museum, Haifa.

5 Gerah.1
Gezer. 2.30 grams.
Dome, quartzite. Five vertical lines on the base.
Context: 'Semitic IV' level, context not clear.
Notes: Scott suggested that the signs mean $^1/5$ = 4 Gerah, or 5 Gerah = $^1/4$. It seems
to me that the five lines on the base mean '5', and have the same value as the
Hieratic numeral on the dome, since both are found on the same weight. This
strengthens the reading of the Hieratic numerals on the Gerah weights at their face
value.
Literature: Macalister 1912: 283; Barrois 1932: 65 no. 18; Scott 1964: 58 no. 4;
1965: 136-37; Kaufman 1967: 40; Eran 1987: App. B.3; Kletter 1991: 152 Table
9D.1.
Location: Not clear, Istanbul (?).

5 Gerah.2
Jerusalem. Reg. no. 3227. 2.57 grams.
Dome, limestone. 10.3 × 22 mm. PS: Fair.
Context: Locus A.672.12. Season 1963.
Literature: Scott 1965: 129, 136, Fig. 9, Pl. 24.9; Kaufman 1967: 40 no. 5; Scott
1985: 199 no. 2, Fig. 78.2; Eran 1987: App. B.4; Kletter 1991: 152 Table 9D.3.
Location: 'Amman 1963'.

5 Gerah.3
Site unknown. 2.87 grams.
Dome, white limestone. 11 × 12.4 × 10.5 mm.
Literature: Lemaire 1976: 38-39 Pl. 1.15; Eran 1987: App. B.3; Kletter 1991: 152
Table 9D.3.
Location: Private collection.

5 Gerah.4 (Fig. 37.4)
Site unknown. Museum no. K-8919. 2.6179 grams.
Dome, limestone. 11 × 13 mm.
Literature: G. Barkay 1981a: 289-90 Pl. 55.3; Eran 1987: App. A.4; Kletter 1991:
152 Table 9D.4.
Location: Eretz Israel Museum, Tel Aviv.

5 Gerah.5
Site unknown. 3.05 grams.
Dome, orange limestone. 11 × 14 mm.
Literature: Qedar 1978: 13 no. 45 = Qedar 1981: no. 80; Eran 1987: App. C.12 =
C.13; Kletter 1991: 152 Table 9D.5.

Notes: This weight was offered twice for sale, thus mentioned in two auction catalogues. Eran treated it as two separate weights.
Location: Private collection.

5 Gerah.6
Site unknown. 2.99 grams.
Dome, limestone. 10 × 18.5 mm.
Literature: Qedar 1978: 14 no. 47; Eran 1987: App. C.14; Kletter 1991: 152 Table 9D.6.
Location: Private collection.

5 Gerah.7
Site unknown. 2.69 grams.
Dome, red limestone. 9.8 × 13.1 mm.
Notes: No drawing or photograph was published, but the inscription was given in the text.
Literature: Kroha (ed.) 1980: no. 82; Eran 1987: App. C.16; Kletter 1991: 152 Table 9D.7.
Location: Private collection.

5 Gerah.a
Site unknown. 2.91 grams.
Dome, blue glass. 11 × 13.5 mm.
Notes: The material is unique, without comparison among Iron Age weights from Judah. Glass was used for weights, but much later. Until similar weights are found in excavations, this object should be treated with caution.
Literature: Kroha (ed.) 1980: no. 83.
Location: Private collection.

5 Gerah.b
Site unknown. 2.5772 grams.
Half-ball, yellow-brown limestone.
Notes: Ben-David saw this weight as ¼ Nsf, but it seems to be 5 Gerah. Since he gave very few details, it may equal one of the weights discussed above (but I could not find proof for this). The photograph does not show any inscription, and it may be an uninscribed weight.
Literature: Ben-David 1979: 42 no. 3.
Location: Private collection.

6 Gerah.1
Jerusalem. Reg. no. 5455. 2.90 grams.
Dome, grey and white limestone. PS: Good.
Context: Locus K.101.5. Season 1965.
Literature: Scott 1985: 199 no. 3, Fig. 78.3; Kletter 1991: 152 Table 9E.1.
Location: Royal Ontario Museum, Toronto.

6 Gerah.2
Lachish. 3.12 grams. PS: Slightly damaged.
Dome, white limestone. $10.2 \times 14 \times 11$ mm.
Context: Locus D.500, a whole area.
Notes: Diringer wrote that the signs are made with ink, a Shekel mark and a numeral above it. He read this as ¼ Shekel or ½ Beqaᶜ. Scott read here ½ Beqaᶜ.
Literature: Diringer 1942: 93; Moscati 1951: 104 no. 17; Diringer 1953: 352 no. 54; Scott 1964: 63 no. 8; Eran 1987: App. B.9; Kletter 1991: 153 Table 9E.2.
Location: Not clear.

6 Gerah.3 (Fig. 37.5)
Malhata. Reg. no. 2037/50. 3.2464 grams.
Dome, limestone. $11 \times 13.5 \times 12$ mm. PS: Excellent.
Context: Locus 1, a brick building, 7th century BCE.
Literature: G. Barkay 1981a: 290-91 no. 5, Pl. 55.1; Eran 1987: App. A.5; Kletter 1991: 153 Table 9E.3; forthcoming b: no. 5.
Location: Tel Aviv University.

6 Gerah.4
Tel el-Far'ah (South). Reg. no. 5661. 3.50 grams.
Dome, limestone.
Context: Locus C.395, dated to the 21st or 22nd dynasties (Macdonald 1932: Plan 80). It is an area in the south of the Tel, but the absolute height (395) better matches the 'Greek' level, B (Petrie 1930: Pls. 59, 60).
Notes: Petrie explained this weight as ¼ Beqaᶜ. Scott read the sign as 7, either 7/20 or 7/24; or as the letter *b* with 2 lines, in the sense of '½ Beqaᶜ'. The reading '6 Gerah' was first proposed by Barkay.
Literature: Petrie 1930: Pl. 49; Scott 1964: 60 no. 40; Kaufman 1967: 40; Dever 1970: Fig. 22; G. Barkay 1981a: Table 4; Eran 1987: App. B.7; Kletter 1991: 153 Table 9E.4.
Location: Petrie Collection, London.

6 Gerah.5
Site unknown (Kh. el Kom?). 3.49 grams.
Dome, light coloured limestone. PS: Damaged.
Literature: Dever 1970: 184 Fig. 15.11; Eran 1987: App. B.8; Kletter 1991: 153 Table 9E.5.
Location: Not clear.

6 Gerah.6
Site unknown. Museum no. K-8917. 3.3306 grams.
Dome, limestone. 10×14.5 mm.
Literature: G. Barkay 1981a: 289-91 no. 6, Pl. 55.5; Eran 1987: App. A.6; Kletter 1991: 153 Table 9E.6.
Location: Eretz Israel Museum, Tel Aviv.

6 Gerah.7
Site unknown. 3.595 grams.
Dome, limestone.
Notes: Scott read the inscription as 8 Gerah, or ²/₆ Shekel, or ²/₅ Nsf, or 7 Gerah.
Kaufman read 2 + 5 = 7.
Literature: Scott 1964: 58-59, Fig. 2a.10; Kaufman 1967: 40; Dever 1970: Fig. 22;
G. Barkay 1981a: Table 4; Eran 1987: App. B.6; Kletter 1991: 153 Table 9E.7.
Location: Private collection.

6 Gerah.8
Site unknown. 3.51 grams.
Dome, red limestone. 12 × 14 mm.
Literature: Qedar 1978: 13 no. 44; Eran 1987: App. C.17; Kletter 1991: 153 Table
9E.8.
Location: Private collection.

6 Gerah.9
Site unknown. 2.94 grams.
Dome, limestone. 11 × 13 mm.
Literature: Qedar 1978: 13 no. 46; Eran 1987: App. C.15; Kletter 1991: 153 Table
9E.9.
Location: Private collection.

6 Gerah.10
Site unknown. 3.22 grams.
Dome, limestone. 11 × 14 mm.
Literature: Qedar 1978: 29 no. 4059; Eran 1987: App. C.20; Kletter 1991: 153
Table 9E.10.
Location: Private collection.

6 Gerah.11
Site unknown. 3.32 grams.
Dome, yellow limestone. 10.3 × 14.2 mm.
Literature: Kroha (ed.) 1980: 79; Eran 1987: App. C.18; Kletter 1991: 153 Table
9E.11.
Location: Private collection.

6 Gerah.12
Site unknown. 3.26 grams.
Dome, grey limestone. 11 × 13.9 mm.
Literature: Kroha (ed.) 1980: 80; Eran 1987: App. C.19; Kletter 1991: 153 Table
9E.12.
Location: Private collection.

6 Gerah.13
Site unknown. 3.07 grams.

Dome, red limestone. 10.4 × 13.5 mm.
Literature: Kroha (ed.) 1980: 81; Eran 1987: App. C.21; Kletter 1991: 153 Table 9E.13.
Location: Private collection.

7 Gerah.1
Site unknown. 3.61 grams.
Dome, bronze. 7 × 12 × 9 mm. PS: Fair.
Literature: Lemaire 1976: 39 Pl. 1.16; G. Barkay 1981a: 290-91; Eran 1987: App. B.24; Kletter 1991: 153 Table 9F.1.
Location: Private collection.

7 Gerah.2 (Fig. 37.6)
Site unknown. Museum no. H-710. 3.22 grams.
Dome, limestone.
Notes: This weight was published by Spaer. The details indicate that it is the same weight in the museum. The Hieratic sign is clear.
Literature: Meshorer in press: no. 36; Spaer 1982: 251 Pl. 41.J; Eran 1987: App. C.22; Kletter 1991: 153 Table 9F.2.
Location: Hecht Museum, Haifa.

8 Gerah.1
Lachish. Reg. no. 7124. 3.820 grams.
Flattened dome, dark grey limestone. 11 × 15.5 × 14.5 mm. PS: Very good.
Context: Locus H.18.1085 (Diringer 1942), a room of level III with *lmlk* jars (Tufnell 1953: Plan 114). In the final report, the weight is ascribed to locus 1084, again a clear locus of level III (Tufnell 1953: 123). Thus, this is an 8th-century-BCE weight.
Notes: Diringer and Scott made all sorts of suggestions for this weight: Hebrew letter $z = 7$, or $2/3$, or $2/x$.
Literature: Diringer 1942: 96 Pl. 12.7; Moscati 1951: 105 no. 16; Diringer 1953: 349 Pl. 51.10; Stern 1963: 872 Table C; Scott 1964: 62 no. 14; Kaufman 1967: 40; Dever 1970: Fig. 21; G. Barkay 1981a: Table 5; Eran 1987: App. B.17; Kletter 1991: 153 Table 9G.1.
Location: British Museum, no. 160030, London.

8 Gerah.2 (Fig. 37.7)
Lachish. 3.770 grams.
Cube, yellow limestone. 12.5 × 13 mm.
Context: Locus J.17.1042, a room of levels III–II. Locus J.17.1073 is also given for this weight, a locus of level III (Tufnell 1953: 11).
Notes: Scott read the signs as $1/6 + 1/6 = 1/3$. Barkay read as Hieratic 8, but the weight (3.77 grams) is exceptional in his view.
Literature: Diringer 1942: 96-97; Moscati 1951: 105 no. 20; Diringer 1953: 352 no. 50, Pl. 51.15; Stern 1963: 872 Table C; Scott 1964: 62 no. 13, Fig. 3d; Kaufman

1967: 40; Dever 1970: Fig. 21; G. Barkay 1981a: Table 5; Eran 1987: App. B.18; Kletter 1991: 153 Table 9G.2.
Location: not clear.

8 Gerah.3 (Fig. 37: 8)
Lachish. Reg. no. 7254. 4.879 grams.
Dome, red-brown limestone.
Context: D/X, out of context.
Notes: Scott gave the weight as 4.95 grams.
Literature: Diringer 1942: 97; 1953: 354 no. 46, Pl. 50.10; Scott 1964: 62 no. 17, Fig. 3f; Kaufman 1967: 40; G. Barkay 1981a: Table 5; Eran 1987: App. B.10; Kletter 1991: 153 Table 9G.3.
Location: Rockefeller 39-380; at the Israel Museum, Jerusalem.

8 Gerah.4
Gezer. 3.84 grams.
Dome, limestone.
Context: Level 8 (Macalister 1905: 192), but this does not help much and the exact context is not clear.
Notes: The form of the Hieratic sign is peculiar. Only a drawing of the script was published, not of the whole weight.
Literature: Macalister 1905: 192; Dalman 1906: 93 Table; Macalister 1912: 285; Pilcher 1912: 191 Table; Barrois 1932: 65 no. 20; Stern 1963: Table C; Scott 1964: 61 no. 15; Kaufman 1967: 40; G. Barkay 1981a: Table 5; Eran 1987: App. B.16; Kletter 1991: 153 Table 9G.4.
Location: Not clear

8 Gerah.5
Unknown. 4.28 grams.
Dome, white limestone. PS: Good.
Notes: There are marks on the base. The published photograph is not good.
Literature: Dever 1970: 184, figs. 15.9, 21; Eran 1987: App. B.12; Kletter 1991: 153 Table 9G.5.
Location: Private collection.

8 Gerah.6
Site unknown. 4.17 grams.
Dome, black bitumen limestone.
Literature: Dever 1970: Fig. 15.10, Eran 1987: App. B.15; Kletter 1991: 153 Table 9G.6.
Location: Private collection.

8 Gerah.7
Site unknown. 4.680 grams.
Dome, limestone. 11.5 × 14 × 16.2 mm.

Literature: Lemaire 1976: 36-37 Pl. 1.2; Eran 1987: App. B.11; Kletter 1991: 153 Table 9G.7.
Location: Private collection.

8 Gerah.8
Site unknown. 4.24 grams.
Dome, limestone. $11.8 \times 13.4 \times 15.4$ mm.
Literature: Lemaire 1976: 37 Pl. 1.12; Eran 1987: App. B.13; Kletter 1991: 153 Table 9G.8.
Location: Private collection.

8 Gerah.9
Site unknown. 4.22 grams.
Dome, limestone. $10 \times 12.5 \times 16$ mm.
Literature: Lemaire 1976: 37 Pl. 1.13; Eran 1987: App. B.14; Kletter 1991: 153 Table 9G.9.
Location: Private collection.

8 Gerah.10
Site unknown. Museum no. K-8915. 4.459 grams.
Dome, dark limestone. 11×16.5 mm.
Literature: G. Barkay 1981a: 291-92 no. 8, Pl. 56.7 Table 5; Eran 1987: App. A.8; Kletter 1991: 153 Table 9G.10.
Location: Eretz Israel Museum, Tel Aviv.

8 Gerah.11
Site unknown. 3.6 grams (?).
Dome, limestone. No drawing or photograph was published.
Notes: Scott read the sign as $4 \times 2 = 8$. The weight does not fit the conception of 20 Gerah per Shekel.
Literature: Dalman 1906: 8; Barrois 1932: 65 no. 19; Scott 1964: 60 no. 11; Kaufman 1967: 40; Eran 1987: App. B.19; Kletter 1991: 153 Table 9G.11.
Location: Private collection.

8 Gerah.12
Site unknown. 4.29 grams.
Dome, limestone.
Literature: Spaer 1982: 251 no. 9, Pl. 41.i; Kletter 1991: 154 Table 9G.12
Location: Private collection.

8 Gerah.13
Site unknown. 4.34 grams.
Dome, red limestone. 11×16 mm.
Literature: Qedar 1979: 28 no. 4057; R. Barkay 1987: 189 Pl.1a; Eran 1987: App. C.26; Kletter 1991: 154 Table 9G.13
Location: Israel Bank, Jerusalem.

8 Gerah.14
Site unknown. 4.55 grams.
Dome, limestone. 12 × 15.5 mm.
Literature: Qedar 1981: 32 no. 79; Eran 1987: App. B.19; Kletter 1991: 154 Table 9G.14
Location: Private collection.

8 Gerah.15
Site unknown. 4.46 grams.
Dome, red-brown limestone. 12 × 15.5 mm.
Literature: Qedar 1983: 25; Eran 1987: App. C.24; Kletter 1991: 154 Table 9G.15
Location: Private collection.

8 Gerah.16
Site unknown. 4.44 grams.
Dome, red limestone. 12.7 × 15.5 mm.
Literature: Kroha (ed.) 1980: no. 75; Eran 1987: App. C.25; Kletter 1991: 154 Table 9G.16
Location: Private collection.

8 Gerah.17
Site unknown. 4.49 grams.
Dome, limestone. 13.7 × 14 mm.
Notes: The inscription is peculiar.
Literature: Kroha (ed.) 1980: no. 74; Kletter 1991: 154 Table 9G.17
Location: Private collection.

10 Gerah.1
Lachish. 5.130 grams. PS: Very good.
Dome, white-yellow limestone. 12.5 × 16.5 mm.
Context: area D/500, out of context.
Notes: Diringer explained this weight as $1/2$ Nsf or $2/3$ Pym, taking the inscription simply as two lines, hence '2'. Scott explained the sign as a Hebrew numeral 8, but could not find of which standard; or perhaps as $1/2$ Nsf.
Literature: Diringer 1942: 95-96 Pl. 12.9; Moscati 1951: 105, no. 18; Diringer 1953: 352 no. 45, Pl. 51.11; Scott 1964: 63 no. 19; Kaufman 1967: 40-41; Eran 1987: App. B.21; Kletter 1991: 154 Table 9H.1.
Location: British Museum, no. 160031.

10 Gerah.2
Site unknown. 5.24 grams.
Dome, limestone. 10.6 × 16 × 17.2 mm.
Literature: Lemaire 1976: 38 Pl. 1.14; Eran 1987: App. B.20; Kletter 1991: 154 Table 9H.2.
Location: Private collection.

10 Gerah.3
Site unknown. Museum no. K-8911. 5.4902 grams.
Dome, limestone. 13 × 16.5 mm.
Literature: G. Barkay 1981a: 292 no. 9, Pl. 56.8 Table 5; Eran 1987: App. A.9; Kletter 1991: 154 Table 9H.3.
Location: Eretz Israel Museum, Tel Aviv.

10 Gerah.4 (Fig. 37.9)
Site unknown. Museum no. K-8913. 5.6567 grams.
Dome, brown limestone. 12.5 × 17.5 mm.
Notes: There is another sign above the numeral (⌁). Barkay suggested that it is the sign of the Gerah unit.
Literature: G. Barkay 1981a: 292 no. 10, Pl. 56.9 Table 5; Eran 1987: App. A.10; Kletter 1991: 154 Table 9H.4.
Location: Eretz Israel Museum, Tel Aviv.

10 Gerah.5
Site unknown. 4.47 grams.
Dome, pink limestone.
Notes: Scott read the sign as $8 = {}^3\!/_8$ Shekel, or $8 + 1 = 9$.
Literature: Scott 1964: 61 no. 16; Kaufman 1967: 41; G. Barkay 1981a: Table 5; Kletter 1991: 154 Table 9H.5.
Location: Private collection.

10 Gerah.6
Site unknown. 5.04 grams.
Dome, orange limestone.
Notes: Qedar explained all the 10 Gerah weights as 8 Gerah.
Literature: Qedar 1978: 13 no. 41; Eran 1987: App. C.31; Kletter 1991: 154 Table 9H.6.
Location: Private collection.

10 Gerah.7
Site unknown. 4.66 grams.
Dome, pink limestone. 14 × 15 mm.
Literature: Qedar 1978: no. 42; Eran 1987: App. C.33; Kletter 1991: 154 Table 9H.7.
Location: Private collection.

10 Gerah.8
Site unknown. 5.39 grams.
Dome, orange limestone. 13 × 17 mm.
Literature: Qedar 1978: no. 43; Eran 1987: App. C.28; Kletter 1991: 154 Table 9H.8.
Location: Private collection.

10 Gerah.9
Site unknown. 4.66 grams.
Dome, yellow limestone. 11 × 16 mm.
Literature: Qedar 1979: 18 no. 4058; Eran 1987: App. C.32; Kletter 1991: 154 Table 9H.9.
Notes: It is not the same as no. 7 (above), since the size and colours are different, and Qedar refers to weight no. 7 in the auction catalogue of no. 9.
Location: Private collection.

10 Gerah.10
Site unknown. 5.62 grams.
Dome, limestone. 16.5 × 13.2 mm.
Literature: Kroha (ed.) 1980: no. 76; Eran 1987: App. C.27; Kletter 1991: 154 Table 9H.10.
Location: Private collection.

10 Gerah.11
Site unknown. 5.31 grams.
Dome, limestone. 11.7 × 16.8 mm.
Literature: Kroha (ed.) 1980: no. 76; Eran 1987: App. C.27; Kletter 1991: 154 Table 9H.10.
Location: Private collection.

10 Gerah.12
Site unknown. 5.21 grams. There is an additional line near the numeral sign.
Dome, limestone. 13 × 16 mm. PS: Very good.
Literature: Qedar 1981: 32 no. 78; R. Barkay 1987: 188 Fig. 10.c; Eran 1987: App. C.30 = C.34; Kletter 1991: 154 Table 9H.12.
Notes: The Israel Bank bought this weight, but Eran was not aware of this, and treated it as two different weights. Loyal to his method, he found different Gerah standards here (first 10 × 0.52, then 11 × 0.4736).
Location: Bank of Israel, Jerusalem.

10 Gerah.13
Site unknown. Museum no. H-1733. 4.88 grams.
Dome, limestone. c. 18 mm diameter.
Literature: Meshorer in press: no. 35; Kletter 1991: 154 Table 9H.13.
Location: Hecht Museum, Haifa.

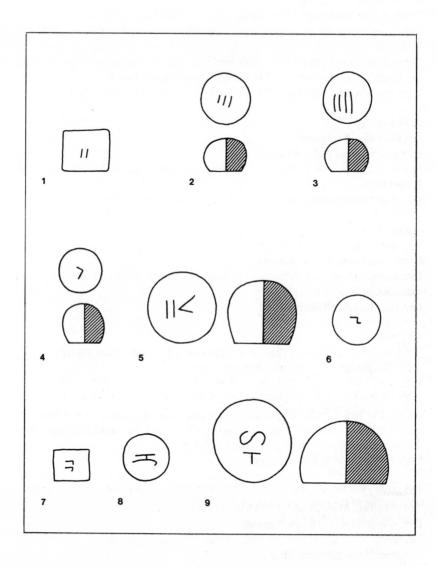

Figure 37. *Selection of Gerah weights.* Legend: 1 Gerah 2.1; 2. Gerah 3.1; 3. Gerah 4.2; 4. Gerah 5.4; 5. Gerah 6.3; 6. Gerah 7.2; 7. Gerah 8.2; 8. Gerah 8.3; 9. Gerah 10.4. Drawings are not to scale (the size of each JIL is given in the catelogue). The weights are referred to according to their catalogue numbers.

Appendix 2

ADDENDA (WEIGHTS ADDED BETWEEN 1991 AND 1996)

ᛝ *1 Weights*

ᛝ *1.35*
Site unknown. 11.25 grams.
Dome, reddish limestone. 19 × 20 mm. PS: Very good.
Literature: Deutsch 1989: 33 no. 86.
Location: Private collection.

ᛝ *1.36*
Site unknown. 11.69 grams.
Dome, reddish limestone. 18 × 20 mm.
Literature: Deutsch 1989: 33 no. 87.
Location: Private collection.

ᛝ *1. 37*
Site unknown.
Dome, limestone. 15 × 21.5 mm.
Literature: courtesy of Y. Meshorer and Hecht Museum (bought in 1992).
Location: Hecht Museum, Haifa, no. H-2375.

ᛝ *1. 38*
Site unknown. 11.45 grams.
Dome, pink limestone.
Notes: There is a danger that it is the same weight as no. 22 above (but the weight and the colour of the stone are stated as different).
Literature: Agora 1974: 8 no. 4.
Location: Private collection.

ᛝ *1: 39*
Site unknown.
Dome, limestone.
Notes: A good photograph was published with the definition 'Herodian weight'. Origin, weight and size were not published.
Literature: Piccirillo 1983: 104.
Location: Franciscan Museum, Jerusalem, no. 6.

ﺵ *1.40*
Malhata. Reg. no. 1904. 11.1664 grams. Season 1993.
Dome, brown-pink limestone. 12 × 20 × 15 mm.
Context: Locus 249, 7th century BC.
Literature: Not yet published, courtesy of I. Beit-Arieh; Kletter forthcoming b: no. 12.
Location: Tel Aviv University.

ﺵ *1.41*
Malhata. Reg. no. 1857. 11.4646 grams. Season 1993.
Dome, brown-grey limestone. 16 × 17 × 13 mm. PS: Very good.
Context: Locus 242, 7th century BC (cf. ﺵ 2.39).
Literature: Not yet published, courtesy of I. Beit-Arieh; Kletter forthcoming b: no. 13.
Location: Tel Aviv University.

ﺵ *1.42*
Site unknown. 12.2 grams.
Dome, reddish limestone. The ﺵ sign is very angular.
Literature: Deutsch 1994: no. 46.
Location: Private collection.

ﺵ *1.b*
Megiddo. 11.75 grams.
Irregular ellipsoid, fossil limestone.
Context: Level IV.
Notes: The weight is marked with the Shekel (?) sign, but the excavators did not refer to it. It may be an accidental scratching.
Literature: Lamon and Shipton 1939: Pl. 104: 37.
Location: Not clear, perhaps Istanbul.

ﺵ *2 Weights*

ﺵ *2.35*
Site unknown. 22.22 grams.
Dome, reddish limestone. Size: 23 × 26 mm. PS: Good.
Literature: Deutsch 1989: 32 no. 84.
Location: Private collection.

ﺵ *2.36*
Site unknown. 22.06 grams.
Dome, white limestone. Size: 24 × 26 mm. PS: Good.
Literature: Deutsch 1989: 32 no. 85.
Location: Private collection.

ﬨ *2.37*
Site unknown. Weight not published.
Dome, limestone. Size: 20.5 × 26.5 mm.
Notes: There is a danger that this weight was bought from Deutsch, thus is already listed above.
Literature: courtesy of Y. Meshorer and the Hecht Museum.
Location: Hecht Museum, H-2374 (bought in 1992). Currently at the Israel Museum, Jerusalem (?).

ﬨ *2.38*
Site unknown. 22.75 grams.
Dome, pink limestone.
Notes: The Shekel sign is very angular at the bottom.
Literature: Agora 1974: 8 no. 3.
Location: Private collection.

ﬨ *2.39*
Malhata. Season 1933. 23.0895 grams.
Dome, dark brown-grey limestone. 22 × 25 × 19 mm.
Context: Locus 242, 7th century BC (cf. ﬨ 1.41).
Notes: There are remains of white paint in the Shekel mark, a unique phenomenon among the JILs.
Literature: Courtesy of I. Beit Arieh; Kletter forthcoming b: no. 10.
Location: Tel Aviv University.

ﬨ *2.40*
Ramot (north of Jerusalem). Reg. no. 1780. 22.60 grams (22.50 after cleaning).
Dome, white-pink limestone.
Context: Locus 181, a domestic context, 8th–7th centuries BC.
Notes: A small part of the dome was not cleaned, to preserved the shallow inscription.
Literature: Courtesy of A. De-Groot; Kletter forthcoming c: no. 1.
Location: IAA.

ﬨ *2.41*
Jerusalem (Shiloh). City of David. Reg. no. E1/9134. 22.80 grams.
PS: Good, few areas of encrustation.
Dome, yellow limestone. 20.5 × 16.8 × 16 mm.
Context: Locus 1310, level 11, 7th century BC.
Literature: Eran 1996: W.96 Fig. 35.8, Pl. 14: 5.
Location: Hebrew University, Jerusalem.

ﬨ *2.42* (Fig. 31.9)
Jerusalem (Shiloh). City of David. Reg. no. G8124. 22.70 grams.
PS: Slightly damaged.

Dome, limestone. 21 × 24 mm.
Context: Surface find.
Literature: Eran 1996: W.199, Fig. 39.12, Pl. 16.7.
Location: Hebrew University, Jerusalem.

४ *4 Weights*

४ *4.48*
Site unknown. 44.37 grams.
Dome, white limestone. Size 3.3 × 3.6 mm.
Notes: The photograph does not show any script, but the text indicate remains of '4 Shekel' inscription. There is a lead filling in the base.
Literature: Deutsch 1989: 32 no. 83.
Location: Private collection.

४ *4.49*
Site unknown. 45.43 grams.
Dome, pink limestone.
Notes: The Shekel sign is very angular.
Literature: Agora 1974: 8 no. 2.
Location: Private collection.

४ *4.50* (Fig. 32.6)
Samaria. Reg. no. Q.1226. 46 grams.
Dome, white limestone. 30 × 32 × 25 mm.
Literature: Not yet published
Location: The Hebrew University, Jerusalem. No. 658.

४ *4.51*
Jericho (?). 44.37 grams.
Dome, limestone.
Literature: Not yet published.
Notes: The weight was registered by Avigad in the 1940s, and was a gift of the late Mrs Market-Krause (for Iron Age remains at Jericho, see Weippert and Weippert 1976).
Location: The Hebrew University, Jerusalem, no. 657.

४ *4.52*
Ein Gedi. 46.5 grams
Dome, limestone. 34 × 40 mm.
Notes: Cf. no. 17 above. It is the one from Avigad's excavations in the 'cave of the pool'.
Literature: Avigad: 1961 Pl. 7.3; Dever 1970: Table.
Location: IAA 67-488.

ষ *4.53*
Jerusalem 'Ophel' (Duncan). 45.23 grams
Dome, orange limestone. c. 22 × 34 mm.
PS: Slightly worn, otherwise good. A natural white mark on the side.
Context: 'Field 7, no. 11, 842'.
Literature: Courtesy of the PEF; Eran 1996: W.211.
Location: PEF London, no. 866 (D17), old no. 50/4841.

ষ *4.54*
Jerusalem 'Ophel' (Duncan). 44.06 grams
Dome, dark grey limestone. c. 22 × 31 × 25 mm.
PS: The dome is slightly worn.
Context: Field 7, no. 5, 845.
Literature: Courtesy of the PEF; Eran 1996: W.209.
Location: PEF London, no. 869, old no. 50/4840.

ষ *4.55*
Jerusalem (Shiloh). City of David. Reg. no. G11597. 44.80 grams.
Dome, limestone. 32.7 × 32 × 28 mm.
Notes: No photograph or drawing has been published.
Context: Locus 967, level 10, 7th century BC.
Literature: Eran 1996: W.147.
Location: Lost.

ষ *4.56*
Jerusalem (Shiloh). City of David. Reg. no. G11598. 46.20 grams.
Dome, limestone. 25 × 34.5 × 24 mm.
Context: Locus 967, see no. 55 above.
Notes: No photograph or drawing has been published.
Literature: Eran 1996: W.148.
Location: Lost.

ষ *8 Weights*

ষ *8.43*
Site unknown. 92.03 grams.
Dome, pink limestone.
Literature: Agora 1974: 8 no. 1.
Location: Not clear.

ষ *8.44*
Jerusalem (the Temple Mount). 88.4 grams.
Dome, limestone.
Notes: No photograph or drawing has been published.
This weight was probably found in B. Mazar's excavations (but does not appear in:

B. Mazar 1972; B. Mazar and E. Mazar 1989).
Literature: Jerusalem City Museum: 1, no. 23.
Location: Not clear.

ℷ 8.45
Jerusalem (Billig). Reg. no. 1023. 86.1812 grams.
Dome, grey limestone. PS: A little damaged.
Context: The weight was discovered in Armon Ha-Naziv (area of the residency of
the British high commissioner during the Mandate period). It was found in a
foundation trench (locus 103) with a few Iron Age sherds (but without clear
stratigraphy).
Literature: Courtesy of Y. Billig (excavation no. 1896).
Location: IAA.

ℷ 8.46 (Fig. 32.8)
Site unknown. 90.3 grams.
Dome, reddish limestone.
Literature: Deutsch 1994: no. 45.
Location: Private collection?

ℷ 8.47
Malhata. Reg. no. 835/1. 89.5145 grams.
Dome, brown limestone. 28 × 41 × 34 mm. PS: Good.
Context: Locus 55.
Notes: The numeral sign is upside-down. The Shekel sign is very angular.
Literature: Courtesy of I. Beit-Arieh and M. Kochavi; Kletter forthcoming b: no. 1.
Location: Tel Aviv University.

ℷ 8.48
Malhata. Reg. no. 328/50. 91.5470 grams.
Season 1993. 33 × 40 × 34 mm.
Dome, brown limestone. PS: Excellent.
Context: Locus 435, 7th century BC.
Literature: Courtesy of I. Beit-Arieh; Kletter forthcoming b: no. 7.
Location: Tel Aviv University.

ℷ 8.49
Jerusalem (Duncan). Reg. NBS 27 825. 90.774 grams.
Dome, yellow-orange limestone. PS: Good, but the dome is damaged.
Context: NBS = steps of the North Step bastion. It was found on 20 November,
1927.
Notes: The Shekel sign is rounded. This weight is different from nos. 1–2 (above).
Literature: Courtesy of the PEF; Eran 1996: W.218.
Location: PEF, London, no. 858.

ᛒ *8.50*

Jerusalem (Duncan). Reg. no. 87, 16. 87.97 grams.

Dome, white limestone. PS: Badly broken and worn. Part of the numeral is missing.

Context: 9B is the area, 'the outer 50 feet north of the sewer'. 22 ft.

Notes: The Shekel sign is rounded. This weight is different from nos. 1–2 (above).

Literature: Courtesy of the PEF; Eran 1996: W.217.

Location: PEF, London, no. 861 (formerly 50/4843).

ᛒ *8.51* (Fig. 32.9)

Jerusalem (Shiloh). City of David. Reg. no. G11001. 92.12 grams.

Dome, limestone. 32 × 42.7 × 33 mm.

Context: Area G, surface find.

Literature: Eran 1996: W.200 Fig. 39.13, Pl. 16.8.

Location: Hebrew University.

ᛒ *8.c*

Site unknown. 90.78 grams.

Dome, limestone. Diameter 42 mm.

Notes: The script is very exceptional: ᛁᚻ.

Literature: Courtesy of Y. Meshorer and the Hecht Museum.

Location: Hecht Museum, Haifa, no. H-1972.

ᛒ *8.d*

Site unknown. 85.5 grams.

Dome, limestone. 32.5 × 40 mm.

Notes: I have not seen this weight, it may be an uninscribed one.

Literature: Courtesy of Y. Meshorer and the Hecht Museum.

Location: Hecht Museum, Haifa, no. H-2371.

ᛒ *12–40 Weights*

ᛒ *16.4* (Fig. 33.4)

Jerusalem (Shiloh). City of David. Reg. no. G2196. 113.75 + x grams. 26 × 53 mm.

PS: Broken, but the upper part with the inscription survived.

Dome, limestone.

Context: Locus 736, level 9, Persian period.

Literature: Eran 1996: W.160 Fig. 38.4.

Location: Hebrew University, Jerusalem.

ᛒ *24.3*

Beit Safafeh. Reg. no. 1394. 287.76 grams.

Dome, hard limestone. 52 × 61 × 43 mm.

Context: Locus 182, depression on the rock, domestic context (on the site, see Feig 1994).

Notes: Only the numeral sign appears on the dome. The weight matches 25, and not

24, Shekel (it is 6.65 heavier than the average of the two known 24 Shekel weights).
Literature: Courtesy of N. Feig; Kletter in press.
Location: IAA no. 94-2443.

४ 40: 3

Jerusalem (Mazar?). 455.80 grams.
Dome, limestone.
Notes: Probably from the excavations of Mazar in Jerusalem. The information is very minimal, and I am not certain that this is an inscribed weight.
Literature: Jerusalem City Museum n.d.: 1 no. 24; cf. ४ 8.44 (above).
Location: not clear.

४ 16.a

Megiddo. 160.8 grams.
Ellipsoid, limestone. PS: Good.
Context: Locus 977, level IV.
Notes: Only part of the sign is seen in the photograph, and this part looks like the Shekel sign. But the sign is drawn in the text as a 'butterfly' sign (▷◁). The weight does not match 16 Judaean Shekel, the form is exceptional, and the origin is outside Judah. Therefore, I preferred not to include it within the JILs.
Literature: Lamon and Shipton 1939: Pl. 104.37.

४ 40: b

Samaria. Weight not published. Inscription: ▬◡ .
Dome, limestone. 106 × 124 mm. PS: Good (?).
Context: Locus LT.1.c.
Notes: The publication is not adequate to define this weight exactly. Puech (1984: 83 Table) claimed that the weight is 4541 grams, but this may relate to another weight. Albright calculated that it is a 200 Shekel weight, by comparing its volume with an uninscribed 400 Shekel weight from Tel Beit Mirsim (Albright 1943: 76 no. 7). This is not certain. Barkay (pers. comm.) noticed that the sign is similar to Hieratic 1000 (cf. Kadesh Barnea ostracon no. 6, written left to right).
Literature: Reisner, Fisher and Lyon 1924: 344 Fig. 217.4a.
Location: Istanbul (?).

Nsf Weights

Nsf.52

Site unknown. Museum no. 1981-124. 10.0 grams.
Dome, pink limestone. Size 18 × 20 mm.
Notes: Bought in Israel, a gift by M. and B. Ratner.
Literature: Ackerman and Braunstein 1982: 72 no. 57.
Location: The Jewish Museum, New York.

Nsf: 53
Site unknown. Reg. no. 3286.
Dome, limestone.
Notes: The weight was bought from a merchant in the 1940s, allegedly found in
'Nebi Daud' in Jerusalem. Avigad made a drawing of this weight in the registration
book.
Literature: Not yet published.
Location: The Hebrew University Collection, Jerusalem.

Nsf.54
Site unknown. 10.1 grams.
Dome, limestone.
Literature: Deutsch 1988: no. 126b.
Location: Not clear.

Nsf: 55
Site unknown. 9.4 grams. Size: 15 × 20 mm.
Dome, red limestone.
Literature: Deutsch 1988: no. 126c.
Notes: It is probably the same weight as Deutsch 1989: no. 88
Location: Not clear.

Nsf.56
Site unknown. c. 10.1 grams.
Dome, limestone. Size: 15 × 20.5 mm.
Notes: A new acquisition of the museum (1992), and it looks different to weight no.
54 (above).
Literature: Not yet published; Meshorer in press.
Location: Hecht Museum, Haifa, H-2373.

Nsf: 57
Site unknown. 9.3 grams.
Dome, white limestone.
Literature: Deutsch 1994: no. 47.
Notes:The colour and the photograph look different from Nsf.55 (above).
According to the text, the inscription is *n*, but the photograph shows at least two
letters, *ns*.
Location: Not clear.

Nsf.58
Site unknown. 9.61 grams.
Dome, limestone.
Literature: Superior Galleries 1992: no. 4587; Elayi 1991: no. 10.
Location: Private collection.

Nsf.59
Site unknown. 8.24 grams.
Dome, brown limestone.
Notes: The low weight is difficult, perhaps an indication of forgery (ancient one).
Literature: Superior Galleries 1992: no. 4588; Elayi 1991: no. 11.
Location: Private hands.

Pym Weights

Pym.48
Pisgat Zeev IV. Reg. no. 6322. 7.9 grams.
Dome, limestone.
Context: Locus 5150.
Literature: Nadelman 1993: 49; courtesy of Y. Nadelman.
Location: IAA.

Pym.49
Site unknown. 7.8 grams.
Dome, red limestone. PS: Good. 8.5 × 14.5 mm.
Context: Locus 5150.
Literature: Deutsch 1989: 33 no. 89.
Location: Private collection.

Pym.50
Site unknown. Museum. no. H-2377. 7.9 grams.
Dome, limestone. 15.5 × 18 mm. Bought in 1992.
Literature: Courtesy of Y. Meshorer and Hecht Museum.
Location: Hecht Museum, Haifa.

Pym.51
Mamila (Jerusalem). Reg. no. 7. 7.38 grams.
Dome, white limestone. 16 × 17 mm. PS: fair.
Context: Tomb 41, L.1.
Notes: the letter *m* is worn.
Literature: Courtesy of R. Reich (for the site, see Reich 1993).
Location: IAA.

Pym.52
Jerusalem (Mazar?). c. 7.5 grams.
Dome, black limestone. Other details not published.
Context: Not published.
Literature: Meshorer in press (?).
Location: IAA no. 86-261, exhibited at the Hecht Museum, Haifa.

Beqaᶜ Weights

Beqaᶜ.30
Nahal Elteke. 6.389 grams.
Dome, limestone.
Context: Survey, surface find, 13528/13334. It was found south of the Chalcolithic site no. 13-13/53/2.
Literature: Courtesy of Y. Dagan.
Location: IAA.

Beqaᶜ.31
Site unknown. Museum no. JM232-68a. 6.1 grams.
Dome, yellow-pink limestone.
Notes: Bought in Israel, gift of Joy Ungerleider in 1968.
Literature: Ackerman and Braunstein 1982: 72 no. 58.
Location: Jewish Museum, New York.

Beqaᶜ.32
Site unknown. 6.49 grams.
Dome, red limestone. 13 × 17 mm.
Literature: Deutsch 1989: 33 no. 90.
Location: Private hands.

Beqaᶜ.33
Site unknown. Museum no. H-2376. Ca. 6.90 grams.
Dome, white limestone. 13 × 18 mm.
Notes: reg. no. N-92-538.
Literature: Courtesy of the Hecht Museum.
Location: Hecht Museum, Haifa.

Beqaᶜ.34
Jerusalem (Mazar).
Dome, black limestone.
Notes: This weight was found in fills in B. Mazar's excavations (not published fully). It may be the same as Beqaᶜ.29 (above), but I am not certain.
Literature: Jerusalem City Museum n.d.: 1 no. 22; B. Mazar 1972: 88.
Location: Not clear.

Beqaᶜ.35
Site unknown. Museum no. E/53051. 6.08 grams.
Dome, dark brown limestone. 12.5 × 17.5 × 17.5 mm.
PS: Very good, polished surfaces, very little damage.
Notes: The weight was bought in 1914 from an Egyptian dealer.
Literature: Courtesy of J.A. Spencer and Pamela Magrill, the British Museum.
Location: British Museum, exhibited in the Palestine Room (no. 1914,0216.113).

Gerah Weights

3 Gerah.10
Site unknown. 1.8 grams.
Dome, grey limestone. 8 × 12 mm.
Literature: Deutsch 1989: 34 no. 96.
Location: Unknown.

3 Gerah.11
Site unknown. 1.8 grams.
Dome, white limestone.
Literature: Deutsch 1994: no. 49.
Location: Unknown.

4 Gerah.9
Malhata. Reg. no. 16492. 2.1874 grams.
Dome, white limestone. 9 × 12 × 10.5 mm. PS: Good.
Context: Locus 1118 (season 1994), 7th century BC.
Literature: Courtesy of I. Beit Arieh; Kletter forthcoming b: no. 14.
Location: Tel Aviv University.

5 Gerah.8
Site unknown. 2.74 grams.
Dome, limestone. 10 × 14 mm.
Literature: Deutsch 1989: 34 no. 94.
Location: Private collection.

5 Gerah.9
Site unknown. 2.63 grams.
Dome, limestone. 9 × 14 mm.
Literature: Deutsch 1989: 34 no. 95.
Location: Private collection.

5 Gerah.10
Site unknown. Museum no. H-2380
Dome, limestone. 10 × 14 mm.
Bought in 1992, reg. no. N92-540.
Literature: Courtesy of the Hecht Museum.
Location: Hecht Museum, Haifa.

5 Gerah.11
Tel Batash. Details not yet published.
Season 1981.
Dome, limestone.

Literature: Courtesy of A. Mazar.
Location: Hebrew University, Jerusalem.

6 Gerah.14
Site unknown. 3.64 grams.
Dome, grey limestone. 12 × 14 mm.
Literature: Deutsch 1989: 34 no. 92.
Location: Private collection.

6 Gerah.15
Site unknown. 3.39 grams.
Dome, red limestone. 12 × 14 mm.
Literature: Deutsch 1989: 34 no. 93.
Location: Private collection.

8 Gerah.18
Site unknown. Museum no. H-2379. 4.3 grams.
Dome, limestone. 12 × 15 mm.
Notes: Bought in 1992, no. N92-539 (?).
Literature: Courtesy of the Hecht Museum.
Location: Hecht Museum, Haifa.

8 Gerah.19
Site unknown. 4.1 grams.
Dome, grey limestone. 13 × 15 mm.
Literature: Deutsch 1990: 27 no. 1.
Location: Eretz Israel Museum, Tel Aviv.

8 Gerah.20
Site unknown. 4.8 grams.
Dome, white limestone.
Literature: Deutsch 1994: no. 48.
Location: Private collection.

8 Gerah.21
Site unknown. 3.77 grams.
Dome, red limestone.
Literature: Superior Galleries 1992: no. 4586.
Location: Private collection.

9 (?) Gerah.1
Site unknown. 5.16 grams.
Dome, grey limestone. 12 × 16 mm.
Notes: According to the text, the inscription is ⬌ ; in the photograph it looks
different (⬌).

Literature: Deutsch 1989: 33 no. 91.
Location: Not clear.

Notes on Further JILs

1. *Accho*. One ȣ weight, unit not clear. Published in a preliminary way (*HadArch* 14 [1965]: 9). It is included in Figs. 1, 3, 5, 6-7, 23 (below).

2. *Ekron*. Two ȣ weights (at least) were mentioned by Gitin (1990: 41). The units are not clear. I have included them in Figs. 1, 3, 5, 6-7, 23 (below).

3. *Jerusalem*, Duncan's excavations. Nine weights were registered by Avigad in the Hebrew University collection (Duncan's nos. 133, 177, 280–282, 316, 735; University nos. 2902–2910). The weights were lost, and it is not clear if they included JILs.

4. *Beer Sheba* (Bedouin *suq* area). A weight of 8 Shekel, inscribed, 46.3463 grams. Courtesy of O. Katz, F. Sontag and O. Salama.

5. *Tel Batash* (Timnah). The weights are now published with drawings and a short discussion (Kelm and Mazar 1995: 169-70).

6. *Tel Hadid*. A few Iron Age weights from this site, outside Judah, were given to the author for publication, courtesy of E. Brand.

7. *Tel Halif* (Lahav). The weights are now published with full details by Seger (1997). This group strengthen the conclusions about the date of the JILs (starting with the 8th century BC). I wish to thank J. Seger for sending the paper in press and allowing me to refer to these weights here.

APPENDIX 3

Judaean Inscribed Weights (Arranged by Sites)

Accho
One Shekel weight, see note at the end of Appendix 2 (above).

Anathot
Nsf.4

Arad
ठ 1.6, 7, ठ 2.16, 17, 18; ठ 4.21, 22; ठ 8.23-26; Nsf.10–11; Pym.9–10.

Armon ha-Naziv
ठ 8.45.

Aroer
ठ 4.18.

Ashdod
Nsf.20; Pym.19; Beqaᶜ.10.

Azeka
ठ 4.25–26; Nsf.15–17.

Beit Safafeh
ठ 24.3.

Beth Shemesh
ठ 2.20.

Beth Zur
Nsf.8–9; Pym.7; Beqaᶜ: 3.

Bethel
ठ 1.12.

Buseirah
Nsf.21.

Dor
ɤ 1.15.

Ekron
ɤ 2.24; ɤ 4.24; Beqaꞓ.11.
Notes: there are at least two more ɤ weights, but their units are not clear. See note at the end of Appendix 2 (above).

En Gedi
ɤ 1.5; ɤ 4.17, 52; ɤ 8.22.

Gezer
ɤ 1.10–11; ɤ 2.22; ɤ 8.34–35; Nsf.19; Pym.17–18; Beqaꞓ.9; 5 Gerah.1; 8 Gerah.4.

Gibeon
ɤ 4.31.

Jericho (?)
ɤ 4.51.

Jerusalem (all weights)
ɤ 1.1–3; ɤ 2.1–11, 13, 41–42; ɤ 4.1–11, 53–56; ɤ 8.1–11, 13, 44, 49–51; ɤ 16.4; ɤ 24.1; ɤ 40.1, 3; Nsf.1–3; Pym.1–3, 51–52; Beqaꞓ.34; 3 Gerah.1; 4 Gerah.1; 5 Gerah.2; 6 Gerah.1.

Notes: Vicinity of Jerusalem (in Fig. 5) includes: Anatot, Armon ha-Naziv, Beit Safafeh, Mevaseret Jerusalem, Moza, Pisgat Ze'ev, Ramot, Repha'im Valley and Shu'eifat.

Jerusalem (Crowford)
ɤ 8.10–11.

Jerusalem (Duncan)
ɤ 2.8–10; ɤ 4.10, 53–54; ɤ 8.1–2, 49–50; ɤ 40.1.

Jerusalem (Guthe)
ɤ 2.12; ɤ 4.12 (see also Jerusalem [Siloam village]).

Jerusalem (Kenyon)
ɤ 1.1–2; ɤ 2.1–7; ɤ 4.1–9; ɤ 8.3–9; ɤ 24.1; Nsf.1–2; Pym.2–3; 3 Gerah.1; 5 Gerah.2; 6 Gerah.1.

Jerusalem (Mazar)
ৎ 8.44; ৎ 40.3; Pym.52 (?); Beqaᶜ.34.

Jerusalem (Reich)
Pym.51.

Jerusalem (Shiloh)
ৎ 1.3; ৎ 2.11, 41–42; ৎ 4.11, 55–56; ৎ 16.4; ৎ 8.51.

Jerusalem (Siloam Village)
Pym.4 (see also Jerusalem [Guthe]).

Jerusalem ([Mt] Zion)
ৎ 2.13; Nsf.3 (?); 4 Gerah.1.

Kh. el-Kom (?)
ৎ 2.19; ৎ 4.27; Beqaᶜ.8.
Notes: I included here weights bought at the site, not those bought at other places.

Kh. Uza
Beqaᶜ.7.

Lachish
ৎ 1.9; ৎ 4.13–16; ৎ 8.12–19; Nsf.14; Pym.11–12; Beqaᶜ.4–6; 2 Gerah.1; 6 Gerah.2; 8 Gerah.1–3; 10 Gerah.1.

Malhata
ৎ 1.40–41; ৎ 2.39; ৎ 8.47–48; Nsf.12; 6 Gerah.3; 4 Gerah.9. See also note after ৎ 4.24.

Mamila
See: Jerusalem (Reich).

Mefalsim
Nsf.18.

Mevaseret Jerusalem
ৎ 1.4.

Mezad Hashavyahu
ৎ 4.30.

Moza
Nsf.5.

Tel el-Far'ah (S)
ö 8.27–28; 6 Gerah.4.

Tel el-Far'ah (north)
ö 1.13.

Tel Halif
See note at the end of Appendix 2.

Tel Haror
Pym.20.

Tel 'Ira
ö 1.8; ö 4.19–20; ö 8.29–30; Pym.8.

Tel Jemmeh
ö 1.16; ö 2.14–15; ö 4.28; Pym.16.

Tel ej-Judeideh
ö 8.33.

Tel Keisan
ö 1.14.

Weights Listed by Letter

Gezer
ö 2.a; Nsf.E.

Jerusalem
ö 4.b.

Lachish
Nsf.f.

Malhata
ö 1.a.

Megiddo
ö 1.b; ö 16.A.

Samaria
ö 40.b.

Tel esh-Shuqaf
Pym.a.

Tel Beer Sheba
Pym.b.

Unknown Sites
♉ 2.b; ♉ 4.a; ♉ 8.a–d; Nsf.a–d.

APPENDIX 4

The Judaean Uninscribed Weights

I have listed the Judaean uninscribed weights (JUL) here, arranged according to units. I have not dealt with possible JULs lighter than Beqaᶜ, since it is difficult to define the smaller units (also, in the drawings/photographs, their details are often not clear). The guiding lines in defining a JUL are: dome-shaped weights, made of limestone, weighing in the range of 5 per cent (give or take a little) of the average of the comparable inscribed weights (e.g. for 1 Shekel, I have included weights in the range of 10.8–11.9 grams). Of course, geographic origin and stratigraphy also help us to define a JUL. For units that lack reliable average (e.g. 12–40 Shekel), I have used a calculation based on the average of inscribed 1 Shekel weights.

Only the most important details are given for each JUL, and the bibliography is limited to the first, or most important publication. Of course, there are some cases of doubt: it is not always possible to be certain that an uninscribed weight is a JUL. For instance, some weights are found in sites outside the heartland of Judah, and may represent Egyptian or local weights. The mass itself is not enough to indicate the standard, since ancient systems were interrelated. Some other weights are not made of limestone, or are half-ball in shape (such exceptions are noted). Sometimes, broken weights are included, as the fragments that remain are enough to identify them as JULs. Most of the doubtful cases are listed separately at the end of each unit (numbered by letters).

4.1. JULs Similar to Beqaᶜ Weights (6.0–6.6 grams)

No.	Site	Weight grams	Locus	Date BCE	Bibliography	Notes
1	Jerusalem	6.51	F.409	7?	Scott 1985: 199 no. 7	Reg. no. 3267. Basalt?
2	City of David	5.8	surface		Eran 1996: W.197, Fig. 39.10	Reg. no. E1/9854
3	Tel en-Nasbeh	6.58	Q.16.14		McCown 1947: 276 no. 7	
4	Lachish	6.135	219	8?	Diringer 1953: no. 39	Irregular. Reg. 4876
5	Gezer	6.20	'Semitic IV'		Macalister 1912: 283	
6	Gezer	6.41	'Persian'		Macalister 1912: 285	
7	Tel Jemmeh	6.065	HF.186		Petrie 1928: Pl. 68	
8	Megiddo	6.0	'Nordburg'		Schumacher 1908: Pl. 15.19	
9	Tel abu-Sleimeh	6.03			Petrie 1937: Pl. 41	Reg. no. 6257
10	Ramot	6.08	surface	8–7?	c/o A. De-Groot	Bronze. Reg. no. 782
a	Unknown	6.08			Qedar 1981.11, no. 17	Bronze
b	Megiddo	6.4			Lamon and Shipton 1939: Pl. 104.33	Cube

4.2. JULs Similar to Pym Weights (7.4–8.2 grams)

No.	Site	Weight grams	Locus	Date BCE	Bibliography	Notes
1	Jerusalem	7.94	L.550.25	7?	Scott 1985: no. 11	Reg. no. 3266
2	Tel en-Nasbeh	7.65	pit 128		McCown 1947: 276 no. 8	
3	Beth Shemesh	7.805	level II	8?	Grant 1931: Pl. 52.20	
4	Gezer	7.8	Semitic 3-4		Macalister 1912: 282	
5	Gezer	7.90	Semitic 3-4		Macalister 1912: 282	
6	Gezer	7.62	'Persian'		Macalister 1912: 285	
7	Tel Abu Sleimeh	8.16	GP.648		Petrie 1937: Pl. 41	Reg. no. 6202

4.3. JULs Similar to Nsf Weights (9.2–10.1 grams)

No.	Site	Weight grams	Locus	Date BCE	Bibliography	Notes
1	Tel en-Nasbeh	9.32	pit 369	8–7?	McCown 1947: 276 no. 10	
2	Gezer	9.73	on rock		Macalister 1912: 280	Semitic II level?
3	Gezer	10.07	on rock		Macalister 1912: 280	Semitic II level?
4	Gezer	9.70	Semitic 3–4		Macalister 1912: 282	
5	Gezer	9.20	Semitic 4		Macalister 1912: 283	
6	Gezer	9.72	Semitic 4		Macalister 1912: 283	
7	Gezer	9.32	'Persian'		Macalister 1912: 285	
8	Azeka	9.75			Bliss and Macalister 1902: 146	No. 17. Bronze
9	Tel Jemmeh	9.597	BE.199		Petrie 1928: Pl. 68.5495	Basalt?
10	Megiddo	9.5	Nordburg		Schumacher 1908: 67	(Pl. 15.19)
11	Megiddo	9.75	Nordburg		Schumacher 1908: 67	(Pl. 15.18)
12	City of David	9.45	823 level X	7	Eran 1996: W.133, Fig. 37.2	Reg. no. G4957

4.4. JULs Similar to 1 Shekel Weights (10.8–11.9 grams)

No.	Site	Weight grams	Locus	Date BCE	Bibliography	Notes
1	Beth Shemesh	11.43	level II	8?	Grant and Wright 1939: 159 no. 31	
2	Tel Beit Mirsim	11.5	1001		Albright 1943: 77 no. 2	
3	Tel Beit Mirsim	11.5	level D	LB?	Albright 1943: n. 9	S.N.1585
4	Gezer	11.29	'Persian'		Macalister 1912: 285	
5	Gezer	11.81	'Persian'		Macalister 1912: 285	
6	Gezer	11.315	Semitic 4		Macalister 1912: 284	
7	Tel Far'ah (south)	11.327			Petrie 1930: Pl. 49	Reg. no. 5642
8	Megiddo	11.75	Nordburg		Schumacher 1908: 67	no. 15
9	Jerusalem ophel	11.1479	area 9b, 832		Eran 1996: W.205	PEF london no. 870

4.4. *(cont.)*

No.	Site	Weight grams	Locus	Date BCE	Bibliography	Notes
a	Unknown	11.04			Qedar 1979: no. 4050	Bronze
b	Lachish	11.230	H.18.1084		Diringer 1953: no. 30	Cylinder. Reg. no. 7123
c	City of David	11.55	1325 lev. 12	8	Eran 1996.W.70	Fig. 33.11. spheroid

4.5. JULs Similar to 2 Shekel Weights (21.5–23.7 grams)

No.	Site	Weight grams	Locus	Date BCE	Bibliography	Notes
1	Jerusalem	22.60	A.669.11b	7	Scott 1985: no. 23	Reg. no. 3239
2	Jerusalem	22.53	A.669.11b	7	Scott 1985: no. 21	Reg. no. 3240
3	Jerusalem	21.50	Late fill		Scott 1985: no. 62	H103.2, Reg. no. 1244
4	Tel en-Nasbeh	22.55			McCown 1947: 276, 17	
5	Lachish	22.856	D/X, surface		Diringer 1953: no. 28	British Museum
6	Tel Jemmeh	23.52	WE.190		Petrie 1928: Pl. 68.5562	
7	Gezer	22.50	Semitic 4		Macalister 1912: 284	
8	Gezer	22.41	Semitic 4		Macalister 1912: 284	
9	Ashdod	22.224	level VIII		Eran 1982: 98 no. 34	
10	Megiddo	22.25	Nordburg		Schumacher 1908: 67	No. 11
11	Megiddo	22.75	Nordburg		Schumacher 1908: 67	No. 12
12	Unknown	23.55			Eretz Israel Museum	No. K-8896
13	Arad	22.44	reg. 174/3		Israel Museum	IAA 64-284

4.6. JULs to the Value of 3 Shekel (32.4–35.8 grams)

No.	Site	Weight grams	Locus	Date BCE	Bibliography	Notes
1	Jerusalem	32.43	A.65.7	7?	Scott 1965: 138	Reg. 3730, little damaged
2	Lachish	33.75			Diringer 1953: no. 23	A little damaged

4.7. JULs Similar to 4 Shekel Weights (43–47.5 grams)

No.	Site	Weight grams	Locus	Date BCE	Bibliography	Notes
1	Jerusalem	44.71	A.676.1a	7	Scott 1985: no. 33	Reg. no. 4441
2	Jerusalem	44.60	A.845.22a	7	Scott 1985: no. 32	Reg. no. 4443
3	Jerusalem	45.50	A.669.a	7	Scott 1985: no. 58	Reg. no. 90
4	Jerusalem	43.39	mixed		Scott 1985: no. 30	Reg. no. 3242
5	Jerusalem	44.34	AA307.4		Scott 1985: no. 31	Reg. no. 6777
6	Jerusalem ophel	c. 45	B22, field 7		(Duncan)	PEF London no. 865
7	Jerusalem ophel	c. 44	NBS 27		50/4846; Eran 1996: W.207	PEF London no. 867
8	Jerusalem ophel	c. 44	9b, 828		50/4845; Eran 1996: W.208	PEF London no. 868
9	City of David	47.0	456, level XII	8	Eran 1996: W.47 Fig. 32.15	Reg. D1/13245
10	City of David	45.33	526, level XII	8	Eran 1996: W.50 Fig. 34.4	Half-ball. D1/13326
11	City of David	43.77 + x	868, level X	7	Eran 1996: W.139 Fig. 37.6	Reg. G768. Hole in base
12	Tel en-Nasbeh	45.70	Room 48 x1		McCown 1947: 276 no. 18	
13	Lachish	45.365	H.14.1002	8	Diringer 1953: no. 18	B.M. 10,125. Reg. 5447
14	Lachish	44.34	D/X surface		Diringer 1953: no. 19	B.M. 10,126, lead fill?
15	Lachish	44.18	pit K.15.94		Diringer 1953: no. 20	B.M. 10,127. Reg. 6360
16	Lachish	47.270	D/X		Diringer 1953: no. 15	B.M. 10,122.
17	Azeka	47.0			Bliss and Macalister 1902	146, no. 12

4.7. (cont.)

No.	Site	Weight grams	Locus	Date BCE	Bibliography	Notes
18	Azeka	45.0			Bliss and Macalister 1902	146, no. 13
19	Tel Beit Mirsim	45.0	level A	8?	Albright 1943: 77 no. 3	SN.1049
20	Tel Beit Mirsim	45.0		8?	Albright 1943: 77 no. 4	
21	Tel Jemmeh	45.04			Petrie 1928: Pl. 68.5465	Flattened dome
22	Tel Jemmeh	44.78	FB.188		Petrie 1928: Pl. 68.5462	
23	Tel Jemmeh	43.82	FG.190		Petrie 1928: Pl. 68.5537	
24	Gezer	44.88	'Persian'		Macalister 1912: 286	
25	Gezer	45.17	'Persian'		Macalister 1912: 286	
26	Gezer	45.69	'Persian'		Macalister 1912: 286	
27	Gezer	45.75	'Persian'		Macalister 1912: 286	
28	Gezer	47.40	'Persian'		Macalister 1912: 286	
29	Gezer	44.10	Semitic 4		Macalister 1912: 284	
30	Gezer	44.90	Semitic 3–4		Macalister 1912: 282	
31	Gezer	43.76	Rock/Sem. 2		Macalister 1912: 281	
32	Tel Keisan	45.2	levels III–IVA		Puech 1980: Pl. 94.16	
33	Unknown	45.0			Hecht Museum H2372	
34	Unknown	44.83			Israel museum, 60-56	
35	Unknown	44.90			Eretz Israel Museum	No. K-8895
36	Unknown	45.1			Eretz Israel Museum	No. K-526
37	Unknown	44.78			Qedar 1979: no. 4046	
38	Unknown	44.76			Kroha (ed.) 1980: 12 no. 65	
a	Ashdod	48.7	levels VIIa-b		Eran 1982: 99 no. 45	
b	Ashdod	43.6	level VIII		Eran 1982: 99 no. 37	
c	Tel 'Ira	44.2090	558	7	c/o I. Beit Arieh	Cylindrical
d	City of David	45.10	1303 level XII	8	Eran 1996: W.63 Fig. 33.8	Spheroid, reg. E1/8538/1
e	Lachish	42.640	G.18.32		Diringer 1953: no. 21	Reg. 6354, BM.10,128

4.8. JULs to the value of 5 Shekel (54–59 grams)

No.	Site	Weight grams	Locus	Date BCE	Bibliography	Notes
1	Beth Shemesh	55.26		8	Grant and Wright 1939: 159 Pl. 53	
2	Tel Far'ah (north)	57.5		10–9?	Puech 1984: 242	Pl. 67.12
3	Tel Keisan	57.02			Puech 1980: no. 26	
4	Lachish	57.155	J.15.1039		Diringer 1953: no. 11	B.M. 'cushion' shape
5	Gezer	58.12	3		Macalister 1912: 282	
6	Gezer	55.74	1		Macalister 1912: 261	

4.9. JULs Similar to 8 Shekel Weights (86.1–95.1 grams)

No.	Site	Weight grams	Locus	Date BCE	Bibliography	Notes
1	Jerusalem	88.38	A.676.5	7	Scott 1985: no. 48	Reg. no. 3727
2	Jerusalem	88.06	A.669.11a	7	Scott 1985: no. 47	Reg. no. 3249
3	Jerusalem	56.63 + x	S.100.20	7	Scott 1985: no. 42	Broken, reg. no. 6557
4	Jerusalem	60.45 + x	L.50.11b	7	Scott 1985: no. 43	Broken, reg. no. 3729
5	Jerusalem	82.24 + x	A.669.11a	7	Scott 1985: no. 44	Broken, reg. no. 3248
6	Jerusalem ophel	88.0		7?	Duncan 1931.216 no. 2	(cf. d below)
7	Jerusalem ophel	85.618	B21, 17.85		PEF London 860 (50/4838)	Eran 1996: W214.
8	City of David	78.35 + x	1585 level X	7	Eran 1996: W.114 Fig. 36.6	Broken, reg. E3/13034
9	City of David	87.58	959 level X	7	Eran 1996: W.144 Fig. 37.11	Reg. G11574
10	City of David	89.25	742 level IX	Per.	Eran 1996: W.162 Fig. 38.6	Reg. G2340, mark '10'
11	City of David	88	1286 level V	late	Eran 1996: W.192 Fig. 36.6	Reg. EI/9121
12	Tel en-Nasbeh	89.06	cistern 159	8–7	McCown 1947: 276	
13	Tel Beer Sheba	88.6636	level II	8	Y. Aharoni (ed.) 1973: Pl. 70.5	
14	Tel Ira	91.85	546	7	c/o I. Beit Arieh	
15	Lachish	88.777	H.17.1089	8	Diringer 1953: no. 6	Reg. 7159, B.M. 10,113

4.9. *(cont.)*

No.	Site	Weight grams	Locus	Date BCE	Bibliography	Notes
16	Lachish	87.735	big pit		Diringer 1953: no. 9	Reg. 7240a, BM 10,116
17	Lachish	49.355 + x	J17.1017		Diringer 1953: no. 12, 6227	Broken. BM 10,119
18	Azeka	91.5			Bliss and Macalister 1902	146, no. 8
19	Azeka	90.0			Bliss and Macalister 1902	146, no. 9
20	Azeka	88.0			Bliss and Macalister 1902	146, no. 10
21	Tel Beit Mirsim	89.0	101 level A	9–8?	Albright 1943: 77 no. 10	
22	Tel Beit Mirsim	89.0	1070 level A	9–8?	Albright 1943: 77 no. 11	
23	Tel Beit Mirsim	89.5			Albright 1943: 77 no. 3	SN.485
24	Tel Jemmeh	90.23	EF.188		Petrie 1928: Pl. 68.5467	White limestone
25	Tel Jemmeh	87.33			PEF London, 1348.4 grains	
26	Tel Far'ah (south)	87.389			Petrie 1930: Pl. 49.5623	
27	Tel Far'ah (south)	90.020	C.926.6		Petrie 1930: Pl. 49.5641	
28	Gezer	88.30	Semitic 3–4		Macalister 1912: 282	
29	Gezer	88.205	'Persian'		Macalister 1912: 286	
30	Gezer	91.43			Macalister 1912: 284, 286	
31	Gezer	91.89	'Persian'		Macalister 1912: 286	
32	Gezer	92.40	Semitic 4		Macalister 1912: 284	
33	Malhata	90.9063	242	7	c/o I. Beit Arieh	
34	Malhata	86.3980	62	7	Formerly 4 Shekel: 24	Reg. no. 2006/50
35	Shephelah	90.7737	264 reg. 3095		c/o Y. Dagan, IAA	White limestone.
36	Megiddo	88.7	level II	6?	Lamon and Shipton 1939: Pl. 104.13	
37	Unknown	92.5			Kroha (ed.) 1980: 12 no. 62	
38	Unknown	94.5			Kroha (ed.) 1980: 12 no. 64	
39	Unknown	85.5			Hecht Museum, H2371	
a	Jerusalem	86.24	L.525.14	7	Scott 1985: no. 46	Reg. no. 4702

4.9. *(cont.)*

No.	Site	Weight grams	Locus	Date BCE	Bibliography	Notes
b	Beth Shemesh	84.73	level II	8	Grant and Wright 1939: 159, Pl. 52	carinated dome
c	Tel Far'ah (south)	86.184			Petrie 1930: Pl. 49.5621	864 (=no. 3 above?)
d	Jerusalem ophel	c. 88	W127, 15.		PEF. Hematite, carinated.	
e	City of David	47.6+x	950, level IX	Per.	Eran 1996: W.172 Fig. 38.14	Broken, reg. G11438
f	City of David	53.3 + x	not clear		Eran 1996: W.195 Fig. 39.8	Broken, reg. E1/6260

4.10. JULs to the Value of 10 Shekel (107.7–119 grams)

No.	Site	Weight grams	Locus	Date BCE	Bibliography	Notes
1	Nahal Zimri	110.0624	204	7	Meitlis 1993: 95	Reg. 2381/1
2	Gezer	113.7			Macalister 1912: 283	
3	Gezer	109.31			Macalister 1912: 283	
4	Gezer	118.7			Macalister 1912: 283	
5	City of David	110.60	419 level XII	8	Eran 1996: W.43 Fig. 32.14	Reg. no. D1/12624
a	Unknown	119			Bliss and Macalister 1902: 146	No. 7. Conus

4.11. JULs Similar to 12 Shekel Weights (130–143 grams)

No.	Site	Weight grams	Locus	Date BCE	Bibliography	Notes
1	Gezer	142.43	Semitic 3-4		Macalister 1912: 283	
2	Gezer	135.52	'Persian'		Macalister 1912: 286	
3	City of David	72.7 + x	surface		Eran 1996: W.196 Fig. 39.9	Broken, reg. E1/9013
a	Unknown	141.0			Eretz Israel Museum	K-8894

4.12. JULs to the Value of 15 Shekel (c. 170 grams)?

No.	Site	Weight grams	Locus	Date BCE	Bibliography	Notes
a	Jerusalem	162.29	A.669.42		Scott 1964: 131 reg. 3251; Eran 1996: W.279	Ashmolean 1965.457

Note: the value of 15 Shekel, to within 5 per cent range, overlaps with weights of 16 Shekels to a certain extent. Many more weights of this unit are needed to prove its existence.

4.13. JULs Similar to 16 Shekel Weights (172.3–181.3 grams)

No.	Site	Weight grams	Locus	Date BCE	Bibliography	Notes
1	Jerusalem ophel	181.5		7	Duncan 1931: 216 no. 3; Eran 1996: W.222	probably = London PEF 857 (50/4837), hematite.
2	City of David	181.20	791 level X	7	Eran 1996: W.124 Fig. 36.11	Reg. no. G4728
3	City of David	131.8 + x	519 lev. VI-VII	late	Eran 1996: W.179 Fig. 38.17	Reg. no. E2/1635
4	Tel 'Ira	179.82		7	c/o I. Beit Arieh	Lead filling, hematite
5	Beth Shemesh	179.495	level II	9–8	Grant and Wright 1939: Pl. 52.41	
6	Tel Jemmeh	183.8	EE.190		Petrie 1928: Pl. 68.5480	
7	Gezer	180.11	Semitic 4		Macalister 1912: 284	
8	Gezer	181.85	Semitic 4		Macalister 1912: 284	
a	Beth Shemesh	173.64		Iron 1?	Grant and Wright 1939: Pl. 53.52	
b	Tel Jemmeh	184.24			Petrie 1928: Pl. 68.5481	Flint
c	Gezer	187.61	Rock/Sem.2		Macalister 1912: 281	Basalt
d	Accho	187.2	Late Bronze		Eran and Edelstein 1977: 58	'Persian Garden'
e	Unknown	178.0			Kroha (ed.) 1980: no. 57	Granite

4.14. JULs Similar to 24 Shekel Weights (261–288 grams)

No.	Site	Weight grams	Locus	Date BCE	Bibliography	Notes
1	Unknown	269.0			Kroha (ed.) 1980: no. 57	
2	City of David	263.90	level IX	Per.	Eran 1996: W.171 Fig. 38.13	Hole for lead? G11361 10882.
3	Jerusalem ophel	269.10			Eran 1996: W.226	
a	Tel Far'ah (N)	270.0	level VIIb	10–9	Puech 1984: 81 no. 12	Egyptian 3 *dbn?*
b	City of David	277.10	level VI	late	Eran 1996: W.188.	Spheroid. Reg. 45185

4.15 JULs to the Values of 30, 32 Shekel (c. 340, 363 grams)?

No.	Site	Weight grams	Locus	Date BCE	Bibliography	Notes
a	City of David	338.20	129 level XII	8	Eran 1996: W.39 Fig. 32.12	Shape exceptional
b	City of David	189.2 + x	surface		Eran 1996: W.202 Fig. 39.15	Broken. 32 Shekel?

Note: the two weights above do not prove the existence of such assumed units (cf. 15 Shekel above).

4.16. JULs Similar to 40 Shekel Weights (432–477 grams)

No.	Site	Weight grams	Locus	Date BCE	Bibliography	Notes
1	Tel Beit Mirsim	436.5	846, level A	9–8	Albright 1943: 77 no. 15	
2	Tel Jemmeh	455.54			Petrie 1928: Pl. 68.5472	
3	Gezer	456.33	Rock/Sem. 2		Macalister 1912: 281	
4	Gezer	453.21	Semitic 3–4		Macalister 1912: 283	
a	Ashdod	426.4	level VIII		Eran 1982: 98 no. 30	Broken

4.16. (cont.)

No.	Site	Weight grams	Locus	Date BCE	Bibliography	Notes
b	Megiddo	424.8	surface		Lamon and Shipton 1939: Pl. 104.52	
c	City of David	57 + x	2015 level XII	8	Eran 1996: W.81 Fig. 35.1	Broken (could be an inscribed weight).

4.17. JULs to the Value of 400 Shekel (4320–4770 grams)

No.	Site	Weight grams	Locus	Date BCE	Bibliography	Notes
a	Tel Beit Mirsim	4564?	Western tower	8	Albright 1943: 76 Pl. 57.d1	
b	Samaria	4541?			Reisner et al. 1924: 344	Rockefeller
c	Jerusalem ophel	4536?			Eran 1996: W.230	Duncan 1931

4.18. Other Weights

No.	Site	Weight grams	Locus	Date BCE	Bibliography	Notes
1	Malhata			7	c/o I. Beit Arieh	125 Shekel. Damaged
a	Jerusalem	1810			Duncan 1931: 221, plate next to p. 229	160 Shekel?
b	Silet Hartiyah	4780			Avigad 1968.	Forgery: Delavault and Lemaire 1979.

Note: See also Eran 1996: W.120, W.145 (hematite, 8 Shekel?); W.229 (100 Shekel?), 1134 grams, from Duncan's excavations); W.184, W.193 (180 Shekel?), W.198, W.201, but their clear identification is doubtful.

BIBLIOGRAPHY

Aberbach, D.

1974 'מנה אחת אפיים' (1 Sam 1.5): A New Interpretation, *VT* 24: 350-53.

Ackerman, S., and S.L. Braunstein

1982 *Israel in Antiquity: From David to Herod* (New York: The Jewish Museum).

Agora

1974 *Agora Catalogue* (Auction 1; Tel Aviv).

1975 *Agora Catalogue* (Auction 2; Tel Aviv: Naidat Press).

Aharoni, M.

1981 'Inscribed Weights and Seals', in Y. Aharoni 1981: 126-27.

Aharoni, Y.

1956 'Excavations at Ramat Rahel 1954', *IEJ* 6: 137-57.

1960 'Excavations at Ramat Rahel (Second Season, 1959)', *Bulletin of the Israel Exploration Society* 24.2-3: 73-119.

1971a 'Arad', *EAEHL* II: 469-477 (Hebrew).

1971b 'A 40 Shekel Weight with a Hieratic Numeral', *BASOR* 201: 35-36.

1971c *The Beer Sheba Excavations* (Tel Aviv: The Institute of Archaeology, Tel Aviv University).

1976 'The Stratification of Judahite Sites in the 8th and 7th Centuries B.C.E', *BASOR* 224: 73-90.

1981 *Arad Inscriptions* (Jerusalem: Israel Exploration Society).

1982 *The Archaeology of the Land of Israel* (trans. A.F. Rainey; Philadelphia: Westminster Press).

Aharoni, Y. (ed.)

1962 *Excavations at Ramat Rahel (Seasons 1959 and 1960)* (Rome: Universita di Roma, Centro di Studi Semitici).

1964 *Excavations at Ramat Rahel (Seasons 1961 and 1962)* (Rome: Universita di Roma, Centro di Studi Semitici).

1966 'The Use of Hieratic Numerals in the Hebrew Ostraca and the Shekel Weights', *BASOR* 184: 13-19. Hebrew version in Abramsky: 309-317.

1973 *Beer Sheba 1* (Tel Aviv: Tel Aviv University, The Institute of Archaeology).

1975 *Investigations at Lachish: The Sanctuary and the Residency (Lachish V)* (Tel Aviv: Gateway Publishers).

Aharoni, Y., and Ruth Amiran

1964 'Arad: A Biblical City in Southern Palestine', *Archaeology* 17.1: 43-53.

Ahlstrom, G. W.

1982 *Royal Administration and National Religion in Ancient Palestine* (Leiden. E.J. Brill).

Albright, W.F.
1937   *The Excavation of Tel Beit Mirsim.* II. *The Bronze Age*, *AASOR*, 17.
1943   *The Excavation of Tel Beit Mirsim.* III. *The Iron Age*, *AASOR*, 21-22.

Archi, A.
1987   'Reflections on the System of Weights from Ebla', in C.H. Gordon, G.A. Rendsburg and N.H. Winter (eds.), *Eblaitica: Essays on the Ebla Archives and Eblaite Languages* (Winona Lake, IN: Eisenbrauns): I, 47-86.

Archi, A., and E. Klengel-Brandt
1984   'I pesi provenienti da Zincirli', *SMEA* 24: 245-61.

Arnaud, D.
1967   'Contribution a l'étude de la métrologie sirienne au IIe millénaire', *RA* 61: 131-69.

Arnaud, D., Y. Calvet and J.L. Huot
1979   'Ilšu: Ibnišu, orfèvre de l'E.BABBAR de Larsa', *Syria* 56: 1-64.

Aviezer, S.
1993   'Shekel or Sheqel?', *The Shekel* 26.5: 24.

Avigad, N.
1961   *Yediot* 25 (Hebrew).
1968   'A Sculptured Hebrew Stone Weight', *IEJ* 18: 181-87.
1986   *Hebrew Bullae from the Time of Jeremiah* (Jerusalem: Israel Exploration Society) (Hebrew).

Balmuth, M.S.
1975   'The Critical Moment: The Transition from Currency to Coinage in the East Mediterranean', *World Archaeology* 6.3: 293-98.

Barag, D.
1987   'The Silver Coin of Yohanan the High Priest and the Coinage of Judah in the Fourth Century B.C.', *Israel Numismatic Journal* 9: 4-21.

Barkay, G.
1978   'A Group of Iron Age Scale Weights', *IEJ* 28: 209-17.
1981a   'Iron Age Gerah Weights', *EI* 15: 288-96 (Hebrew).
1981b   'The Museum of the Jesuite Fathers', in G. Barkay and E. Shiler (eds.) *Unknown Jerusalem* (Qardom 16-17: 42-44) (Hebrew).
1985   'Northern and Western Jerusalem in the End of the Iron Age' (PhD thesis; Tel Aviv University) (Hebrew).
1987   'Gerah', in B.A. Levin (ed.), *Encyclopedia of the Biblical World: Leviticus* (Jerusalem: Revivim): 218-19 (Hebrew).
1990   'Iron Age II–III: Unit 9', in A. Ben-Tor (ed.), *The Archaeology of Ancient Israel in the Biblical Period* (Tel Aviv: The Open University): 77-233 (Hebrew; ET Harvard University)
1992   'A Scale-Beam from Lachish', *The 18th Archaeological Congress: Abstracts of Lectures* (Hebrew).
1993   'The Redefining of Archaeological Periods: Does the Date 588/586 BCE indeed Mark the End of the Iron Age Culture?', in Biran and Aviram: 106-109.
1994   'Burial Caves and Burial Practices in the Iron Age', in I. Singer (ed.), *Graves and Burial Practices in Israel in the Ancient Period* (Jerusalem: Yad Izhak Ben Zvi): 96-164 (Hebrew).

1996   'A Balance Beam from Tel Lachish', *Tel Aviv* 23.1: 75-82.

Barkay, Rachel
1987   'The Museum Collection of the Bank of Israel', *Cathedra* 42: 184-97 (Hebrew).

Barnett, R.D.
1968   *Illustrations of Old Testament History* (London: The Trustees of the British Museum).

Barrois, A.
1932   'La métrologie dans la Bible', *RB* 41: 50-76.
1953   'Poids', *Manuel d'archéologie biblique* (Paris: A. Picard): II, 252-58.

Barton, A.
1903   'New Hebrew Weights 1: A Unique Hebrew Weight', *JAOS* 24: 384-87.
1937.   *Archaeology and the Bible* (Philadelphia: American Sunday School Union, rev. edn [1st edn 1916]).

Bass, G.F.
1967   *Cape Gelidonia: A Bronze Age Shipwreck* (Philadelphia. American Philosophical Society).

Beck, P.
1996   'Horvat Qitmit Revisited Via 'En Hazeva', *Tel Aviv* 23.1: 102-14.

Becking, B.
1992   *The Fall of Samaria: A Historical and Archaeological Study* (Leiden. E.J. Brill).

Beit-Arieh, I.
1985   'Tel 'Ira: A Fortified City of the Kingdom of Judah', *Qedem* 18 (69-70): 17-24 (Hebrew).
1987   'Tell 'Ira and Horvat 'Uza: Negev Cities in the Late Israelite Period', *Cathedra* 42: 34-38 (Hebrew).

Beit Arieh, I., and B.C. Cresson
1991   'Horvat 'Uza: A Fortified Outpost on the Eastern Negev Border', *BA* 54: 126-35.

Ben-David, A.
1973   'A Rare Inscribed N-c-f Weight', *IEJ* 23: 176-77.
1975   'A Rare Inscribed Phoenician Weight', *PEQ* 107: 21-27.
1979   'The Philistine Talent from Ashdod, the Ugarit Talent from Ras Shamra, the PYM and the NSF', *UF* 11: 29-45.

Bennett, C.M.
1966   'Fouilles d'Umm el Biyara', *RB* 73: 372-403.
1973   'Excavations at Buseirah, Southern Jordan, 1971', *Levant* 5: 1-11.
1978   'Some Reflections on Neo Assyrian Influence in Transjordan', in P.R.S. Moorey (ed.), *Archaeology in the Levant* (Festschrift K. Kenyon; Warminster: Arris & Phillips): 164-71.
1983   'Excavations at Buseirah', in J.F.A. Sawyer *et al.* (eds.), *Midian, Moab and Edom* (JSOTSup, 24; Sheffield: JSOT Press: 9-17.

Berrimen, A.E.
1955   'A New Approach to the Study of Ancient Metrology', *RA* 49: 193-201.

Betlyon, J.W.
1986   'The Provincial Government of Persian Period Judah and the Yehud
            Coins', *JBL* 105: 633-42.
Bewer, J.A.
1942.   'Notes on 1 Sam. 13.21; 2 Sam. 23.1 and Psalms 48.8', *JBL* 61: 45-50.
Bienkowski, P. (ed.)
1992   *Early Edom and Moab: The Beginning of the Iron Age in Southern
            Jordan* (Sheffield: Sheffield Academic Press).
Biran, A.
1987   'Tel 'Ira and 'Aroer towards the End of the Judean Monarchy', *Cathedra*
            42: 26-33 (Hebrew).
Biran, A., and J. Aviram (eds.)
1993   *Biblical Archaeology Today* (Jersusalem: Keter)
Biran, A., and R. Cohen
1975   'Aroer: Notes and News', *IEJ* 25: 171-17.
1978   'Aroer in the Negev', *Qadmoniot* 41: 20-24 (Hebrew).
1981   'Aroer in the Negev', *EI* 15: 250-73 (Hebrew).
Bjorkman, Judith K.
1993   'The Larsa Goldsmith's Hoards: New Interpretations', *JNES* 52.1: 1-23.
1994   'Hoards and Deposits in Bronze Age Mesopotamia' (PhD thesis; Univer-
            sity of Pennsylvania).
Bliss, F.J.
1899   'Second/Third Report on the Excavations of Tell Zakariya', *PEFQS*: 89-
            111, 170-87.
Bliss, F.J., and A.C. Dickie
1898   *Excavations at Jerusalem* (London: Palestine Exploration Fund).
Bliss, F.J., and R.A.S. Macalister
1902   *Excavations in Palestine* (London. Palestine Exploration Fund.).
Bordereuil, P.
1983   'Expotions', *Syria* 60: 340-41.
Borowski, O.
1995   'Hezekiah's Reforms and the Revolt against Assyria', *BA* 58.3: 148-53.
Brewer, D.I.
1991   'Mene Mene Teqel Uparsin Daniel 5.25 in Cuneiform', *Tyndale Bulletin*
            42.2: 310-16.
Briend, J.
1992   'Bible et archéologie: Dialogue entre deux disciplines', *Le Monde du
            Bible* 75: 37-41.
Briend, J., and J.P Humbert (eds.)
1980   *Tell Keisan (1971-1976): Une cité phénicienne en Galilee* (Paris: J.
            Gabalda).
Bron, F., and A. Lemaire
1983   'Poids inscrits phénico-araméens du 8e siècle av. J.C.', *Atti del 1
            Congresso Internationale di studi Fenici e Punici* (Rome): III, 763-70.
Broshi, M.
1977   'Nasbeh, Tell el-', *EAEHL* III: 912-18.
Broshi, M., and I. Finkelstein
1992   'The Population of Palestine in Iron Age II', *BASOR* 287: 47-60.

Buhl, M.L.
1983   *Sukas VIII: The North-Eastern Pottery and Objects of Other Materials from the Upper Strata* (Copenhagen: Publications of the Carlsberg Expedition to Phoenicia 9. det Kongelige Danske Viedenskabernes Salskab: Munksgaard).

Bulbach, S.W.
1981   *Judah in the Reign of Mannasseh* (PhD dissertation; New York University).

Burimovitz, S. and Z. Lederman
1993   'Beth-Shemesh: The New Excavations', *EAEHL* NS I: 251-53.

Cahill, J.
1995   'Rosette Stamp Seal Impressions from Ancient Judah', *IEJ* 45.4: 230-52.

Castle, E.W.
1992   'Shipping and Trade in Ramesside Egypt', *JESHO* 35: 230-77.

Cerny, J.
1953   'Prices and Wages in the Ramesside Period', *JWH* 1.

Chambon, A. (ed.)
1984   *Tell el-Far'ah. I. L'Âge du Fer* (Paris: J. Gabalda).

Chaplin, T.
1890   'An Ancient Hebrew Weight from Samaria', *PEFQS*: 267-68.
1894   'The Ancient Hematite Weight from Samaria', *PEFQS* 26: 286-87.

Chapman, R.L.
1995   'The Defences of Tell as-Saba (Beersheba): A Stratigraphic Analysis', *Levant* 27: 127-42.

Chavane, Marie José
1987   'Poids zoomorphe', in MargueriteYon, *Ras Shamra-Ougarit. III. Le centre du ville* (Paris: Editions recherches sur les civilisations): 367-74.

Chester, G.J.
1871   'Notes on Miscalleneous Objects Found in the Excavations', in R.E. Wilson and R.E. Warren (eds.), *The Recovery of Jerusalem* (London: Richard Bentley): 491-93.

Clermont-Ganneau, Ch.
1884   'Antiquities of Palestine in London', *PEFQS*: 222-30.
1896   *Archaeological Researches in Palestine during the Years 1873–4, Vol. II* (London).
1901   'Cinq poids israelites à inscriptions', *Recueil d'archéologie orientale* 4: 25-35.
1924   'Deux inscriptions israelites archaïques de Gezer', *Recueil d'archéologie orientale* 8: 105-12.

Codrigan, K. de B.
1964   'The Origins of Coinage', *Bulletin of the Institute of Archaeology, London University College* 4: 1-24.

Cohen, R.
1983   'Kadesh-Barnea: A Fortress from the Time of the Judean Kingdom', *The Israel Museum Catalogue* 233 (Jerusalem: The Israel Museum).

Conder, C.R.
1891   'Notes 2: The Hebrew Weight', *PEFQS*: 69-70.

270 _Economic Keystones_

Cook, S.A.
1909 'The Old Hebrew Alphabeth and the Gezer Tablet', *PEFQS*: 284-309.
Cooper, M.
1980 'Gold, Silver, Copper and Iron in the Old Testament' (PhD dissertation; New York University).
Cour-Marty, M.
1983 'Une norme ponderale dominante en Egypte pharaonique', *GM* 69: 27-30.
1985 'La collection du musée du Caire revisité', *REg* 36: 189-200.
1990 'Les poids egyptiens, de precieux jalons archéologiques', *Cahiers de recherches de l'institut de papyrologie et d'egyptologie de Lille* 12: 17-55.
1991 'Weights in Ancient Egypt: A Method of Study', in Sylvia Schoske (ed.), *Studien zur Altägyptischen Kultur* (Hamburg: H. Buske Verlag): 137-45.
Courtois, J.C.
1983 'Le poids de Palaepaphos-Skales', in V. Karageorghis (ed.), *Palaepaphos-Skales: An Iron Age Cemetery in Cyprus* (Konstantz: Universitätsverlag): 424-25.
1984 'Poids en pierre', in *idem, Alashia III: Les objects de niveaux stratifiés d'Enkomi* (Paris: Mission archéologique d'Alasia): 107-34.
Cré, L.
1892 'Conférence sur le Kikkar ou Talent Hébreu découvert a Sainte-Anne de Jerusalem', *RB* 1: 416-32.
Cross, F.M.
1962 'Epigraphical Notes on Hebrew Documents of the Eighth–Sixth Centuries B.C. Part 3: The Inscribed Handles from Gibeon', *BASOR* 168: 18-23.
1981 *An Inscribed Weight*, AASOR, 47: 27-30.
1986 'An Unpublished Ammonite Ostracon from Heshbon', in L.T. Geraty and L.G. Herr (eds.), *The Archaeology of Transjordan and Other Essays Presented to S.H. Horn* (Berrien Springs: Andrews University Press): 475-89.
1995 'A "Neo-Philistine" Ostracon from Seventh-Century Ashkelon', *BARev* 22: 64-65.
Crowfoot, J.W., and G.M. Fitzgerald
1929 *Excavations in the Tyropoeon Valley, Jerusalem, 1927*, PEFA, 4.
Culican, W.
1973 *The Graves at Tell er-Ruqeish*, AJBI, 2.2: 66-105.
Curtin, P.
1984 *Cross Cultural Trade in World History* (Cambridge: Cambridge University Press).
Dagan, Y.
1992 'The Shephelah During the Period of the Monarchy in Light of Archaeological Excavations and Survey' (Unpublished M.A. thesis, Tel-Aviv University) (Hebrew).
Dahood, M.
1966 'Hebrew-Ugaritic Lexicography IV', *Biblica* 47: 403-19.

Dalman, G.
1906 'Neugefundene Gewichte', *ZDPV* 29: 92-94.
Dandamayev, M.A.
1979 'State and Temple in Babylonia in the First Millenium B.C.', in E. Lipiński (ed.), *State and Temple Economy in the Ancient Near East* (OLA, 6; Leuven: Department Oriëntalistick): 589-96.
1988 'Wages and Prices in Babylonia in the 6th and 5th Centuries B.C.', *Altorientalische Forschungen* 15: 53-58.
Daumas, F.
1977 'La problème de la monnaie dans l'Egypte antique', *Mélange de l'école française de Rome* 89: 425-42.
Dayton, J.
1974 'Money in the Near East before Coinage', *Berytus* 23: 41-52.
De Cenival, J.L.
1982 'Vie économique', in B.A. Leicknam and C. Ziegler (eds.), *Naissance de l'écriture* (Paris: Ministère de la Culture. Editions de la Réunion des Musées Nationeaux): 273-74.
De Vaux, R.
1939 'Titres et fonctionnaires égyptiens à la cour de David et de Solomon', *RB* 48: 394-405.
1957 'Les fouilles de Tell el Far'ah, près Nablouse', *RB* 64: 552-80.
1958 *Les institutions de l'ancient Testament* 61 (Paris: Cerf, 2nd rev. edn).
Delavault, B., and A. Lemaire
1979 'Les inscriptionnes phéniciennes de Palsetine', *Rivista di Study Fenici* 7: 30-33.
Demski, A.
1976 'Literacy in Israel and among Neighboring Peoples in the Biblical Period' (PhD thesis, Hebrew University, Jerusalem) (Hebrew).
Deutsch, R.
1988 *Ancient Coins and Antiquties* (Auction no. 45; Tel Aviv: Archaeological Centre).
1989 *Ancient Coins and Antiquities* (Auction no. 55; Tel Aviv: Matsa Company) (Hebrew).
1990 *Auction no. 65* (Tel Aviv: Archaeological Centre).
1994 *Auction no. 12* (Tel Aviv: Archaeological Centre).
Deutsch, R., and M. Heltzer
1994 *Forty New Ancient West Semitic Inscriptions* (Tel Aviv: Archaeological Centre).
Dever, W.G.
1970 'Iron Age Epigraphic Materials from the Area of Khirbet el-Kom', *HUCA* 40-41: 139-204.
1990 *Recent Archaeological Discoveries and Biblical Research* (Seattle: University of Washington Press).
1991 'Archaeology, Material Culture and the Early Monarchical Period in Israel', in Diana Edelman (ed.), *The Fabric of History* (JSOTSup, 127; Sheffield: JSOT Press): 103-115.
1994 'Ancient Israelite Religion: How to Reconcile the Differing Textual and Artifactual Portraits?', in W. Dietrich and M.A. Klopfenstein (eds.), *Ein*

Gott allein? (OBO, 139; Freiburg: Universitätsverlag): 105-25.

Dever, W.G., *et. al.* (eds.)
1970   *Gezer I* (HUCA Annual, I).
1970   *Gezer III* (HUCA Annual, III).
1970   *Gezer IV* (HUCA Annual, IV).

Di Segni, Lea.
1990   'The Systems of Weights in the Land of Israel', in Kedar, Dothan and Safari: 202-22 (Hebrew).

Diakonoff, I.M.
1992.   'The Naval Power and Trade of Tyre', *IEJ* 42: 168-93.

Diringer, D.
1934   *Le iscrizioni antico: Ebraiche palestinensi* (Florence: Felice le Monnier).
1942   'The Hebrew Weights found at Lachish', *PEQ* 74: 82-103.
1949   'The Royal Jar Handle Stamps of Ancient Judah', *BA* 12: 70-86.
1953   'Weights', *Lachish* 3: 348-56.
1958   'Weights', in D. Winton-Thomas (ed.), *Documents from Old Testaments Times* (London: Thomas Nelson & Sons): 227-30.

Dothan, M.
1951   'Archaeological Survey of the Nahr Rubin Area', *Bulletin of the Israel Exploration Society* 16: 37-46 (Hebrew).

Dothan, M. (ed.)
1971   'Ashdod II–III: The Second and Third Seasons of Excavations 1963, 1965', *'Atiqot* 9-10.

Dothan, M., and D.N. Freedman
1967   'Ashdod I: The First Season of Excavations 1962', *'Atiqot* 7.

Duncan, J.G.
1924   'Fourth Quarterly Report on the Excavation of the Eastern Hill of Jerusalem', *PEFQS*: 163-80.
1925   'Fifth Quarterly Report on the Excavation of the Eastern Hill of Jerusalem', *PEFQS*: 8-24.
1931   *Digging up Biblical History* (London: Society for Promoting Christian Knowledge).

Einzig, P.
1949   *Primitive Money in its Ethnological, Historical and Economic Aspects* (London: Eyre & Spottiswoode).

Eitam, D.
1990   'Royal Industry in Ancient Israel during the Iron Age Period', in E. Aerts and H. Klengel (eds.), *The Town as Regional Economic Centre in the Ancient Near East* (Leuven: Leuven University Press): 56-73.

Eitan-Katz, H.
1994   *Specialized Economy of Judah in the 8th–7th Centuries B.C.E.* (MA thesis; Tel Aviv: Tel Aviv University) (Hebrew).

Elat, M.
1977   *Economical Relations in the Lands of the Bible c. 1000–539 BC* (Jerusalem: Bialik Institute and the Israel Exploration Society).
1990   'The International Trade in Eretz Israel under Assyrian Rule', in Kedar, Dothan and Safrai 1990: 67-88 (Hebrew).

1994   'International Trade and its Merchants in the Assyrian Empire', *EI* 24: 12-17.

Elayi, Josette
1991   'Quelques poids nord-ouest sémitiques inédits', *Semitica* 40: 31-38.

Eph'al, I.
1996   *Siege and its Ancient Near Eastern Manifestations* (Jerusalem: The Hebrew University) (Hebrew).

Eph'al, I., and J. Naveh
1993   'The Jar of the Gate', *BASOR* 289: 59-65.

Eran, E.
1974   'Appendix B: A Group of Weights from Gezer', in Dever *et. al.* 1974: 131-32.

1982   'The Weights', in M. Dothan and Y. Porat, 'Ashdod IV', *'Atiqot* 15: 91-100.

1985   'The Old Egyptian Weight Unit "Deben"', in G. Otruba (ed.), *Acta Metrologiae Historica* (Lynz: Travaux des 3e congrés internationale de la métrologie historique): 94-116.

1987   'The Part Weights of the Hebrew Iron Age', in G. Otruba (ed.), *Acta Metrologiae Historica II* (Lynz): 68-85

1990   'Appendix A: A Metrological Consideration of the Eshtemo'a Hoard', *'Atiqot* 10: 58-60 (Hebrew).

1994   'Weights from the Excavations 1981–1984 at Shiloh', *ZDPV* 110.2: 151-57.

1996   'Weights and Weighing in the City of David: The Early Weights from the Bronze Age to the Persian Period', in D.T. Ariel and A. De-Groot (eds.), 'City of David IV', *Qedem* 35: 204-56.

Eran, E., and G. Edelstein
1977   'The Weights', in S. Ben Arieh and G. Edelstein (eds.), 'Akko-Tombs near the Persian Garden', *'Atiqot* 12: 52-62.

Eshel, I.
1978   'The Excavations of Petrie at Tell Gemmeh: Ceramic Assemblages and Chronology of the Iron Age Strata' (MA thesis, Tel Aviv University) (Hebrew).

1986   *The Chronology of Selected Late Iron Age Pottery Groups from Judah* (PhD thesis; Tel Aviv University) (Hebrew).

Eshel, I., and K. Prag (eds.)
1995   *Excavations by K.M. Kenyon in Jerusalem 1961–1967. IV. The Iron Age Cave Deposits in the South East Hill and Isolated Burials and Cemeteries Elsewhere* (Oxford: Oxford University Press).

Feig, Nurit.
1994   'Beit Safafeh: The Agricultural Hinterground of Jerusalem', *Twentieth Archaeological Conference in Israel, Abstracts of Lectures* (Jerusalem: Israel Exploration Society): 19.

Finkel, I.L.
1987   'An Issue of Weights from the Reign of Amar Sin', *ZA*: 192-93.

Finkelstein, I.
1992   'Horvat Qitmit and the Southern Trade in the Late Iron Age II', *ZDPV* 108.2: 156-70.

1993 'Environmental Archaeology and Social History: Demographic and Economic Aspects of the Monarchic Period', in Biran and Aviram: II, 56-66.

1996 'The Archaeology of the United Monarchy: An Alternative View', *Levant* 28: 177-87.

Fitzgerald, M.
1996 'Laboratory Research and Analysis', *INA Quarterly* 23.1: 7.

Forrer, E.
1920 *Die Provinzeinteilung des assyrischen Reiches* (Leipzig: S.C. Hinrichs.

Franken, H.J., and M.M. Ibrahim
1978 'Two Seasons of Excavations at Tell Deir 'Alla', *ADAJ* 22: 57-80.

Franken, H.J. and M.L. Steiner (eds.)
1990 *Excavations in Jerusalem 1961–1967. II. The Iron Age Extramural Quarter on the South West Hill* (Oxford: Oxford University Press).

Fritz, V.
1994a *An Introduction to Biblical Archaeology* (JSOTSup, 172; Sheffield: JSOT Press)

1994b 'Vorbericht über die Grabungen in Barqa el-Hetiye im Gebiet von Fenan, Wadi el-'Araba (Jordanien 1990)', *ZDPV* 110.2: 125-50.

Galil, G.
1992 'Judah and Assyria in the Sargonic Period', *Zion* 57.2: 111-33 (Hebrew).

Gandz, S.
1933 'Hebrew Numerals', *Proceedings of the American Academy for Jewish Research* 4: 54-112.

Gardiner, A.
1950 *Egyptian Grammar* (London: Oxford University Press, 2nd. edn).

Garfinkel, Y.
1984 'The Distribution of Identical Seal Impressions and the Settlement Pattern in Judah before Sennacherib's Campaign', *Cathedra* 32: 35-53 (Hebrew).

1985 'A Hierarchic Pattern of the Private Seal Impressions on the "LMLK" Jar-Handles', *EI* 18: 108-15 (Hebrew).

Gelb, I.J.
1969 'On the Alleged Temple and State Economies in Ancient Mesopotamia', *Studi in onore di Edwardo Volterra* 4: 137-54.

Gibson, J.C.L.
1971 *Textbook of Syrian Semitic Inscription* (Oxford: Clarendon Press): I, 67-70.

Ginsberg, H.L.
1950 'Judah and the Transjordan State from 734 to 582 BCE', in *Alexander Marx Jubilee Volume* (New York: The Jewish Theological Seminary of America): 347-68.

Gitin, S.
1989 'Tel Miqne–Ekron: a Type Site for the Inner Coastal Plain in the Iron Age 2 Period', in S. Gitin and W.G. Dever (eds.), *Recent Excavations in Israel: Studies in Iron Age Archaeology*, AASOR, 49: 23-58.

1990 'Ekron of the Philistines Part 2: Olive Oil Supplies to the World', *BARev* 16.2: 32-43.

1993 'Seventh Century BCE Cultic Elements at Ekron', in Biran and Aviram 1993: 248-58.

1995   'Tee Miqne-Ekron in the 7th Century B.C.E', in S. Gitin (ed.) *Recent Excavations in Israel: A View to the West* (Dubuque, IO: Archaeological Institute of America): 61-79.

Gitin, S., and Trude Dothan
1987   'The Rise and Fall of Ekron of the Philistines', *BA* 50: 197-222.

Glanville, S.R.K.
1935   'Weights and Balances in Ancient Egypt', *Royal Institution of Great Britain Proceedings* 29.136: 10-40.

Glueck, N.
1959   'A Seal-Weight from Nebi Rubin', *BASOR* 153: 53-58.

Goff, Beatrice.
1979   *Symbols of Ancient Egypt in the Late Period* (The Hague: Mouton).

Goetze, A.
1948   'Thirty Tablets from the Reign of Abī-ešuh and Ammi-ditānā', *JCS* 2: 73-112.

Goldwasser, O.
1984   'Hieratic Inscriptions from Tel Shera in Southern Canaan', *Tel Aviv* 11: 77-93.
1991   'An Egyptian Scribe from Lachish and Hieratic Tradition of the Hebrew Kingdom', *Tel Aviv* 18: 248-53.

Gophna, R.
1970   'Some Iron Age II Sites in Southern Philistia', *'Atiqot* 6: 25-30 (Hebrew).

Gordis, R.
1942   'A Note on 1 Sam. 13.21', *JBL* 61: 209-11.

Gordon, C.H.
1965   *Ugaritic Textbook* (Rome: Pontificial Biblical Institute).

Grant, E.
1931   *Ain Shems Excavations I* (Haverford: College Press).
1932   *Ain Shems Excavations 1928–1931 Part II* (Haverford: College Press).
1934   *Rumeilah, being Ain Shems Excavations Part III* (Haverford: College Press).
1938   *Ain Shems Excavations Part IV: Pottery* (Haverford: College Press).

Grant, E., and G.E. Wright
1939   *Ain Shems Excavations Part V: Text* (Haverford: College Press).

Gray, J.
1964   *I and II Kings: A Commentary* (OTL; London: SCM Press).

Griffith, F.L.
1892   'Notes on Egyptian Weights and Measures', *Proceedings of the Society of Biblical Archaeology* 14: 403-50.
1893   'Notes on Egyptian Weights and Measures', *Proceedings of the Society of Biblical Archaeology* 15: 301-16.

Guthe, H.
1882   'Ausgrabungen bei Jerusalem', *ZDPV* 5: 7-204, 271-378.

Hachlili, R., and Y. Meshorer
1986   *Selected Objects from the Collections of the Reuben and Edith Hecht Museum* (Catalogue no. 1; Haifa) (Hebrew).

Heltzer, M.
1978 *Goods, Prices and the Organization of the Trade in Ugarit* (Wiesbaden: Reichert).
1996 'The "Unification" of Weight and Measure Systems in Foreign Trade in the Eastern Mediterranean (1500–700 BCE)', *Michmanim* 9: 31-38.

Hemmy, A.S.
1935 'The Statistical Treatment of Ancient Weights', *Ancient Egypt and the East* 89: 83-93.
1937 'An Analysis of the Petrie Collection of Egyptian Weights', *JEA* 23: 39-56.

Herzfeld, L.
1863 *Metrologische Voruntersuchungen zur eine Geschichte des ibräischen resp. altjüdischen Handels* (Leipzig: C. Willsserodt).

Herzog, Z., *et al.*
1984 'The Israelite Fortress at Arad', *BASOR* 254: 1-34.
1987 'The Stratigraphy of Israelite Arad: A Rejoinder', *BASOR* 267: 77-80.

Herzog, Z., and L. Singer-Avitz
1995 'Abuse of Typology: The Case of Stratum V at Tel Baer Seba (Tell es-Seba')', *ZDPV* 111: 83-84.

Hestrin, Ruth
1963 *Inscriptions Reveal: Documents from the Time of the Bible, the Mishna and the Talmud* (Israel Museum Catalogue no. 100; Jerusalem) (Hebrew).

Holladay, J.S.
1987 'Religion in Israel and Judah Under the Monarchy: An Explicitly Archaeological Approach', in P.D.Miller, P.D. Hanson and S.D. McBride (eds.), *Ancient Israelite Religion: Essays in Honor of F.M. Cross* (Philadelphia: Fortress Press): 249-99.

Holland, T.A.
1975 'An Inscribed Weight from Tell Sweyhat, Syria', *Iraq* 37: 75-76.

Hoyrup, Af.J.
1995 *Mellem gide og videnskab: Et essay om noget der blevtil algebra* (Roskilde Universitetscenter).

Hultsch, F.
1882 *Griechische und römische Metrologie* (Berlin: Weidman; 2nd edn).
1898 *Die Gewichte des Alterthums* (Leipzig: B.G. Teubner).

Hurowitz, A.
1996 'Kaesaep 'ober lassoher', *ZAW* 108.1: 12-19.

Ifrah, G.
1981 *From One to Zero: A Universal History of Numbers* (ET New York: Viking).

Illife, J.H.
1936 'A Hoard of Bronzes from Ascalon', *QDAP* 5: 61-68.

Jackson, K.P.
1980 'The Ammonite Language of the Iron Age' (PhD dissertation, Michigan University).

Jackson, K.P., and J.A. Dearman
1989 'The Text of the Mesha' Inscription', in J.A. Dearman (ed.), *Studies in the Mesha' Inscription and Moab* (Atlanta, GA: Scholars Press): 92-95.

James, Francis W.
1966   *The Iron Age at Beth Shean: A Study of Levels VI-IV* (Philadelphia: The University Museum).
James, T.G.H.
1984   *Pharaoh's People: Scenes from Life in Ancient Egypt* (London: Bodley Head).
Janssen, J.J.
1975   *Commodity Prices from the Ramside Period* (Leiden. E.J. Brill).
1979   'The Role of the Temple in the Egyptian Economy during the New King-dom', in E. Lipiński (ed.), *State and Temple Economy in the Ancient Near East* (OLA, 6; Leuven: Department Oriëntalistiek): 505-15.
1988   'On Prices and Wages in Egypt', *Altorientalische Forschung* 15: 10-23.
Jaros, K.
1976   *Sichem* (OBO, 11; Göttingen: Vandenhoeck & Ruprecht).
Jericke, D.
1992   'Tell es-Seba' Stratum V', *ZDPV* 108: 122-48.
Jerusalem City Museum
n.d.   *Exhibition of Finds from the Archaeological Excavations Near the Temple Mount* (Jerusalem: Jerusalem City Museum).
Joannès, F.
1989   'La culture materielle a Mari (IV): Les méthodes de pesée', *RA* 83: 113-52.
Kaufman, I.T.
1967   'New Evidence for Hieratic Numerals on Hebrew Weights', *BASOR* 188: 39-41.
Kaufman, S.A.
1986   'The Pitfalls of Typology: On the Early History of the Alphabet', *HUCA* 57: 1-14.
Kedar, B.Z., T. Dothan and S. Safrai (eds.)
1990   *Commerce in Palestine throughout the Ages* (Jerusalem: Yadlzhak Ben Zvi) (Hebrew)
Kelm, G.L., and A. Mazar
1982   'Three Seasons of Excavations at Tel Batash—Biblical Timna', *BASOR* 248: 1-36.
1991   *Tel Batash (Timnah) Excavations: Third Preliminary Report, 1984–1989*, AASOR, Supplement 27: 47-67.
1995   *Timnah: A Biblical City in the Sorek Valley* (Winona Lake, IN: Eisenbrauns).
Kelso, J.L.
1968   *The Excavation of Bethel (1934-1960)*, AASOR, 39.
Kempinski, A.
1987   'Some Philistine Names from the Kingdom of Gaza', *IEJ* 37: 20-24.
Kenyon, K.M.
1967   *Jerusalem: Excavating 3000 Years of History* (London: Thames & Hudson).
1974   *Digging up Jerusalem* (New York: Praeger).
1976   'The Date of the Destruction of Iron Age Beer Sheba', *PEQ* 108: 63-64.

Kerkhof, Vera
1966 'An Inscribed Stone Weight from Shechem', *BASOR* 184: 20-21.
1969 'Catalogue of the Shechem Collection in the Rijksmuseum Van Oudheden in Leiden', *Oudheidkundige Mededelingen* 50: 28-109.

Kindler, A.
1967 'New Acquisitions to Kadman Numismatic Museum', *Alon* (Quarterly of the Israel Numismatic Society) 2: 17-18 (Hebrew).

Kisch, B.
1965 *Scales and Weights: A Historical Outline* (New York: Yale University Press).

Kitchen, K.A.
1986 'Egypt and Israel during the First Millenium B.C.', in J. Emerton (ed.), *Supplement to VT 40 (Congress Volume)* (Leiden. E.J. Brill): 107-23.

Klengel, H.
1988 'Einige Bemerkungen zu Löhnen und Preisen in hethitischen Anatolien', *Altorientalische Forschungen* 15: 76-81.

Kletter, R.
1991 'The Iscribed Weights of the Kingdom of Judah', *Tel Aviv* 18: 121-63.
1994 'Phoenician (?) Weights from Horvat Rosh Zayit', *'Atiqot* 25: 33-43.
1995 'Selected Material Remains of Judah at the End of the Iron Age in Relation to its Political Borders' (PhD thesis, Tel Aviv University).
1996 *The Judean Pillar-Figurines and the Archaeology of Asherah* (BAR International Series, 636; Oxford: Tempus Reparatum).
1997 'Clay Figurines and Scale-Weights from Tel Jezreel', *Tel Aviv* 24: 110-21.
in press a 'Appendix: A 24 Sheqel Weight from Beit Safafah', *'Atiqot*.
forthcoming a 'A Weight of 110.0624 Grammes from Nahal Zimri', *'Atiqot*.
forthcoming b 'The Weights from Malhata'.
forthcoming c 'The Weights from Ramot', *'Atiqot*.
forthcoming d 'Pots and Polities: Material Remains of Late Iron Judah in Relation to its Political Borders'.

Kletter, R., W. Galili and Y. Sharvit
forthcoming 'The Weights from the underwater Site of Palmahim', *'Atiqot*.

Kochavi, M.
1970 'The First Season of Excavations at Tell Malhata', *Qadmoniot* 9: 22-24.

Kochman, M.
1982 '"Yehud Medinta" in the Light of the Seal Impressions YHWD-PHW', *Cathedra* 24: 3-30 (Hebrew).

Kohl, P.L.
1975 'The Archaeology of Trade', *Dialectical Anthropology* 1.1: 43-50.
1978 'The Balance of Trade in Southwestern Asia in the Mid-Third Millenium BC', *Current Anthropology* 19: 463-92.

Kroha, T. (ed.)
1980 *Kölner Münzkabinett 28* (Auction catalogue: Cologne).

Kyle-McCarter, P.
1980 *1 Samuel: A New Translation with Introduction, Notes and Commentary* (Anchor Bible; New York: Doubleday).

Laato, A.
1992   *Josiah and David Redivitus* (Stockholm: Almqvist & Wiksell).
Lahav, M.
1968   'The Royal Estates in Israel', in H. Gvaryahu (ed.), *Zer Kavod Book* (Jerusalem): 207-45 (Hebrew).
Lamon, R.S., and G.M. Shipton (eds.)
1939   *Megiddo I: Seasons of 1925-34* (Chicago: Chicago University Press).
Lane, W. R.
1961   'Newly Recognized Occurences of the Weight Name PYM', *BASOR* 164: 21-23.
Lawton, R.
1984   'Israelite Personal Names on Pre-Exilic Hebrew Inscriptions', *Biblica* 65: 330-46.
Layard, A.H.
1853   *Discoveries among the Ruins of Nineveh and Babylon* (New York: Harper).
Lehman-Haupt, C.F.
1893   *Das altbabylonische Mass- und Gewichtssystem (als Grundlage der antiken Gewichts-, Münz- und Maassysteme* (Leiden: E.J. Brill).
1910   'Zum Wertverhältnis von Gold und Silber', *Klio* 10.2: 243-48.
1912   *Vergleichende Metrologie und keilinschriftliche Gewichtskunde* (Leipzig: F.A. Brokhaus; repr. from *ZDMG* 66: 607-96).
1956   'Talent', *Realencyclopedia Pauly-Wissowa*, Suppl. VIII: 791-848.
Lemaire, A.
1972   'L'ostracon C.1101 de Samaria: Nouvel essai', *RB* 79: 565-70.
1976   'Poid inscrits inédits de Palestine', *Semitica* 26: 33-44.
1977   *Inscriptions hebraïques. I. Les ostraca* (Paris: Cerf).
1978   'Les ostraca paléo-hébreux de fouilles de l'Ophel', *Levant* 10: 158-61.
1980   'Notes d'épigraphiques nord-ouest sémitiques', *Semitica* 32: 19-20.
1982   'Nouveaux poids PYM en bronze', *Semitica* 32: 19-20.
1988   'Recherches actuelles sur les sceaux nord-ouest sémitiques', *VT* 38: 220-30.
Lemaire, A., and P. Vernus
1978   'L'origine égyptiennes du signe ɤ des poids inscrits de l'époque royale israelite', *Semitica* 28: 53-58.
1980   'Les ostraca paléo-hébreux de Qadesh-Barnéa', *Orientalia* 49: 341-45.
1983   'L'ostracon paléo-hébreu n.6 de Tell Qudeirat (Qadesh-Barnéa)', in M. Gorg (ed.), *Fonte atques pontes* (Festschrift für H. Brunner; Wiesbaden: Otto Harrassowitz): 302-26.
Lipiński, E.
1979   'Les temples neó-assyriens et les origines du monnayage', in E. Lipiński (ed.) *State and Temple Economy in the Ancient Near East* (OLA, 5-6; Leuven: Department Oriëntalistiek): 565-88.
Liverani, M.
1972   'Il talento di Ashdod', *OA* 11: 193-99.
1990   *Prestige and Interest: International Relations in the Near East ca. 1600–1100 BC.* (Padova: Sargon SRL).

1991   'The Trade Network of Tyre', in M. Coogan, and I. Eph'al (eds.), *Ah, Assyria...Studies in Assyrian History and Ancient Near Eastern Historiography Presented to H. Tadmor* (Scripta Hierosolymitana; Jerusalem: Magnes Press, 33): 65-79.

Lloyd, A.
1983   'The Late Period', in B.G. Trigger *et al.* (eds.), *Ancient Egypt: A Social History* (Cambridge: Cambridge University Press).

Loud, G. (ed.)
1948   *Megiddo II: Seasons of 1935–39* (Chicago: Chicago University Press).

Macalister, R.A.S.
1904a   '8th Quarterly Report on the Excavation at Gezer', *PEFQS*: 194-228.
1904b   '9th Quarterly Report on the Excavation at Gezer', *PEFQS*: 320-57.
1905   '11th–12th Quarterly Report on the Excavation at Gezer', *PEFQS*: 97-115, 183-98.
1908   '19th Quarterly Report on the Excavation at Gezer', *PEFQS*: 272-90.
1909   'Excavations at Gezer: Supplementary Details', *PEFQS*: 189.
1912   *The Excavation of Gezer Vols. II–III* (London: J. Murray).

Macalister, R.A.S., and J.G. Duncan
1926   *Excavations on the Hill of Ophel* (PEFA, IV; Jerusalem).

Macdonald, E.
1932   *Beth Pelet II* (London: British School of Archaeology in Egypt).

Mackenzie, D.
1912–13   *Excavations at Ain Shems (Beth Shemesh)* (PEFA, II; Jerusalem).

Malinine, M.
1972   'L'Hiératique anormal', in *Textes et langages de l'Egypte pharaonique* (Festschrift J.F. Champollion; Cairo: Institut française d'archéologie orientale du Caire): 31-35.

Mallowan, M.E.L.
1966   *Nimrud and its Remains, Vol. I* (London: Collins).

Man, N.
1988   'The Date of 2 Chronicles 11.5-10: A Reply to Y. Garfinkel', *BASOR* 271: 74-77.

Mayers, W.R.
1988   'Erwägungen zur Unterteilung des Shekels im spätzeitlischen Babylonia', *Orientalia* 57: 70-75.

Mazar, A.
1985   'Between Judah and Philistia: Timnah (Tel Batash) in the Iron Age II', *EI* 18: 300-24 (Hebrew).
1990   *Archaeology of the Land of the Bible* (Garden City, NY: Doubleday).

Mazar, A., and E. Netzer
1986   'On the Israelite Fortress at Arad', *BASOR* 263: 87-90.

Mazar (Maizler), B.
1951   'The Excavations at Tel Qasile: Preliminary Report III', *IEJ* 1.4: 194-218.

Mazar, B. *et al.*
1963   *Ein Gedi Archaeological Excavations 1961–1962* (Jerusalem: Israel Exploration Society) ET in *'Atiqot* 5 (1966).

1972   'Excavations near the Temple Mount', *Qadmoniot* 19–20: 74-90 (Hebrew).

Mazar, Eilat, and B. Mazar

1989   'Excavations in the South of the Temple Mount', *Qedem* 29.

Mazzoni, Stephanie

1980   'Un peso in forma di leone dal palazzo Q', *Studi Eblaiti* 3: 157-60.

McCown, C. (ed.)

1947   *Tell en Nasbeh. I. Archaeological and Historical Results* (Berkeley, CA: Pacific Schools of Religion and the AASOR).

McKenzie, J.L.

1968   *Second Isaiah: A Study of the Civil Government Officials of the Israelites* (Garden City, NY: Doubleday).

Meitlis, Y.

1993   'The "Hazer" (Court) at Nahal Zimri', in Z.H. Erlich (ed.), *Samaria and Benjamin*, III (Qdumim: Judah and Samaria College): 91-99 (Hebrew).

1976   'Means of Payment Prior to Coinage and the First Coinage?', *Qadmoniot* 34–35: 51-60 (Hebrew).

Meshorer, Y.

1976   'Means of Payment Prior to Coinage and the First Coinage', *Qadmoniot* 34-35: 51-60 (Hebrew).

in press   *Catalogue of the Hecht Museum* (Hecht Museum: University of Haifa).

Mettinger, T.N.D.

1971   *Solomonic State Officials* (Lund: C.W.K. Gleerup).

Millard, A.R.

1984   'An Assessment of the Evidence for Writing in Ancient Israel', in *Biblical Archaeology Today* (Jerusalem: Israel Exloration Society): 301-11.

Mildenberg, L.

1985a   'Baana: Preliminary Studies of the Local Coinage in the Fifth Satrapy, Part II', *EI* 19: 28*-35*.

1985b   'Schekel Fragen', in *Festschrift H. Cahn* (Basel): 83ff.

1988   'Yahud Münzen', in H. Weippert (ed.), *Palästina in vorhellenistischer Zeit* (Munich: C.H. Beck): 721-28.

1991   'Palästina in der persischen Zeit', in T. Hackens *et. al.* (eds.), *A Survey of Numismatic Research 1985–1990* (Brussels: International Numismatic Commission): 102-105.

Mitchell, T.C.

1988   *The Bible in the British Museum* (London: British Museum Publications).

Mittmann, S.

1990   'Hizkia und die Philister', *JNSL* 16: 91-106.

1992   'Königliches "bat" und "ṭēt-Symbol": Mit einem Beitrag zu Micha 1,14b und 1 Chronik 4, 21-23', *ZDPV* 107: 59-76.

Molina, M.

1989   'Una mina di Narām Sîn', *Aula Orientalis* 7.1: 125-27.

Möller, G.

1936   *Hieratische Paläographie*, III (Leipzig: J.C. Hinrichs).

Momigliano, Nicoletta

1996   'Duncan Mackenzie and the Palestinian Exploration Fund', *PEQ* 128: 139-70.

Moscati, S.
1951   *L'Epigraphia ebraica antica 1935–1950* (Rome: Pontificial Biblical
                Institute).
Muller, W.W.
1904   'Notices on Foreign Publications', *PEQ*: 177-79.

Na'aman, N.
1979   'Sennacherib's Letter to God on his Campaign to Judah', *BASOR* 214:
                25-39.
1981   'Royal Estates in the Jezreel Valley in the Late Bronze Age and under the
                Israelite Monarchy', *EI* 15: 140-44 (Hebrew).
1986a   'Hezekiah's Fortified Cities and the Lmlk Stamps', *BASOR* 261: 5-21.
1986b   *Borders and Districts in Biblical Historiography* (Jerusalem Biblical
                Studies, 4; Jerusalem: Simor).
1987   'The Negev in the Last Century of the Kingdom of Judah', *Cathedra* 42:
                3-15 (Hebrew).
1988   'The Date of 2 Chronicles 11.5-10: A Reply to Y. Garfinkel', *BASOR*
                271: 74-77.
1989   'The Kingdom of Judah under Josiah', *Zion* 50: 17-71 (Hebrew). ET in
                Tel Aviv 18 (1990).
1996   'Sources and Composition in the History of David', in V. Fritz and P.R.
                Davies (eds.), *The Origins of the Ancient Israelite States* (JSOTSup, 228;
                Sheffield: Sheffield Academic Press): 170-86.
Na'aman, N., and R. Zadok
1988   'Sargon II's Deportations to Israel and Philistia (716–708 B.C.)', *JCS* 40:
                36-46.
Nadelman, J.
1993   'Pisgat Ze'ev D', *Had. Arch.* 99: 49 (Hebrew).
Naveh, J.
1958   'Khirbat al-Muqanna‘-Ekron: An Archaeological Survey', *IEJ* 8: 87-100.
1962   'More Hebrew Inscriptions from Mezad Hashavyahu', *IEJ* 12: 27-32.
1985   'Writing and Script in Seventh Century Philistia: The New Evidence
                from Tell Jemmeh', *IEJ* 35: 11-15.
1989   *Early History of the Alphabeth* (Jerusalem: Magnes Press) (Hebrew).
1992   'The Numbers of *bat* in the Arad Ostraca', *IEJ* 42: 52-54.
Negbi, Ora.
1970   'The Cemetery of Biblical Moza', in Abramsky *et al.* (1970): 358-70
                (Hebrew).

Nogah, Rivka
1992   'The Daily Life in the Time of the Bible' (PhD thesis; Newport
                University) (Hebrew).
Noth, M.
1934   'Das Krongut der israelitischen Könige und seine Verwaltung (Exkursus
                über die Zahlzeichen auf den Ostraca)', *ZDPV* 50: 240-44.
Olivier, J.P.
1994   'Money Matters: Some Remarks on the Economic Situation in the King-
                dom of Judah during the Seventh Century BC', *BN* 73: 90-100.

Oren, E.D.
1986a   'Land of Gerar Expedition: Preliminary Report for the Seasons of 1982
          and 1983', *BASOR* Supplement 24: 57-87.
1986b   'A Phoenician Emporium on the Border of Egypt', *Qadmoniot* 75–76:
          83-91.
1993   'Ethnicity and Regional Archaeology: The Western Negev under Assyr-
          ian Rule', in Biran and Aviram : II, 102-105.
Oren, E.D., et. al.
1991   'Tel Haror—: After Six Seasons', *Qadmoniot* 93–94: 2-19 (Hebrew).
Parayre, Dominique
1993   'Les cachets ouest-sémitiques à travers l'image du disque solaire ailé',
          Syria 67.2: 269-301.
Parise, N.F.
1971   'Per uno studio del systema ponderale Ugaritico', *Dialoghy di Arche-
          ologia* 4–5: 3-36.
1981   'Mina di Ugarit, mina di Karkemish, mina di Khatti', *Dialoghy di
          Archeologia* NS 3: 155-60. ET 'The Mina of Ugarit, the Mina of
          Karkemish, the Mina of Khatti', in C. Zaccagnini (ed.), *Production and
          Consumption in the Ancient Near East* (Budapest: Le chaire d'Egyp-
          tologie de l'universite Eotvos Lorand de Budapest): 333-41.
1984   'Unità ponderali di cambio nella Siria del nord', in A. Archi (ed.),
          Circulation of Goods in Non Palatial Context in the Ancient Near East
          (Incunabula Graeca, 82: Rome: Edizioni dell'Ateneo): 125-38.
1991   'Unità ponderali e circulazione metallica nell' oriente mediterraneo', in
          T. Hackens *et al.* (eds.), *A Survey of Numismatical Research 1985–1990*
          (Brussels: International Numismatic Commission): I, 28-34.
Parpola, S.
1981   'Assyrian Royal Inscriptions and Neo-Assyrian Letters', in F.M. Falles
          (ed.), *Assyrian Royal Inscriptions* (Rome: Istituto per l'Oriente): 120-24.
Petrie, W.M.F.
1885   *Tanis Part I* (London: Egypt Exploration Fund).
1886   *Naukratis Part I* (London: Egypt Exploration Fund).
1888.   *Nebeshe and Defenneh* (London: Egypt Exploration Fund.)
1926   *Ancient Weights and Measures* (London: Arris & Phillips).
1928   *Gerar* (London: British School of Archaeology in Egypt).
1930   *Beth Pelet I* (London: British School of Archaeology in Egypt).
1931   *Ancient Gaza I* (London: British School of Archaeology in Egypt).
1933   *Ancient Gaza III* (London: British School of Archaeology in Egypt).
1934a   *Measures and Weights* (London: Methuen).
1934b   *Ancient Gaza IV* (London: British School of Archaeology in Egypt).
1937   *Anthedon* (London: British School of Archaeology in Egypt).
1952   *Ancient Gaza V* (London: British School of Archaeology in Egypt).
Petruso, K.M.
1981   'Early Weights and Weighing in Egypt and the Indus Valley', *Bulletin of
          the Museum of Fine Arts, Boston* 79: 44-51.
1984   'Prolegomena to Late Cypriot Metrology', *AJA* 88: 293-304.
1992   *Aiya Irini: The Balance Weights* (Keos, VIII; Results of the Excavations
          carried out by the University of Cincinnati under the Auspices of the

American School of Classical Studies at Athens; Mainz: Von Zabern Verlag).

Piccirillo, M.
1983   *Studium Biblicum Franciscanum Museum, No. 6* (Jerusalem: The Museum).

Pilcher, E.J.
1912   'Weights of Ancient Palestine', *PEFQS* 44: 136-44, 178-95.
1914   'A New Hebrew Weight', *PEFQS*: 99.
1915   'The Shekel of the Sanctuary', *PEFQS* 47: 186-95.
1916   'Hebrew Weights in the Book of Samuel', *PEFQS*: 77-85.

Polzin, R.
1989   *Samuel and the Deuteronomist* (San Francisco: Harper & Row).

Powell, M.A.
1971   'Sumerian Numeration and Metrology' (PhD thesis, University of Minnesota).
1979   'Ancient Mesopotamian Metrology: Methods, Problems and Prospects', in M.A. Powell and R.H. Sack (eds.), *Studies in Honor of J.B. Jones* (AOAT, 203; Kevelaer: Butzon & Bercker): 71-110.
1984   'Late Babylonian Surface Mensuration', *AfO* 31: 32-66.
1987–90 'Masse und Gewichte', *RLA* 7: 508-17.
1992   'Weights and Measures', *ABD*: VI, 898-908.

Pritchard, J.B.
1958   *The Ancient Near East: An Anthology of Texts and Pictures* (Princeton, NJ: Princeton University Press).
1959   *Hebrew Inscriptions and Stamps from Gibeon* (Philadelphia: The University Museum).
1961   *The Water System of Gibeon* (Philadelphia: University Museum).
1969   *ANET: Supplementary Texts and Pictures Relating to the Old Testament* (Princeton, NJ: Princeton University Press).
1985   *Tell el-Sa'idiyeh* (Excavations on the Tell 1964–1966 (Philadelphia: University Museum).

Pryor, F.L.
1977   *The Origins of the Economy: A Comparative Study of Distribution in Primitive and Peasant Economies* (New York: Academic Press).

Puech, E.
1977   'Documents épigraphiques de Buseirah', *Levant* 9: 11-20.
1980   'Poids', in Briend and Humbert 1980: 306-308.
1984   'Les poids', in Chambon 1984: 79-84.
1985   'L'inscription de la statue d'Amman et la paléographie Ammonite', *RB* 92: 5-24.

Qedar, S.
1978   *Gewichte aus drei Jahrtausenden* (32 Auktion; Cologne: Münz Zentrum).
1979   *Gewichte aus drei Jahrtausenden 2* (37 Auktion; Cologne: Münz Zentrum).
1981   *Gewichte aus drei Jahrtausenden 3* (45 Auktion; Cologne: Münz Zentrum).
1983   *Gewichte aus drei Jahrtausenden 4* (49 Auktion; Cologne: Münz Zentrum).

Raban, A.
1992   'A Group of Objects from a Wreckage Site at Athlit', *Michmanim* 6: 31-53.
Raffaeli, S.
1920   'The Ancient Hebrew Weights', *JPOS* 1: 22-24.
Rainey, A.F.
1965   'Royal Weights and Measures', *BASOR* 179: 34-36.
1982   'Wine from the Royal Vineyards', *BASOR* 245: 57-62 (Hebrew version in *EI* 16 [1981]: 177-81).
1983   'The Biblical Shephelah of Judah', *BASOR* 251: 1-22.
Reich, R.
1984   'On the Identification of the "Sealed Karu" of Egypt', *IEJ* 34: 32-38.
1989   'A Third Season of Excavations at Mesad Hashavyahu', *EI* 20: 228-32.
1993   'The Cemetery in the Mamilla Area of Jerusalem', *Qadmoniot* 103–104: 103-109 (Hebrew).
Reich, R., and B. Brandl
1985   'Gezer under Assyrian Rule', *PEQ* 117: 41-54.
Reifenberg, A.
1925   'Notes and Queries', *PEFQS*: 107.
1936   'Ein neues hebräisches Gewicht', *JPOS* 16: 39-43 (Hebrew version, 'The Legend "Shekel" on Hebrew Weights', *Bulletin of the Jewish Palestine Exploration Society* 15.3-4 [1940]: 70-71; repr. in 1965, Reader Vol. A [1965]: 264).
Reisner, G.A., C.S. Fisher and D.G. Lyon (eds.)
1924   *Harvard Excavations at Samaria, 1908–1910*, I (Cambridge, MA: Harvard University Press).
Renfrew, C.
1969   'Trade and Cultural Process in European Prehistory', *Current Anthropology* 10: 51-169.
1975   'Trade as Action at a Distance', in J.A. Sabloff and C.C. Lamberg-Karlovsy (eds.), *Ancient Civilization and Trade* (Albuquerque: University of New Mexico Press): 3-59.
1977   'Alternative Models for Exchange and Spatial Distribution', in *Trade and Interaction?*: 135-53.
Restö, J.
1991   'The Domestication of the Camel and the Establishment of the Frankincense Road from South Arabia', *Orientalia Suecana* 40: 187-219.
Ridgeway, W.
1970   *The Origin of Metallic Currency and Weight Standards* (Detroit: Singing Tree Press).
Riis, P.J., and M.L. Buhl
1990   *Hama II, 2: Les objets de la période dite syro-hittite (Age du Fer)* (Nationalmuseet Skrifter; Copenhagen: Nationalmuseet, 12).
Robson, E.
1996   *Old Babylonian Coefficient Lists and the Wider Context of Mathematics in Ancient Mesopotamia, 2100–1600 BC* (DPhil; Oxford University).

Rockefeller Museum.
1940   *Palestine Archaeological Museum Gallery Book: The Iron Age* (Jerusalem: Department of Antiquities, Government of Palestine).

Ronen, A.
1996   'The Enigma of the Shekel Weights of the Judean Kingdom', *BA* 59.2: 122-25.

Rose, M.
1975   *Der Ausschliesslichkeitsanspruch Jahwes deuteronomische Schultheologie und die Volksfrömmigkeit in der späten Königszeit* (Stuttgart: W. Kohlhammer).

Rütherswörden, U.
1985   *Die Beamten der israelitischen Königszeit* (Stuttgart: W. Kohlhammer).

Sauer, J.A.
1995   'Artistic and Faunal Evidence for the Influence of the Domestication of Donkeys and Camels in the Archaeological History of Jordan and Arabia', in *SIHAJ*, V: 39-47.

Sayce, A.H.
1893   'On an Inscribed Bead from Palestine', *PEFQS*: 32-33.
1894   'The Hematite Weight', *PEFQS*: 220-31, 284.
1904   'Inscribed Weights', *PEFQS*: 357-59.

Schumacher, G.
1908   *Tell el Mutesellim* (Leipzig: R. Haupt).

Scott, R.B.Y.
1959a   'The Shekel Sign on Stone Weights', *BASOR* 153: 32-35.
1959b   'Weights and Measures of the Bible', *BA* 22: 22-40.
1964   'Shekel Fraction Markings on Hebrew Weights', *BASOR* 173: 53-64.
1965   'The Scale Weights from Ophel 1963-4', *PEQ*: 128-39.
1970   'The N-s-f Weights from Judah', *BASOR* 200: 62-66.
1971   'Balance', *Encyclopaedia Judaica* 48: 127-28.
1985   'Weights from Jerusalem', in Tushingham 1985: I, 197-212.

Segal, M.H.
1915   'A New Hebrew Weight', *PEFQS*: 40f.

Segal, Ruth.
1971   'Unmarked Ancient Weights in the Kadman Numismatic Museum', *Museum Haaretz, Tel Aviv, Bulletin* 13: 33-38 (Hebrew).

Seger, J.
1987   'Tel Gezer: Phase II Excavations 1972-1994', in L.G., Perdue, G.L. Toombs and G.L. Johnson (eds.), *Archaeological and Biblical Interpretation* (Atlanta, GA: John Knox Press): 113-127.
1997   'Stone Scale Weights of the Judean Standard from Tel Halif', in J. Magness *et al.* (eds.), *Festschrift Dr E.S. Frerichs* (in press).

Sellers, O.R.
1933   *The Citadel of Beth Zur* (Philadelphia: Westminster Press).

Sellers, O.R., and W.F. Albright
1931   'The First Campaign of Excavation at Beth Zur', *BASOR* 43: 2-13.

Sellers, O.R. *et.al.*
1968   *The 1957 Excavation at Beth Zur* (AASOR, 38; Cambridge, MA).

Shany, A.
1967　'A New Unpublished "Beqaʿ" Weight in the Collection of the Pontifical Biblical Institute, Jerusalem, Israel', *PEQ* 99: 54-55 (Hebrew version *Beit Miqra* 22.1 [1964]: 64-67).

Shea, W.H.
1985　'Israelite Chronology and the Samaria Ostraca', *ZDPV* 101: 9-20.

Shiloh, Y.
1979　'New Excavations in the City of David', *Qadmoniot* 45: 12-19.
1981　'Past and Present in Archaeological Research on the City of David', in B. Mazar (ed.), *Thirty Years of Archaeology in Eretz Israel, 1948–1978* (Jerusalem: Israel Exploration Society): 172-81.
1989　*Judah and Jerusalem in the Eighth–Sixth Centuries B.C.E.* (AASOR, 49): 97-105.

Silver, M.
1983　*Prophets and Markets: The Political Economy of Ancient Israel* (Boston).

Skinner, F.G.
1967　*Weights and Measures* (London: HMSO).

Smith, H.P.
1889　*A Critical and Exegetical Commentary on the Book of Samuel* (Edinburgh: T. & T. Clark).

Spaer, A.
1982　'A Group of Iron Age Stone Weights', *IEJ* 32: 251.

Speiser, E.A.
1967　'Of Shoes and Shekels', in J.J. Finkelstein and M. Greenberg (eds.), *Oriental and Biblical Studies: Collected Writings of E.A. Speiser* (Philadelphia: University of Pennsylvania Press): 151-59. (*BASOR* 7 [1940]: 15-20).

Spencer, A.J.
1993　*Excavations at el-Ashmunein III: The Town* (BM Expedition to Middle Egypt; London: British Museum).

Spieckermann, H.
1982　*Juda unter Assur in den Sargonidenzeit* (Göttingen: Vandenhoeck & Ruprecht).

Stager, L.E.
1991　*Ashkelon Rediscovered* (Washington: Biblical Archaeology Society).
1996　'Ashkelon and the Archaeology of Destruction: Kislev 604 BCE', *EI* 25: 61*-74*.

Stern, E.
1963　'Weights and Measures', *EncMiqr* IV: 861-76 (Hebrew). ET in *Encyclopaedia Judaica* 16 (1971): 376-88.
1973a　'Eretz Israel at the End of the Period of the Monarchy', *Qadmoniot* 21: 2-17 (Hebrew).
1973b　*The Material Culture of the Land of the Bible in the Persian Period, 538–332 BCE* (Jerusalem; Bialik Institute and the Israel Exploration Society) (Hebrew).
1992　*Dor: The Ruler of the Seas* (Jerusalem: Bialik Institute) (Hebrew).
1994　'The Jericho Region and the Eastern Border of the Judean Kingdom in its Last Days', *EI* 24: 192-97 (Hebrew).

Stieglitz, R.B.
1979   'Commodity Prices at Ugarit', *JAOS* 99: 15-23.
Superior Galleries
1992   *The June 2nd 1992 Sale: Ancient Coins, Antiquities and Coins of the World*: 86.
Suzuki, Y.
1992   'A New Aspect on Occupation Policy by King Josiah', *AJBI* 18: 31-61.
Thompson, J.A.
1986   'Weights and Measures', in *Handbook of Life in Bible Times* (Leicester: Inter-Varsity Press): 167-73.
Thomsen, P.
1926   'Gewicht und Gewichtssystem', in M. Ebert, *Reallexikon der Vorgeschichte* 4.1 (Berlin: W. de Gruyter): 311-15.
Torczyner (Tur Sinai), H.
1938   *Lachish I: The Lachish Letters* (Oxford: Oxford University Press).
1948   'The Raqiᶜa and the Šeḥakim', *Leshonenu* 16.1-2: 12-19 (Hebrew).
1952   'Šḥq', in E. Ben Iehuda (ed.), *Thesaurus Totis Hebraitatis et Veteris et Recentioris* (Jerusalem): XIX (Hebrew).
1987   *The Lachish Ostraca: A New Enlarged Edition* (Jerusalem: The Bialik Institute and the Israel Exploration Society [1940]) (Hebrew).
Torrey, C.C.
1903   'An Inscribed Hebrew Weight', *JAOS* 24: 206-208.
Trinquet, J.
1957   'Métrologie biblique: Measures de poids', *Supplément au dictionnaire de la Bible* 5: 1240-50.
Tufnell, Olga (ed.)
1953   *Lachish III. The Iron Age* (London: Oxford University Press).
Tushingham, A.D. (ed.)
1985   *Excavations in Jerusalem 1961–1967, Vol. 1* (Toronto: Royal Ontario Museum).
1988   'The 1961–1967 Excavations in the Armenian Garden, Jerusalem: A Response', *PEQ*: 142-45.
Ussishkin, D.
1976   '"Lamelech" Store-Jars and the Excavations at Lachish', *Qadmoniot* 34-35: 63-68 (Hebrew).
1977   'The Destruction of Lachish by Sennacherib and the Date of the Royal Judean Storage Jars', *Tel Aviv* 4: 28-57.
1982   *The Conquest of Lachish by Sennacherib* (Tel Aviv: The Institute of Archaeology, Tel Aviv University).
1983   'Excavations at Tel Lachish 1978–1983: Second Preliminary Report', *Tel Aviv* 10.2: 97-185.
1988   'The Date of the Judean Shrine at Arad', *IEJ* 38: 14: 2-57.
Valbelle, Dominique
1977   *Catalogue des poids à inscriptions hiératiques de Deir El-Médineh Nos. 5001-423* (Institut français d'archéologie orientale).
Van Beek, G.W.
1973   'Assyria Vaulted Buildings at Tell Jerumeh', *Qadmoniot* 21: 23-27 (Hebrew).

Van der Kooij, G., and M.M. Ibrahim
1989   *Picking up the Threads* (Leiden: University of Leiden Archaeological Centre).

Veenhof, K.R.
1985   'SAG.ÌL.LA = SAGGILÛ, "Difference Asserted" on Measuring and Accounting in some Old Babylonian Texts', in J.M. Durand and J.R. Kupper (eds.), *Miscellanea Babylonica* (Festschrift Maurice Birot; Paris: Editions recherches sur les civilisations): 285-306.

Viedebannt, O.
1923   'Zur hebräische, phönizischen und syrischen Gewichtskunde', *ZDPV* 45-46: 1-22.

Wampler, J.C. (ed.)
1947   *Tell en Nasbeh Vol. II (The Pottery)* (Berkeley, CA: Pacific Schools of Religion and the AASOR).

Warburton, D.A.
1997   *State and Economy in Ancient Egypt: Fiscal Vocabulary of the New Kingdom* (OBO, 151; Fribourg: University Press; Göttingen: Vandenhoek & Ruprecht).

Ward, W.A.
1989   'Some Foreign Personal Names and Loan-Words from the Deir el Medinah Ostraca', in A. Leonard and B.B. Williams (eds.), *Essays on Ancient Civilization Presented to H.J. Kantor* (Chicago: University of Chicago Press): 301.

Warren, C.
1870   'List of Weights and Other Stones', *PEFQS*: 330.
1903   *The Ancient Cubit and our Weights* (London: Palestine Exploration Fund).

Weigall, A.E.P.
1908   *Weights and Balances* (Cairo: Catalogue général des antiquités égyptiennes du musée du Caire).

Weippert, M., and Helga Weippert
1976   'Jericho in der Eisenzeit', *ZDPV* 92: 105-48.

Weissbach, F.H.
1907   'Über die babylonischen, assyrischen und altpersischen Gewichte', *ZDMG* 61: 379-402, 948-50.
1916   'Neue Beiträge zur keilinschriftlichen Gewichtkunde', *ZDMG* 70: 49-91, 354-402.

Wenning, R.
1989   'Meṣad Hashavyahu: Ein Stutzpunkt des Jojakim?', in F.L. Hossfeld (ed.), *Vom Sinai zum Horeb* (Wurzburg: Echter Verlag): 169-96.

Westermann, C.
1969   *Isaiah* (OTL; London: SCM Press).

Wightman, G.D.
1985a   *Studies in the Stratigraphy and Chronology of the Iron Age 2-3 in Palestine* (PhD dissertation; Sydney University).
1985b   'Megiddo VIIa-III: Associated Structures and Chronology', *Levant* 17: 117-29.

Williams, R.J.
1974   'A People Come out of Egypt: An Egyptological Look at the Old Testament', *VT Supplement* 28: 231-52.

Williamson, H.G.M.
1982   *1 and 2 Chronicles* (The New Century Bible Commentary; Grand Rapids: Eerdmans).

Wright, G.E.
1965   *Shechem: The Biography of a Biblical City* (London: Gerald Duckworth).
1978   'Shechem', *EAEHL* IV: 1083-94.

Yadin, Y., *et al.* (eds.)
1959–62   *Hazor I–IV* (3 vols.; Hebrew University: Magnes Press).

Yadin, Y.
1960   'Ancient Judean Weights and the Date of the Samaria Ostraca', *Scripta Hierosolimitana* 8: 9-25 (Hebrew version in Y. Kaufman *et al.* [eds.], *Oz le-David: Studies in the Bible Presented to D. Ben Gurion* [Jerusalem, 1964]: 322-34).
1985   'The Archaeological Aspect', in J. Amitai (ed.), *Biblical Archaeology Today* (Jerusalem: Keter): 21-27.

Yadin, Y., and Sh. Geva
1983   'The Cities of the Negev during Josiah's Days', in Y. Hoffman (ed.), *Encyclopaedia of the Biblical World: Jeremiah* (Jerusalem: Revivim): 247-55.

Yassine, Kh.
1988   'Tell el Mazar, Field I. Preliminary Report of Area G, H, L and M: The Summit', in *idem*, *Archaeology of Jordan: Essays and Reports* (Amman: University of Jordan, Department of Archaeology): 75-113.

Yisraeli, Y.
1978   'Sharuhen, Tell', *EAEHL* IV: 1074-82 (= EAEHL NS II [1993]: 441-44).

Zaccagnini, C.
1988   'On Prices and Wages at Nuzi', *Altorientalische Forschungen* 15: 42-52.
1995   War and Famine at Emar', *Orientalia* 64.2: 92-109.

Zertal, A.
1988   *The Israelite Settlement in the Hill Country of Manasseh* (Haifa: Haifa University) (Hebrew).
1989   'The Wedge-Shaped Decorated Bowl and the Origin of the Samaritans', *BASOR* 276: 77-84.

Zimhoni, Orna
1985   'The Iron Age Pottery of Tel 'Eton and its Relation to the Lachish, Tell Beit Mirsim and Arad Assemblages', *Tel Aviv* 12.1: 63-90.
1990   'Two Ceramic Assemblages from Lachish Levels III and II', *Tel Aviv* 17.1: 3-52.

Zippor, M.
1984   'I Sam. 13.20-21 in the Light of the Ancient Versions: A Textual Study', *Textus* 11: 1-50 (Hebrew).

Zorn, J.R.
1993   'Tell en-Nasbeh: A Re-evaluation of the Architecture and Stratigraphy of the Early Bronze Age, Iron Age and Later Periods' (PhD thesis, University of California, Berkeley).

INDEXES

INDEX OF REFERENCES

BIBLE

INDEX OF AUTHORS

INDEX OF PLACE NAMES

The names are arranged alphabetically; the index includes the main text (Chapters 1–12), but not the appendices. It does not include forms such as Cypriot, Persian, etc. (But Cyprus, Persia…).

JOURNAL FOR THE STUDY OF THE OLD TESTAMENT
SUPPLEMENT SERIES